A Lexicon of Economics

Social Science Lexicons

Key Thinkers, Past and Present
Key Topics of Study
A Lexicon of Economics
A Lexicon of Psychology, Psychiatry and Psychoanalysis
Methods, Ethics and Models
Political Science and Political Theory
Social Problems and Mental Health

A Lexicon of Economics

Edited by
Phyllis Deane and Jessica Kuper

ROUTLEDGE
LONDON AND NEW YORK

First published in 1988 by
Routledge
2 Park Square, Milton Park, Abingdon, Oxon, OX14 4RN
29 West 35th Street, New York, NY 10001

Transferred to Digital Printing 2004

Set in Linotron Baskerville
by Input Typesetting Ltd., London SW19 8DR

Library of Congress Cataloging in Publication Data

A lexicon of economics.
    (Social science lexicons)
    1. Economics—Dictionaries.   I. Deane, Phyllis.
II. Kuper, Jessica.   III. Series.
HB61.L427   1988   330′.03′21   *88–18401*
ISBN 0–415–00234–6 (pbk.)

British Library CIP Data also available

Contents

A Lexicon of Economics: the entries

Contributor List

General Editors: Phyllis Deane and Jessica Kuper

Armstrong, A G	Dept of Economics, University of Bristol
Asimakopulos, A	Dept of Economics, McGill University, Montreal
Bain, Andrew D	Dept of Economics, University of Strathclyde
Barrell, Ray	Dept of Economics, University of Southampton
Black, R D C	Queen's University College, Belfast
Bliss, Christopher	Nuffield College and Dept of Economics, Oxford
Boland, Lawrence A	Dept of Economics, Simon Fraser University, Burnaby, British Columbia
Bray, Margaret	Faculty of Economics and Politics, University of Cambridge
Brown, Arthur J	Emeritus Professor of Economics, University of Leeds
Brown, C V	Dept of Economics, University of Stirling
Bronfenbrenner, Martin	Dept of Economics, Durham University, North Carolina and Aoyama Gakuin University, Tokyo
Button, Kenneth J	Dept of Economics, Loughborough University
Casson, Mark	Dept of Economics, University of Reading
Chick, Victoria	Dept of Political Economy, University College London
Chisholm, Michael	Dept of Geography, University of Cambridge
Clark, J A	Science Policy Research Unit, University of Sussex

Coats, A W	Dept of Economics, University of Nottingham
Collard, David A	School of Humanities and Social Sciences, University of Bath
Cornwall, John	Dept of Economics, Dalhousie University, Halifax, Nova Scotia
Cowell, Frank A	Dept of Economics, The London School of Economics and Political Science
Currie, J M	Dept of Economics, University of Manchester
Davidson, Paul	Dept of Economics, Rutgers, The State University of New Jersey
Davies, S W	School of Economic and Social Studies, University of East Anglia
Deane, Phyllis	Emeritus Professor of Economic History, University of Cambridge
Dilnot, Andrew	Institute of Fiscal Studies, London
Douglas, Susan P	Graduate School of Business Administration, New York University
Duller, H J	Dept of Development Sociology, University of Leiden
Engerman, Stanley	Dept of Economics, University of Rochester
Estrin, Saul	Dept of Economics, University of Southampton
Evans, H David	Institute of Development Studies, University of Sussex
Fitzgerald, E V K	Institute of Social Studies, The Hague
Freeman, C	Social Policy Research Unit, University of Sussex
Frey, Bruno	Institute of Empirical Economics, University of Zurich
Gregory, Mary B	St Hilda's College, University of Oxford

Gruchy, Allan G	Dept of Economics, University of Maryland
Gudeman, Stephen	Dept of Anthropology, University of Minnesota
Hansson, Bjorn	Dept of Economics, University of Lund
Heertje, Arnold	Dept of Economics, University of Amsterdam
Hughes, Gordon	Faculty of Economics and Politics, University of Cambridge
Humphries, Jane	Faculty of Economics and Politics, University of Cambridge
Hunt, E K	Dept of Economics, University of Utah
Jackson, Dudley	Dept of Economics, University of Wollongong, New South Wales
Joshi, Heather	Centre for Population Studies, London School of Hygiene and Tropical Medicine, University of London
Kanbur, S M Ravi	Dept of Economics, University of Essex
Kindleberger, Charles P	Emeritus Ford International Professor of Economics, Massachusetts Institute of Technology
Kregel, J A	Dept of Economics, University of Groningen, The Netherlands
Lecomber, Richard	Formerly of the Dept of Economics, University of Bristol
Llewellyn, David T	Dept of Economics, University of Loughborough
Loasby, Brian J	Dept of Economics, University of Stirling
McLellan, David	Eliot College, University of Kent
Maynard, Alan	Centre for Health Economics, University of York
Millward, Robert	Dept of Economics, University of Salford

Mishan, Ezra J	London
Moggridge, Donald	Royal Economic Society, University of Toronto
Moore, Basil J	Dept of Economics, Wesleyan University, Middletown, Connecticut
Muellbauer, John	Nuffield College, University of Oxford
Mullineaux, Andy W	Dept of Economics, University of Birmingham
Neale, Sir Alan	London
Neary, Peter J	Dept of Political Economy, University College, Dublin
Nell, Edward J	Dept of Economics, New School for Social Research, New York
O'Brien, D P	Dept of Economics, University of Durham
Peach, Terry	Faculty of Economic and Social Studies, University of Manchester
Pearce, David	Dept of Economics, University College, London
Reekie, W Duncan	Dept of Business Studies, University of the Witwatersrand, Johannesburg
Revell, Jack R S	Institute of European Finance, University College of North Wales, Bangor
Rose, Hilary	Dept of Applied Social Studies, University of Bradford
Rothschild, Kurt W	Dept of Economics, Johannes Kepler University, Linz, Austria
Shaw, G K	Dept of Economics, University of Buckingham
Shone, Ronald	Dept of Economics, University of Stirling
Singer, H W	Institute of Development Studies, University of Sussex

Skinner, Andrew S	Dept of Political Economy, University of Glasgow
Stoneman, Paul	Dept of Economics, University of Warwick
Streissler, Erich	Dept of Economics, University of Vienna
Tarascio, Vincent J	Dept of Economics, University of North Carolina at Chapel Hill
Thirlwall, A P	Keynes College, University of Kent
Toye, John	Centre for Development Studies, University College of Wales, Swansea
Vines, David	Dept of Applied Economics, University of Glasgow
Ward, Michael	OECD, Paris
Weale, Martin	Dept of Applied Economics, University of Cambridge
Whitaker, John K	Dept of Economics, University of Virginia
Whittington, Geoffrey	Dept of Economics, University of Bristol

Economics

The Ancient Greeks who gave to us the name of this subject lacked the concept of what we now call economics. *Oeconomicus* would be 'Household Management' in modern English, the domain of Mrs Beeton rather than J. S. Mill. Of course, what we would now recognize as economic questions are certainly ancient, but such questions and particular answers to them amount to less than the kind of knowledge that in Schumpeter's elegant description, '. . . has been the object of conscious efforts to improve it'. In that sense, which is of a science in the broad and generous use of that term, economics is a young discipline. The term now usually employed is even younger than the modern form of the subject itself. Earlier writers described themselves as '*political economists*'. Too much can be and has been made of this distinction. In an age in which the educated knew Greek, it was pertinent to remind the reader what the term did not mean. However, any terminological distinction between economics and political economy must be questioned. The unadorned 'economic' had long been in use, and was frequently employed by Marx, while 'political economy' has continued in use into the twentieth century and has enjoyed something of a revival lately from writers wishing to advertise that their work has not treated its subject in isolation from the political system.

It is customary to associate the beginning of modern economics with the publication of Adam Smith's *The Wealth of Nations* (1776). As this attribution sets aside more than a thousand years of economic writing, ancient, Christian and Islamic, it calls for justification. However, a study of the earlier literature will not leave the reader long in doubt concerning the claim that a radical shift of method had taken place. What we recognize in Adam Smith's work, and what sets it apart from that which had gone before, is the characteristic imprint of the eighteenth century in which the Grand Idea finds its expression in the language of exact scholarship. We recognize the same spirit in reading Gibbon's *History*.

Adam Smith's writing represents the source of a stream which runs to the present day. This is true of modern economics in general but more particularly of a style of approaching the subject which was his own. Its distinguishing characteristic is its limited use of the method of simplification and abstraction. The strengths of the method are obvious, but experience has revealed its weaknesses. Description needs a strong guiding principle if it is not to deteriorate into the unenlightening elaboration of a mass of incoherent fact. One could illustrate this point from *The Wealth of Nations* itself, where illustrations are sometimes developed to the point of tedium, but that would do less than justice to a writer whose genius generally enabled him to surmount this problem. Better illustrations of the point might be provided from much later work by the Institutionalist School which made its influence felt in Germany and in the United States in the late nineteenth and early twentieth centuries.

A problem inherent in Adam Smith's method is that it provides no guidance concerning the resolution of disagreements. The arguments make use of persuasive reasoning and examples to back them up. If the number and quality of these is overwhelming there will clearly be no difficulty, but such cannot always be the case, and as economics grew the triumph of ideas by acclamation was far from being the rule. What was required were more refined methods of economic reasoning and more powerful methods of evaluating the kinds of claim to which that reasoning gave rise. The first development preceded the second but they were ultimately seen to be closely related.

The method of studying economic questions by means of simplification and abstraction was developed, and even taken to extremes, by David Ricardo. So important was his innovation of method that writers for two generations acknowledged his influence even when they propounded conclusions quite contrary to his own. The kind of abstraction that Ricardo developed took the form of what today would be called an 'economic model'. This consists in a formal, more or less simple, invented economy which is claimed to illustrate a point or to capture the essence of the true, and of course more complicated, economy of real life. One illustration would be a numerical example. Another would be the stylized story, such as the Tribe of Hunters by means of which Adam Smith illustrated his theory of the division of labour. The numbers of an example are not taken by their inventor to be the values of real life, while stories can be taken to be schematic accounts of true history. For the present purpose, however, this distinction is less important than the fact that both are examples of model building.

Ricardo was not the first or the only economist to employ a model in his work. What makes him stand out in that model-building was not a method to which he had occasional recourse: it was his typical and usual method of reasoning. Moreover, an examination of his arguments will show that the model is essential to the argument; it is not there to add colour or verisimilitude. Thus Ricardo's work sometimes reveals an almost mathematical quality, being concerned with the development of the logical implications of certain postulates. The apparent power and objectivity of this kind of reasoning could not fail to impress those who came to it anew.

From the beginning of the modern subject, then, certain important distinctions are already apparent, notably that between realism and abstraction, and between description and model building. The method of economics for another hundred years was to be very largely historical (historical, that is, in the sense that the kind of evidence employed and the manner in which it was made use of were both the same as would characterize historical enquiry). Ricardo used invented numbers, partly because his argument was general and not dependent upon the particular values selected, but also because the availability of statistics in his time was extremely limited and haphazard. But it would be wrong to suppose that this made economics a non-empirical subject. Malthus, for example, was certainly influenced by the observation that population was growing at an unprecedented rate in the England of his time, and the correctness of that observation cannot be questioned. He estimated that population unchecked by restraints would double every 25 years, which corresponds to an annual rate of increase of 2.8 per cent per annum. The latter estimate has stood up well for a population which is balanced in age composition at the start and then accelerates in its growth.

The work of Petty in gathering statistics is frequently cited, but it stands out more for being pioneering than for being representative. It was government that was to collect statistics, and government was still exceedingly small by later standards. A growing science normally demands measurement, if not experiment, as a young child calls for food. Economics, however, was nourished for a long time by such observations as were available to the informed citizen and chiefly by its own ideas. In this respect it resembled Greek science or modern physics when the latter has outreached the possibility of experiment. Most of all, it resembled philosophy to which its close affinity was recorded in the term 'moral sciences' for long in use in the ancient universities of Britain. One could characterize the 150 years and beyond following the publication of *The Wealth of Nations* as having been preoccupied with working out the logical implications of certain assumptions about economic reality, while at the same time those assumptions themselves were in the process of being changed and influenced by far-reaching alterations in economic institutions. This was no small task. The logical implications of economic assumptions can be rich and complex, and they readily give rise to controversy. Some have attributed these problems to the inherent difficulty of the subject, others to the powerful ideological content of the questions involved – both are partly correct.

The difficulties of economic theory do not consist simply of the intellectual demands that it makes, which do not compare with those of physics or pure mathematics. It is rather that economics requires a body of analytical tools and a technique of reasoning without which even simple questions cannot be accurately answered. The uninitiated constantly demonstrate the truth of that claim. However, the development of these tools and methods took some considerable time. One need only compare the writings of John Stuart Mill with those of some indifferent economist of the turn of the century to see what a difference the accumulation of technique had made. In Mill we see one of the finest intellects of the nineteenth century struggling to cut his way through a jungle. In the plain economist of the later years we would see an unskilled craftsman no doubt, but one working with what by then had become a thoroughly useful box of tools. There are even tasks for which the latter would be better employed.

The ideological problem is ever present. Economists have sometimes seen it as a distraction, as a diversion from the important questions on which economics could speak, but there is no justification for such a simple separation. Through experience and through the application of the same apparatus that he uses to resolve other matters, the economist is uniquely placed to say useful things about the type of political conflict which is concerned with the division of economic goods. That does not mean, of course, that he should play God, or pretend to more expertise than he has, but equally he cannot push such questions aside and say that because they are not all to do with him, they are therefore not at all to do with him.

The problem is naturally not peculiar to economics. It arises in any field in which the expert must address himself to issues concerning which people, including the practitioners themselves, their students, their employers and others, have strong feelings. Certain principles are obvious if economics is not to be sucked into the political whirlpool. The pursuit of objectivity and scholarly integrity clearly belong among them. These principles are under attack from two sides. On the one side will be some who will argue that there is no detachment, no standing apart, and that science should serve progressive forces in society, however those may be defined at the time. On the other side will be those who claim to accept these principles, only to discredit them by advancing under the guise of the objective and the detached what is patently the ideological.

Economics has been assaulted to its foundations during its still short history by the claim that its doctrines are no more than 'false ideology'. Marx attacked what he called 'bourgeois political economy' as mere apologetics for the existing social order. He said the most wounding thing that can be said about a science – that his opponents were concerned only with the superficial, the surface appearance of things. The importance of Marx's contribution will ultimately be judged by what he put in the place of the economics which he attacked, and not by the attacks as such, memorable though their invective may be to anyone who has read them. It was Marx's political activity, and his political writing, that changed the world, as indeed they did, and not his economic theory. This is to insist on making a distinction to which the master would have strongly objected, but make it we must. Within the narrow field of economic theory he retains his followers to the present day, but Marxist economics, recent revivals notwithstanding, remains a backwater and a curiosum beside mainstream economics. The fact that it has failed to propose an alternative system to orthodoxy with anything like the same reach and the same richness, and probably could not as it is formulated, may alone explain this fact.

The last third of the nineteenth century witnesses a huge burgeoning of economic theory and the beginnings of systematic empirical investigation. The theoretical movement has been unhappily named 'neo-classical'. It was not 'neo' if that prefix means a revival of an earlier period, and it is difficult to see what meaning of the term 'classical' would usefully connect it with the early writers. Naturally, however, no movement is unconnected with the past. The use of abstraction and model-building was now freely employed, sometimes again to excess, but more fruitfully, generally speaking, than ever before. Most importantly, perhaps, the ultimately inescapable, mathematical character of economic reasoning was becoming clear. Diagrams were employed, not without resistance at first, and the concept of 'elasticity of demand' made its appearance. The 'marginalism' sometimes taken to characterize the period was more the result of the new approach than its generator. It may nevertheless be the most powerful single organizing principle that economics has yet seen.

These developments which established economics as we know it today began to change the appearance of the discipline. It came to stand apart from its neighbouring fields, not in every respect or in every part of the field to be sure, but noticeably all the same. Its employment of mathematics in particular, or mathematical-like reasoning, sometimes made it resemble physics more than it resembled law, philosophy, politics, history or sociology. On closer examination, however, economics did not seem to resemble any other discipline at all closely. The quantification of its theoretical relations, for example, without which a 'natural' science was not counted as having established itself, was still at a primitive stage of development. Still more, it was far from clear that the theoretical relationships of economics would ever attain to the status of those of physics or chemistry. The latter had arrived at powerful 'laws' which seemed to hold without exception and to a degree of approximation defined by the resolving power of the measuring instruments. True amendments to these laws were later shown to be necessary, but they were corrections and often unimportant ones. In economics, few 'laws' worth stating could be expected to hold except as tendencies. Science certainly could investigate weak effects or tendencies but it liked to have a great deal of preferably reliable data to undertake this task. But reliable data was in short supply and often small in quantity.

Had economists reached the point at which they demanded a testable implication of every new theory, they would undoubtedly have become completely discouraged by the formidable difficulties which confront the testing of economic hypotheses. Fortunately, perhaps, they have not yet arrived at that point. Many economic models are seen as following in the tradition established by Ricardo and illustrated by his model of comparative advantage. They are not designed to produce a hypothesis to be compared with the observation of reality, so much as they aim to explore the implications of making a set of assumptions, simplified by intention but equally meant to be realistic enough to capture something of reality. The ultimate aim of such an exercise is to influence the way in which people think about the world. There are so many examples of what such reasoning might be doing that it is not easy to find an instance that stands for more than its own type. However, the following case is certainly encountered rather frequently. An economist, drawing on observation formal or informal, says to himself: 'I think that people behave in such and such a way. What would follow if I was right in that belief?'

Why should the economist worry about the subsidiary question, which may very well involve him in a lot of work? The answer is that it is a check on the reasonableness of his initial assumption. It is no different in kind, though surely less monumental in import, than Newton asking himself what would happen if bodies moved in straight lines at constant velocity unless acted upon by a force. Interesting assumptions need to have their plausibility tested in a thoroughgoing manner. Otherwise people who believe that the wealth of a nation is measured by its balance of payments surplus, have too much influence.

Economic theory in the twentieth century has been altered by a major intellectual revolution, associated with the name of Keynes, of which more will be said below. However, the effect of the Keynesian revolution, important though it has been, should not be allowed to detract from certain advances which have gone on more or less continually, and not directly influenced by the new ways of thinking. Nineteenth-century economic theory was based on abstraction and on bringing economic concepts to bear on practical questions. These tendencies were continued in the twentieth century, which has witnessed some of the greatest successes of formalization and generalization which the subject has known, at the same time as it has seen a growing interest in bringing economic theory to bear directly on important real matters. In an age in which econometrics was increasingly available as a research tool, the old presumptions about realism and unrealism have sometimes been upset. Mathematically rich models have sometimes, though not always, lent themselves better to empirical implementation than have homely and realistic ones. An important example of this is the new mathematical method of linear programming, which has made complex maximization problems, even of large size, highly soluble.

Nineteenth-century economic theory borrowed from ethics the notion of 'utility' as measuring or representing the level of satisfaction or well-being of the household or consumer. It no doubt struck the students of the time as reasonable and sensible, as did Marshall's assumption that the marginal utility of income would be approximately constant, and it was useful in deriving simply the so-called 'law of demand'. Eventually this was too out of touch with reality for the twentieth-century taste, which had become more positivistic. How was utility to be measured? The outcome of these doubts was the realization that utility could only be an ordinal quantity, that this was all that was required to derive the consumer's behaviour, and the eventual understanding of income and substitution effects in a general framework.

The implication of this change of view did not stop with demand theory. Economic policy, or welfare economics, had previously been conceived as an application of utilitarian principles to economic questions. The application concerned, however, was a quantitative one; it supposed the measurability of utility. If that was now called into question, how were policy recommendations to be justified? A radical sceptical view said that they could only be justified as value judgements, that any claimed scientific basis to economic recommendations was unfounded. A more constructive approach set out to delineate which properties a recommendation would have to fulfil so as not to require value judgements for its validation. It was not so much that many interesting recommendations could be value-free that made this exercise of importance; rather the whole investigation greatly clarified how value judgements enter into economic reasoning and for the first time put welfare economics on a sound basis.

The earlier welfare economics of the nineteenth century was now seen to be, to a great extent, the economics of efficiency. The problem of distribution, of equity, one could say, had been treated as something separate, independent of efficiency. One of the major advances of the twentieth century, particularly the period following the Second World War, has been the development of a theory of economic policy, much closer to reality in its conception and in its method than traditional welfare economics. Efficiency has not been shown to be an irrelevant consideration – far from it – but the role that efficiency plays in a system constrained by perhaps a bad distribution of incomes, or constrained to depart from efficiency in certain directions, has been clarified. Economic policy has become the art of maximizing the possible, second-best optimization, in the jargon of today's economics.

A settled interpretation and assessment of the contribution of Keynes is still elusive nearly fifty years after the publication of his great work, *The General Theory*, in 1936. That this should be so is a measure partly of problems and obscurities in that work, and partly of the value which has been conceded to its ideas even by those who have undertaken to attack them. Only recently have wholehearted rejections arisen in the main countries of economic research, rejections not based simply on ideological revulsion. Many earlier critiques, notably that associated with Milton Friedman's monetarism, were more revisionist than completely counter to Keynes's method as well as to his conclusions. One reason is that Keynes posed some sharp and important questions to the then orthodoxy which it was at the time wholly unable to answer. To these questions Keynes provided answers. There are no more potent ingredients for an intellectual revolution and its rapid dissemination.

Keynesian ideas found their expression in a new field, macroeconomics. This division of economic theory into separate and largely non-communicating sectors was readily accepted at the time but was later felt to be unhealthy. While setting itself apart from much existing theory, the new ideas very easily connected with applied economics and econometrics, and the new macroeconomics was an applied subject from the outset. Economic forecasting models were constructed, sometimes of huge scale, and governments and private users began to pay for their results. Just as it was applied in spirit, so was the new theory interventionist in outlook. According to Keynesian doctrine a wise government could stabilize the economy close to full employment and avoid fluctuations and inflation. Later the numerous problems associated with such a programme became apparent. From early optimism there has been a pessimistic reaction in which stress has been laid on the powerlessness of governments to have any useful influence in a world whose individual actors have become more sophisticated and far-seeing. It is too early yet to forecast where these latest ideas themselves will lead, but one may note a development which is unlikely to be harmful in the end. The apparently well-established division between macroeconomics and microeconomics is breaking down. On the one hand, macro-theorists are no longer willing to accept that agents act in not very intelligent rule-of-thumb ways when it comes to determining employment and wages and asset prices, or assessing the influence of government policies on their futures, while attributing considerable sophistication to those agents when discussing price determination in individual markets. On the other hand, microeconomic theorists are more interested in building models of the price rigidities and rationing that sometimes seem to characterize markets, rather than dismissing such cases as freaks.

Meanwhile, at the practical level, economists are in a state of intellectual ferment, which manifests itself to the outsider as chaotic disunity, concerning fundamental questions of macroeconomic management. On the basic question of the consequences of a large government deficit, for example, reputable spokesmen can be found to claim that the deficit as such is unimportant, that only the supply-side, somehow defined, matters; that the deficit matters only if translated to excessive growth in the money supply; or that the deficit is expansionary, if not perhaps in the most healthy manner. The world and the profession must derive what comfort it can from the fact that such widespread disagreements tend to resolve themselves, usually as the result of the accumulation of new evidence, but sometimes of new ideas as well. Modern economics has huge resources in its techniques and in its methods of evaluating empirical evidence. These should eventually enable it to emerge from the present 'crisis of confidence' stronger and in better shape. If, as seems likely, the public never quite recovers an excessive confidence which it may have placed in the pronouncements of economists, there will be no harm in that.

Economics began as a British subject and remained so for many years. Today it is an international discipline including scholars from most countries of the world and from all regions. Its chief centre is in the US, and papers originating from there account for a sizeable proportion of those appearing in the major journals. Economists everywhere advise governments and private institutions, and they frequently write in newspapers and appear on the radio and on television. Another important development, particularly since the Second World War, has been the use of economics in new and unexpected fields. Thus the economics of medicine, to cite one example, has now become a specialism with its own practitioners and its own journals. Through optional courses at universities, more people now have some exposure to economics than ever before. While co-operating well with workers from other disciplines in applied work, economists still stand apart when it comes to theory, and fruitful cross-disciplinary co-operation, while it happens, is not at all common. A growing tendency towards specialization within the field has been evident. Few scholars are economists and econometricians, for example, and many define their field of interest surprisingly narrowly. In part this state of affairs is imposed by the huge amount of literature now appearing in every field which demands the attention of the serious worker. While it would be rash to predict the future of the subject very far ahead, it is interesting to note that the loss of an excessive confidence in economists' abilities to pronounce the truth has not been accompanied by a loss of interest in employing them. Although academic openings in the 1980s compare unfavourably with the rich possibilities of the 1960s, many other employment opportunities continue to attract economists.

Christopher Bliss
University of Oxford

Further Reading

Blaug, M. (1980), *The Methodology of Economics, or How Economists Explain*, Cambridge.

Friedman, M. (1969), *The Optimal Quantity of Money and Other Essays*, Chicago.

Keynes, J. M. (1931), *Essays in Persuasion*, London.

Keynes, J. M. (1936), *The General Theory of Employment, Interest and Money*, London.

Koopmans, T. C. (1957), *Three Essays on the State of Economic Science*, New York.

Little, I. M. D. (1982), *Economic Development: Theory, Politics and International Relations*, New York.

Luce, R. D. and Riaffa, H. (1967), *Games and Decisions*, New York.

Meade, J. E. (1975), *The Intelligent Radical's Guide to Economic Policy: The Mixed Economy*, London.

Robinson, J. (1966), *An Essay on Marxian Economics*, London.

Samuelson, P. A. (1980), *Economics: An Introductory Analysis*, 11th edn, New York.

Schumpeter, J. S. (1952), *Ten Great Economists*, London.

Schumpeter, J. S. (1954), *History of Economic Analysis*, Oxford.

Sen, A. K. (1982), *Choice, Welfare and Measurement*, Oxford.

Shackle, G. L. S. (1967), *The Years of High Theory*, Cambridge.

See also: *Political economy*.

Accelerator Principle

In contrast to the (Keynesian) multiplier, which relates output to changes in investment, the accelerator models investment as determined by changes in output. As the principle that investment responds to the changes in output which imply pressure on capacity, the accelerator has a long history, but its formal development dates from the realization that its combination with the multiplier could produce neat models of cyclical behaviour. J. M. Clark originally noted the possibilities inherent in such models, but their first formal development was by Lundberg and Harrod, and subsequently by Samuelson, with Hicks and Goodwin and others providing refinements.

Suppose the optimal capital stock stands in fixed proportion to output, that is, formally:

$$K^* = \alpha Y$$

where K^* is the desired stock of fixed capital

Y is annual output

α is the average and marginal ratio of optimal capital to output i.e. $(K^* / Y = \Delta K^* / Y)$

Now let the subscripts t and t-1 refer to the variables in years t and $t-1$

$$K^*_{t-1} = \alpha Y_{t-1}$$
$$K^*_t = \alpha Y_t$$
$$\text{so } K^*_t - K^*_{t-1} = \alpha(Y_t - Y_{t-1})$$

Assume that the optimal capital stock was achieved in year $t-1$,

$$K_{t-1} = K^*_{t-1}$$

therefore $K^*_t - K_{t-1} = \alpha(Y_t - Y_{t-1})$

To understand investment, that is, the flow of expenditure on capital goods, it is necessary to know how quickly investors intend to close any gap between the actual and optimal capital stocks. Let λ be an adjustment coefficient which represents the extent to which the gap between the realized and the desired capital stocks is to be closed.

Then

$$I_t = \lambda\alpha(Y_t - Y_{t-1})$$
or $I_t = V(Y_t - Y_{t-1})$

The λ and α coefficients together link investment to first differences in output levels and are described as the accelerator coefficient, here V. Even at this elementary level the accelerator has several interesting implications. First, net investment determined by the accelerator will be positive (negative and zero respectively) if and only if $(Y_t - Y_{t-1})$ is positive (negative and zero resepectively). Second, such net investment will fall if the *rate* at which output is increasing declines.

However, even at this simple level the weaknesses of the approach are also apparent. First, the results above relate *only* to investment determined by the accelerator, that is motivated as described above by a desire to expand capacity in line with output. It may well be that while entrepreneurs are influenced by relative pressure on their capital stocks, other factors also act as an inducement/disincentive to investment such as expectations, availability of new technology, and so on. Thus, the accelerator describes only a part of investment which might not stand in any fixed relation to total investment. Furthermore, the capacity argument really only models the *optimal capital stock*. To make the jump to the flow of investment requires the introduction of the λ coefficient which can only be justified by *ad hoc* references to supply conditions in the investment goods industries and/or the state of expectations. In the absence of such additional assumptions it would only be possible to say that $I \lesseqgtr O$ according to whether $K^*_t \lesseqgtr K_{t-1}$.

As suggested above, the accelerator has been fruitfully combined with the multiplier in models designed to explicate economic dynamics. Here the problem has been that while such models are useful in understanding the origins of cyclical fluctuation, realistic estimates of V predict an unreasonable degree of dynamic instability. This problem has generally been solved by combining the accelerator with other determinants of investment in more general models, and more specifically by theorizing the existence of 'floors' and 'ceilings' to income fluctuation, hence constraining potentially explosive accelerator multiplier interactions. In addition, generalized accelerator models themselves have provided the basis for empirical investigation of investment behaviour.

Jane Humphries
University of Cambridge

Further Reading

Goodwin, R. M. (1948), 'Secular and cyclical aspects of the multiplier and the accelerator', in *Income Employment and Public Policy: Essays in Honor of Alvin H. Hansen*, New York.

Harrod, R. F. (1936), *The Trade Cycle: An Essay*, Oxford.

Hicks, J. R. (1949), 'Mr Harrod's dynamic theory', *Economica*, XVI.

Hicks, J. R. (1950), *A Contribution to the Theory of the Trade Cycle*, Oxford.

Lundberg, E. (1937), *Studies in the Theory of Economic Expansion*, London.

Samuelson, P. A. (1939), 'A synthesis of the principle of acceleration and the multiplier', *Journal of Political Economy*, 47.

Samuelson, P. A. (1939), 'Interactions between the multiplier analysis and the principle of acceleration', *Review of Economic Statistics*, 21.

Accounting

Accounting deals with the provision of information about the economic activities of various accounting entities, the largest of which is the whole economy, for which national accounts are prepared. However, the traditional province of the accountant is the smaller unit, typically a business firm. Here, a distinction is often made between financial accounting and management accounting.

(1) *Financial accounting* deals with the provision of information to providers of finance (shareholders and creditors) and other interested parties who do not participate in the management of the firm (such as trade unions and consumer groups). This usually takes the form of a balance sheet (a statement of assets and claims thereon at a point in time), and a profit and loss account (a statement of revenue, expenses and profit over a period of time), supplemented by various other statements and notes. The form of financial accounting by companies is, in most countries, laid down by statute, and the contents are usually checked and certified independently by auditors. In some countries, there are also accounting standards laid down by the accounting profession or by the independent bodies which it supports, such as the United States Financial Accounting Standards Board, which determine the form and content of financial accounts.

(2) *Management accounting* is concerned with the provision of information to management, to assist with planning, decision making and control within the business. Because planning and decision making are inevitably directed to the future, management accounting often involves making future projections, usually called budgets. Important applications of this are capital budgeting, which deals with the appraisal of investments, and cash budgeting, which deals with the projection of future cash inflows and outflows and the consequent financial requirements of the entity. Management accounting is also concerned with controlling and appraising the outcome of past plans, for example, by analysing costs, and with assessing the economic performance of particular divisions or activities of the entity. Because the demand for management accounting information varies according to the activities, size and management structure of the entity, and because the supply of such information is not subject to statutory regulation or audit, there

is a much greater variety both of techniques and of practice in management accounting than in financial accounting.

Both management accounts and financial accounts derive from an accounting system which records the basic data relating to the transactions of the entity. The degree to which management accounting and financial accounting information can both derive from a common set of records depends on the circumstances of the individual accounting entity and, in particular, on the form of its management accounting. However, all accounting systems have a common root in double-entry book-keeping, a self-balancing system, based on the principle that all assets of the entity ('debits') can be attributed to an owner (a claim on the entity by a creditor or the owners' 'equity' interest in the residual assets of the entity, both of which are 'credits'). This system owes its origin to Italian merchants of the fifteenth century, but it is still fundamental to accounting systems, although records are now often kept on computers, so that debits and credits take the form of different axes of a matrix, rather than different sides of the page in a handwritten ledger. The design of accounting systems to avoid fraud and error is an important aspect of the work of the accountant.

The traditional orientation of accounting was to record transactions at their historical cost, that is, in terms of the monetary units in which transactions took place. Thus, an asset would be recorded at the amount originally paid for it. Inflation and changing prices in recent years have called into question the relevance of historical cost, and inflation accounting has become an important subject. It has been proposed at various times and in different countries that accounts should show current values, that is, the specific current prices of individual assets, or that they should be adjusted by a general price level index to reflect the impact of inflation on the value of the monetary unit, or that a combination of both types of adjustment should be employed. Intervention by standard-setting bodies on this subject has been specifically directed at financial accounting, but it has been hoped that the change of method would also affect management accounting.

Financial accounting has also been affected, in recent years, by an increased public demand for information about business activities often supported by governments. Associated with this has been demand for information outside the scope of traditional profit-oriented accounts, resulting in research and experimentation in such areas as human asset accounting and corporate social reporting. There has also been more interest in accounting for public-sector activities and not-for-profit organizations. Recent developments in management accounting, facilitated by the increased use of computers, include the greater employment of the mathematical and statistical methods of operational research for such uses as the control of stock levels. This development has, however, been matched by a growing interest in behavioural aspects of accounting, for example, studies of the human response to budgets and other targets set by management accountants. The whole area of accounting is currently one of rapid change, both in research and in practice.

Geoffrey Whittington
University of Bristol

Further Reading
Arnold, J., Carsberg, B. and Scapens, R. (1980), *Topics in Management Accounting*, Oxford.
Barton, A. D. (1977), *The Anatomy of Accounting*, St Lucia, Queensland.
Bull, R. J. (1980), *Accounting in Business*, London.
Carsberg, B. and Hope A. (1977), *Current Issues in Accounting*, Oxford.
Edwards, E. O., Bell, P. W. and Johnson, L. T. (1979), *Accounting for Economic Events*, Houston.
See also: *capital consumption; stock-flow analysis*.

Advertising

Advertising is a way of drawing attention to goods offered for sale. Its aim may include the enhancing of a reputation as well as inducing immediate purchase, for example, political and charitable advertising, announcement of corporate trading results, and the sponsorship of sports or cultural events. Media employed include journals, newspapers, television, radio, cinema, bill hoardings and direct mail. Advertising grew in importance with the Industrial Revolution, mass production and, later, self-service retailing. As these replaced traditional methods of manufacture and distribution, so salesmen 'pushing' goods to a relatively small number of retailers were gradually and partially displaced by advertising aimed at large numbers of final consumers who, if convinced of a product's merits, would 'pull' it through the marketing channel. Retailers would stock goods which had been 'presold' by manufacturers' advertising.

Since the advent of television and the abolition of newsprint rationing after World War II, the economic importance of advertising has changed little. Total UK expenditure was 1.43 per cent of GNP in 1960; in 1981 1.34 per cent. In the US, the 1981 figure was 1.38 per cent. In the UK in 1981 the press accounted for 65 per cent of all expenditure, television for 28.7 per cent. For the US corresponding figures were 54.7 per cent and 31.3 per cent. The most obtrusive form is MCA (manufacturers' advertising directed at consumers) which excludes financial, employment, trade, classified (or personal), retailer and charitable advertising. The 1981 MCA component was 42 per cent of the UK total.

Advertising presupposes free consumer choice and consequentially provides problems to both practitioners and economists. Businesses must decide what to spend on advertising in terms of results. These are difficult to measure and so unambiguously to link the input with sales or profits. Economists have different concerns, such as advertising's link with competition, resource allocation and choice distortion. The traditional 'informative' and 'persuasive' distinction exemplifies that disquiet. The dichotomy for many is useful but non-operational. J. K. Galbraith (1962) popularized it by awarding the outcome of 'persuasive' advertising the title of the 'Dependence Effect'. Thus, consumer wants depend not on innate human needs but on advertising; producers must 'create' these wants to dispose of their output, and were it not for advertising, people would have no important, unsatisfied desires. However, the argument's force lies in its originator's persuasive semantics and not in empirical proof.

In the last three decades a large amount of empirical work has been conducted. On balance it is indecisive. Advertising has not been found to be conclusively associated or otherwise with a range of economic variables: for example, measures of industrial concentration, entry barriers, competitive mobility, monopoly profits, price-cost margins or aggregate demand. Other controversies have been settled. Advertising appears to be closely linked to technological innovation and diffusion (whether this is to be approved of will vary with the view adopted regarding the Dependence Effect). Advertising also provides a guarantee of quality since a brand name can be relied upon to denote product consistency; conversely, some brand names would indicate products to avoid. An unadvertised product would not be so identifiable. Again, however, consensus is wanting since, unless the assumption is made that persistent purchasing of a brand *vis à vis* a cheaper non-advertised product is free of the Dependence Effect, then no agreement can be reached that branding and advertising guarantee value *vis à vis* quality.

One way out of the theoretical and empirical impasse is the suggestion by economists of the Austrian school that advertising should be seen as part of the total product package bought, or not bought, by the consumer. Without advertising, the product either ceases to exist or is a different product, just as it would be if a tangible input was removed. Littlechild (1981) claims that the relevant (practical) alternatives then become the product as it stands or no product at all. The concept of the product with or without advertising is not a real world choice. Although this approach could resolve many of the economic debates and could also bring economists into agreement with practitioners, it seems unlikely to command a consensus.

W. Duncan Reekie
University of the Witwatersrand

Further Reading
Broadbent, S. (1979), *Spending Advertising Money*, 3rd edn, London.
Galbraith, J. K. (1962), *The Affluent Society*, London.
Littlechild, S. C. (1981), 'The social costs of monopoly power', *Economic Journal*.
Reekie, W. D. (1981), *The Economics of Advertising*, London.
See also: *marketing research*.

Aid

The terms aid or development aid (often also foreign aid or development assistance) are not entirely unambiguous and are often used with slightly different meanings by different writers and organizations. However, there is agreement that in essence resource transfers from a more developed to a less developed country (or from a richer country to a poorer country) qualify for inclusion in 'aid' provided they meet three criteria:

(1) The objective should be developmental or charitable rather than military.
(2) The donor's objective should be non-commercial.
(3) The terms of the transfer should have a concessional element ('grant element').

Each of these criteria gives rise to some conceptual difficulty. The first one neglects the factor of 'fungibility', that is, that up to a point the use of resources by the recipient country is somewhat flexible. For example, aid may be given and ostensibly used for developmental purposes, but in fact the recipient country may use its own resources set free by this transaction in order to buy armaments; or the aid may lead to leakages and abuses and result in the building up of bank accounts in Switzerland, rather than to the ostensible developmental objectives. Such frustrations of aid objectives are impossible to allow for statistically.

The second criterion, that the objective should be non-commercial, also presents difficulties. Much of the bilateral aid, that is, aid given by a single government to another government, is 'tied', which means that the proceeds must be spent on classified goods produced in the donor country. Here we clearly have a commercial objective mixed in with the developmental objective; it is again impossible to decide statistically at what point the transaction becomes a commercial transaction rather than aid. The line of division between export credits and tied aid of this kind is clearly a thin one. Moreover, many acts of commercial policy, such as reduction of tariffs or preferential tariff treatment given to developing countries under the internationally agreed GSP (Generalized System of Preferences) can be more effective aid than many transactions listed as aid – yet they are excluded from the aid concept.

The third criterion – that the aid should be concessional and include a grant element – is also not easy to define. What, for example, is a full commercial rate of interest at which the transaction ceases to be aid? The grant element may also lie in the duration of any loan, in the granting of a 'grace period' (a time-lag between the granting of the loan and the date at which the first repayment is due). The DAC (Development Assistance Committee of the OECD, the Organization for Economic Cooperation and Development in Paris) makes a valiant attempt to combine all these different aspects of concessionality into one single calculation of the grant element. However, such calculations are subject to the objection that the grant element in aid from the donor's point of view may differ from that from the recipient's point of view. In DAC aid in 1981, some 75 per cent was direct grants and the loans had a 58 per cent grant element, resulting in an 'overall grant element' for total aid of 89 per cent.

The Development Assistance Committee is the main source of aid statistics, and its tabulations and definitions are generally recognized as authoritative. DAC publishes an Annual Report under the title 'Development Cooperation'; the 1983 volume contains detailed tables and breakdowns of aid flows. The OECD countries (the Western industrial countries including Japan, Australia and New Zealand) and the international organizations supported by them, such as the World Bank, the Regional Development Banks, the UN Development Programme, and so on, account for the bulk of global aid. DAC also provides some data on other aid flows such as from OPEC

(Organization of Petroleum Exporting Countries) countries and from the Eastern bloc.

Private investment, lending by commercial banks, and private export credits are by definition treated as commercial and thus excluded from aid. In recent years such private flows have been larger than aid, although this has only been the case since 1974 when some of the big surpluses of the OPEC countries were recycled by commercial banks to developing countries.

One of the main distinctions is between bilateral aid and multilateral aid (contributions of multilateral institutions such as the World Bank, the Regional Development Banks, and so forth). This distinction is also not entirely clear. For example, the Western European countries give some of their aid through the EEC (European Economic Community). EEC aid is not bilateral nor is it fully multilateral as the World Bank is; it is therefore to some extent a matter of arbitrary definition whether EEC aid should be counted as bilateral or multilateral. Multilateral aid is more valuable to the recipient than tied bilateral aid, because it gives a wider choice of options to obtain the imports financed by aid from the cheapest possible source. Untied bilateral aid would be equally valuable to the recipient – however, on political grounds, the recipient (and some donors, too) may prefer the multilateral route. In recent years multilateral aid has constituted about 25 per cent of total aid.

It has been frequently pointed out that aid donors could increase the value of their aid to the recipients without any real cost to themselves, either by channelling it multilaterally or by mutually untying their aid by reciprocal agreement. However, this might lose bilateral aid some of the political support which it acquires by tying and which gives national producers and workers a vested interest in aid. This is particularly important in the case of food aid.

H. W. Singer
University of Sussex

Reference
OECD (1983), *Development Cooperation in 1983 Review*, Paris.

Further Reading
Bhagwati, J. and Eckaus, R. S. (eds) (1970), *Foreign Aid. Selected Readings*, Harmondsworth.
Brandt Commission (1983), *Common Crisis. North-South Co-operation for World Recovery*, London.
Pincus, J. (1967), *Trade, Aid and Development*, New York.

Antitrust Legislation

Capitalist economies rely primarily on free markets to allocate resources efficiently and make suppliers responsive to consumer preferences. If individual businesses or combinations of suppliers (cartels) are able to restrict output and raise prices, resources will be misallocated and consumer choice may be limited. For these reasons, most countries with free market economies have some form of law or regulation aimed at preventing or curbing undue exercise of monopoly power. In framing such legislation the question arises whether to lay down clear rules of law proscribing monopolistic conduct, or whether to provide that the legality of such conduct should depend on some assessment of its economic effects.

Clear rules of law are best exemplified in the antitrust legislation of the United States of America, reflecting the strong American preference for settling issues through the courts rather than by administrative action. Thus the Sherman Act (1890) declares illegal (Section 1) 'every contract, combination . . . or conspiracy in restraint of trade or commerce among the several States or with foreign nations' and makes it a misdemeanour (Section 2) for any person 'to monopolize or attempt to monopolize . . . any part of the trade or commerce. . .'. The Clayton Act (1914) with later amendments makes illegal exclusive dealing, price discrimination and acquisitions where the effect may be 'to substantially lessen competition or tend to create a monopoly', and the Federal Trade Commission Act (1914) prohibits 'unfair methods of competition in commerce'.

The courts interpret these broad provisions according to a

'rule of reason', but this is concerned only to establish that the purpose of the defendants is truly anti-competitive; it does not permit deliberate restrictions of competition to be defended on the ground that they are economically reasonable. In the 1980s, however, under the influence of the Chicago school of economics, an important section of legal opinion holds that enforcement action should be shown to be in the interests of economic efficiency. A notable feature of antitrust enforcement is that private suits may be undertaken and plaintiffs, if successful, can obtain treble damages, that is three times the damage caused to them by the antitrust offence, as well as their costs.

In economies smaller than the United States and more dependent on international trade, it may appear that the domestic market cannot sustain a number of competitors of adequate strength to compete in world markets, and hence that the exercise of monopoly power should not be condemned without careful analysis of its economic effects. In the United Kingdom, for example, under the Restrictive Trade Practices Act (1976) restrictive agreements and cartels are brought before the Restrictive Practices Court, and there is a presumption that they operate against the public interest; but the presumption is rebuttable if certain economic justifications for them can be established. No such presumption operates against monopolies or proposed mergers, but cases may be referred under the Fair Trading Act (1973) to the Monopolies and Mergers Commission which advises on broad economic grounds whether such arrangements operate or may be expected to operate against the public interest. Where it finds this to be so, the government has powers of remedial action.

The legislation in the European Economic Community lies between these poles. Under Article 85 of the Treaty of Rome, all agreements and concerted practices restricting competition within the common market are prohibited as 'incompatible with the common market', and Article 86 prohibits 'any abuse by one or more undertakings of a dominant position within the common market. . .'. At first sight these provisions look similar to the clear rules of law of the Sherman Act and they are enforced by decisions of the European Court. There are, however, significant differences. Article 85(3) provides that agreements may be exempted from the general prohibition where they promote technical or economic progress and do not affect competition unduly. Article 86 operates against the abuse of dominant positions, not as Section 2 of the Sherman Act against acquiring and taking steps to maintain a monopoly position. Moreover, the operation of the Treaty relies heavily on administrative action by the European Commission which has, for example, promulgated significant exemptions from Article 85 for classes of restrictive agreement, and which has the responsibility with relatively meagre resources for selecting and preparing cases to be brought before the Court. For these reasons the impact of the legislation on business in the Community is markedly less than that of antitrust in the United States, and the main emphasis so far has been on preventing types of restrictive practice which have the effect of re-establishing trade barriers between the member countries.

Alan Neale
London

Further Reading
Neale, A. D. and Goyder, D. G. (1980), *The Antitrust Laws of the USA* (3rd edn), Cambridge.
Hawk, B. E. (1979), *United States, Common Market and International Antitrust: A Comparative Guide*, New York.
See also: *business concentration; cartels and trade associations; competition; monopoly; oligopoly.*

Austrian School

The Austrian School of Economics is one of the branches of economic thought which grew out of the Marginalist or neoclassical revolution (1870–1890). Although basically similar to the teachings stemming from Jevons, Leon Walras and Marshall, the Austrian School's unique ideas were already contained in Menger's relatively slim volume, *Grundsätze der Volkswirtschaftslehreo* (1871), thus giving the school its alternative name, the 'Menger School'. Menger was the sole professor of economic theory in the law faculty of Vienna University between 1873 and 1903. Wieser succeeded him in 1904 and held the position until 1922. But from 1904 until 1913, Böhm-Bawerk, too, was an economics professor in the university, which is why the school is also known as the 'Vienna School'.

Menger (1950 [1871]) tried to create a unified theory of prices, encompassing commodity as well as distributional prices. He based this on subjective valuation of the buyers at the moment of purchase, that is, on their direct utility for consumption goods or their indirect utility for productive services. These ideas are similar to other marginalist traditions. But what was unique to Menger's approach was his stress on problems of information in economics (taken up later by Hayek), consequent upon the time structure of production which entails the likelihood of forecasting errors, especially by producers of 'higher order commodities' – those far removed from final demand ('first order commodities'). From this developed the Austrians' concern with both capital and business cycle theory, the two being seen as closely linked (Böhm-Bawerk, Mises, Hayek, Schumpeter). Another unique contribution by Menger was his vision of price formation, with monopolistic pricing or even individual bargains at the fore, and perfect competition only a limiting case. Thus prices are not fully determinate, but subject to bargaining – this approach developed via Morgenstern into the Theory of Games. Menger regarded commodities as typically unhomogeneous; the constant creation of new varieties of final commodities, aside from offering insights into productive possibilities, were to him the most important aspects of development, another idea taken up by Schumpeter. Finally, Menger was the first of many Austrians to be concerned with monetary theory: he saw in money the most marketable commodity, and a medium of reserve held for precautionary reasons, with, consequently, a volatile velocity of circulation.

The best-known contributions of Menger's successors are Böhm-Bawerk's (1959) attempts to measure capital in terms of waiting time, and his determinants of 'the' rate of interest. Wieser (1927 [1914]) should be remembered for his notion that prices are, above all, informative, and therefore necessary for all private and social calculations (an idea which is now usually associated with Mises's strictures on the impossibility of efficient socialist economies without market prices). Wieser also propounded the leadership role of the creative entrepreneur, an idea which Schumpeter (1952 [1912]) expanded into his theory of innovation and economic development. Mises (1949) and Hayek created a monetary ('Austrian') theory of the business cycle: investment booms are caused by bouts of bank credit at a market rate of interest below the rate of return on capital, a credit creation which cannot be prolonged indefinitely without additional saving, so that much new capital formation must be prematurely terminated.

More recently, a new 'Austrian School' has developed, particularly in the US. Taking up the strands of Austrian thought, it stresses the non-static nature of economic processes and the informational uniqueness of entrepreneurial decision taking. It must be noted, however, that both in respect of the full scope of thought and in its personal links, its connection with the now defunct former Austrian School is rather tenuous.

Erich Streissler
University of Vienna

References
Böhm-Bawerk, E. (1890), 'The Austrian economists', *Annals of the American Academy of Political and Social Science*, 1.
Böhm-Bawerk, E. (1959), *Capital and Interest*, 3 vols, South Holland, 1.
Menger, C. (1950 [1871]), *Principles of Economics: First General Part*, ed J. Dingwall and B. F. Hoselitz, Glencoe, Ill. (Original German edn, *Grundsätze der Volkswirtschaftslehre*, Vienna.)
Mises, L. (1949), *Human Action: A Treatise on Economics*, 3rd edn, New Haven.
Schumpeter, J. (1952 [1912]), *The Theory of Economic Development: An Inquiry into Profits, Capital, Credit, Interest and the Business Cycle*, 5th edn, Cambridge, Mass. (Original German edn, *Theorie der wirtschaftlichen Entwicklung*, Leipzig.)

Wieser, F. (1927 [1914]), *Social Economics*, New York. (Original German edn, 'Theorie der gesellschaftlichen Wirtschaft' in *Grundriss der Sozialökonomik*, Tübingen.)

Further Reading

Hicks, J. R. and Weber, W. (eds) (1973), *Carl Menger and the Austrian School of Economics*, Oxford.

Streissler, E. (1969), 'Structural economic thought – on the significance of the Austrian School today', *Zeitschrift für Nationalökonomie*, 29.

See also: *Schumpeter*.

Automation

The key feature of an automated production process is its control, either total or partial, by machines. Although over the years it has been used in widely differing ways (Rezler, 1969), automation can be considered an extension to, although not necessarily an evolution of, mechanization, the application of machines to previously human or animal tasks. Mechanization becomes automation when the human operator is partially or totally replaced by automatic controls. Automation may involve, as general examples, the automatic transfer of materials within a production process; or the automatic provision of information on the state of a production process and automatic reaction to divergences from pre-set norms; or the collection, processing and transmission of data and information either without, or with only limited, human intervention.

Although early embodiments of the automation concept, such as the thermostat, can be found, it now largely concerns the application of computer technology in production (widely defined). Thus present-day examples of automated processes include computer-numerically-controlled machine tools, automatic transfer lines, automated warehousing systems, flexible manufacturing systems, computer-aided design and manufacture (CAD/CAM), robots, word processing, electronic funds transfer and information networks. Given the computer-based nature of most automated processes and the information processing principles embodied in these processes, the current terminology of computerization or information technology is synonymous with automation. Such synonyms have the advantage of correctly suggesting that the technology can be applied to any economic sector, not just manufacturing.

Since the advent of electronic computers in the late 1940s, enormous advances based largely on developments in the technology of electronic components have generated machines that are physically smaller, more powerful and with greater logic and storage capacity, in many cases the improvements being by factors measured in thousands. Extensive miniaturization and improvements in information-processing ability have opened up the technological possibility of automating processes that it was not previously possible to automate. One must be careful, however. The hardware advances must be matched by suitable software (programming) before their application is possible, and software advances have not in general kept pace with hardware improvements. The improvements in computer technology have also been matched by significant price reductions. These changes make automation economically as well as technologically feasible.

Attitudes to automation vary across a wide spectrum. The potential that automation provides for replacing men by machines conjures up two possible extreme scenarios for the future of industrial society:

(1) A future is envisaged where automation ensures an unlimited growth of labour productivity, man is increasingly dispensable in the production process, goods and services will be supplied in unlimited amounts by machines, and man can devote his efforts to the arts and the higher levels of human experience rather than be tied to machines. It is a vision of a society where most material wants can be satisfied, where there is no poverty and unlimited leisure time.

(2) At the other extreme is the vision of a society of mass unemployment, with wide disparities in income distribution and, consequently, an underlying threat of violence in society. Those who own the machines, or the few

still employed, will be the wealthy. The masses will be
unemployed and impoverished.

Such science-fiction type visions are probably more fiction
than science, at least in a medium-term view. These visions
imply such enormous increases in productivity as a corollary
to automation that they can really only be extremely long-term
projections. In the shorter term, the impact on productivity of
extensions to the use of new information technology is much
more moderate. If one thinks of automation as something
additional to the 'normal' processes leading to productivity
increase (which itself is not really certain), rough approximations suggest that labour productivity may only be 10 per
cent higher in 1990 than if the potential for automation did not
exist (Stoneman *et al.*, 1982). This does not seem particularly
revolutionary. This is not to deny, however, the strength of
feeling behind the discussions of the impact of automation on
society, in particular the fear of potential mass unemployment.
   The impact of technological change on employment has been
raised many times since Ricardo's original contribution to the
subject. The parallel between modern discussions and Ricardo's
work suggests that we have not proceeded far in finding an
answer to the problem (David, 1982). (For a fuller discussion
see Stoneman, 1983.) However the following points are salient
to the debate:

(1) The adoption of any new technology will not be instan-
    taneous. Diffusion processes are slow.
(2) Given that the new technology increases labour
    productivity, the impact on employment depends upon
    what happens to output. If it increases, then the direct
    labour demand-reducing effects may be offset.
(3) The impact of new technology in any one economy will
    depend on what happens in others through the inter-
    national trading nexus.
(4) New technology may affect the quality of products rather
    than costs, and the repercussions of product innovation
    may differ from those of process innovations.

(5) It is clear that most technologies when introduced change the required skill mix of the labour force. Such changes will almost definitely generate at least transitional unemployment.

On the positive side, automation can, although not necessarily will, reduce the need for work in harsh physical environments, increase the potential for leisure in society, generate new products, expand the potential for scientific advance, open up the frontiers of space or help tap new sources of energy (for example, solar power). Here again diffusion is slow, and one cannot expect instantaneous results.

Perhaps one of the most interesting impacts of automation or information technology will be its effect on the industrial structure of the economy. As automation proceeds, the proportion of the work force employed in the information sector will increase further. Moreover, traditional dividing lines between industries will become less distinct. The distinction between telecommunications and computers has almost disappeared. Data networks and electronic fund transfer already integrate data transfer into source industries. Within specific industries the classic phases in the production process of design, development, manufacture and inventory management have already, through CAD/CAM and computerized stock control systems, been shown to be capable of integration. As such changes occur so we should expect changes in both the organization of work and the location of industry.

It is clear that further extensions to computer use, automation and the application of new information technology can potentially, in the long term, affect dramatically the nature of industrial society. A vision of the future depends largely upon one's faith in the automaticity of the economy's responses to disequilibria, and one's view of the degree of inequality in the distribution of the costs and benefits of automation.

P. Stoneman
University of Warwick

References

David, P. A. (1982), 'Comments', in *Micro-Electronics, Robotics and Jobs*, ICCP, No. 7, Paris.

Rezler, J. (1969), *Automation and Industrial Labour*, New York.

Stoneman, P., Blattner, N. and Pastre, O. (1982), 'Major findings on and policy responses to the impact of information technologies on productivity and employment', in *Micro-Electronics, Robotics and Jobs*, ICCP, No. 7, Paris.

Stoneman, P. (1983), *The Economic Analysis of Technological Change*, Oxford.

Further Reading

Gourvitch, A. (1966), *Survey of Economic Theory on Technological Change* and (1940), *Employment*, New York.

Heertje, A. (1977), *Economics and Technical Change*, London.

Jones, T. (ed.) (1980), *Microelectronics and Society*, Milton Keynes.

See also: *technological progress*.

Balance of Payments

A balance of payments is an accounting record of a country's international transactions with the rest of the world. Foreign currency receipts from the sale of goods and services are called exports and appear as a credit item in what is termed the current account of the balance of payments. Foreign currency payments for purchases of goods and services are called imports and appear as a debit item in the current account. In addition, there are transactions in capital which appear in a separate capital account. Outflows of capital, to finance overseas investment, for example, are treated as debits, and inflows of capital are treated as credits. A deficit on current account may be offset or 'financed' by a surplus on capital account and vice versa. Since the foreign exchange rate is the price of one currency in terms of another, total credits (the supply of foreign exchange) and debits (the demand for foreign exchange) must be equal if the exchange rate is allowed to fluctuate freely to balance the supply of and demand for foreign currency. If the exchange rate is not free to vary, however, deficits or surpluses of foreign currency will arise. Deficits may be financed by government borrowing from international banks and monetary institutions, such as the International Monetary Fund, or by selling gold and foreign currency reserves. Surpluses may be dissipated by accumulating reserves or lending overseas.

The fact that a flexible exchange rate guarantees a balance in the foreign exchange market does not mean a country is immune from balance of payments difficulties. A country may experience a decline in real income and employment because of the inability of exports to pay for imports on current account. Such a deficit financed by capital inflows will not preserve jobs, nor will a depreciating currency necessarily guarantee that the current account deficit will be rectified. Neither can a country be indifferent to the international value of its currency. Widely fluctuating exchange rates may adversely affect international trade. A rapidly depreciating currency, which raises the domestic price of imports, can be highly inflationary, which necessitates further depreciation, and so on.

In considering measures to adjust the balance of payments, therefore, it is highly desirable that countries should focus on the current account if they are concerned with the functioning of the real economy, and (if in deficit) wish to avoid turbulent exchange rates round a declining trend. Three major approaches to balance of payments adjustment have been developed by economists, corresponding to how deficits are viewed. (1) The elasticities approach sees deficits as a result of distorted relative prices or uncompetitiveness in trade. Adjustment should work through exchange rate depreciation provided the sum of the price elasticities of demand for imports and exports exceeds unity. (2) The absorption approach views deficits as a result of excessive expenditure relative to domestic output, so that favourable adjustment must imply that expenditure falls relative to output. (3) The monetary approach ascribes deficits to an excess supply of money relative to demand, so that adjustment can be successful only if it raises the demand for money relative to the supply. In many contexts, particularly in developing countries, none of the approaches may be relevant where the problem is one of the characteristics of goods produced and exported, so that the price of balance of payments equilibrium is always slow growth. In this case, there is an argument for structural adjustment through planning and protection. If economic objectives are to be obtained simultaneously, a necessary condition is that the form of adjustment should be related to the initial cause of the disequilibrium.

A. P. Thirlwall
University of Kent

Further Reading
Thirlwall, A. P. (1982); *Balance of Payments, Theory and the United Kingdom Experience*, 2nd edn, London.
See also: *devaluation; exchange rate; international monetary system; international trade.*

Banking

The word for a bank is recognizably the same in virtually all European languages, and is derived from a word meaning 'bench' or 'counter'. The bench in question appears to have been that of the money-changer at the medieval fairs rather than that of the usurer, and the link of banking with trade between nations and communities has been maintained. The early banks were often started as a subsidiary business by merchants, shippers, cattle drovers and, more recently, by travel agents. Other banks grew out of the business of the goldsmiths, and some of the earliest were founded for charitable reasons. In the last two centuries, however, banking has become a recognizable trade in its own right, and companies and partnerships have been founded to carry on the specific business of banking.

Each legal system has its own definition of a bank. One common element present in nearly all definitions is the taking of deposits and the making of loans for the profit of the owners of the bank, although in some cases the proviso is made that both the deposits and the loans should be short term. An economist would be more likely to seize on the fact that a banker is able to use a relatively small capital of his own to pass large sums from ultimate lenders to ultimate borrowers, taking a margin on each transaction in the form of higher interest rates for loans than for deposits. Both these approaches credit banks with only one function, the macroeconomic function of intermediation. In reality all banks perform many more functions, while some recognized banks are not particularly active as intermediaries. Many provide payment services, and most act as insurers by giving guarantees on behalf of their customers. Services of this sort could plausibly be regarded as facilitating intermediation, but there are many other services that are purely incidental – investment management, computer services and travel agency are among them. Increasingly important in many countries is the part of the bank's income that comes from fees and commission rather than from the interest margin.

Because the liabilities of banks form a large part of the accepted definitions of the money supply, banks attract government regulation on a scale that is greater than that applying to almost every other sector. This regulation can be divided into two main areas. The first is regulation for the purposes of furthering monetary policy. The other area of regulation covers the prudent behaviour of banks in an effort to ensure the safe and efficient functioning of the banking system.

Monetary policy seeks to influence the behaviour of the real economy by changing various financial variables like interest rates, the stock of money, the volume of credit and the direction of credit. Since bank deposits account for a large part of the stock of money, and since bank loans are a very important part of the total volume of credit, it is only natural that banks should be the most important channel for monetary policy measures. The measures that have been imposed on banks include control of their interest rates, primary and secondary requirements on holdings of reserves with the central bank and of government securities, limitation of the amount of credit extended, and control over the direction of credit. Many of these measures built on constraints that the banks had previously observed on their own initiative for prudential reasons.

Banking is a business that depends completely on the confidence of the public, and for the most part banks have always been very careful not to endanger that confidence. After the banking crisis of the early 1930s, the self-regulation that banks had practised for prudential reasons was supplemented in most countries by an elaborate set of prudential regulations and often by detailed supervision; the same intensification of prudential regulation and supervision occurred after the 1974–5 banking crisis. The various measures adopted are often said to be motivated by a desire to protect the interests of the depositor, but an even more important motive is the need for any government to protect the stability and soundness of the entire financial system. The measures laid down in regulations are designed to prevent bank failures by ensuring that the capital and reserves are adequate to cover all likely risks of loss, and that there are sufficient sources of liquidity to meet cash demands day by day. Many sets of regulations seek to achieve these aims by detailed and rigid balance-sheet ratios, but the real problem is to ensure that no banks indulge in bad banking practices.

Over the past twenty or thirty years the banking systems of most developed countries have changed considerably in several directions. The first major trend has been the internationalization of banking. Until the middle of this century banks conducted most of their international business through correspondent banks in the various countries, but most large and many medium-sized banks now reckon to have branches in all important international financial centres. This move was led by the large banks from the United States, and they and branches of banks from other countries have introduced new techniques and been the catalysts for change in many countries whose banking markets were previously sheltered. Banking has also become internationalized through the establishment of a pool of international bank deposits (the so-called eurodollar market) and through syndicated lending by numbers of large banks to multinational corporations and to governments. During the recession that started in 1978, the inability of many governments and other borrowers to meet the conditions of loan repayments has been a considerable source of instability.

On the domestic scene the methods of operation of the international banking market have been adopted in what is termed 'wholesale' banking, in which banks deal with large organizations. The technique is essentially the mobilization of large deposits through an interbank money market to provide funds for loans of up to ten years, often at rates of interest that change every three or six months.

In 'retail' banking, with households and small businesses, the number of personal customers has increased, especially through the payment of wages into bank accounts rather than by cash. Competition has intensified, and savings banks, building societies and co-operative banks are becoming more like the main banks in their powers and kinds of business. The new electronic technology of payments, using the plastic card, will further increase competition, because it will enable institutions without branch networks to compete successfully with those that have branches.

Jack Revell
University College of North Wales
Bangor

Further Reading
Pecchioli, R. (1983), *The Internationalisation of Banking*, Paris.
Revell, J. R. S. (1973), *The British Financial System*, London.
Revell, J. R. S. (1983), *Banking and Electronic Fund Transfers: A Study of the Implications*, Paris.
See also: *credit; financial crises; financial system.*

Black Economy

In the strict sense, the black economy refers to that part of the economy based on illegal transactions, or to economic behaviour that is against the law. This covers income earned through criminal activities or undeclared but legally acquired income. In a broader sense, the black economy encompasses all kinds of economic transactions not reflected in the official statistics. Dealing with the black economy in this broader sense, one must also consider tax evasion, whereby people avoid the intended level of taxation through loopholes in the law. Other terms in use are 'unobserved economy', 'underground economy', and 'secondary economy', which all make clear that the concept is not only concerned with illegal but also with legal transactions that may result in a difference between the actual workings of an economy and the picture provided of it by the official data.

Official employment figures do not fully reflect the unemployment situation. People who receive social payments because they are sick or handicapped are not actually part of the labour market, so they contribute to hidden unemployment. Conversely, others who are registered as unemployed are gainfully occupied, in which case there is greater employment than officially registered.

We have similar problems when we investigate private consumption. Those who acquire black money by not declaring their income to the tax authorities also spend part of it. If shops do not invoice purchases, then actual consumption will be higher than registered consumption. Consequently, in many countries the depression seems actually to have been less severe for consumers than one would expect on the basis of reported developments. Real income distribution is also different from what the records suggest. Registered salaries fail to take into account the various fringe benefits such as free telephone, free meals and travel perks, while, at the lower end of the income scale, people often receive unrecorded payments. This also applies to production, national income and the economic growth rate, where official estimates fall below the actual.

The black economy has always existed, but there are strong indications, supported by econometric research in Europe and the US, that it has grown from a marginal phenomenon to a major feature of modern welfare states only since World War II. It is not easy to quantify the significance of the black economy, because this depends largely on what aspects of it are being considered. If one considers only non-declared income and/or hidden production, empirical studies suggest that it amounts to between 20 and 30 per cent of the real national income.

The theoretical economists' explanation of why an individual would choose to participate in the black economy is based on a calculation of expected costs and benefits, rather than on any moral judgements. Looked at from this perspective, it is clear that heavy taxes play a role. Nevertheless, in the US where taxes are lower and the consequences of being caught more severe, the size of the black economy seems to be roughly the same as in Europe. It may be significant that people nowadays are more critical of government spending than in the past. Furthermore, the government may create situations in which both parties benefit if one party were to act illegally. There may also be a tendency for individuals to defer less to the views and decisions of authorities and to place greater reliance on individual opinions and participation in decision making.

If policy makers react by tightening the laws and punishing offenders, export of capital may be stimulated, and people will seek other ways of avoiding taxes. By basing policy measures on an economic analysis of the decision-making process in the black economy, it might be possible to predict individual reactions, and in this way to establish optimal rules and norms. One could, for example, avoid formulating laws that would enable both parties to benefit from illegal behaviour. But as long as governments are not prepared to base policy measures on an analysis of the phenomenon itself, the black economy will continue to grow.

A. Heertje
University of Amsterdam

Further Reading
Heertje, A., Allen, M. and Cohen, A. (1982), *The Black Economy*, London.
Mars, G. (1983), *Cheats at Work*, London.

Business Concentration

Business seller concentration refers to the extent to which sales in a market, or economy, are concentrated in the hands of a few large firms. At the level of an individual market or industry, *market concentration* is thus an (imperfect) indicator of the *degree of oligopoly*, and measures thereof are widely used by industrial economists in empirical tests of oligopoly theory. The most popular operational measure is the *concentration ratio*, which records the share of industry size (usually sales, but sometimes employment or value added) accounted for by the k largest firms (where, usually, k = 3 or 4 or 5). Its popularity derives more from its regular publication in Production Census reports than from a belief in its desirable properties (either economic or statistical). The multitude of other concentration measures include the Hirschman-Herfindahl index, which is the sum of squared market shares of all firms in the industry, the Hannah-Kay index, a generalization of the former, and various statistical inequality measures borrowed from the study of personal income distribution. While there is general agreement that a respectable measure of concentration should be inversely related to the number of sellers and positively related to the magnitude of size inequalities, these criteria are satisfied by a large number of the alternative indexes, and there is no consensus on what is the ideal measure.

Evidence on market concentration is readily available for most Western economies, and although differences in methods of data collection and definitions make most international comparisons hazardous, some broad facts are indisputable:

(1) The pattern of concentration is similar within most countries, with high concentration prevalent in consumer good and capital-intensive industries.

(2) Typical levels of market concentration are higher in smaller economies.

(3) In-depth studies of the UK and the US suggest that, on average, the 5 firm ratio may be as much as 14 points higher in the UK. Studies of trends over time show a steady and pronounced increase in the UK from 1935 to 1968, with a levelling off in the 1970s. In the US, on the other hand, market concentration has remained fairly constant since World War II.

Theories on the causes of concentration include the technology and entry barrier explanation (emanating from the Structure-Conduct-Performance paradigm), and a range of stochastic models based on Gibrat's Law of Proportionate Effect. The latter are largely (statistically) successful in accounting for the characteristic positive skew observed in most firm size distributions and for the steady increase in concentration ('spontaneous drift'). They do not, however, provide a true economic understanding of the forces at work. Empirically, mergers have also been identified as a major source of concentration increases.

Aggregate concentration is often measured as the share in G.D.P, or aggregate manufacturing of the top 100 corporations. In the UK this rose dramatically from 16 per cent in 1909 to 40 per cent in 1968 and then remained constant up to 1980.

S. W. Davies
University of East Anglia

Further Reading
Curry, B. and George, K. D. (1983), 'Industrial concentration: a survey', *Journal of Industrial Economics*, 31.
See also: *antitrust legislation; competition; corporate enterprise; monopoly; oligopoly.*

Business Cycles

Business cycles are recurring cycles of economic events involving a period of more rapid than normal or average growth (the *expansionary phase*) and culminating in a peak, followed by a phase of slower than average growth (a *recession*), or a period of negative growth (a *depression*) culminating in a trough. In the post-war literature, business cycles are normally assumed to be forty to sixty months in duration distinguishable from various longer cycles that have been discussed in the economics literature, such as the six to eight year Major trade cycle, the fifteen to twenty-five year Kuznets or building cycle, and the fifty to sixty year Kondratieff wave.

Business cycles have commonly been viewed as evolving around a long-term growth trend, especially in the post-war period, and this has typically led to a divorce of 'business cycle theory', which attempts to explain the fluctuations around the trend, from 'growth theory', which attempts to explain the trend growth itself. In the 1970s, interest in long waves revived, and an alternative view is that business cycles are short-term fluctuations in economic activity around longer cycles or waves. In this case, business cycles will be analysed as growth cycles, with alternating rapid growth expansionary phases and slower growth contractionary phases (or recessions) during the upswing of the long wave; while during the downswing of the long wave they will involve periods of positive growth in the expansionary phase followed by periods of zero or negative growth in the contractionary phase (or depression).

There has been some debate about whether business cycles are systematic economic fluctuations, or whether they are instead purely random fluctuations in economic activity. It is certainly true that business cycles are not regular, in the sense of a sine wave with constant period and amplitude. But the weight of evidence, largely due to the accumulated studies produced through the National Bureau of Economic Research, indicates that business cycles are sufficiently uniform to warrant serious study.

Business cycle modelling in the post-war period has usually adopted the approach, suggested by the work of Frisch and Slutsky, of regarding the economic system as fundamentally stable but being bombarded by a series of shocks or unexpected events. Thus business cycle models have commonly attempted to devise a 'propagation model' of the economy capable of converting shocks, generated by an impulse model, into a cycle. Using this strategy, many different models have been devised; these vary according to the degree of stability assumed in the 'propagation model', the form of the series of shocks emanating from the 'impulse model', and the sources of the shocks and sectors of the economy described by the propagation model. The various models have commonly involved linear stochastic second order equation systems. The linearity assumption serves both to simplify analysis and to allow an easy separation of business cycle and growth theory, because growth can be represented by a linear or log linear trend. There have been exceptions to this general modelling strategy that have used nonlinear equation systems capable of generating – in the absence of shocks – self-sustaining 'limit cycles'. These can be stable and self-repeating even in the face of shocks, which merely impart some additional irregularity. Such contributions have been relatively rare but may become more common as economists increasingly familiarize themselves with nonlinear techniques of mathematical and statistical analysis. The possibility of modelling the business cycle as a limit cycle, as an alternative to the Frisch-Slutsky approach, raises the general question of whether the business cycle is something that would die out in the absence of shocks, or whether it is endogenous to the economic system.

The nonlinear models have also commonly treated business cycles and growth theory as separable. There is, however, an alternative view, which is that business cycles and growth should be explained together, and that a theory of dynamic economic development is required. This view is most frequently associated with Marxist writings, but other students of the business cycle have suggested that the work of Schumpeter might provide a useful starting point.

In 1975, a series of published papers discussing the political and the equilibrium theories of the business cycle had a major impact. The political theory of the business cycle argues that business cycles are in fact electoral economic cycles which result from governments manipulating the economy in order to win elections. This contrasts with the broad Keynesian consensus view of the mid 1960s that governments, through anti-cyclical demand management policies, had on the whole been successful in reducing the amplitude of the cycle, although it was accepted that at times they may have aggravated it because of the problems involved in allowing for the lag in the effect of policy interventions. The equilibrium theory of the business cycle assumes that economic agents are endowed with 'rational expectations' but must make decisions based on inadequate information about whether price changes are purely inflationary, so that no real response is required, or whether they indicate a profitable opportunity. In models based on this theory, systematic anti-cyclical monetary policy can have no effect, and the only contribution the government can make is to reduce the shocks to the economy by pursuing a systematic monetary policy. The equilibrium theory of the business cycle contrasts with most other theories, which view business cycles as being fundamentally a disequilibrium phenomenon. Although the political and equilibrium theories have many contrasting features, they both raise questions concerning the appropriate treatment of the government in business cycle models. The Keynesian consensus view was that the government could be treated exogenously. In contrast, the political and equilibrium theories of the business cycle indicate that the government should be treated endogenously in business cycle models. A possible route for progress in business cycle modelling might involve game theoretic analyses of government policy making.

Both the political and equilibrium theories of the business cycle have their origins in much earlier literature and the evidence in support of each of them is rather less than conclusive. Nevertheless, these modern theories have revived interest in the controversial subject concerning the nature and causes of business cycles.

Andy Mullineux
University of Birmingham

Further Reading

Hansen, A. H. (1964), *Business Cycles and National Income* (enlarged edn), New York.

Harberler, G. (1964), *Prosperity and Depression* (5th edn), London.

Kuhne, K. (1979), *Economics and Marxism: Vol. II – The Dynamics of the Marxian System*, London.

Mandel, E. (1980), *Long Waves of Capitalist Development: The Marxist Interpretation*, Cambridge.

Mullineux, A. W. (1984), *The Business Cycle After Keynes: A Contemporary Analysis*, Brighton.

Schumpeter, J. A. (1939), *Business Cycles*.

See also: *accelerator principle; financial crises; stagflation.*

Cambridge School of Economics

In his 1922 Introduction to the Cambridge Economic Handbooks, Keynes defined 'The Cambridge School of Economics' as lecturers in the University of Cambridge (UK) whose 'ideas . . . are traceable to . . . the two economists who have chiefly influenced Cambridge thought . . . , Dr Marshall and Professor Pigou' (successor in Marshall's Chair of Political Economy), and included F. Lavington, H. D. Henderson, D. H. Robertson (Pigou's successor), and G. F. Shove.

A process of rejuvenation and internal criticism started in 1927 when Keynes imported a young Italian, P. Sraffa, who committed 'the sacrilege of pointing out inconsistencies in Marshall', as Joan Robinson put it. Combining work by Shove, E. A. G. Robinson, and R. F. Kahn, Joan Robinson developed these inconsistencies into a 1933 book which launched the 'Imperfect Competition Revolution'. Shortly after, with the help of these young economists (and J. E. Meade, an Oxford visitor who eventually succeeded Robertson), Keynes himself challenged the established views of Marshall and Pigou in his revolutionary *General Theory*.

The new generation, joined by Kaldor in the 1950s, and Pasinetti in the 1960s, propagated and extended Keynes's theory, formulating original approaches to capital, growth and distribution theory. Together with Sraffa's 1960 theory of prices, which built on his earlier work, the process of internal criticism of the 1930s reached maturity in a coherent approach (although Robertson and Meade defended the traditional positions) which superseded traditional marginal analysis and provoked the 'Cambridge Controversies', which dominated economics in the 1960s and 1970s. In the 1980s Cambridge economists exhibit no unified approach, yet the Cambridge tradition is preserved in the post-Keynesian and Surplus approaches in universities around the world.

J. A. Kregel
University of Groningen

References

Keynes, J. M. (1922), 'Introduction' to H. D. Henderson, *Supply and Demand*, vol. I, London.

Keynes, J. M. (1936), *The General Theory of Employment, Interest and Money*, London.

Robinson, J. (1933), *The Economics of Imperfect Competition*, London.

Sraffa, P. (1960), *Production of Commodities by Means of Commodities*, Cambridge.

See also: *capital theory; economic dynamics; Keynes; Keynesian economics.*

Capital Consumption

Understanding capital consumption (that is, the using up of fixed capital) must be based on an understanding of the distinction between fixed capital and circulating capital. In this context, the word 'capital' refers to tangible assets (i.e. as excluding financial assets). Items of circulating capital have only a once-for-all (or 'once-over') use in the process of production; items of fixed capital have a continuing and repeated use in the process of production. A dressmaker has a stock of cloth and a sewing machine: the cloth has a once-for-all use in the process of dressmaking; the sewing machine can be used repeatedly. The cloth is *circulating capital*; the sewing machine is *fixed capital*. The universal feature of items of fixed capital (apart from land) is that, for more than one reason, they have finite working lifetimes and will eventually have to be replaced (as the cloth has immediately to be replaced) if the production process is to continue.

Suppose the working lifetime of a sewing machine is ten years: at the beginning of Year 1 the dressmaker starts business with a (new) sewing machine valued at $1,000 and at the end of Year 10 the sewing machine is worth nothing (assuming it has no residual scrap-metal value). In order to continue in business, the dressmaker has then to spend $1,000 on replacing the sewing machine (abstracting from inflation – a very significant proviso). Now, if over the years the dressmaker has not gathered in from all the customers an aggregate amount of

$1,000, then the effect is that those customers have had the free gift of the services of the sewing machine. Therefore, customers should be charged for the use of fixed capital. Suppose the dressmaker makes 200 dresses a year; over ten years 2,000 dresses will have been made and customers should be charged 50 cents per dress, reckoned as: $1,000 (original capital cost of sewing machine) *divided by* 2,000 (dresses) *equals* $0.50 per dress. The 50 cents is the charge for (fixed) capital consumption per dress, and is analogous to the charge made for the cloth used. The price charged must include the cost of capital consumption per dress.

However, most enterprises do not proceed in this direct way to incorporate capital consumption into the price(s) of the item(s) they produce. Instead, the same result may be achieved by making an overall deduction of annual capital consumption from annual gross income (income gross of – including – capital consumption). The dressmaker may deduct from gross income an *annual* charge for capital consumption, reckoned as: $1,000 (original capital cost of sewing machine) *divided by* 10 (years – the lifetime of the sewing machine) *equals* $100 per annum.

If 'income' is to be taxed, then net income rather than gross income is the appropriate tax-base. Hence tax authorities have regulations concerning the deduction of (annual) capital consumption, otherwise known as depreciation provisions.

There are various methods of calculating the flow of depreciation provisions. The formula just given is known as the 'straight-line' method because it gives a linear decline in the depreciated value of the fixed capital stock and a linear increase in the cumulated depreciation provisions (that is, there is a constant annual charge for depreciation), as follows: beginning Year 1, $1,000 capital, $0 cumulated depreciation provisions; end Year 1, $900 depreciated value of capital, $100 cumulated depreciation provisions; end Year 2, $800 depreciated value of capital, $200 cumulated depreciation provisions; and so on until end Year 10, $0 depreciated value of capital, $1,000 cumulated depreciation provisions. Together, the sum of depreciated capital and cumulated depreciation provisions always equal $1,000 and so 'maintains' capital (i.e. wealth) intact.

This arithmetic example illustrates the definitions that: 'Depreciation is the measure of the wearing out, consumption or other loss of value of a fixed asset' *(Accounting Standards*, 1982); or that capital consumption is the fall in the value of fixed capital between two accounting dates; or that charging depreciation provisions is a method of allocating the (original) cost of a long-lived asset to the time periods in which the asset is 'used up'. It also illustrates how the purpose of charging capital consumption against gross income to arrive at net (true) profit is to prevent an enterprise from 'living off its capital': 'A provision for depreciation reduces profit by an amount which might otherwise have been seen as available for distribution as a dividend' (Pizzey, 1980). It is not essential that the depreciation provisions be re-invested in the same item: it is quite in order for the dressmaker to invest in an ongoing way the depreciation provisions in, say, a knitting machine – what is essential is that sufficient capital equipment for production purposes continues to be available.

Dudley Jackson
University of Wollongong, Australia

References
Accounting Standards (1982), *Statements of Standard Accounting Practice 12*, 'Accounting for depreciation', London.
Pizzey, A. (1980), *Accounting and Finance: A Firm Foundation*, London.
See also: *capital theory; stock-flow analysis.*

Capitalism
The term capitalism relates to a particular system of socioeconomic organization (generally contrasted with feudalism on the one hand and socialism on the other), the nature of which is more often defined implicitly than explicitly. In common with other value-loaded concepts of political controversy, its definition – whether implicit or explicit – shows a chameleon-like tendency to vary with the ideological bias of the user. Even when treated as a historical category and precisely defined for

the purpose of objective analysis, the definition adopted is often associated with a distinctive view of the temporal sequence and character of historical development. Thus historians such as Sombart, Weber and Tawney, who were concerned to relate changes in economic organization to shifts in religious and ethical attitudes, found the essence of capitalism in the acquisitive spirit of profit-making enterprise and focused on developments occurring in the sixteenth, seventeenth and early eighteenth centuries. Probably a majority of historians have seen capitalism as reaching its fullest development in the course of the Industrial Revolution and have treated the earlier period as part of a long transition between feudalism and capitalism. Marxist historians have identified a series of stages in the evolution of capitalism – for example, merchant capitalism, agrarian capitalism, industrial capitalism, state capitalism – and much of the recent debate on origins and progress has hinged on differing views of the significance, timing and characteristics of each stage. Thus Wallerstein (1979), who adopts a world-economy perspective, locates its origins in the agrarian capitalism that characterized Europe of the sixteenth, seventeenth and eighteenth centuries; while Tribe (1981), who also takes agrarian capitalism as the original mode of capitalist production, sees the essence of capitalism in a national economy where production is separated from consumption and is co-ordinated according to the profitability of enterprises operating in competition with each other.

Whatever the historical or polemical objective of the writer, however, his definition is likely to be strongly influenced by Karl Marx, who was the first to attempt a systematic analysis of the 'economic law of motion' of capitalist society and from whom most of the subsequent controversy on the nature and role of capitalism has stemmed. For Marx, capitalism was a 'mode of production' in which there are basically two classes of producers: (1) the capitalists, who own the means of production (capital or land), make the strategic day-to-day economic decisions on technology, output and marketing, and appropriate the profits of production and distribution; and (2) the labourers, who own no property but are free to dispose of their labour for wages on terms which depend on the numbers seeking work and the demand for their services. This was essentially the definition adopted, for example, by non-Marxist economic historians such as Lipson and Cunningham and by Marxists such as Dobb.   Given this perspective, it is primarily the emergence of a dominant class of entrepreneurs supplying the capital necessary to activate a substantial body of workers which marks the birth of capitalism.

Orthodox economic theorists eschew the concept of capitalism – it is too broad for their purposes in that it takes into account the social relations of production. Modern economic historians adhering to an orthodox framework of economic theory also tend to avoid the term. They do, however, recognize a significant aspect of capitalism by emphasizing the rational, profit-maximizing, double bookkeeping characteristics of capitalist enterprise; and in the post-Second World War debates on economic development from a backward starting-point, there has been a tendency to regard the emergence of this 'capitalist spirit' as an essential prerequisite to the process of sustained economic growth in non-socialist countries. (See, for example, Landes, 1969; North and Thomas, 1973; Morishima, 1982.)

The modern debate on capitalism in contemporary advanced economies has revolved around its being an alternative to socialism. Marxist economists follow Marx in seeing capitalism as a mode of production whose internal contradictions determine that it will eventually be replaced by socialism. In the aftermath of the Second World War, when the governments of most developed countries took full employment and faster economic growth as explicit objectives of national economic policy, there was a marked propensity for the governments of capitalist economies to intervene actively and extensively in the process of production. At that stage the interesting issues for most Western economists seemed to be the changing balance of private and public economic power (see Shonfield, 1965), and the extent to which it was either desirable or inevitable for the increasingly 'mixed' capitalist economies to converge towards socialism. In the late 1960s and 1970s, when the unprecedented post-war boom in world economic activity came to an end, Marxist economists were able to point confidently to the 'crisis of capitalism' for which they found evidence in rising unemployment and inflation in capitalist countries; but non-Marxist economists had lost their earlier consensus. The economic debate on capitalism is now taking place in a political context which is relatively hostile to state intervention; and those economists who believe that the 'spirit of capitalism', or free private enterprise, is the key to sustained technological progress and that it is weakened by socialist economic policies, seem to carry more conviction than they did in the 1950s and 1960s.

Phyllis Deane
University of Cambridge

References

Dobb, M. (1946), *Studies in the Development of Capitalism*, London.

Landes, D. (1969), *Prometheus Unbound*, Cambridge.

Morishima, M. (1982), *Why has Japan Succeeded?*, Cambridge.

North, D. C. and Thomas, R. P. (1973), *The Rise of the Western World*, Cambridge.

Shonfield, A. (1965), *Modern Capitalism*, London.

Sombart, W. (1915), *The Quintessence of Capitalism*, New York.

Tawney, R. H. (1926), *Religion and the Rise of Capitalism*, London.

Tribe, K. (1981), *Genealogies of Capitalism*, London.

Wallerstein, I. (1979), *The Capitalist World-Economy*, Cambridge.

Weber, M. (1930), *The Protestant Ethic and the Spirit of Capitalism*, New York. (Original German, 1922, Tübingen.)

Capital Theory

Capital's role in the technological specification of production and as a source of income called interest or profit encompasses theories of production and accumulation and theories of value and distribution. The subject has perplexed economists because capital produces a return which keeps capital intact and yields an interest or profit which is thus permanent, while consumption goods produce a unique return (utility) equal to cost and are destroyed in use.

The pre-industrial Classical economists thought of capital as stocks of food and provisions advanced to labour; it was the accumulation of stocks making possible the division of labour which was of importance. This position is reflected in J. S. Mill's (1848) statement that to 'speak of the "productive powers of capital" . . . is not literally correct. The only productive powers are those of labour and natural agents.' Capital was at best an intermediate good determined by technology and thus subject to exogenous or 'natural' laws, rather than human or economic 'laws'.

By Marx's time, factory labour working with fixed machinery had become widespread, and he was impressed by the increase in the ratio of 'dead' labour, which had gone into producing the machines, to the living labour which operated them. Marx's idea of a 'mode of production' made capital a social, rather than a purely technological, relation; it was not the machinery, but the operation of the laws of value and distribution under capitalism that produced revolutionary implications. This integration of production and distribution challenged Mills's separation and clearly raised the question of the justification for profit or interest as a permanent return to capital.

Jevons was among the first to note the importance of the time that labour was accumulated in stock. Böhm-Bawerk's Austrian theory of capital built on time as a justification for interest in answer to Marx. The Austrians considered human and natural powers as the original productive factors, but 'time', which allowed more 'roundabout' production processes using intermediate inputs, was also productive. Longer average periods of production would produce greater output, but in decreasing proportion. It was the capitalists' ability to wait for the greater product of longer processes, and the workers' haste to consume, which explained the former's profit.

Clark extended Ricardo's Classical theory of differential rent of land to physical capital goods, considering diminishing returns to be a 'natural law' of production. In Clark's explanation it is the capital goods themselves which are considered productive, their return equal to their marginal product. Determination of capital's 'marginal' contribution requires that it be 'fixed' while the amount of labour employed varies, but 'transmutable' into the appropriate technical form when different quantities are used with a 'fixed' quantity of labour.

L. Walras shifted emphasis from physical capital goods to their services as the 'productive' inputs and the return to owning the goods themselves which can then be analysed as the exchange and valuation of the permanent net revenues they produce.

Wicksell was critical of Walras, rejected 'time' as a productive factor, and was sceptical of the application of marginal theory to aggregate capital, for the 'margin' of the capital stock could not be clearly defined. The problem was in the fact that 'land and labour are measured each in terms of their own technical unit' while 'capital . . . is reckoned as a sum of exchange value . . . each particular capital good is measured by a unit extraneous to itself', which meant that the value of capital, equal in equilibrium to its costs of production, could not be used to define the quantity used to calculate its marginal return because 'these costs of production include capital and interest. . . . We should therefore be arguing in a circle' (1934). Wicksell's argument recalls the original Classical view of capital as an intermediate good, a produced means of production, rather than an 'original' productive factor.

Fisher made a sharp distinction between the flow of income and the capital stock that produced it; since discounting future income converts one into the other, the key to the problem is in the role of individual preferences of present over future consumption, or the 'rate of time preference' in determining the rate of interest. The greater the preference for present goods, the higher the rate of time discount and the lower the present value of future goods represented by the stock of capital.

Keynes's *General Theory* assumption of a fixed stock of capital and the absence of a clear theory of distribution left open the analysis of capital and the determination of the rate of interest or profit to complement the theory. Neoclassical theorists (based in Cambridge, US) added a simplified version of Clark's theory via an aggregate production function relating homogeneous output to the 'productive' factors: labour and aggregate capital, in which the 'quantity' of capital would be negatively associated with its price, the rate of interest. This preserved the negative relation between price and quantity of traditional demand theory. Cambridge (UK) economists rejected capital as a productive factor, arguing that the value of the heterogeneous produced means of production comprising 'aggregate capital' could not be measured independently of its price, which was a determinant of the value used to identify its quantity. These theoretical disputes came to be known as the 'Cambridge Controversies' in capital theory.

A crucial role was played in these debates by Sraffa's 1960 theory of prices, which furnished formal proof of Wicksell's criticisms by demonstrating that changes in the rate of interest (or profit) in an interdependent system could affect the prices of the goods making up the means of production in such a way that the sum of their values representing the aggregate 'quantity' of capital might rise or fall, or even take on the same value at two different rates of interest. These demonstrations came to be known as 'capital reversal' and 'reswitching' and clearly demonstrated that the negative relation between the quantity of aggregate capital and the rate of interest had no general application. Such criticism does not apply to the analysis of individual capital goods, although a general equilibrium in which the rate of return is uniform requires the comparison of competing rates of return and thus ratios of profits to the value of the capital goods that produce them. Modern theorists only agree on the inappropriateness of aggregate capital concepts.

J. A. Kregel
University of Groningen

References
Mill, J. S. (1886 [1848]), *Principles of Political Economy*, London.
Wicksell, K. (1934), *Lectures on Political Economy*, London.

Sraffa, P. (1960), *Production of Commodities by Means of Commodities*, Cambridge.

Further Reading
Harcourt, G. C. (1972), *Some Cambridge Controversies in the Theory of Capital*, Cambridge.
Kregel, J. A. (1976), *Theory of Capital*, London.
See also: *capital consumption; capitalism; human capital; Keynesian economics; Marxian economics.*

Cartels and Trade Associations

Cartels are a common form of collusion in oligopolistic markets. In a market with many sellers (perfect competition) each seller can take the market price as parametric, but in an oligopolistic market firms will be aware that their pricing decisions will affect the decisions of others. It is commonly agreed that isolated profit maximization in an oligopolistic market will lead all producers to have lower profits than would be possible if they colluded. Cartels and trade associations are descriptions for collusion, the former in markets with a small number of firms, the latter in markets where there are many (100). Cartels vary from gentleman's agreements to legally binding contracts. In most countries they are illegal, but have often also been formed at government behest, as in Germany and the US in the 1930s. The objective of a cartel is to raise price and cut quantity to increase industry profits. Although they are commonly observed (and more commonly exist), they are often unstable, as each firm has an incentive to cheat by offering small discounts to gain increased sales. Because every firm can cheat, many will, and cheating will occur unless the cartel is properly policed. Cartels can take many forms, from overt (or covert) agreements to tacit agreements on price leadership in the market. Agreement appears to be easier to reach when numbers involved are modest, products are homogeneous and government regulation lax. Recent developments in the theory of games, using infinite dynamic game theory with time discounting and plausible retaliation for cheating, have aided our understanding of the topic (See Friedman, 1982), but have only served to emphasize the indeterminateness of possible solutions in cartelized markets.

Ray Barrell
University of Southampton

Reference
Friedman, J. (1982), *Oligopoly Theory*, Cambridge.

Further Reading
Scherer, F. M. (1980), *Industrial Structure and Economic Performance*, 2nd edn, Chicago.
See also: *antitrust legislation; business concentration; monopoly; oligopoly.*

Chicago School of Economics

The so-called Chicago School of economics, chiefly American, is a neoclassical counter-revolution against institutionalism in economic methodology, against Keynesian macroeconomics, and against 'twentieth-century liberalism', i.e. interventionism and *dirigisme*, in economic policy generally. Its centre has been the University of Chicago, where it first achieved prominence in the 1930s. Its intellectual leaders until about 1950 were Frank H. Knight in matters of theory and methodology and Henry C. Simons in matters of economic policy. During the next generation, the leaders have been Milton Friedman, George Stigler and Gary Becker. Many economists not trained at Chicago have aligned themselves with many 'Chicago' positions, and many members of the Chicago economics faculty, to say nothing of its graduates, have dissociated themselves from 'Chicago' doctrine.

Some characteristic Chicago School views have been:

(1) Methodological positivism. The validity of a theory depends neither upon its generality nor upon the plausibility of its initial assumptions, but exclusively upon the confirmation or disconfirmation (primarily statistical) of such of its implications as diverge from the implications of alternative theories.

(2) Acceptance of market solutions for economic problems, not in any Utopian or optimal sense but in aid of political and

intellectual freedom. Chicago School economists see the market economy as a *necessary* condition for free societies generally. It is not, however, a *sufficient* condition.

(3) Distrust of administrative discretion and *ad hoc* intervention in economic policy. Preference for 'rules versus authorities' in matters of monetary and fiscal policy.

(4) Monetarism rather than fiscalism in macroeconomic regulation.

(5) The use of fiscal measures to alleviate poverty, but distrust of redistributionism above the poverty line.

(6) Disciplinary imperialism, by which is meant the applicability of economic analysis by economists to problems normally restricted to other disciplines, particularly law and sociology.

The school's positions with regard to a number of topics, especially trade regulation and monetary policy, have changed over the years. Simons, for example, believed in the active maintenance of competition by a strong anti-monopoly or 'trust-busting' policy, while Friedman and Stigler thought monopoly and oligopoly to be only short-term problems of minor long-term significance. Simons also believed that monetary policy should be guided by a price-level rule – expansionary when the price level was falling and contractionary when it was rising. Friedman, impressed by the long and variable time lags involved in price-level reactions to monetary change, has favoured a constant rate of monetary growth.

The two best summaries of Chicago doctrine are Simons's *Economic Policy for a Free Society* and Friedman's *Capitalism and Freedom*.

Martin Bronfenbrenner
Duke University
and Aoyama Gakuin
University, Tokyo

Further Reading
Patinkin, D. (1981), *Essay On and In the Chicago Tradition*, Durham, N.C.
See also: *monetarism*.

Classical Economics

The term Classical Economics, although sometimes given the rather broader meaning of any economics which is not Keynesian, is generally taken to refer to the body of economic ideas stemming from the work of David Hume, whose most important work was published in 1752, and Adam Smith whose great *Wealth of Nations* was published in 1776. These ideas came to dominate economics particularly, but far from exclusively, in Britain throughout the last quarter of the eighteenth and the first three quarters of the nineteenth century.

Hume's contributions principally concerned money and the balance of payments. But Smith's work is a virtual compendium of economics, focusing on the key question of economic growth, and covering division of labour, distribution, capital accumulation, trade and colonial policy, and public finance. Amongst their successors was T. R. Malthus; though chiefly famous for his writings on population, he covered the whole field of economic inquiry. A major impetus to the development of Classical economics was provided by David Ricardo. He read Smith's work critically and from it constructed a 'model' which, unlike Smith's work, produced fairly clear and definite predictions. Ricardo succeeded initially in attracting disciples, notably J. Mill and – though he later drifted away from Ricardo's influence – J. R. McCulloch as well as Thomas De Quincey. But his influence waned after his death and the work of J. Mill's son, J. S. Mill, is much closer to Smith in range, reliance upon empirical material, and the avoidance of precise predictions.

Classical economics covered the whole field of economic enquiry, but with an emphasis on questions dealing with large aggregates – economic growth, international trade, monetary economics, public finance – rather than with the analysis of the behaviour of the maximizing individual which came to be of dominant interest after 1870. (In the field of value theory, in particular, the Classical economists generally made do with various sorts of production theories emphasizing, in varying degrees, the importance of labour cost in total cost.) At the same time a fundamental premise lying behind the analysis of aggregates, and stemming from Smith, was that individuals were motivated by the pursuit of self-interest, and that their pursuit had to be limited by a framework of law, religion and custom, to ensure coincidence of private and social interest. This in turn meant that in the field of economic policy Classical economics, while predisposed against government interference (partly because of the way in which such interference could be used for purely sectional interest, and partly because of a belief that decentralized individual knowledge was superior to State knowledge), was pragmatic – the necessary legislative framework could only be learnt by experience and enquiry.

At the heart of the Classical vision is the idea of economic growth occurring through the interaction of capital accumulation and division of labour. Capital accumulation made it possible to postpone the sale of output, permitting the development of specialization and division of labour. Division of labour in turn increased total output, permitting further capital accumulation. Economic growth would be increased by allowing capital to flow to where it was most productive; thus, other things being equal, it was desirable to remove restraints on the free allocation of resources. Division of labour itself was limited by the extent of the market. The extent of the home market depended on population and income per head. As capital was accumulated, the available labour supply found itself in greater demand and wages rose above the necessary minimum – 'subsistence' which could be either psychological or physiological. Population responded to the rise in wages by increasing; this in turn increased the labour supply which pushed wages back towards subsistence, though, if subsistence was a psychological variable – as it was with many Classical writers – population growth might well stop before wages had fallen to the old level of subsistence. As wages rose, profits fell; this might check capital accumulation, but as long as profits were above a necessary minimum, capital accumulation would continue. Output, population, and capital thus all grew together. However, a brake on growth was provided by the shortage of a third input, land. With the progress of economic growth, food became more and more expensive to produce, while landlords enjoyed the benefit of an unearned rent arising from ownership of this scarce but vital resource – this aspect was particularly stressed by Malthus and Ricardo. The rising cost of food also meant that the floor below which subsistence could not fall – the minimum wage necessary to procure basic physical necessities of life – rose; and Ricardo in particular emphasized that such a rise would depress profits and might eventually stop capital accumulation and growth altogether. (Smith had believed that growth would only stop when investment opportunities were exhausted.) He then argued that repeal of the Corn Laws (restricting food imports) was urgent, since subsistence could be obtained more cheaply abroad. (Later Classical economists such as McCulloch and J. S. Mill were, however, optimistic about technical progress in agriculture which could postpone any slowdown in economic growth by lowering the cost of agricultural output.)

The argument for repeal of the Corn Laws provided one part of a general Classical case for freedom of trade; the desire to widen the market to maximize possible division of labour provided another. However, a more general and sophisticated argument for freedom of trade was provided by R. Torrens and Ricardo, in the form of the theory of comparative costs (later refined and developed by J. S. Mill) which showed that a country could gain from importing even those commodities in which it had a competitive advantage if it had an even greater competitive advantage in the production of other commodities – it should concentrate its scarce resources on the latter.

Balance of payments equilibrium was ensured by a mechanism which was due to David Hume, and which was also basic to Classical monetary theory, the price-specie-flow mechanism. A balance of payments deficit would, through gold outflow, reduce the money supply, and thus the price level, making exports competitive and imports less attractive, and this equilibrating mechanism would continue until the gold outflow stopped and payments came into balance. The price level was thus dependent on the money supply: and the predominant Classical view from Ricardo to Lord Overstone was that the note issue, as part of the money supply, should be contracted if gold was flowing out, since the outflow was a symptom of a price level which was too high. Monetary control was also necessary to dampen the effects of an endogenous trade cycle, an element introduced into Classical economics, chiefly by Overstone, from the late 1830s. (A minority of Classical economists however viewed the money supply as demand-determined.)

Classical economics represented a major intellectual achievement. The foundations which it laid in the fields of monetary and trade theory, in particular, are still with economics today. Eventually however it lost some of its momentum; it was always policy-orientated, and as the policy questions were settled – usually along the lines indicated by the Classical analyses – and as economists came to take continuing economic growth for granted, they turned their attention to different questions requiring different techniques of analysis.

D. P. O'Brien
University of Durham

Further Reading
Blaug, M. (1958), *Ricardian Economics*, New Haven.
O'Brien, D. P. (1975), *The Classical Economists*, Oxford.
See also: *Malthus; Ricardo; Smith.*

Cliometrics
The term cliometrics (a neologism linking the concept of measurement to the muse of history) was apparently coined at Purdue University, Indiana, US, in the late 1950s. Originally applied to the study of economic history as undertaken by scholars trained as economists (and also called, by its practitioners and others, the 'new economic history', 'econometric history', and 'quantitative economic history'), more recently cliometrics has been applied to a broader range of historical studies (including the 'new political history', the 'new social history', and, most inclusively, 'social science history').

The historians' early interest in cliometrics partly reflects the impact of two important works in United States economic history. The detailed estimates by Conrad and Meyer (1958) of the profitability of slavery before the Civil War and the quantitative evaluation of the role of the railroads in economic growth by Fogel (1964) triggered wide-ranging debate, with much attention to questions of method as well as substance. While these two works, combining economic theory and quantitative analysis, attracted the most attention, two other books published at about the same time also highlighted the quantitative aspect, although in a more traditional (and less controversial) manner. A National Bureau of Economic Research conference volume, edited by Parker (1960), presented a number of important studies (by, among others, Easterlin, Gallman, Lebergott, and North) pushing back many important times series on economic variables to the early nineteenth century, an effort complemented by the publication, several years later, of another NBER conference dealing mainly with nineteenth-century economic change (1966). North (1961) combined his new estimates of pre-1860 foreign trade with a familiar regional approach to describe the basic contours of United States economic growth from 1790 to the Civil War. These works had important implications for discussions of economic growth in the United States, particularly in the period before the Civil War. The concentration of major publications within a short time period, together with the start of an annual conference of cliometricians at Purdue University (which, with several changes of venue, still continues), generated the momentum which led to major shifts in the nature of the writing of American economic history, as well as revisions of many interpretations of past developments. The late 1950s and 1960s saw similar changes in other subfields of history, particularly political and social history, although it was in economic history that the concentration on theory, quantitative data, and statistical methods was most complete.

The most general characteristics of cliometric work (in economic history) have been the systematic use of economic theory and its concepts to examine economic growth in the past, and the widespread preparation and formal statistical analysis of quantitative material. While none of this may seem to provide a new approach in historical studies (as is often pointed out in criticizing claims of novelty), the more explicit attention to theory and the more frequent reliance on quantitative materials and statistical procedures have had an important impact upon the manner in which historical questions have been approached and interpreted. However, cliometricians still differ in how they make use of quantitative and statistical methods. To some, the major work is the preparation of quantitative data, either of detailed information for a particular time period (e.g., the samples of population, agriculture, and manufacturing records drawn from the decadal federal census) or of long-period time series (e.g., national income and wealth, wages, labour force) to be used in measuring and understanding past economic changes. These estimates require imaginative reconstructions from the available samples of past data, but do not often involve sophisticated statistical tools. Others emphasize the use of more formal statistical methods, most frequently regression analysis, to test hypotheses. And some cliometricians restrict themselves to the use of economic theory to analyse institutional and economic changes, which are not described quantitatively.

Continued interest in economic (and political and sociological) theory has led to a more frequent attempt to find historical generalizations based upon social science concepts and methods than some, more traditionally-trained, historians seem comfortable with. Nevertheless, the ability to collect and examine data, from archival and published sources, furthered by the development of the computer, has permitted a considerable expansion in the amount of material relevant to questions of interest to historians, as well as better methods of organizing, analysing, and testing data. In recent years, the heat of earlier debates on method has apparently declined as the use of quantitative methods and theoretical constructs has become a part of the standard 'tool-kit' of historians, while cliometricians have broadened the range of questions they have discussed and the varieties of evidence utilized.

While the first cliometric studies were done principally by North American scholars and, for reasons of data availability, most frequently concerned the United States in the nineteenth century, over the past two decades the temporal and geographic scope has widened, as has the types of questions to which cliometric analysis is applied. Much work has been done on the colonial period, as well as the twentieth century, in the United States. And, not only have the interests of American cliometricians expanded to include studies of other parts of the world, but cliometric work has developed in a number of other countries, most particularly in Britain and in Western Europe. Although, as with most attempts at categorization, a sharp dividing line is often difficult to draw, cliometric history continues to emphasize the systematic application of social science theory and the use of quantitative data and statistical analysis to understand the historical past.

Stanley L. Engerman
University of Rochester

References

Conrad, A. H. and Meyer, J. R. (1958), 'The economics of slavery in the ante-bellum South', *Journal of Political Economy*.

Fogel, R. W. (1964), *Railroads and American Economic Growth: Essays in Econometric History*, Baltimore.

National Bureau of Economic Research, Conference in Research in Income and Wealth (1960), *Trends in the American Economy in the Nineteenth Century*, Princeton.

National Bureau of Economic Research, Conference on Research in Income and Wealth (1966), *Output, Employment, and Productivity in the United States after 1800*, New York.

North, D. C. (1961), *The Economic Growth of the United States, 1790–1860*, Englewood Cliffs, NJ.

Further Reading

Engerman, S. L. (1977), 'Recent developments in American economic history', *Social Science History*.

Kousser, J. M. (1980), 'Quantitative social-scientific history', in M. Kammen (ed.), *The Past Before Us*, Ithaca.

McCloskey, D. N. (1978), 'The achievements of the cliometric school', *Journal of Economic History*.

McCloskey, D. N. and Hersh, G. (1985), *The Bibliography of Historical Economics, 1957–1980*, Cambridge.

Commodity Stabilization Schemes

Schemes for the stabilization of primary commodity prices have always been an important item on the agenda of international policy discussions. This is because the prices of these commodities are volatile, and because exports of them are large sources of revenue for many countries, particularly those of the Third World. One of the most famous schemes was proposed by Keynes in 1942, as a companion to his International Clearing Union (which later became the IMF). Keynes's argument for commodity price stabilization led to political opposition from those opposed to market intervention and had to be shelved. More recently the same fate has befallen the Integral Program for Commodities put forward by UNCTAD (the United Nations Conference on Trade and Development). Those schemes which exist have developed in a piecemeal fashion. 'Only [schemes for] wheat, sugar, tea and coffee have lasted a number of years, and few appear to have achieved much before their demise' (MacBean and Snowden, 1981).

Price stabilization is usually put forward as a means of stabilizing the incomes of producers and consumers. It could also be used as a means of raising the average incomes of producers, but would then need to be buttressed by quota schemes to restrict production.

Price stabilization will normally succeed in stabilizing revenues to producers in the face of shifts in demand for commodities of the kind which occur because of the world business cycle. The managers of the scheme need to operate some kind of buffer stock. When demand is high, the extra can be satisfied by sales from the buffer stock: producers' revenue is unaltered by the demand increase. The reverse is true when demand falls. Stabilization of prices will, it is true, allow fluctuations in producers' incomes to remain in the face of fluctuations in the quantity produced, as a result, say, of changes in harvests.

However, without stabilization of prices, producers' incomes might be even more unstable, if good harvest produced very large falls in prices (and vice versa). Price stabilization will also isolate consumers of primary commodities from shocks to the purchasing power of their incomes in a wide variety of circumstances.

Economists differ in their assessment of the benefits to be obtained from such stabilization of prices. Newbery and Stiglitz (1981) have argued, in a powerful modern study, that the benefits to producers are small. Newbery and Stiglitz would clearly be correct if producers could adjust their spending in line with fluctuations in their income. However, they ignore the great hardships which could arise when primary commodity producers (both individuals and nations) have to make unexpected cuts in expenditures. Such hardships will indeed arise when average incomes are not much above subsistence or when the revenue from sales of primary commodities is used to pay for development projects which are hard to stop and start at will. Newbery and Stiglitz also argue that the potential benefits to consumers would be small. But they largely ignore the inflationary difficulties for consumers which primary-commodity-price instability creates, and it was those which concerned Keynes. It must be admitted that contemporary proponents of primary commodity price stabilization schemes have been slow to produce good evidence about the size of those effects which Newbery and Stiglitz ignore.

There are fundamental difficulties in the way of setting up any stabilization scheme. It is necessary to choose (1) the price level at which stabilization is to take place, and (2) the optimum size for the buffer stock. An obvious candidate for the price level is that one which would balance supply with demand, averaging over the normal fluctuations in both supply and demand. But the amount of information required accurately to determine this price would be formidable for most commodities. As for the buffer stock, it should presumably be able to deal with the normal fluctuations in supply and demand. But in order to avoid running absurdly large stocks the objective of *complete* price stabilization would need to be abandoned, at least in extreme circumstances. Even so, the cost of operating the required buffer stock might be very large for many commodities. It is thus easy to see why those stabilization schemes which have been established have always been on the verge of breaking down.

David Vines
University of Glasgow

References

Newbery, D. M. G. and Stiglitz, J. E. (1981), *The Theory of Commodity Price Stabilization: A Study on the Economics of Risk*, Oxford.

MacBean, A. I. and Snowden, P. N. (1981), *International Institutions in Trade and Finance*, London.

See also: *cartels and trade associations*.

Compensation Principle

The compensation principle is an ingenious device for getting around the view that interpersonal comparisons of utility are unscientific. If everyone gains, real income has unambiguously increased and so has economic welfare. There has been a Pareto-improvement. But suppose, as is usually the case, that some gain and some lose. What has happened to real income and to economic welfare? It was to deal with this problem that Kaldor (1939), endorsed by Hicks, formulated the compensation principle: there will be a potential improvement if the gainers from a change are able to compensate the losers and yet still be better off – i.e. they can 'over-compensate' the losers. Without some such rule one is powerless to make judgements about change, even when it makes almost everyone much better off. There were early technical criticisms and suggestions for improvement by Scitovsky, who noticed that losers might at the same time be able to bribe gainers to return to the initial situation, and the principle has continued to be controversial because of its ambiguous status. It has long been recognized that either compensation is hypothetical only – in which case it is contentious – or it is actual – in which case it is anodyne.

Further is it a *test* for increases in real income or a *criterion* of policy? As a criterion of policy it forms the basis, though in simplified form, for much of cost-benefit analysis. The debate among cost-benefit analysts about whether distributional weights should be included, exactly reflects the ambiguities of the compensation principle itself.

David Collard
University of Bath

Reference
Kaldor, N. (1939), 'Welfare propositions of economic and interpersonal comparisons of utility', *Economic Journal*, 49.

Further Reading
Mishan, E. J. (1981), *Introduction to Normative Economics*, Oxford.
See also: *cost-benefit analysis; welfare economics*.

Competition

Competition and its different aspects have maintained a central place in economic reality and economic theory for well over two hundred years. Competition – always to some extent a motivating force in economic affairs (as in other fields of human endeavour) – rose to prominence when the static and regulated world of medieval and feudal days, with its guilds and restrictions, began to decline and gave way to the dynamics of the Industrial Revolution bringing division of labour, capital accumulation, free markets and mobile workers.

When the foundations of economic theory were built in eighteenth-century Britain – above all with the publication of Adam Smith's pathbreaking work *Wealth of Nations* (1776) – competition in the leading capitalist country was already so pronounced that it could not escape the attention of any realistic economist. But from the very beginning competition was not only seen as a real-world phenomenon whose working had to be explained ('positive' economics). It also rapidly acquired the status of a norm, a standard of efficiency to which economic systems should aspire ('normative' economics). This was already true for Adam Smith. He tried to analyse the working of competitive markets – the formation of demand, supply, and prices. At the same time, he was intrigued by the moral problem of how the multitude of isolated actions of egotistic, profit-seeking individuals could result in a common good, the growing wealth of nations. He saw competition as the force, the hidden hand, which brings about this socially desirable transformation.

This double vision of competition has remained typical for all so-called classical and neo-classical schools of economic theory. They try to *explain* the variations in demands, supplies and relative prices through increasingly sophisticated theories of competitive processes, and they *advocate* the adoption of competitive policies by pointing out the alleged advantages of competition: efficient allocation of resources through prices signalling the desires of consumers and producers (if backed by purchasing power); pressure on producers to lower production costs and prices in order to be able to compete; dynamic efficiency, because competition enforces a constant search for new products and marketing opportunities.

While real world competition is a complex phenomenon and always coexisted with other economic mechanisms (as Smith clearly saw), economic *theory* tended more and more towards a highly formalistic and abstract model of 'perfect competition' which soon became the basic standard for both 'positive' and 'normative' investigations of economic processes. 'Perfect competition' denotes a market situation where large numbers of fully informed ('transparent markets') producers and consumers meet in order to sell or buy clearly defined and uniform goods and services ('homogeneous markets'). The very large number of economic agents implies that a single seller or buyer is such a small fraction of the market that his individual action (purchase or sale – entry or withdrawal) is so infini-tesimal that it cannot noticeably affect the market situation and the market price ('atomistic competition').

Full information means that no seller will sell below the going (equilibrium) price and no buyer will be prepared to pay more than that price. There will thus be at any moment just one price for a given commodity ('Law of One Price') and this price will serve as a basis for the decision-making process of economic agents. If we assume a general network of such 'perfect markets', and add a general competitive search for high profits (in the case of firms) and low costs of provisioning (in the case of households), we obtain a picture of the efficiency of a 'perfectly competitive' system. Suppose, for instance, that the demand for commodity A increases. More buyers enter the A-market and this causes a shortage of supplies. As a consequence prices rise (flexibility of market prices being another assumption of perfect competition). The ensuing super-profits attract firms from other branches. Supplies in the A-market increase, price and profits fall until the super-profits are wiped out. Perfect competition and its price system has brought about a rearrangement of the production structure to suit a changed demand and has at the same time – by permitting free entry of new firms – forced a return to lower prices and 'normal' profits.

The 'idyllic' features of perfect competition – a theoretical construct – lie behind the age-old advocacy of free markets, free competition, and free trade by members of the economic profession. Monopoly, where the producer can raise prices by keeping out competitors and keeping goods in short supply, was to be fought with all means. But the forces making for monopolistic inroads on competition are very strong. It was already becoming clear in the nineteenth century that techno-logical changes leading to extensive capital equipment and mass production methods involved a concentration process in many industries, reducing the number of firms. In the place of 'atom-istic' (perfect) competition there is a steadily growing trend towards 'oligopolistic competition', the 'Competition among the Few' (Fellner, 1949). Here prices and profits are no longer regulated by competition alone, but also by conventions and agreements between powerful agents. The chance for higher profits is a strong urge – apart from technological factors – towards concentration, and this urge has proved more effective than the anti-monopoly legislation that was started approxi-mately one hundred years ago in the US (Sherman Act 1890) and later spread to other countries.

But the 'ideal' of perfect competition is not only threatened by concentration and oligopoly. Even where markets are characterized by a large number of firms, the conditions of perfect competition are frequently missing because products are not homogeneous and information is incomplete. In many markets, *technically* similar goods (e.g. motor cars, toothpastes, and so on) are markedly differentiated through trademarks, make-up, advertising. The heterogeneous goods are no longer perfect substitutes. Their prices can differ, and although there is competition between them, it is by no means perfect. Each firm has some influence on the sales, prices and profits of its 'own' product. This fragmentation of markets is intensified by the insufficient information of consumers regarding prices and quality differences. As a consequence 'perfect competition' gives way to 'imperfect' or 'monopolistic competition' (Robinson, 1933; Chamberlin, 1932) which no longer 'guarantees' efficient allocation and low costs.

The gap between the idealized model of 'perfect competition' and real-world developments has led to various criticisms of the 'normative' bias towards competitive rules in traditional theories. One line of reasoning, the 'Theory of the Second Best' (Lipsey and Lancaster, 1956), has shown that once perfect competition is not the *general* rule, non-competitive measures in other fields may turn out to be preferable. An example is the 'Theory of Countervailing Power' (Galbraith, 1952), which discusses the creation of big units as effective answer to already existing monopolies. The 'Theory of Market Failures' has shown that while competition for high profits may be efficient within the framework of a single market, it may lead to 'external effects', i.e. to positive or negative developments in other fields which are not sufficiently taken into account in a purely competitive adjustment process. This factor, which has acquired important dimensions in the ecological context, indicates that public intervention and collective action might be advantageous. They become imperative in the case of the so-called Public Goods (e.g. public security, law courts, etc.) which by their very nature cannot be regulated in a competitive manner. Finally, we have to mention the socioeconomic reform movements, like some Christian social theories and – above all

– the socialist movements, which criticize the uneven distribution of income resulting from private capital and competitive
markets. They would prefer to replace – at least partly – the
competition-plus-profit mechanism of economic regulation by
more collective and solidaric methods, both for economic and
general humanitarian reasons.

Kurt W. Rothschild
Johannes Kepler University, Linz

References
Chamberlin, E. H. (1932), *The Theory of Monopolistic
Competition*, Cambridge, Mass.
Fellner, W. (1949), *Competition among the Few*, New York.
Galbraith, J. K. (1952), *American Capitalism. The Concept of
Countervailing Power*, Oxford.
Lipsey, R. G. and Lancaster, K. (1956/57), 'The general
theory of the second best', *Review of Economic Studies*, 24.
Robinson, J. (1933), *The Economics of Imperfect Competition*,
London.
See also: *Smith*.

Conservation
Conservation is essentially a stockholding activity. Holding
back today allows greater use tomorrow or perhaps 100 years
hence. Economists' attention, and ours, is generally focused
on natural phenomena – fish, oil, environmental quality, and
suchlike – although machines, literature, culture may also be
conserved and many of the same principles apply.

The earth is finite, its resources and its ability to carry population and absorb pollution are limited. Some economists
believe that continued growth in output and population will
bring the world to these limits perhaps rather quickly.
According to this view both nonrenewable stocks (such as oils
and metals) and renewable resources (for example, fish and
land) will come under increasing and perhaps irreparable
strain. Environmental damage (through erosion, build-up of
carbon dioxide) will likewise become excessive, and habits of

high consumption, once built up, will be difficult to break. Radical and Marxist economists often blame such problems on capitalism, even if the Eastern bloc appears to have fared equally badly.

A more characteristic view among economists is that *markets* provide adequate incentives to conservation. Resource use will be determined mainly by expected price movements and the discount rate. Scarcity involves high prices, expected scarcity expected high prices, increasing the advantage both of conserving the resource and of taking other resource-saving measures such as recycling and appropriate technical change. Only where market failure occurs is there perhaps cause to worry, and even then such failure may tend to excessive conservation. Moreover, market failure can generally be recognized and alleviated. Occasionally the view emerges that such difficulties present a challenge, which mighty man must and will overcome. Wise use of resources to build up capital and develop new techniques and skills may be a crucial part of this fight.

The 1973 oil crisis exhibited vividly the possibilities and dangers of a resource crisis. The sudden fourfold rise in oil prices caused worldwide disruption; the ensuing slumpflation (though doubtless partly due to earlier causes) has been an obvious disaster, economically, medically, and socially, Even an oil-rich country like Britain has been depressed. Recent econometric studies have indicated great responsiveness to price, but building up slowly over decades as capital, technologies and habits change. It is the slowness of these changes that has created the current crisis, while in the longer run technological changes may bring unwelcome side effects.

Renewable resources (like fish) are constantly replenished by nature, hence permitting (up to a point) continued use without depletion. There is a maximum sustainable yield, although it may be desirable to hold yield below this level because of harvesting cost, or above it becaue of discounting. With nonrenewable resources (like oil), use now precludes use later, although reserves can be extended by improved extraction techniques and by exploration. Metals are normally considered nonrenewable, although recycling can extend their use.

The natural environment is another kind of resource. To some extent it is the concern of the rich, for example, as a source of landscape and recreational experiences. However, in this it differs little from other parts of market and indeed non-market systems. But not all environmental problems are of this type. Water pollution and air pollution damage those who live in the areas concerned – often the poor, as the rich can afford to move away (into 'Conservation Areas' perhaps). Erosion, flooding and pesticides will affect everyone. There are also international problems, such as global overheating and the excessive build-up of carbon dioxide leading to difficult-to-reverse melting of the polar ice caps and very extensive flooding. Problems associated with nuclear radiation are widely feared.

There are two reasons for including population in this discussion: (1) Population size and growth are major determinants of problems of resources and environment; (2) Child-bearing involves the characteristic externality problem of unpaid burdens on others, especially if fiscal help is given to large families. Currently the world's population is doubling every 40 years. In some countries, such as China and Taiwan, dramatic downward shifts in birthrate are occurring. But elsewhere, as in India and most Muslim and Roman Catholic countries, signs of change are very weak. Even in most developed countries population growth continues, with particularly strong resource effects. The causes are complex and poorly understood, although cost has been found relevant.

Many factors underlie inadequate conservation (see Pearce, 1976), for example, difficulties of prediction and the appropriate treatment of uncertainty. Particularly important are common access problems, applying not only to fishing, but to forestry, hunting, extraction of oil and deep sea nodule mining, and to population growth. Tax regimes can be strongly anti-conservationist – childbearing and US mining are important examples. Another possible problem is that the discount rate used is too high, giving undue favour to the present; the difficulties here are: (1) that this is an economy-wide problem, by no means confined to resources, and indeed some writers have used it to justify greater investment and faster growth; (2) governments may hesitate to override the preferences of the current generation; and (3) more radical authors suggest that growth itself uses resources and damages the environment, although this is disputed.

Remedies are difficult to summarize. Characteristically those used (and supported by most non-economists) are regulations, whereas much of the economic debate is over the superiority of taxes. Regulations include net size, limited seasons and outright bans in fishing, limits or bans for pollution, including pesticides, and planning regulations for building and land use. The objection is that lack of discrimination leads to inefficiency; sometimes extreme inefficiency, as when limited fishing seasons invite the multiplication of boats, which stand idle over the rest of the year. Direct controls also tend to be narrowly specific, leaving no incentive to achieve more than the specified cutback or to undertake R & D to improve control. Fiscal measures are occasionally used but with little finesse, and subsidies or tax concessions (as for airlines, heavy industries, children) are generally preferred to taxes. More promising examples, such as fuel-saving subsidies and also the emerging systems of penalizing pollution in several European countries, incidentally (and unlike controls) generating substantial revenue. There are many other possible remedies, such as nationalization, diversification (often favoured by ecologists) indirect measures (recycling, durability and curbs on advertising and so on), auctioned rights (for example to cull a resource or to pollute), public expenditure (on sewage or agricultural infrastructure and so on), provision of information, including forecasts, and attempts to influence attitudes. As Baumol and Oates (1979) emphasize, each of these methods, or indeed various combinations, will be appropriate in particular circumstances.

Richard Lecomber
University of Bristol

References

Baumol, W. J. and Oates, W. E. (1979), *Economics, Environmental Policy and the Quality of Life*, Englewood Cliffs, N.J.

O'Riordan, T. (1976), *Environmentalism*, London.

Pearce, D. W. (1976), *Environmental Economics*, London.

Schultz, T. P. (1981), *Economics of Population*, Reading, Mass.

Consumer Behaviour

In his authoritative review of the development of utility theory, Stigler (1950) wrote, 'If consumers do not buy less of a commodity when their incomes rise, they will surely buy less when the price of the commodity rises. This was the chief product – so far as the hypotheses on economic behaviour go of the long labours of a very large number of able economists . . . [who] had known all along that demand curves have negative slopes, quite independently of their utility theorizing.' So what use is utility theory, the reigning paradigm among economists interested in consumer behaviour?

Thirty-five years on, data on consumer behaviour have expanded enormously, computing costs have plummetted, statistical numeracy has spread and the range of applied studies has multiplied. Simultaneously more content has been put into choice theory and more accessible links forged via the cost and other 'dual' functions between the structure of preferences and behaviour. A comprehensive modern treatment of choice theory and its application to most types of consumer behaviour can be found in Deaton and Muellbauer (1980).

The existence of an ordinal utility function defined on bundles of goods implies that certain axioms of choice are fulfilled, the key ones being transitivity or consistency of choice, continuity (small differences matter only a little) and nonsatiation. Preferences can also be represented through the cost function. This defines the minimum cost of reaching a given utility level for a consumer facing given prices. Among its properties: it is concave in prices and its price derivatives give purchases as functions of prices and the utility level i.e., compensated demands. The great advantage is that a simple step – differentiation – leads from a representation of preferences to a description of the behaviour of a consumer faced with a linear budget constraint. Concavity then immediately implies the law of demand described above. In fact, considerably more is implied: the matrix of compensated price derivatives is symmetric negative semidefinite. A great deal of econometric effort has gone into applying and testing these very considerable restrictions on behaviour.

Systems of demand equations are usually estimated for annual or quarterly observations on aggregate consumer spending on such categories as food, clothing, housing, fuel, etc. More is now understood about the links between individual and aggregate behaviour. For example, under quite restrictive conditions, average behaviour is like that of a single consumer so that then one can say a 'representative consumer' exists. Specific assumptions on the structure of preferences yield further implications. Thus an additive utility function strongly restricts the cross-price responses of demands. These and many other properties are analysed in Gorman (1976) who makes elegant use of cost and profit functions. Almost invariably, some kind of separability assumptions are made in applied work: thus, preferences for current period goods need to be separable from the allocation of leisure and of consumption in other periods if demands are functions only of current prices and total expenditure on these goods. On the other hand, such static demand functions are, by most empirical evidence, mis-specified. A widely applied hypothesis which can explain why is that preferences are conditioned by past behaviour, not only of the consumer but of others, so that demand functions are dynamic (more on this below).

By assuming the consumer can lend or borrow at the same interest rate, the utility maximizing consumer's intertemporal choices are subject to a linear budget constraint. In this life-cycle theory of consumption, developed by Modigliani and his co-workers, the budget is life-cycle wealth consisting of initial asset holdings, income and discounted expected income, and relative prices depend on real interest rates. Extensions to the demand for money and durables have yielded interesting insights into, for example, the role of interest rates.

The treatment of income expectations has been the most controversial issue for empirical workers using this theory. The simple treatment by Friedman in his book on the permanent income hypothesis of consumption, as well as his suppression of a separate role for assets, is now seen as less than satisfactory. Hall (1978) has shown that, under certain conditions, the life-cycle model together with rational expectations implies that consumption follows a random walk which seems not a bad empirical approximation for some countries.

One of the major criticisms of life-cycle theory is that the budget constraints are not in fact linear for credit constrained consumers, though the implications are hard to model on aggregate data. Much attention has been paid to non-linear budget constraints in the analysis of behaviour from household surveys. Labour supply decisions are the major example; others are the choice of housing tenure and transport models where choice has discrete elements. An integrated statistical framework with rational and random elements for such decisions now exists. In this context too, restrictions on preferences have major empirical content, for example, additive preferences allow great simplifications in the analysis of repeated surveys of the same households. A more traditional use of household budget surveys collected to derive weights for cost of living indices and to analyse inequality has been the derivation of Engel functions which link expenditures on different goods with the total budget and household demography. A major use has been derivation of equivalence scales used to standardize budgets in studies of poverty and inequality for variations in household size and structure.

Another way to put more content into the theory is to regard the household as a producer using market goods and time of utility yielding commodities. This household production approach has proved useful, for example, in the measurement of quality change, in welfare measurement of the provision of public leisure facilities, and in the economics of fertility and other aspects of family life. There has been little work, however, on how decisions by individual family members are co-ordinated, an important lacuna.

Most decisions are, of course, made under uncertainty and the expected utility approach has been widely used by economists. Under the axioms assumed here, subjective probabilities are themselves defined and this gives rise to a theory of learning founded on Bayes' Theorem. The intuitive notion of risk averting behaviour here has a formal basis and applications to the behaviour of financial markets have proved particularly popular. In recent years, evidence against some of the axioms has accumulated from laboratory experiments on volunteers. So far no agreement exists on a better set of axioms.

There have been many criticisms of the utility maximizing approach ranging from 'it is tautologous' to the introspective doubt that anyone could be so good at absorbing and storing information and then computing consistent decisions. H. A. Simon's notion of bounded rationality has much intuitive appeal. Certainly one can interpret the role of costs of adjustment or habits based on own or others' behaviour in this light. The implication of a stimulus response smaller in the short run than in the long is suggestive. Psychologists have suggested models such as that of 'cognitive dissonance' which appeal in particular contexts but do not yield a general behavioural theory. Market researchers have developed distinct approaches of their own based on the interpretation of attitude surveys used as marketing tools and with the major focus on brand choice, repeat buying and the introduction of new varieties. They have drawn relatively little out of the utility maximizing hypothesis, though not all these approaches are necessarily inconsistent with it.

John Muellbauer
Nuffield College, University of Oxford

References

Deaton, A. and Muellbauer, J. (1980), *Economics and Consumer Behavior*, New York.

Gorman, W. M. (1976), 'Tricks with utility functions', in M.

Artis and R. Nobay (eds), *Essays in Economic Analysis*, Cambridge.

Hall, R. E. (1978), 'Stochastic implications of the life cycle-permanent income hypothesis: theory and evidence', *Journal of Political Economy*, 86.

Stigler, G. (1950), 'The development of utility theory', *Journal of Political Economy*, 58.

See also: *consumer surplus; consumption function; marketing research; maximization.*

Consumer Surplus

There can be few areas of economics where more ink has been spilled in obfuscating an essentially simple idea. The basic idea of the change in consumer surplus is to measure the loss or gain to a consumer from a change in consumption or from a change in one or more prices. The early formulation by Dupuit in 1844 was justified by Marshall in 1880. It consists of taking the area under the demand curve which traces out the effect of changes in the good's price, holding constant the budget in order to measure the change in utility in money terms. Already in 1892 Pareto criticized Marshall's assumption of a constant marginal utility of the budget. Indeed, there are only two circumstances where Marshall's formulation is correct: either the proportions in which goods are consumed are independent of the budget, which is grossly untrue empirically, or, for the particular good whose price is changing, the demand is unaffected by changes in the budget.

Hicks in 1939 recognized that the correct measure is to take the change in area under the compensated demand curve. However, as Samuelson remarked in 1947, consumer surplus was essentially a superfluous concept since there was already an established theory of economic index numbers. The modern theory of index numbers is based on the cost or expenditure function which gives the minimum cost of reaching a given indifference curve at a specified set of prices. The money value of a change in utility is then given by the change in cost at some reference prices. When the change in utility is caused by some price changes, Hicks's 'compensating variation' can be viewed as the measure which uses the new prices as reference and his 'equivalent variation' as that which uses the old prices as reference.

There is a widespread impression that the computation of such correct concepts is intrinsically harder or requires more information than computing Marshallian consumer surplus. However, simple and accurate approximations to the correct measures are available, and straightforward algorithms exist to calculate them with any required degree of accuracy. Finally, it should be noted that *aggregating* utility changes over different consumers raises a new issue: is a dollar to the poor worth the same in social terms as a dollar to the rich? Consumer surplus as such does not address this question, though it is an inescapable one in cost benefit analysis.

John Muellbauer
Nuffield College, University of Oxford

Reference
Deaton, A. and Muellbauer, J. (1980), *Economics and Consumer Behavior*, New York.
See also: *consumer behaviour*; *consumption function*.

Consumption Function

The consumption function expresses the functional dependence of consumption on variables thought to influence the level of consumption expenditure by individuals, such as income, wealth and the rate of interest. The consumption function was an important innovation introduced into economic theory by J. M. Keynes in his *General Theory of Employment, Interest and Money* (1936), to undermine the classical orthodoxy that the rate of interest acts to equilibriate savings and investment at the full employment level of income. Keynes made consumption, and therefore saving, a function of income, and by doing so divorced the savings function from the investment function. He then showed that if plans to invest fall short of plans to save out of the full employment level of income, there will be a tendency for the level of income (not the rate of interest) to fall to bring saving and investment into equilibrium again, the extent of the fall being given by the value of the income multiplier which is the reciprocal of the marginal propensity to save. By means of the consumption function, Keynes had apparently demonstrated the possibility that an economy may find itself in an equilibrium state at less than full employment. This demonstration was part of the Keynesian revolution of thought which undermined the idea that there are macroeconomic forces at work which automatically guarantee that economies tend to long run full employment. This is the theoretical importance of the consumption function.

The practical interest in the consumption function relates to the relation between consumption and income through time. Keynes seemed to suggest that the long run consumption function was non-proportional, so that as societies became richer they would spend proportionately less on consumption, implying that a higher proportion of income would have to be invested if economies were not to stagnate. Fears were expressed that mature economic societies might run out of profitable investment opportunities. The international cross section evidence reveals an interesting pattern. The savings ratio does rise with the level of development but at a decreasing rate, levelling off in maturity at about 25 per cent of national income. There is a voluminous literature concerning why this should be the case. It is as if saving is a luxury good which then loses its appeal. James Duesenberry (1949) developed the relative income hypothesis, which predicts that the savings-income ratio will remain unchanged through time if the personal distribution of income remains unchanged. Ando and Modigliani (1963) developed the life-cycle hypothesis of saving, which predicts a constant savings ratio if the rate of growth of population and per capita income are steady. Milton Friedman (1957) developed the permanent income hypothesis, arguing that individuals wish to maintain a constant relation between their consumption and a measure of permanent income determined by wealth and other factors. To discriminate between the hypotheses is virtually impossible. As societies develop, both growth and income inequality first increase and then decelerate and stabilize, which would explain the historical savings behaviour observed. Other factors that might be important relate to the increased monetization of an economy, which then yields diminishing returns. However, the fears of a lack of investment opportunities to match growing saving, owing to the saturation of markets, seems to be unfounded.

A. P. Thirlwall
University of Kent

References
Ando, A. and Modigliani, F. (1963), 'The life cycle hypothesis of saving: aggregate implications and tests', *American Economic Review*.
Duesenberry, J. (1949), *Income, Saving and the Theory of Consumer Behavior*, Cambridge, Mass.
Friedman, M. (1957), *A Theory of the Consumption Function*, Washington.
See also: *consumer behaviour; consumer surplus*.

Co-operatives

Co-operatives are economic organizations run by their members on the basis of one person, one vote, with their trading surplus being distributed among the membership in an agreed manner. Membership can therefore be seen as an extention of corporate shareholding except that, in co-operatives, decision making is based on democratic principles, and a capital stake is not necessarily the crucial element in joining. Indeed, the return on capital holdings is generally fixed at a low level, leaving the bulk of the surplus to be allocated according to member transactions. For example, in consumer co-operatives, membership derives from the act of purchase and profits are distributed according to the amount spent. In agricultural co-ops, the members are private farmers who join forces for production, retailing and services. Other important co-operative forms include credit unions and housing co-operatives, in which the membership are borrowers and lenders and tenants respectively, and producer co-operatives, in which the workers control the business through some democratic process and jointly share the profits as income.

The first co-operative was opened by twenty-eight Lancashire workers in Toad Lane, Rochdale, in 1844, who developed the seven 'Co-operative Principles' which still form the basis of the international co-operative movement. These are open membership; one member, one vote; limited return on capital; allocation of surplus in proportion to member transactions; cash trading; stress on education; and religious and political neutrality. They were reviewed by the International Co-operative Alliance (ICA), the world-wide organization of all co-ops, in 1966, and the latter two principles were dropped in favour of a new one supporting inter-co-operative collaboration. The international co-operative movement has now grown to enormous proportions, with the more than 700,000 co-operatives affiliated to the ICA in 1980 containing some 350 million members in 65 countries. The largest number of societies were agricultural and credit co-operatives, with a quarter of a million each world-wide covering some 180 million members between them. However, the largest number of members are in consumer co-operatives, containing some 130 million in around 60,000 societies. There are also some 45,000 industrial co-operatives with a labour force in excess of five and a half million workers.

Inspired by the Yugoslav system of workers' self-management of industry and following the seminal work of Ward (1958) and Vanek (1970), these producer co-operatives, or labour-managed firms as they have become known, have been studied extensively in recent years (see Ireland and Law (1982) for a survey). Analysts interested in how enterprise decisions change when the interests of workers replace profitability as the corporate objective, have focused on four main areas: the possibility of sluggish or even 'perverse' production responses to shifts in demand and cost conditions, of insufficient investment, of managerial deficiencies and unwillingness to bear risks, and of a boost to performance due to higher worker morale. The latter prospect has stimulated interest in schemes for worker participation in management as a way of obtaining the positive incentive effects without the presumed deficiencies of full workers' control.

There are producer co-operative sectors in most Western economies, the largest and most successful being the Mondragon group in the Basque area of Spain. Since its formation in the mid-1950s, an integrated productive, retail, financial and educational structure has emerged providing around 16,000 industrial jobs. Empirical work establishes the group to be relatively more productive and profitable than comparable capitalist firms, as well as being better able to meet social goals (see Thomas in Jones and Svejnar, 1982). Other studies isolate a positive productivity effect in the 20,000 Italian producer co-operatives, the 700 French ones and the 800 societies in the United States (see Jones and Svejnar, 1982). However, apart from Mondragon, producer co-operatives have tended to be relatively small, under-capitalized, concentrated in traditional sectors like textiles and processing, and short-lived. The co-operative form has probably failed to displace joint stock companies despite their democratic structure and the productivity benefits because of difficulties with risk-bearing: entrepreneurial workers cannot spread their risks by working in a number of activities in the way that capital owners can spread theirs by holding a diversified portfolio of assets. Hence capital has historically hired workers rather than labour hiring capital, but recently many new producer co-operatives have been founded as a way of maintaining employment – some 400 in the UK between 1975 and 1980 – and if risk-bearing problems can be solved this may prove to be an important type of enterprise in the future.

Saul Estrin
University of Southampton

References
Ireland, N. J. and Law, P. J. (1982), *The Economics of Labour-Managed Enterprises*, London.
Jones, D. C. and Svejnar, J. (1982), *Participatory and Self-Managed Firms*, Lexington, Mass.

Vanek, J. (1970), *The General Theory of Labour-Managed Market Economics*, Ithaca, N.Y.

Ward, B. (1958), 'The Firm in Illyria; market syndicalism', *American Economic Review*, 55.

Corporate Enterprise

Corporations as an important business form appeared in large numbers after the institution of limited liability. Prior to that, and still numerically important today, most businesses were conducted by sole traders (that is, generally owner-managers) and unlimited partnerships of two or more people. Incorporation encouraged firm growth and as a corollary, except in the smallest corporations, shareholders participated less in day-to-day management. In the UK this growth continued well into the twentieth century resulting in an increasing concentration of industry. In 1949, 22 per cent of manufacturing net output emanated from the 100 largest firms, and by 1976, 42 per cent. This trend levelled elsewere, and in the US the share of value added by the 100 largest manufacturing firms remained at around one-third from the early 1950s. Small firms (under 200 employees) are still important in the UK, accounting for 95 per cent of firms in manufacturing and around 20 per cent of net output and employment. Their prominence is even greater in service sectors of the economy.

Firms initially grew to obtain the advantages of scale economies and of monopoly power. The latter was perceived to be especially true in the US where men like Rockefeller and Carnegie built industrial empires in the oil and steel industries. Congress, fearful of the consequences of industrial size, passed the Sherman Anti-trust Act in 1890, and firms such as Standard Oil and American Tobacco were ordered to divest themselves of assets and split into separate firms. In the next three-quarters of a century many American firms took alternative growth routes, partly to minimize their visibility to 'trust-busters' and partly to obtain the benefits of diversification. Risk-avoidance was obtained by spreading the company's efforts over a range of domestic markets for different products, or by expanding abroad with the original product range. These activities were mirrored elsewhere by British, German, Dutch and Swiss firms such as ICI, Hoechst, Philips, and Nestlé respectively.

Many students of industrial structure are concerned at the levels of concentration now ruling. They argue that as a consequence prices are uncompetitively high, that very large firms become inefficient and reluctant to change and innovate. Others argue that concentration varies industry by industry and is determined by technology or is a reward for innovation and efficiency. Large firms only become large by winning the consumer's approval. The identities of the leading firms are also changing, and the leading 100 firms of 1900 are different in both identity and in ranking from the leading 100 in 1980. Thus firms must either change as demand and supply conditions change or forfeit any position they have won through previous successful responsiveness to market conditions. This school believes that provided entry to and exit from an industry are easy, concentration levels need not be a cause for concern. The issue of whether industrial structure determines firm conduct and performance, or whether firm performance and conduct determines industrial structure is still unsettled. If there are barriers to entry imposed by regulations, the truth may embody both theses.

A further area of debate is the degree to which incorporation and what Berle and Means (1968) called the consequential 'divorce of ownership from control' has resulted in managers pursuing goals different from the maximization of profit which the owner-manager is presumed to do in the standard theory of the firm. Alternative theories have been put forward suggesting that managers pursue sales or asset growth, size *per se*, or maximize utility functions containing both financial and psychic variables. In most cases these alternative goals are subject to a minimum profit constraint which, if not met, would result in a takeover by another firm, loss of managerial job security and a return to a profit target closer to that of maximization. Proponents of these views argue that these alternative goals result in different patterns of firm behaviour if the external environment changes (for example, a tax on profits does not affect a profit maximizer's behaviour, but a sales maximizer subject to a minimum profits constraint would reduce output and raise price). Defenders of the traditional theory argue that efficient stock markets, *via* the takeover mechanism, ensure that managers depart but little from profit maximization. To the extent that they do, this is a cost borne willingly by owners to achieve the net benefits of specialization of function between the risk-capital providers and the more risk-averse providers of managerial expertise.

W. Duncan Reekie
University of the Witwatersrand, Johannesburg

Reference
Berle, A. A. and Means, G. C. (1968), *The Modern Corporation and Private Property* (rev. edn), New York.

Further Reading
Brozen, Y. (1982), *Concentration, Mergers and Public Policy*, New York.
Reekie, W. D. (1978), *Industry, Prices and Markets*, Oxford.
Scherer, F M. (1980), *Industrial Market Structure and Economic Performance* (2nd edn), Chicago.
See also: *business concentration; monopoly.*

Cost-Benefit Analysis

In terms of its practical application, cost-benefit analysis (CBA) is usually regarded as having its origins in the United States Flood Control Act of 1936. Without reference to the body of welfare economics that had already arisen by then, and before the introduction of compensation criteria into the literature, the Act argued that flood control projects had their social justification in a weighing up of the costs and benefits, with the latter being summed regardless of to whom they accrued. It is this reference to the *social* dimension of investment appraisal that distinguishes CBA from the more orthodox techniques which deal with the cash flow to a firm or single agency.

Oddly, CBA grew in advance of the theoretical foundations obtained from welfare economics that subsequently provided its underpinning. The notion that the benefits to individuals should be measured according to some indicator of consumer's surplus was well established by nineteenth-century writers especially Dupuit and Marshall, but Hicks's work (1943) established the exact requirements for such measures. Similarly, the notion of a *shadow price* is crucial to CBA since, even if a project's output is marketed, CBA does not necessarily use market prices as indicators of value. Rather, reference is made to the marginal cost of providing the extra output in question. Despite the ambiguous relationship between marginal cost pricing in an economy where some sectors have unregulated pricing policies which force price above marginal cost, CBA and shadow pricing has flourished as an appraisal technique. It secured widespread adoption in US public agencies in the 1950s and 1960s, and was both used and advocated in Europe in the 1960s. It suffered a mild demise in the early 1970s in light of critiques based on the alleged fallacy of applying monetary values to 'intangible' items such as peace and quiet, clean air and the general 'quality of life'. Significantly, post-1973 recession revived its use as governments sought 'value for money' in public expenditure. Unease with the monetization of many unmarketed costs and benefits has, however, remained, resulting in a proliferation of alternative techniques such as environmental impact assessment, cost-effectiveness analysis (in which only resource costs are expressed in money and benefits remain in non-monetary units), and some 'multi-objective' approaches. CBA retains its strength because of its ability potentially to identify optimal expenditures (where net benefits are maximized) and to secure a well-defined project ranking. However, few practitioners would argue that it has a role outside the ranking of expenditures within a given budget. That is, it has a highly limited role in comparing the efficiency of expenditures across major budget areas such as defence, education, health and so on.

As generally formulated, CBA operates with the efficiency objectives of welfare economics. The maximization of net social benefits is formally equivalent to securing the largest net welfare gain as defined by the Kaldor-Hicks compensation principle. Academic debate in this respect has centred on the appropriate choice of the measure of consumer's surplus, with the dominant advocacy being of the use of the 'compensating variation' measure introduced by Hicks (1943). It seems fair to say, however, that the philosophical basis of CBA remains a source of professional confusion. Use of social prices based on consumer valuations implicitly assumes that the distribution of market power within the relevant economy is itself optimal. Since this is a value judgement, it is open to anyone to substitute it with an alternative distributional judgement. Some would argue that this apparent arbitrariness defines the inadequacies of CBA, while others suggest that no society has ever operated with disregard for distributional criteria and that distributional judgements are no less arbitrary than efficiency judgements.

Much of the practical effort in CBA has gone into actual mechanisms for discovering individuals' preferences in contexts where there is no explicit market. The most successful have been the hedonic price technique and the use of bidding techniques. Hedonic prices refer to the coefficients defining the relationship between property prices and changes in some unmarketed variable affecting property prices. An example would be clean air which should raise the price of a property, other things being equal. Bidding techniques involve the use of questionnaires which ask directly for consumers' valuations of the benefits.

Since costs and benefits accrue over time, CBA tends to adopt a discounting approach whereby future cash and non-cash flows are discounted back to a present value by use of a discount rate. The determination of the discount rate has occupied a substantial literature. In theory, one would expect consumers to prefer the present to the future because of impatience ('myopia') and expectations of higher incomes in the future (thus lowering their marginal valuation of a unit of benefit in the future). In turn, the resulting rate of time preference should be equal to interest rates ruling in the market which also reflect the productivity of capital. In practice, time preference rates and cost of capital estimates can vary significantly because of imperfections in capital markets. Moreover, the rate of discount relevant to *social* decisions can differ from the average of individual valuations, because choices made as members of society will differ when compared to choices made on an individualist basis. Further controversy surrounds the issue of intergenerational fairness since positive discount rates have the potential for shifting cost burdens forward to future generations. Thus the risks of, say, storing nuclear waste appear small when discounted back to the present and expressed as a present value. Conversely, zero discount rates may discriminate against projects which offer the highest potential for leaving accumulated capital for the use of future generations. To pursue the nuclear power example, non-investment because of the waste disposal problem could reduce the inherited stock of energy availability to future generations, by forcing a rapid depletion of finite stock resources such as coal or oil. The intergenerational issue is thus complex and raises the fundamental issue of just how far into the future CBA should look. Because of its foundations in consumer sovereignty, there is a temptation to argue that the time horizon is set by the existing generation and, at most, the succeeding one or two generations.

CBA remains a controversial appraisal technique. As an aid to rational thinking its credentials are higher than any of the alternatives so far advanced. That it cannot substitute for political decisions is not in question, but social science has a duty to inform public choice, and it is in this respect that CBA has its role to play.

David Pearce
University College London

Reference
Hicks, J. (1943), 'The four consumer's surplus', *The Review of Economic Studies*, LL.

Further Reading
Mishan, E. J. (1975), *Cost Benefit Analysis*, 2nd edn, London.
Pearce, D. W. (1983), *Cost Benefit Analysis*, 2nd edn, London.
See also: *project analysis; transport economics and planning; welfare economics.*

Credit

'Credit', derived from the Latin *credere* (to believe), has several meanings, many of which are outside the field of finances. Even in finance it can be used to indicate a positive accounting entry, an increase in wealth or income, but the main use, with which we are concerned here, involves an element of deferred payment. It thus covers not only formal loans but also the multitude of informal arrangements whereby payment for a transaction is made some time after the physical transfer of the goods or services, and by extension it is also used where payment is made in advance. In accounting terms it refers not only to trade credit between businesses but also to the various items known as accruals. Examples of such accruals are the payment of salaries after a person has worked for a week or a month and, on the other side, the advance payment of a year's premium for insurance.

In macroeconomics the term is used with a special meaning to refer to those items of credit that are measurable for the economy as a whole; in practice this restricts it to credit extended by the banking system. As bank loans are made, the proceeds are used to pay for goods and services, and the recipients of these payments pass the cheques to the credit of their own bank deposits: bank loans can be said to create bank deposits. By controlling the volume of bank credit, the monetary authorities can thus indirectly control the volume of bank deposits, which are the most important element in the money supply. The control of bank credit, both in total volume and in the selection of favoured and unfavoured borrowing sectors, is thus often a weapon of monetary policy.

Credit plays an important part in the theory of financial intermediation. The first stage of development of a financial system can be taken as the move from barter to the use of commodity money. Although this move frees the exchange of commodities from the restrictions of barter, by itself it does nothing for the growth of business enterprises because the only funds available for capital investment come from the current income or the previously accumulated money balances of the entrepreneur himself. The development of credit, in the form of direct lending and borrowing, enables the accumulated money balances of others to be transferred to the entrepreneur, who can thus put to profitable use the savings of many other people. Because this development was associated with the levying of interest, it faced religious and social obstacles; these still persist in Muslim countries, where an alternative form of banking (Islamic banking) has been developed on the basis of profit-sharing by the depositor.

For several centuries, credit, both as formal loans and as trade credit, was restricted to businesses and the wealthier households, but in the past 50 years all but the poorest households have obtained access to formal and informal credit. This extension of credit has been achieved by a number of innovations in the forms in which credit is granted. Few of these forms were completely new; the innovations came in the use to which they were put and in the ways in which they were combined.

All lenders need to satisfy themselves on two points before granting credit: these are the ability of the borrower to repay and his willingness to do so. Traditionally, the ability to repay was assured by requiring the borrower to give the lender a mortgage or charge on assets to a value greater than that of the loan, and willingness to repay was assessed on the past record of the borrower and personal knowledge of his character. Unless the loan is for the purchase of a house, the problem raised in giving credit to the ordinary household is that there are no suitable assets to pledge as security. The solution has taken several forms. The first was to obtain a mortgage on the asset (car or television set, for example) that was being purchased with the loan; where the legal system did not permit this (as under English law), the asset was hired to the 'borrower', with a final nominal payment to transfer ownership – hire purchase. Even where this legal subterfuge was not necessary, there was a growth in leasing and straight hiring to households to overcome many of the credit problems.

The key change in this form of consumer lending was a realization that current income rather than accumulated assets was the real security for a loan. In lending on consumer durables this came about because there is a poor second-hand market, but even with houses lenders prefer to avoid the trouble of auctioning the property to secure repayment. During the 1960s this change of attitude towards the nature of the security for a loan was also adopted in corporate lending; it came to be known as lending on the cash flow. For large corporate loans, banks often use their computers for simulating the cash flows of prospective borrowers under a number of hypothetical conditions.

It is obvious from the previous analysis that the key point in granting credit is the assessment of the creditworthiness of the borrower. In the past much of this depended on the personal judgement of local bank managers and on adequate collateral. With the growth in the number of customers, no branch manager can now claim a close knowledge of all his customers, and more formal methods of assessment have become necessary. This is particularly necessary when loans can be obtained by post through the filling in of a simple questionnaire or even through answering questions posed by an electronic terminal. Most of the methods used are based on credit scoring, which uses a statistical technique known as multivariate discriminant analysis (MDA) or one of its variants. Applicants are scored according to such characteristics as ownership of their home, steady employment, and possession of a telephone, and the loan is granted if the score exceeds a predetermined level based on past experience of bad debts.

Jack Revell
University College of North Wales, Bangor

Further Reading
Beckman, T. N. (1969), *Credits and Collections: Management and Theory*, 8th edn, New York.
Gurley, J. G. and Shaw, E. S. (1960), *Money in a Theory of Finance*, Washington, D.C.
See also: *banking*.

Crowding Out

The concept of the crowding out of private sector activity by expansions of government sector has become increasingly important in recent political/ academic debates. All participants in the debate accept that if the economy is at full employment, then an increase in government spending will reduce private sector spending. The debate is concentrated on the effect of increases in government spending away from full employment. If government spending rises by $100 million and national income increases by less than $100 million, then crowding out is said to have occurred. In other words, crowding out is associated with a *multiplier* of less than unity. Even if national income rises by more than $100 million, it would normally be the case that the higher interest rates associated with higher borrowing will reduce productive private sector investment and so 'crowd out' some elements of national income.

The resurgence of interest in crowding out has been associated with the monetarist critique of macroeconomic policy and has received its main theoretical (Carlson and Spencer, 1975) and empirical (Anderson and Jordan, 1968) support from work undertaken at the Federal Reserve Bank of St Louis in the US. Although much of this work has been discredited (see Goldfeld and Blinder, 1972), the political impact has been increasing. Apart from the interest rate effect on investment, a number of other possible sources for crowding out have been suggested. Increased government expenditure may have a depressing effect on people's expectations about the future possible productivity of the economy, and so causing them to reduce investment. Alternatively, investment could be so interest sensitive that even a small rise in the interest rate will reduce investment fully in line with the increase in government spending (this is sometimes known as the Knight case after the Chicago economist Frank Knight).

The major case emphasized by monetarist economists comes from an analysis of the financing of a government deficit. To have an impact on the economy a deficit has to be sustained for a number of years, but each year that deficit has to be financed by borrowing or printing money. Continual financing by borrowing will raise interest rates as the government competes for funds, and the gradual increase in interest rates will reduce investment. As well as this effect, it may be stressed that government debt is safer than private debt, so dollar for dollar substitution will increase the liquidity of the economy and reduce the impulsion to save (and therefore reduce investment funds).

However lacking in persuasiveness these arguments may be, there is strong empirical support for the proposition that multipliers are very low in the UK at least (see Taylor in Cook and Jackson, 1979). In versions of the Treasury Model and the Keynesian National Institute model, long run multipliers vary from 1. 1 to .4 giving considerable credence to the arguments in favour of crowding out. This does not demonstrate that fiscal policy is impossible, but that it is just difficult to sustain.

Ray Barrell
University of Southampton

References

Anderson, L. C. and Jordan, J. L. (1968), 'Monetary and fiscal actions: a test of their relative importance in economic stabilisation', *Federal Reserve Bank of St Louis Review*.

Carlson, K. M. and Spencer, R. W. (1975), 'Crowding out and its critics', *Federal Reserve Bank of St Louis Review*.

Cook, S. T. and Jackson, P. M. (eds), *Government Issues in Fiscal Policy*, London.

Goldfeld, S. and Blinden, A. (1972), 'Some implications of endogenous stabilisation policy', *Brookings Papers on Economic Activity*.

See also: *fiscal policy; monetarism*.

Deflation as a Statistical Device

Economists are interested in abstracting from the effects of price changes when studying movements in economic variables. Deflation is the division of a value variable by an appropriate price index so as to obtain a quantity variable. When the value variable represents a purchase of goods or services the problem

is relatively straightforward. A price index can be clearly identified and, although the result will depend on the choice of index,
the question is relatively uncontroversial.

But the problem of deflating a variable which does not have
any clearly identified flow of goods as its counterpart is much
harder to solve. This has arisen particularly from attempts to
measure the effect on national income of a change in the terms
of trade. If the price of imports rises a country's income must
fall, although there may be no change in the volume of its
output measured (as output volume usually is) by a Laspeyres
quantity index. If a country goes into trade deficit because of
a rise in the price of oil, it is little comfort to observe that in
base period prices it would still be in surplus. Following from
work of Stuvel (1959), it has been pointed out that if one
deflates all goods flows by their appropriate price index and all
other flows in the national accounts by the ratio of
GDP/deflated GDP, then a set of national accounts will be
obtained which add up and in which terms like the 'real trade
balance' and 'real profit' can be given some meaning.

Martin Weale
University of Cambridge

Reference
Stuvel, G. (1959), 'Asset revaluation and terms of trade effects
in the framework of the national assets', *Economic Journal*.

Further Reading
Hibbert, J. (1975), 'Measuring changes in the nation's real
income', *Economic Trends*.
See also: *index numbers; national income analysis.*

Devaluation
The reduction in the official rate of exchange of one currency
for another is called devaluation. The term is used in connection
with exchange-rate reduction, in a fixed exchange-rate system,
and corresponds to the depreciation of a currency in a floating
exchange-rate system.

A fixed exchange-rate system operated between 1944, following the 'Bretton Woods Agreement', until 1973, when a floating exchange-rate system took its place, following the collapse of the 1971 'Smithsonian Agreement'. Under the Bretton Woods Agreement, member countries agreed to stabilize their exchange rates within a 1 per cent band around the agreed per exchange rate against the dollar. This band was widened to 2.25 per cent, following the Smithsonian Agreement. Countries in 'fundamental balance of payments disequilibrium' could apply to the International Monetary Fund for permission to devalue or revalue their currencies. Revaluation involved the raising of the official exchange rate against the dollar.

Britain devalued its currency twice in the period of the Bretton Woods Agreement: in September 1949 the rate of exchange against the US dollar was reduced from $4.03 to $2.80; and in November 1967 it was reduced to $2.40. In 1982, the French franc and the Italian lira were devalued within the European Monetary System, which incorporates a fixed exchange-rate system called the Exchange Rate Mechanism.

Devaluation (or currency depreciation) has the effect of reducing the price of exports, in terms of foreign currencies, and raising the price of imports in the home market. If this results in a rise in exports and a fall in imports, in value terms, then it will help to overcome a country's trade deficit with the rest of the world. There has been considerable debate concerning the likelihood that the domestic and foreign markets will respond in the desired manner and about the inflationary effects of devaluation, following the rise in import prices.

Andy Mullineux
University of Birmingham

Further Reading
Group of Thirty (1982), *The Problem of Exchange Rates*, New York.
Grubel, H. (1984), *The International Monetary System*, 4th edn, Harmondsworth.
See also: *exchange rate.*

Distribution of Incomes and Wealth

The distribution of income is usually understood by economists in two main senses: (1) the distribution of income amongst *factors* (sometimes known as the *functional* distribution of income), and (2) the distribution of income amongst *persons* (alternatively known as the *size* distribution of income).

(1) The distribution of income amongst factors is an integral part of the economic analysis of relative prices, output and employment. In this sense there are several 'Theories of Income Distribution' corresponding to different theoretical and ideological stances on these central issues. However these various analyses usually focus on the same basic economic concepts: employment of the 'factors of production' – land, labour and capital – and the rates of remuneration of their services – rent, wages and profit. It should be understood that this tripartite classification is by no means the only functional decomposition which is useful in economic theory; in some analyses, for example, a finer subdivision is attempted, distinguishing specifically between interest and profits as rewards to 'waiting' and 'entrepreneurship' respectively, or distinguishing between rewards to different types of labour. Moreover, in many practical applications the characteristics of national data make it expedient to subdivide the functional categories simply as income from work and income from property. Note that when these categories are applied to the income of an individual, household or subgroup of the population, a third type must be added, transfer income, although items in this category, such as welfare payments and alimony, net out when the economy as a whole is considered. Some macroeconomists gave much attention to the supposed constancy or stability of the share of wages in national income. This interest now appears to have been somewhat misplaced, since it is clear that over long periods this share does change significantly. In many industrialized countries during the present century it has been increasing, and now stands at about three-quarters (UK) to four-fifths (USA).

(2) The distribution of income amongst persons – the size distribution – and the distribution of wealth may both be thought of as particular applications of a statistical frequency

distribution, although they are often represented by other statistical devices such as the Lorenz curve (which in the case of income distribution graphs cumulative proportions of income received against cumulative proportions of income receivers). The frequency distribution of each quantity is generally positively skewed with a long 'upper tail' indicating the presence of relatively small numbers of very well-off people. The dispersion of these frequency distributions, which can be measured in a number of ways, is taken as an indicator of the inequality of the size distributions of income and of wealth.

The size distribution of income is noted almost everywhere for two remarkable qualities: the great inequality of personal incomes that is revealed, and the stability of the distribution over time. This is true even though the exact shape of the size distribution is significantly affected by the particular definition of income one employs (for example whether one includes transfer incomes and incomes received in 'kind' rather than cash, and deducts personal taxes), and the definition of the income-receiving 'unit' (for example, whether one looks at the distribution of income amongst households, or incomes amongst persons). In the case of the US, the top one-fifth of income receivers in 1947 received about 45.5 per cent of total personal income before tax and the bottom fifth then received about 3.5 per cent of total income; in 1977 the shares in total personal income of these two groups were about 45 and 4 per cent respectively (although there was some variation in intervening years) (Blinder, 1980). Whilst the composition of personal incomes in the lower tail of the distribution has changed substantially as the scope of government transfers has altered, it is still true to say that in most Western-style economies the component of personal income that comes from various forms of property is primarily associated with the upper tail of the distribution. In order to understand the size distribution of *incomes* in the upper tail, therefore, it is important to examine the size distribution of wealth.

One of the most difficult problems in analysing the wealth distribution within any community with reasonably extensive holdings of private property is to decide exactly what one means by wealth. This is not a point of semantics, nor is it one of purely arcane, theoretical interest. While *marketable* wealth – including financial assets such as stocks and cash balances, and physical assets such as land, houses and jewellery – is fairly readily recognizable for what it is, other forms of wealth may also need to be taken into account in estimating the people's effective command over economic resources. These include various pension rights, which represent substantial *future* claims against economic goods (and are thus in that sense substitutes for cash or negotiable securities that have been held as a precaution against old age), but which may have little or no immediate surrender value. As is the case with the size distribution of incomes, estimates of the distribution of wealth are sensitive to assumptions one makes about the definition of wealth itself and the 'units' of population amongst whom the wealth is distributed. Moreover, parts of the wealth distribution are also very sensitive to different methods of valuing the components of wealth and to short-term changes in the prices of assets. However, it is virtually incontestable that the size distribution of wealth is much more unequal than the size distribution of income. For example, in the UK in 1976 the top 1 per cent of wealth holders possessed at least 14 per cent of personal wealth (this is on the most generous assumptions which include state and occupational pension rights as personal wealth; were these to be excluded the figure would have been 25 per cent), but the top 1 per cent of income recipients received about 5.5 per cent of personal income before tax (3.5 per cent after tax). Furthermore, it is clear that a substantial proportion of this implied inequality in the distribution of wealth is attributable to the effects of inheritance, rather than to the process of wealth accumulation that takes place during the course of people's lives (Harbury and Hitchens, 1979).

Finally if one switches one's attention from the analysis of the size distribution of income (or wealth) within national economies to the size distribution in the world as a whole, not only do the problems of measurement and comparison become much greater, so also does the dispersion. However one resolves the difficult practical questions of defining and quantifying personal or household incomes on this inter-country basis, it is clear that income inequality within national economies is usually much smaller than the income inequality that persists between countries.

Frank A. Cowell
London School of Economics and Political Science

References
Blinder, A. S. (1980), 'The level and distribution of economic well-being', in M. Feldstein (ed.), *The American Economy in Transition*, Chicago.
Harbury, C. and Hitchins, D. M. W. N. (1979), *Inheritance and Wealth Inequality in Britain*, London.

Further Reading
Atkinson, A. B. and Harrison, A. J. (1978), *Distribution of Personal Wealth in Britain*, Cambridge.
Pen, J. (1971), *Income Distribution*, London.
See also: *income distribution, theory of*.

Dual Economy

The term dual economy has at once a technical academic meaning and a broader, more general meaning. In the former sense it relates to the simultaneous coexistence within the same economy of two different sectors, divided by different culture, different laws of development, different technology, different demand patterns, and so on. In certain models or theories of development, such a two-sector division, and the interaction between the two sectors, that is, a dual economy is taken as a foundation for theoretical analysis.

The best-known of such models is the Arthur Lewis model, based on his famous article 'Economic development with unlimited supply of labour' (1954). Lewis distinguishes between a rural low-income subsistence type sector in which there is surplus population (zero or very low marginal productivity of labour), and a developing urban capitalist sector in which wages are held down by the pressure of rural surplus population with resulting rapid development, ultimately exhausting the labour surplus. A considerable literature has followed in the wake of the Lewis model. The main modification of this model has been through Harris and Todaro (1970), who pointed out that the transfer of the labour surplus from rural to urban sectors could lead to urban unemployment and the development of an urban 'informal sector' rather than a reduction in wages in the capitalist sector to subsistence level.

The concept of the dual economy was originally developed by Boeke (1953), to describe the coexistence of modern and traditional sectors in a colonial economy. Today the term dual (or more frequently dualistic) economy is applied more broadly to the coexistence of rich and poor sectors (either rich and poor countries in the global economy or rich and poor people in the national economy), where there is often a tendency for the 'rich to become richer, while the poor remain poor or become poorer'. For a discussion and literature survey of the concept in this broader sense, see Singer (1970).

H. W. Singer
Institute of Development Studies
University of Sussex

References

Boeke, J. H. (1953), *Economics and Economic Policy of Dual Societies*, New York.

Harris, J. R. and Todaro, M. P. (1970), 'Migration, unemployment and development: a two-sector analysis', *American Economic Review*.

Lewis, W. A. (1954), 'Economic development with unlimited supply of labour', *The Manchester School*.

Singer, H. W. (1970), 'Dualism revisited: a new approach to the problems of dual society in developing countries', *Journal of Development Studies*, 7.

Econometrics

As the main concern of economics has shifted away from description and institutional analysis, economists have sought to quantify the relationships underpinning their models more precisely. In part this concern has been prompted by the desire to forecast the future behaviour of economic variables – for example, the response of aggregate consumption expenditure to changes in disposable income, or the effect of income tax changes on labour supply and the willingness of individuals to participate in the labour market. For such quantitative forecasts to have any value, it is essential that the empirical relationships on which the predictions rest should be relatively stable, both in terms of their structural characteristics and their coefficient values. On the other hand, it is less important that the empirical relationships should conform to the specification of a fully articulated economic model of the phenomenon under consideration, since, in practice, 'naive' models may yield good forecasts and it may be quite impossible to observe the variables or to estimate the parameters in an elaborate model. There is, however, another reason for quantifying economic relationships which necessarily implies that careful model specification is essential if the resulting empirical estimates are to be of any value. This arises when the economist wishes to use the estimates to test hypotheses about the relative importance of different factors or economic variables which simultaneously determine some particular aspect of economic behaviour.

These distinct uses of quantitative economic relationships – i.e. forecasting and the investigation of economic hypotheses – have meant that econometrics, which is the branch of economics and statistics devoted to the empirical estimation of economic models, has developed in a number of quite separate directions. This tendency has been encouraged by the nature of the data available to econometricians. Much of classical statistical theory was developed for the purpose of making inferences from data collected in controlled experiments, typically involving some kind of randomized design in which all combinations of variables have an equal – or, at least, a known – probability of occurring. Economists must be satisfied either with time series data produced by governments or other bodies, or with responses to sample surveys of a cross-section of the population during some period of time. Because their data is not experimentally generated, econometricians have been obliged to develop special techniques to deal with the characteristics of different types of data. For example, the user of aggregate time series data must always check for the possibility that the errors about a particular equation are systematically correlated over time – this is called serial correlation. For the user of cross-section data, there is the consistent problem that the sample of observations may be non-random because, for example, self-selection means that certain types of individuals either refused to answer the questions or were excluded from the sample.

These and many other similar considerations mean that it is never simple to interpret data concerning economic relationships. Since the classical statistical assumptions rarely hold, the econometrician is unable to separate questions concerning the validity of his statistical assumptions from issues relating to the specification of the model which he is estimating. As a result, the progress of empirical economic work has been characterized by interlocking disputes about econometric methodology and the relevance of the equations modelling aspects of eocnomic behaviour. This means that it is often difficult to set up decisive econometric tests of particular hypotheses, especially as the underlying theoretical models may be specified in terms of variables which can, at best, only be approximately measured in practice. Nonetheless, econometric work has frequently prompted economists to reformulate or extend their models, either because the estimated equations had a poor forecasting record or because their explanatory power was rather low.

Historically, the development of econometric techniques has run parallel with changes in the availability of economic data and in the amount of computing power. Econometrics began to establish itself as a distinct discipline in the late 1920s and early 1930s – the Econometric Society was founded in 1931 with help from Alfred Cowles who was interested in forecasting stock market price movements – but it grew most rapidly in the years after the Second World War. This was because the political commitment to full employment using Keynesian policies prompted governments to monitor macroeconomic developments much more closely. The availability of time series data on aggregate economic variables, and interest in forecasting aggregate demand encouraged econometric work on the relationships which comprise a simple Keynesian model of the economy. Two elements of such a model attracted particular attention: (1) the consumption function in which consumption (or saving) is linked to disposable income, and (2) the investment function which expresses aggregate investment in terms of the growth of aggregate demand (or production), interest rates, and other variables. While there are a number of competing formulations of the consumption function, econometric work on this has always appeared to be much more successful than that dealing with the investment function. It was found to be very difficult to forecast aggregate investment reliably, and estimated relationships differ significantly between time periods so that even after more than thirty years of work there is no general agreement on the best specification for this relationship.

Interest in making forecasts of individual components of effective demand gradually evolved into the estimation of large macroeconometric models designed to forecast the overall macroeconomic behaviour of particular economies, as well as to investigate the implications of changes in aggregate variables for specific sectors of the economy or categories of expenditure. Work of this kind was initiated by Klein in the early 1950s, but by the late 1960s advances in data and computing power had allowed econometricians to compile and simulate large-scale macroeconometric models. Despite considerable scepticism about the reliability of the forecasts produced by these models, their use has become an indispensable part of the process of making macroeconomic policy in all developed countries, so that argument tends now to revolve around the merits of competing models rather than about the value of making such forecasts. As macroeconomic models have become larger and more specialized, it has also become increasingly difficult to understand the factors which determine the way in which they behave as a whole. Hence, during the 1970s, econometricians started to focus more on the properties of complete models rather than on the performance of individual equations within the model.

Another application of econometrics that has been developing since the 1950s combines the interest in forecasting with the scope provided by econometric models for testing propositions derived from theoretical models. This is the estimation of single, or systems of, demand equations using either aggregate data on prices and consumption patterns or information collected in surveys of household expenditure. Initially, the main purpose of this work was to estimate income and price elasticities of demand for specific goods. This remains an important consideration, but theoretical work on consumer behaviour has shown that, if consumer expenditure decisions are derived from some kind of maximizing model, it is necessary to impose quite stringent conditions on the specification and parameter values of systems of demand equations. These restrictions include homogeneity in income and prices, symmetry of cross-price effects, and negative substitution effects. The results of testing these restrictions illustrate the difficulties of using econometric work to test theoretical models. Most studies have found that some or all of these restrictions are rejected by the data, but the response of economists has not been to discard the maximizing model of consumer behaviour but rather to investigate more elaborate specifications of the demand equations until the restrictions are not rejected. It is never possible to test the general restrictions implied by theoretical analysis except by adopting specific functional forms for the equations under investigation, so that statistical evidence against some hypothesis may be interpreted as implying either that the functional specification is inadequate, or that the basic theoretical model is wrong. In cases such as demand analysis, where the underlying theory is highly developed, econometricians have inevitably tended to regard their results as tests of specification rather than of general theoretical propositions. Only by the accumulation of negative evidence for a wide range of specifications is it possible to regard such work as undermining prior theoretical assumptions.

The availability of large-scale cross-section surveys – and of panel data sets in which individuals/households are interviewed at regular intervals over a period of years – has prompted the recent development of econometric techniques to deal with qualitative or limited dependent variables. These are variables which take on discrete values – e.g. 0 or 1 corresponding to 'no' or 'yes' responses to certain choices – or for which the range of permissible values is limited – e.g. it is not possible to work for a negative number of hours. The estimation of such microeconometric models is typically much more expensive than for classical regression models, and in most cases the amount of data to be handled is many times greater than·for macroeconometric work. Hence, this work would have been impossible without the great improvements in computer hardware and software since the late 1960s. The principal applications of these techniques have been in the area of labour economics to the analysis of choices concerning labour supply and participation, education, job movement, retirement and migration. The results of this work have generated much interest among economists working on other topics so that the range of applications may be expected to continue to increase rapidly as also will the techniques of analysis and estimation.

Econometrics has developed to the extent that it dominates applied work in most branches of economics. Indeed, even economic historians use econometric analysis – often under the title 'cliometrics' – in discussing issues such as the impact of railways on US or British economic growth, and of technical change in both agriculture and industry. The major improvements in the volume and quality of economic statistics and in the availability of large-scale sample surveys which stimulated many econometric developments during the period 1950–80 are not likely to be repeated. Thus, future developments in the subject will necessarily focus on methods of extracting more information from the data which is available. In practice, this will mean that applied economists and econometricians will have to devote more attention to the theoretical and statistical specification of their models in order to clarify the assumptions underpinning tests of particular hypotheses. Fortunately, the speed of technical change in computing is such that the cost of investigating more complex models, which has been prohibitive in the past, will not be a significant consideration in the future.

Gordon Hughes
University of Cambridge

Further Reading
Griliches, Z. (1983), *Handbook of Econometrics*, vols I and III, Amsterdam.
Harvey, A. C. (1981), *The Econometric Analysis of Time Series*, Oxford.
Maddala, G. S. (1983), *Limited–Dependent and Qualitative Variables in Econometrics*, Cambridge.
Pindyck, R. S. and Rubinfeld, D. (1981), *Econometric Models and Economic Forecasts*, 2nd edn, New York.
See also: *cliometrics; macroeconomics; microeconomics.*

Economic Anthropology

The field of economic anthropology falls somewhere between economic history and economics proper. Like economic history, it is a descriptive discipline in which other economies and their transformations are carefully documented; like economics proper, it is a field in which competing theories of human behaviour are elaborated and intensely debated.

The substantive differences among exotic economies have been recorded by anthropologists for more than sixty years. Systems of production, for example, exhibit great variation. Considerable attention has been given to hunting and gathering, but anthropologists also have examined forms of pastoralism and patterns of agriculture, including slash-and-burn, terrace, and irrigation systems. Trade, exchange and distribution take many forms. For example, in capitalist economies distribution occurs through market pricing of wage, profit and rent, but this is not a universal custom. In some societies distribution is carried out by dividing animals joint by joint and allocating each to specific social roles. The link between economic processes and social formations also is highly variable. In the simplest case all economic functions may be performed within a single household unit; but usually larger groupings such as lineages, bands and villages are involved. Sometimes production will involve units at one level of the society, but property control, distribution and consumption may bring into play other social aggregations. A descriptive and analytic task for economic anthropologists, therefore, is to show how the several economic functions are fitted together within the social organization of a particular society.

Most exotic economies are now undergoing change due to penetration by the world market system. In recent years, therefore, anthropologists have been studying shifting conceptions of wealth, labour and gender, as well as the ways nonmonetary economies become reorganized when brought into contact with systems based on the use of cash and arranged according to different principles.

The very fact that differences exist in the ways people gain and use their livelihood poses questions about the economic models that anthropologists employ. Can we, for example, extend Western economic categories to the analysis of other cultures? What assumptions are involved? Is anthropology a testing ground for the development of universal theories of the economy?

Many economic anthropologists use theories derived from neoclassical economics. Their central assumption is that actors choose among alternatives to maximize preferences or utility; the model has a rationalist basis. For example, input-output or production functions are sometimes employed to show how pastoralists produce cattle or foragers select game. Similarly, a neoclassical analysis of bridewealth transactions will focus on the exchange rate of women and cattle and the ways in which it is responsive to conditions of supply and demand.

Institutionalists, whose approach is more empiricist, pay greater attention to the organizational differences that are found among economies. Karl Polanyi (1968) suggested that land and labour comprise the bedrock for all economies; but these underlying elements, he argued, are institutionally organized according to different patterns of exchange. Polanyi isolated three such patterns: reciprocity, redistribution and market haggling. According to the Polanyi view, the analyst should try to reveal the connection between the substratum of land and labour and the visible but differing modes of exchange. In the case of bridewealth, an institutionalist might attempt to show how the exchange is linked to land and labour, yet is unlike other transactions in society. In nonmarket economies, each exchange is embedded in a distinct social context; different patterns of exchange are not reducible, one to another, through the solvent of the market.

Marxists commence with the assumption that the human is a material maker, that he produces things of value only through labouring. The organization of this capacity provides the base for the superstructural parts of social life. On this view, there exists a relation between modes of exploiting labour and other sectors of society, such as religion, ideology or kinship. In the case of bridewealth, for example, neo-Marxists have emphasized that control of cattle by elder males sustains their position of power and their ability to extract labour from younger males as well as females.

Despite their differences, the three models resemble one another in a crucial respect. Each starts from a supposed core feature of human behaviour and attempts to show how the ethnographic data can be fitted to or derived from it. The three models continuously reproduce their own assumptions in the exotic materials.

One alternative to this style of analysis is to assume that a people model their own actions just as Western economists model our behaviour. Exotic lives and thoughts, which are a residue of the past and a plan for the future, constitute a model for ethnographers to examine. Exotic economic actions have their own meanings. According to this view the task is to 'understand' other economic patterns rather than 'explain' how well they fit a supposed pan-cultural characteristic. For example, in many societies where bridewealth is found, women and cattle are constructed as metaphors of one another; cattle both are and are not women. Because both are constructed as being like each other but unlike other 'goods', they are mutually and exclusively exchanged. Similarly, other wealth items and economic practices have their particular formulations. According to such a constructivist view, the economy is a symbolic sphere filled with cultural information. Therefore, Western assumptions and categories such as maximization, exploitation, production and consumption must be put in abeyance in favour of the particular constructions which the ethnographer encounters and tries to translate to his Western audience. This final approach is more distinctly anthropological than the other three, which derive from one or another form of modern economics; it is not, however, widely used.

Stephen Gudeman
University of Minnesota

Reference
Polanyi, K. (1968), *Primitive, Archaic and Modern Economies*, Boston.

Further Reading
Sahlins, M. (1972), *Stone Age Economics*, Chicago.

Economic Development

The central question in the study of economic development has turned out to be 'in what *precisely* does the economic development of a society consist?' For many years, the accepted view was that the prolonged and steady increase of national income was an adequate indicator of economic development. This was held to be so because it was believed that such an increase could only be sustained over long periods if specific economic (and social) processes were at work.

These processes, which were supposed to be basic to development, can be briefly summarized as follows:

(1) The share of investment in national expenditure rises, leading to a rise in capital stock per person employed;

(2) The structure of national production changes, becoming more diversified as industry, utilities and services take a larger relative share, compared with agriculture and other forms of primary production;

(3) The foreign trade sector expands relative to the whole economy, particularly as manufactured exports take a larger share in an increased export total;

(4) The government budget rises relative to national income, as the government undertakes expanded commitments to construct economic and social infrastructure.

Accompanying these structural changes in the economy, major changes of social structure also occur:

(5) The population expands rapidly as death rates fall in advance of birth rates. Thereafter, a demographic transition occurs in which improved living conditions in turn bring the birth rate down, to check the rate of overall population increase;

(6) The population living in urban areas changes from a small minority to a large majority;

(7) Literacy, skills and other forms of educational attainment are spread rapidly through the population.

This conceptualization of economic development as the inter-relation of capital accumulation, industrialization, government growth, urbanization and education can still be found in many contemporary writers. It seems to make most sense when one has very long runs of historical statistics to look back over. Then the uniformities which this view implies are most likely to be visible. One doubt has always been whether generalizing retrospectively from statistics is not an ahistorical, rather than a truly historical, approach. It almost always presupposes some 'theory of history' which links the past to the future in an unsubtly mechanistic and deterministic manner.

Another major doubt about the adequacy of the view of development described in 1–7 above centres around the question of income distribution. If the basic development processes described above either do not make the distribution of income more equal, or actually worsen the degree of inequality for more than a short period, some theorists would argue that economic development has not taken place. They prefer to distinguish economic growth from economic development which, by their definition, cannot leave the majority of the population as impoverished as they originally were. For them, measures of growth and structural change must be complemented by measures of improvement in the quality of everyday life for most people.

Such measures can be of various kinds. They can focus on the availability of basic needs goods – food, shelter, clean water, clothing and household utensils. Or they can focus on life expectation tables and statistics of morbidity. The availability and cost of educational opportunities are also relevant. Although the distribution of income may be a good starting point, the distribution of entitlements (to use a concept expounded by A. K. Sen (1981)) to consume of all kinds is the terminus. The difficulty here is clearly with weighting all of the different indices involved to arrive at a single measure of the degree of development in this extended sense. Perhaps it cannot be done; and perhaps, if policy rather than international league tables is our main concern, this failure is not very important.

Similar kinds of consideration arise when one examines the role of political liberty in economic development. Is rapid growth and structural change induced by an oppressive, authoritarian regime true development? Those who object to the 'costs' of the development strategies of the USSR or the People's Republic of China do not think so. From a libertarian standpoint, they refuse to accept the standard account of 'economic development' as sufficiently comprehensive.

These wider concerns with the meaning of 'development' inevitably influence the many debates about how economic development can be actively promoted. Disagreement has focused on the following issues:

(1) Whether the government should confine itself to its so-called 'traditional functions' and the creation of incentives for development by private enterprise, or whether some overall co-ordination through economic planning, plus an expanded sphere for government investment in manufacturing industry is required.

(2) How much emphasis should be placed on the creation of physical capital, compared with human capital – the education and good health of the labour force. Where physical capital is involved, how should the investments be phased? In a single big push, so that they create demand for each other (as

recommended by Rosenstein-Rodan, 1943)? Or, as shortages and bottlenecks reveal the need for each (Hirschman's (1958) unbalanced growth)?

(3) Should greater priority in investment be given to a particular sector of the economy – the capital goods sector (suggested by Maurice Dobb, 1955) or agriculture (as argued by Lipton, 1977)? Or should investments be selected, regardless of sector, solely in accordance with a calculation of their social profitability, the criterion for the appraisal of projects devised by Little and Mirrlees (1974)?

(4) What role should the foreign sector play in development? Has isolation from the world economy triggered off economic development, as is argued of Meiji Japan (by Baran, 1973) and Latin America during the Depression of the 1930s (by Frank, 1969)? Or do countries like Taiwan and South Korea, which deliberately organize their economy to be competitive in world markets, develop faster? The utility of foreign financial and technical assistance from governments and international agencies and foreign private investment through multinational companies is also debated in this context, with strong views being held both for and against, often on flimsy empirical evidence.

Somewhat greater agreement exists on the facts of recent economic development than on the methods of bringing it about. That many poor countries have experienced much economic growth and structural change since 1945 is widely accepted. A few still claim that growth in developed countries actually causes increased poverty in other, poorer countries. This suggests a trend of global polarization of income and wealth, combined with the immiserization of the poorest people/countries. A weaker version of this thesis is that there is an ever-widening gap between richest and poorest, which can arise when the welfare of the poorest is constant or rising. Even this weaker version is controversial, on the grounds that countries are ranged evenly along a spectrum of wealth/poverty, and thus to split this spectrum into two groups of 'rich' and 'poor' in order to compare group statistics of economic performance can be somewhat arbitrary. In fact, the measured growth rates of 'developed' and 'developing' countries over the last thirty odd years show relatively small differences and ones that may well lie within the margins of error that attach to such estimates.

But, although the overall record of economic growth at least need not give cause for deep gloom, certain geographical regions do appear to have markedly unfavourable development prospects. Such regions include sub-Saharan Africa and South Asia, and parts of Central and South America. The reasons for their poor prospects vary from place to place. Some are held back by severe pressure of population on cultivable land; some by inability to generate indigenous sources of appropriate technical progress; some by the persistence of intense social and political conflict; some by unenlightened policy making; and some by the continuing failure to evolve a world-wide financial system which does not tend to amplify the inherent unevenness (over place and time) of economic development.

J. F. J. Toye
University College of Swansea
University of Wales

References

Baran, P. (1973), *The Political Economy of Growth*, Harmondsworth.

Dobb, M. (1955), *On Economic Theory and Socialism*, London.

Frank, A. G. (1969), *Latin America: Underdevelopment or Revolution?*, New York.

Hirschman, A. (1958), *The Strategy of Economic Development*, New Haven.

Lipton, M. (1977), *Why Poor People Stay Poor*, London.

Little, I. M. D. and Mirrlees, J. A. (1974), *Project Appraisal and Planning for Developing Countries*, London.

Rosenstein-Rodan, P. N. (1943), 'Problems of industrialisation of Eastern and South-Eastern Europe', *Economic Journal*, June–September.

Sen, A. K. (1981), *Poverty and Famines; An Essay on Entitlement and Deprivation*, Oxford.

Further Reading

Kitching, G. (1982), *Development and Underdevelopment in Historical Perspective*, London.

Little, I. M. D. (1983), *Economic Development: Theory, Policy and International Relations*, New York.

See also: *aid; economic growth; technical assistance; underdevelopment.*

Economic Dynamics

Comte's 'social dynamics' appears to have stimulated J. S. Mill's original distinction between statics, the theory of equilibrium, and dynamics, the theory of the laws of the progress of society. On this definition the classical theories of Smith, Ricardo and Marx represent the first economic dynamics. By 1890, however, J. M. Keynes reported that 'the main body of economic science' was concerned with statics. Analogy with physical mechanics displaced Comte's ideas, and the great neoclassical economists (Clark, Marshall, Walras) all promised, but never produced, dynamic theories. Marshall even suggested a biological analogy might be more appropriate for dynamics. The problem was important, for the mechanical analogy not only implied use of deduction in place of the induction of the evolutionary (or biological) approach; it also implied a new definition of dynamics (as in Samuelson's 'correspondence principle') as the stability properties of equilibrium.

Keynes's *General Theory* (1936) interrupted development of the dynamic implications of lagged relationships in quantitative business cycle models (Kalecki, Tinbergen, Frisch), while von Neumann's theory of an expanding general economic equilibrium did not create interest until its post-war publication in English. Hicks (1939) defined dynamics as the study of 'dated' quantities and 'the way changes in these dates affect the relations between factors and products', but his static 'temporary equilibrium' created most interest. Harrod's (1939) 'fundamental relation': $G=s/C$ (where s is the ratio of saving to income and C the ratio of an extra pound invested to the additional income it generates), used to explain trend growth rates had more success. If s, determined by households, generates growth in demand which satisfies entrepreneurs' expected returns on new investment, G is a 'warranted' rate, for it will be maintained (provided it does not exceed a maximum, 'natural' rate given by population and productivity growth). Comparison of its actual and warranted rates indicates an economy's future movement. Domar's post-war analysis of whether short-run Keynesian demand management could assure full employment over time produced a similar equation.

In the 1950s Harrod-Domar theory was extended by the Cambridge School (e.g. Robinson, Kaldor, Pasinetti) who suggested that if s were an average of savings propensities from wages and profits, then the distribution of income adjusts to make saving equal to the rate of investment implied by the rate of growth, which thus determined distribution and the rate of return to capital. Neoclassical economists (e.g. Swan, Solow, Meade) argued that if relative prices affect the proportions of capital to labour used in production, C will be affected, via an aggregate production function linking output to aggregate capital and labour inputs. Here input prices adjust capital intensity to the available savings given the rate of growth. The differences in the explanation of distribution and in the role of aggregate capital in the two approaches reflected different conceptions of dynamics which surfaced in the 'Cambridge Controversies'.

In the mid-1970s both Hicks and Lowe attempted, without success, to bridge these differences by specifying a 'traverse' adjustment path in terms of an 'Austrian' time-pattern of inputs. These debates suggest that economics still has no accepted definition or theory of dynamics.

J. A. Kregel
University of Groningen

References

Domar, E. D. (1946), 'Capital expansion, rate of growth and employment', *Econometrica*, 14.

Harrod, R. F. (1939), 'An essay in dynamic theory', *Economic Journal*, 49.

Hicks, J. R. (1939), *Value and Capital*, Oxford.

Hicks, J. R. (1973), *Capital and Time*, Oxford.

Keynes, J. M. (1890), *The Scope and Method of Political Economy*, London.

Keynes, J. M. (1936), *The General Theory of Employment, Interest and Money*, London.

Lowe, A. (1976), *The Path of Economic Growth*, London.

Marshall, A. (1925), 'Mechanical and biological analogies in economics', in A. C. Pigou (ed.), *Memorials of Alfred Marshall*, London.

Mill, J. S. (1848), *Principles of Political Economy*, London.

Samuelson, P. A. (1947), *Foundations of Economic Analysis*, Cambridge, Mass.

Von Neumann, J. (1945–6), 'A model of general economic equilibrium', *Review of Economic Studies*, 13.

Further Reading
Jones, H. (1975), *Modern Theories of Economic Growth*, London.
Kregel, J. A. (1972), *Theory of Economic Growth*, London.
See also: *economic growth; equilibrium*.

Economic Efficiency

A machine is more efficient if it generates more powers or more product for a given amount of fuel or input. Although this more obvious notion of efficiency is contained within the concept of economic efficiency, it plays only an intermediate role inasmuch as the latter addresses itself broadly to the goal of bringing the limited resources of society into proper relation with the desired ends. The ends themselves are expressed through the pattern of social valuation or demand for finished goods, which pattern is determined in part through the market mechanisms of the private sector of the economy and in part through the political mechanisms that control expenditures in the public sector.

There are heuristic advantages in decomposing the concept of economic efficiency into three components, the first two being subsidiary to and subsumed in the third.

(1) *Exchange Efficiency* is increased if, beginning with a collection of goods divided arbitrarily among a number of persons, the exchange of goods between them makes at least one person

better off and nobody worse off (hereafter abridged to '"everyone" better off'). Such an economic change is said to meet an actual Pareto improvement.

Provided the exchange of goods incurred no costs, the process of exchange would culminate in a set of relative prices that were common to all. This resulting situation, one in which no opportunity remains for making 'everyone' better off, is described as an 'exchange optimum'.

(2) *Production Efficiency* is increased if, with given supplies of the factors of production, the factor proportions used in the various goods are altered so as to produce more of 'every good'. Once all such opportunities are exhausted, a 'production optimum' obtains.

An economy where each firm minimizes the production costs of its goods in the presence of a common set of factor prices is sufficient to realize a production optimum.

(3) *Top-Level Efficiency*: Allowing that exchange and production optima are met, as a result of which society is faced with a 'production frontier' of alternative collections of goods – each collection associated with a particular set of goods and factor prices – a movement from an existing collection of goods to another, in consequence of which 'everyone' *could* be made better off (by a costless redistribution of the goods), identifies an increase in top-level efficiency. Such increase in efficiency may properly be described as a *potential* Pareto improvement.

A sufficient condition for a movement from an existing goods collection (I) to a new collection (II) to meet a potential Pareto improvement (or increase in top-level efficiency) is that, valued at the goods prices of the I collection, the goods contained in the II collection have a higher aggregate value.

A situation in which all opportunities for top-level efficiency increases are exhausted is one described as a 'Top-Level Optimum'. A sufficient condition for the existence of top-level optimum is that at the prevailing set of goods prices no other collection of goods (producible with the given supplies of factors) has a higher aggregate value.

It must be borne in mind, however, that there can be any number of possible top-level optimum collections, each associated with a particular set of goods prices, which in general alter with changes in taste and with redistributions of purchasing power. Thus an existing top-level optimum assumes given tastes and a given distribution of purchasing power.

One last point in this connection: since the range of alternative collections of goods along a large part of the production frontier qualify – in virtue of all conceivable patterns of distribution of purchasing power – as potential optima, some economists have embraced the notion of a 'social welfare function' in order to rank these alternative possible optima and, consequently, to identify a 'best' optimum or 'optimum optimorum'. While the idea has formal appeal, it has no 'operational value' – no acceptable way having been discovered for identifying such a position.

Ezra J. Mishan
London

Further Reading
Graaf, J. de V. (1957), *Theoretical Welfare Economics*, Cambridge.
Mishan, E. J. (1981), *Introduction to Normative Economics*, Oxford.
Winch, D. M. (1971), *Analytic Welfare Economics*,
    Harmondsworth.
See also: *welfare economics*.

Economic Geography
Economic geography is a discipline that deals with economic phenomena in a spatial context, examining the interrelationships of man and the environment as mediated by the economic processes of production, exchange, and consumption.

Modern economic geography is a fusion of three strands of scholarship. The oldest of these is the compilation of factual accounts of where useful commodities are produced and how they are traded, information that was widely regarded as of major importance in the nineteenth-century days of colonial empire. *The Handbook of Commercial Geography* by G. G. Chisholm, first published in 1889 and running to many editions over almost a century, is probably the best known of these writings; much of the work of Stamp was in the same tradition. These and other authors pioneered the systematic collation of descriptive data about the distribution of economic activities, primarily the production of agricultural, mineral and industrial goods. The second and third strands represent attempts to provide explanatory frameworks for the mass of descriptive data. In 1935 Buchanan applied the tools of formal economic analysis to the dairy industry of New Zealand, but it was not until 1966 that the first geographical text was published which systematically applied neoclassical economic ideas to the explanation of geographical patterns of production and exchange. The third strand can be described as the discovery by geographers of the locational models for agriculture, published by von Thünen in 1826, A. Weber's 1909 systematization of industrial location decisions, and seminal work in the same idiom by the geographer Christaller on models of central places, published in 1933.

Economic geography came of age in the 1950s and 1960s. The single most important problem addressed has been the analysis of industrial and office location and especially changes in the distribution of firms. What causes some regions to specialize in the manufacture of steel, vehicles, textiles or electronic goods? To answer this question, it is necessary to examine the manufacturing requirements – raw materials, fuel, labour, research information, etc. – and the markets for the products, as well as the transport needs. If entrepreneurs were fully rational 'economic men', they would compile the relevant cost surfaces and calculate the location which would maximize their profits. In practice, other considerations necessarily carry some weight. A first question, therefore, is to determine what the optimal location pattern should be, and several practical algorithms have been devised for this purpose. Real-world patterns diverge from this ideal, and a major theme has been to examine the reasons for this divergence. This leads to an examination of the actual decision process for location choices and the factors that weigh with managers. Empirical evidence shows that larger firms are more 'rational' in their location choices and are willing to move longer distances than small firms, which have fewer resources to devote to a careful evaluation of opportunities. In the last decade or two, a widespread trend has been observed for manufacturing firms to leave the larger conurbations in favour of smaller cities and even rural areas. Problems of space and traffic congestion in big cities provide one reason for this trend; another reason lies in the nature of new industrial and office businesses and their greater need to locate where their workers like to live.

The location decision of any one firm is taken in the light of the existing distribution of firms and facilities, and expectations about the future decisions of others. Actual or expected external economies of scale play an important part in this decision process, providing a major reason for the agglomeration of activities into growth centres. The same mechanism provides the justification for using growth poles as an instrument of policy in the development of less prosperous regions within countries. However, it now appears that diseconomies arising from congestion, etc., are beginning to outweigh the advantages of agglomeration in the more developed nations, though not yet in Third-World countries. At the wider regional scale within nations, the progressive concentration of activity is now often less evident than the development of new regions, suitable for the new generation of industries.

The primary sector continues to receive attention, but proportionately less than hitherto – reflecting the declining proportion of the work-force engaged in primary activities in most developed nations. On the other hand, the interplay of environmental conditions, technological change and economic circumstances is more clearly seen in the agricultural, forestry and mining industries than in much modern manufacturing, making it easier to maintain the geographer's traditional interest in man/land relationships. To accommodate changes in farming practice, major changes in the settlement pattern and layout of farms has been necessary in much of Europe and elsewhere, effecting a drastic alteration of the rural landscape.

At the international level, economic geographers have contributed major studies to the processes of agrarian change and industrialization, in a context of changing comparative advantage. A theme of considerable interest is the interrelationships of the world 'core' and the 'periphery' (often called the North and South respectively). Debate focuses around questions such as: Does the core drain resources from the periphery? What has been the impact of the core on the nature and scale of development in the periphery? Economic geographers approach questions such as these through aggregate data and also by means of national and intra-national case studies.

Commercial production depends on transport. Therefore, transport systems deserve study in their own right and as part of wider studies of the economy. In the less developed world, the close association of transport and development is readily apparent; it is harder to disentangle in more advanced nations. Indeed, in a small country such as Britain geographical differences in the cost of transport seem to be too small significantly to affect location choices. The movement of people, intra-regionally and inter-regionally, has been assuming greater significance and provides the basis for many firms to locate near international airports. Studies of freight and passenger movements show a very clear decline of inter-action as distance increases.

Governments have become major agents shaping the geography of nations, through their policies of redistribution, of direct involvement in production and the provision of services, and through procurement. Some policies have an explicitly spatial purpose, and it is important to evaluate their success or otherwise; other policies have unintentional spatial consequences which need to be recognized.

Two areas are emerging as important foci of enquiry. Economic geographers are interested in the functioning of cities and city systems, especially the processes by which land uses change and cities grow or decline, both in the more advanced nations and the Third World. Secondly, as the pressure on natural resources grows, so does the need for rational management – of energy resources and recreational facilities, of minerals and agricultural land, and so on.

Michael Chisholm
University of Cambridge

Further Reading

Abler, R., Adams, J. S. and Gould, P. (1971), *Spatial Organization. The Geographer's View of the World*, Englewood Cliffs, N.J.

Blunden, J., Brook, C., Edge, G. and Hay, A. (eds) (1973), *Regional Analysis and Development*, London.

Chisholm, M. (1970), *Geography and Economics*, 2nd edn, London.

Cox, K. (1972), *Man, Location and Behavior*, New York.

Hodder, B. W. and Lee, R. (1974), *Economic Geography*, London.

Lloyd, P. E. and Dicken, P. (1977), *Location in Space: A Theoretical Approach to Economic Geography*, 2nd edn, New York.

Morrill, R. L. (1974), *The Spatial Organization of Society*, Belmont, Calif.

Paterson, J. H. (1972), *Land, Work and Resources*, London.

Smith, R. H. T., Taaffe, E. J. and King, L. J. (eds) (1968), *Readings in Economic Geography. The Location of Economic Activity*, Chicago.

See also: *transport economics and planning*.

Economic Growth

Economic growth can be measured and defined in various ways. One of the most common is the rate at which aggregate production and spending, i.e., GNP or GDP grows. Alternatively, the rate of growth of per capita GNP or GDP is used because of its closer proximity to the growth of living standards and economic welfare. The recognition of growth so measured as a natural part of the economic history of a nation is fairly new, dating more or less from the Industrial Revolution. By the First World War enough countries had experienced periods of sustained growth that its achievement had become a goal of highest priority in those countries yet to experience a 'take-off' into modernity. During the quarter of a century following the Second World War many economies, capitalist and communist alike, experienced historically high rates of economic growth. A comparison of relative growth rates between capitalist and communist countries became a standard practice in determining the relative worth of alternative economic systems.

With the recognition of economic growth as a natural part of the evolution of an economy came the desire to explain differences in growth patterns and growth rates. Attempts to discern differences and similarities in patterns of growth have merged with efforts to discover 'stages of growth' common to countries that have experienced growing per capita incomes. Marx was one of the earliest to see distinct historical processes and stages in the growth process. His vision was so comprehensive as to encompass distinct changes in the legal, social and economic systems that would evolve as a natural part of the growth process. Less sweeping have been the more recent writings of Schumpeter and Svennilson who, nevertheless, saw economic growth largely in terms of a 'transformation' in which the unbalanced nature of growth leads to changing patterns of output, resource allocation and regional development. For example, those economies experiencing rising per capita incomes have at the same time undergone a relative decline in agriculture accompanied by the rise of industry and manufacturing employment and output. The increasing importance of the service sector was also apparent.

The immediate causal factor behind this transformation has been rising per capita incomes and affluence. As living standards rise, households rearrange their expenditures towards 'luxuries' and away from 'necessities'. For example, the demand for food and clothing declines relatively as living standards rise, while consumer durable goods become a more important item in consumer budgets. Moreover, the more rapidly that per capita incomes rise, the more rapidly has been the rate at which the economy transforms itself. Thus, more rapid growth should be viewed as a more rapid rate of transformation of an economy.

Until very recently, economists wishing to explain why growth and transformation rates differed have stressed the importance of capital formation. The development of new processes, goods, industries and regions was seen to require new plant and equipment of a qualitatively different kind. The more rapid was this rate of capital formation (as measured typically by the rate of investment to GNP) the more rapid was growth and transformation. With the increased popularity of mathematics in economic theory, highly abstract models of growth have been developed. By their very structure they downplay the importance of investment. The influence of this kind of theorizing on policy has been slight.

The Keynesian revolution, as well as the stagnation of the capitalist economies in more recent times, has led to an interest in the relative importance of demand and supply in the determining rates of growth. The important issue today, of whether economies can ever resume the growth performance of the 1950s and 1960s while unemployment is so high and capital utilization so low, is very much a part of this debate. For example, a currently popular view about growth, supply-side economics, argues that even under conditions of depressed aggregate demand and stagnation, policies can be implemented that stimulate the rate of growth of capital and productivity and somehow also cause demand to grow rapidly. Modern Keynesians, by contrast, find little hope in ever ending the current stagnation of growth rates without first greatly reducing the slack in the economy.

Rising per capita incomes, while conferring benefits such as the reduction of poverty, have also led to new problems. As Keynes pointed out over a half century ago, when incomes have risen enough to allow savings to become a significant portion of incomes, problems of effective demand arise. If these are not handled through government intervention, widespread unemployment becomes a distinct possibility.

The prolonged period of full employment and substained growth following the Second World War permitted rapidly rising living standards, increased savings and expanded public welfare programmes including unemployment insurance. One result was to increase vastly the power of labour, thereby intensifying the conflict between capital and labour over the distribution of incomes. This has led to a marked acceleration of inflation rates in the post-war period compared to earlier 'normal' periods. It has also resulted in governments in capitalist countries repressing aggregate demand in the interests of fighting inflation. Unfortunately, this has caused stagnation and the virtual end to economic growth. Unless new policies can be devised to stabilize wages and prices when the economy reaches full employment, it is unlikely that stimulative policies will be pursued with any vigour. The result may be little or no economic growth for some time to come.

John Cornwall
Dalhousie University

Further Reading
Duesenberry, J. (1958), *Business Cycles and Economic Growth*, New York.
Kaldor, N. (1967), *Strategic Factors in Economic Development*, Ithaca.
Schumpeter, J. (1961), *The Theory of Economic Development*, New York.
Svennilson, I. (1954), *Growth and Stagnation in the European Economy*.
See also: *business cycles; planning, economic; stagflation.*

Economies of Scale
The term economies of scale refers to the situation in which, at a given and unchanging set of input prices, the unit cost of production is lower in a plant of larger scale of (annual) output than in a plant of smaller scale. This is sometimes called 'real economies of scale' and is contrasted with 'pecuniary economies of scale' in which the plant of larger scale may obtain inputs, including finance for investment, at a lower price. Economies of scale usually obtain in unit labour cost and unit capital costs, but scarcely ever in unit materials cost. An example of economies of scale may be given for ethylene production (Jackson, 1982).

In this real-world example (c. 1970), unit operating costs are 6 per cent lower in a plant of capacity 200 thousand tons per annum than in a plant of capacity 100 thousand tons per annum, and 11 per cent lower in a plant of capacity 300 thousand tons per annum; while there is no alteration in unit feed-

Scale of ethylene plant, thousand tons per annum	100	200	300
Operating cost per ton of ethylene			
Feedstock costs, chemicals, and utilities, £ per ton	41.2	41.2	41.2
Labour costs, £ per ton	3.5	2.7	2.1
Capital cost (depreciation and interest), £ per ton	15.1	12.3	10.1
Total operating costs, £ per ton	59.8	56.2	53.4
Index of operating costs (59.8 taken as 100)	100	94	89

stock etc, costs, unit labour costs are 40 per cent lower in the 300 thousand ton plant, and unit capital costs are 33 per cent lower.

The main reason for lower unit labour costs is that an increase in the scale of this process plant does not require an equi-proportionate increase in the number of workers. In manufacturing plants, a larger scale of output may facilitate changes in the organization and/or mechanization of work which makes labour more productive. The introduction by Henry Ford of assembly-line mass-production techniques and matching organization of work is a famous example. Between 1909 and 1911, Ford moved from its original small Piquette Street plant to the much larger Highland Park plant and introduced the moving assembly-line. As Ford (1926) remarked of this change: 'You will note that men were not employed in proportion to the output.'

	1908	*1911*
Factory output, number of cars	6,181	34,528
Number of employees	1,908	4,110
Labour productivity, cars per employee per annum	3.2	8.4
Unit labour cost (estimated at annual earnings in 1910 of $651 per full-time employee in manufacturing), $ per car	201	77

The main reason for lower unit capital cost is likewise that an increase in the scale of output does not require an equi-proportionate increase in the initial investment. For the ethylene plants, the initial capital costs were, respectively, £8.4 million, £13.5 million, and £16.6 million; as the scale of output doubles the fixed capital cost rises by 61 per cent, and as it increases by a further 50 per cent the capital cost rises by a further 23 per cent. The investment cost per ton capacity thus declines from £84 to £67.5 to £55.3. The reasons for declining investment cost per unit of capacity are many and complex. One commonly cited reason is that much capital equipment takes the general form of a container, the cost of which is related to surface area while production capacity is related to volume: e.g. a box 1m × 1m × 1m has a surface area of 6 square metres and a volume of 1 cubic metre; a box 2m × 2m × 2m has an eightfold increase in volume (in production capacity) for only a fourfold increase in surface area (in cost). Such relationships explain economies of scale in, for example, steel-making. Or to take another example, increasing the carrying capacity of a goods vehicle is unlikely to require an increase in the cost of gearbox, axles, electrics, and so on, so that the capital cost of the vehicle will not rise commensurately with the increase in its carrying capacity.

The economic implications of economies of scale are consider-able and reasonably obvious: plants of bigger scale will tend to have a price/profitability advantage over smaller plants, which have to seek a specialized niche in the market if they are to survive.

Dudley Jackson
University of Wollongong
Australia

References
Ford, H. (1926), *My Life and Work*, London.
Jackson, D. (1982), *Introduction to Economics: Theory and Data*, London.
US Department of Commerce, Bureau of the Census (1975),

Historical Statistics of the United States: Colonial Times to 1970,
Washington.

Efficiency
See Economic Efficiency.

Elasticity
Many propositions in economics are in the form of a relationship between two variables. We may write the relationship in
general as $y = f(x)$, which reads 'y is a function of x'. 'Quantity
consumed (y) is a function of price (x)' is an example of such
a proposition. One important feature of any such relationship
is how y responds to a change in x. If we let Δx be the change
in x and Δy the corresponding change in y, then the sign of
$\frac{\Delta y}{\Delta x}$ tells us whether y increases or decreases for a given increase
in x. Thus 'quantity consumed falls when price rises' would be
represented by a negative sign of $\frac{\Delta y}{\Delta x}$.

For many purposes, it is not enough simply to know the
direction of the response of y to a given change in x – we also
need to know the *magnitude* of this response. How is this to be
measured? One candidate is the absolute value $\frac{\Delta y}{\Delta x}$. The problem with this measure is that it is not free of the units in which
y and x are measured, since Δx, and Δy are both measured in
their respective units. However $\frac{\Delta x}{x}$ and $\frac{\Delta y}{y}$ are unit free measures of the change in x and the corresponding change in y.
Hence

$\dfrac{\dfrac{\Delta y}{y}}{\dfrac{\Delta x}{x}}$ is a unit free measure of the responsiveness of y to a change

in x. The absolute value of this is known as the *elasticity* of y
with respect to x. The expression can be rewritten as $\left(\dfrac{\Delta y}{\Delta x}\right)\left(\dfrac{x}{y}\right)$

and, for a small change in x it becomes $\frac{dy}{dx} \cdot \frac{x}{y}$, where $\frac{dy}{dx}$ is the derivative of y with respect to x.

It is not surprising that elasticity – the responsiveness of one variable to another – has widespread uses in economics. To take just two examples, 'Price elasticity of demand' and 'Income elasticity of demand' are central concepts in consumer theory; 'Price elasticity of Imports' and 'Price elasticity of Exports' are used, for example, in the famous Marshall-Lerner conditions in International Trade Theory.

S. M. Ravi Kanbur
University of Essex

Employment and Underemployment

Most generally, employment is the process of devoting human time and energy to production. It is the labour input to the economy, the performance and organization of work by people in an economic system. In economics the term is normally used in a restricted sense, to describe the creation of goods and services that fall within whatever convention is in use to define the National Product. Economists conventionally exclude unpaid domestic or voluntary services and remunerated activities such as crime, gambling or prostitution which are not considered 'productive'.

The term employment, strictly speaking, derives from the capitalist and wage-labour mode of production. On a narrower definition, it refers to the contractual arrangements which bring workers together with materials and equipment which are not their own property. The term is extended by analogy to other modes of production to cover self-employment, people working in collective enterprises and – at a stretch – family-based production and other pre-capitalist institutions like sharecropping.

The corollary of employment being a productive activity is that it entitles the performer to income – wages in the capitalist mode. Sen (1975) draws attention to these production and income aspects of the notion of employment, to which he adds a third perspective, that it entitles the worker to recognition, or self- and social-esteem, as doing something worthwhile. There is thus a threefold cause for concern if an economy is deemed to have an 'employment problem': production is unnecessarily low, some incomes are unnecessarily low and some people may be deprived of the recognition, or status, that employment would give them.

For wage-labour economies, where employment is organized on a regular full-time basis, 'employment' can be roughly measured as the number of people holding jobs. The suitability of this simplification for any actual situation will depend on how much the quantity of work actually varies between workers. The following exposition also abstracts from heterogeneity in the quality of workers and employment. Employment is the minimum of labour supply and labour demand. On a head-count measure, it is the numbers required by employers or the numbers available for work (at the going wage rate), whichever is smaller. Labour supply in this context is equivalent to the 'labour force' – the total numbers willing to perform paid work, consisting of people in employment plus those available for employment but unable to find it, that is, the unemployed. The classic criterion for unemployment is therefore unsuccessful job search.

The Keynesian notion of 'full employment' in such a labour market is that the effective demand for labour is at a level where productive capacity is fully utilized and unemployment is at a minimum. This minimum consists of at least one element, 'frictional unemployment', people spending a relatively short time finding a suitable job where labour market information is, perhaps inevitably, not good enough to match all vacancies and job seekers instantaneously. Under some circumstances, keeping employment at this frictional minimum would satisfy another definition of full employment as that level of demand for labour which does not aggravate inflation. This level of employment will, however, only ensure maximal utilization of the labour force if there is enough material capital to equip each job. Ideally, capital would accumulate embodying techniques (capital: labour ratios) which utilize available labour resources.

But in the short run the stock of capital is fixed, and often the techniques by which it can be operated are also virtually fixed. This sets an upper limit to the amount of labour an economy can absorb in the short run. If available labour supplies exceed this limit there is said to be 'structural' unemployment, as it could only be eliminated by changes in the structure or size of the capital stock. 'Structural unemployment' also arises when the quality of labour required differs from the quality of the labour on offer in respects such as skill, education or location.

In economies not dominated by the simplified sort of labour market postulated above, underemployment (or the underutiliz-ation of labour) and its attendant problems need not take the form of 'open unemployment'. Indeed, unless there are insti-tutions (such as social insurance or the family) which transfer resources to the jobless, open unemployment is a luxury which few can afford. Unemployment may be hidden in various ways.

(1) Potential workers may drop out of the labour force altoge-ther, labelling themselves as 'retired', 'housewife', or 'student', though they might be available for employment should the demand arise.

(2) Work and income may be shared by members of the labour force working fewer hours, fewer days or less intensively than they would otherwise.

(3) The 'underemployed' may actually work hard and long in inferior, low productivity occupations for want of access to employment in well equipped and well paid sectors of the economy.

The first type of hidden unemployment (or 'discouraged workers') avoids the recognition aspect (if people really do think of themselves in the social accountant's mutually exclusive categories), and is sometimes regarded as none too pressing a social problem, particularly as it is certainly problematic to discover how many people fall into this category at any given time.

The second, work sharing, version typically arises in family-run modes of production such as peasant agriculture when faced either by deficiencies of market demand for output, or, in the classic 'surplus labour' situation, by limited availability of land.

The third type of underemployment is characteristic of 'informal' employment in the urban sectors of developing countries, though it was an example from a mature economy – match selling on the streets of London – that Joan Robinson (1937) used when advancing the idea of disguised unemployment in the 1930s. The notion of dual or segmented labour markets harbouring sectors where underprivileged participants labour at a disadvantage and form an underutilized reserve to a more productive part of the labour market has found applications for both rich and poor countries in the current economic literature. 'Discouraged' housewives might also be regarded as a subset of the third type if their domestic work were a less productive use of their time than their potential market employment.

'Employment policies' are interventions designed to alleviate 'employment problems'. They comprise a very wide set of measures, just as the diagnosis can cover a very wide range of circumstances. Macroeconomic policy can alleviate (or exacerbate) the part of underemployment attributable to deficient aggregate demand. Then there are measures to improve labour market information, to assist labour and employer mobility and to train and retrain the available manpower. In the long run, labour demand can be affected by interventions in the wage formation process, development planning, international trade policy and fiscal policy which favours either capital or labour intensive techniques. From the classic job-creation measure of public works, the list of employment policies now extends to those which redistribute earning opportunities, promote or protect the employment of special groups, encourage work-sharing and develop intermediate techniques.

Heather Joshi
London School of Hygiene and Tropical Medicine

References
Robinson, J. (1937), *Essays on the Theory of Employment*, London.
Sen, A. K. (1975), *Employment, Technology and Development*, Oxford.

Further Reading
Garraty, J. (1979), *Unemployment in History*, New York.
Greenhalgh, C. A., Layard, P. R. G. and Oswald, A. S. (eds) (1983), *The Causes of Unemployment*, Oxford.
I.L.O. (1984), *World Labour Report 1: Employment, Incomes, Social Protection, New Information Technology*, Geneva.
Squire, L. (1981), *Employment Policy in Developing Countries: A · Survey of Issues and Evidence*, New York.
See also: *labour market analysis; productivity.*

Entrepreneurship

The term entrepreneur seems to have been introduced into economic theory by Cantillon (1755), and was first accorded prominence by Say (1803). It was variously translated into English as 'merchant', 'adventurer', or 'employer', though the precise meaning is the undertaker of a project. John Stuart Mill (1848) popularized the term in England.

In the neoclassical theory of the firm, entrepreneurial ability is analogous to a fixed factor endowment because it sets a limit to the efficient size of the firm. The static and passive role of the entrepreneur in the neoclassical theory reflects the theory's emphasis on perfect information – which trivializes management and decision-making – and on perfect markets – which do all the co-ordination that is necessary and leave nothing for the entrepreneur.

According to Schumpeter (1934), the entrepreneur is the prime mover in economic development, and his function is to innovate, or 'carry out new combinations'. Five types of innovation are distinguished: (1) the introduction of a new good (or an improvement in the quality of an existing good); (2) the introduction of a new method of production; (3) the opening of a new market – in particular an export market in new territory; (4) the 'conquest of a new source of supply of raw materials or half-manufactured goods'; (5) the creating of a new type of industrial organization – in particular the formation of a trust or some other type of monopoly.

Schumpeter is also very clear about what the entrepreneur is *not*: he is not an inventor, but someone who decides to allocate resources to the exploitation of an invention; nor is he a risk-bearer: risk-bearing is the function of the capitalist who lends funds to the entrepreneur. Essentially, therefore, Schumpeter's entrepreneur has a managerial or decision-making role.

This view receives qualified support from Hayek (1937) and Kirzner (1973), who emphasize the role of the entrepreneur in acquiring and using information. The entrepreneur's alertness to profit-opportunities, and his readiness to exploit them through arbitrage-type operations, makes him the key element in the 'market process'. Hayek and Kirzner regard the entrepreneur as responding to change – as reflected in the information he receives – whilst Schumpeter emphasizes the role of the entrepreneur as a source of change. These two views are not incompatible: a change effected by one entrepreneur may cause spill-over effects, which alter the environment of other entrepreneurs. Hayek and Kirzner do not insist on the novelty of entrepreneurial activity, however, and it is certainly true that a correct decision is not always a decision to innovate; premature innovation may be commercially disastrous. Schumpeter begs the question of whether someone who is the first to evaluate an innovation, but decides (correctly) not to innovate, qualifies as an entrepreneur.

Knight (1921) insists that decision making involves uncertainty. Each business situation is unique, and the relative frequencies of past events cannot be used to evaluate the probabilities of future outcomes. According to Knight, measurable risks can be diversified – or 'laid off' – through insurance markets, but uncertainties cannot. Those who take decisions in highly uncertain environments must bear the full consequences of those decisions themselves. These people are entrepreneurs: they are the owners of businesses and not the salaried managers that make the day-to-day decisions.

Leibenstein (1968) regards the entrepreneur as someone who

achieves success by avoiding the inefficiencies to which other people – or the organizations to which they belong – are prone. Leibenstein's approach has the virtue of emphasizing that, in the real world, success is exceptional and failure is the norm.

Casson (1982) defines the entrepreneur as someone who specializes in taking decisions where, because of unequal access to information, different people would opt for different strategies. He shows that the evaluation of innovations, as discussed by Schumpeter, and the assessment of arbitrage opportunities, as discussed by Hayek and Kirzner, can be regarded as special cases. He also shows that if Knight's emphasis on the uniqueness of business situations is used to establish that differences of opinion are very likely in all business decisions, then the Knightian entrepreneur can be embraced within his definition as well. Because the definition identifies the *function* of the entrepreneur, it is possible to use conventional economic concepts to discuss the valuation of entrepreneurial services and many other aspects of the market for entrepreneurs.

Perhaps the aspect of entrepreneurship that has attracted most attention is the motivation of the entrepreneur. Hayek and Kirzner take the Austrian view that the entrepreneur typifies purposeful human action directed towards individualistic ends. Schumpeter, however, refers to the dream and will to found a private dynasty, the will to conquer and the joy of creating, whilst Weber (1930) emphasizes the Protestant Ethic and the concept of calling, and Redlich (1956) the role of militaristic values in the culture of the entrepreneur. Writers of business biographies have ascribed a whole range of different motives to people they describe as entrepreneurs. For many students of business behaviour, it seems that the entrepreneur is simply someone who finds adventure and personal fulfilment in the world of business. The persistence of this heroic concept suggests that many people do not want a scientific account of the role of the entrepreneur.

Successful entrepreneurship provides an avenue of social advancement that is particularly attractive to people who are denied opportunities elsewhere. This may explain why it is claimed that immigrants, religious minorities and people denied higher education are over-represented amongst entrepreneurs. Hypotheses of this kind are difficult to test without carefully controlled sampling procedures. The limited evidence available suggests that, in absolute terms, the most common type of entrepreneur is the son of an entrepreneur.

Mark Casson
University of Reading

References

Cantillon, R. (1755), *Essai sur la nature du commerce en générale* (ed. H. Higgs, London, 1931).

Casson, M. C. (1982), *The Entrepreneur: An Economic Theory*, Oxford.

Hayek, F. A. von (1937), 'Economics and knowledge', *Economica* (N.S.), 4.

Kirzner, I. M. (1973), *Competition and Entrepreneurship*, Chicago.

Knight, F. H. (1921), *Risk, Uncertainty and Profit* (ed. G. J. Stigler), Chicago.

Leibenstein, H. (1968), 'Entrepreneurship and development', *American Economic Review*, 58.

Redlich, F. (1956), 'The military enterpriser: a neglected area of research', *Explorations in Entrepreneurial History* (series 1), 8.

Schumpeter, J. A. (1934), *The Theory of Economic Development* (trans. R. Opie), Cambridge, Mass.

Weber, M. (1930), *The Protestant Ethic and the Spirit of Capitalism* (trans. by T. Parsons), London.

See also: *economic growth; Schumpeter.*

Equilibrium

Ever since philosophers replaced divine intervention with rational man, economists have been intrigued that uncoordinated individual decision making does not produce economic anarchy. Adam Smith (1776) was among the first to posit free will based in self-interest, but he also noted that the specialization associated with the division of labour implied co-ordination among individuals. Quesnay's (1766) earlier physiocratic system of circulation reflected a particular form of economic interdependence centred on the surplus net product of agricultural land.

General equilibrium theory attempts to explain how the price mechanism in a free market operates to resolve this seeming paradox of increasing independence in decision making requiring increased co-ordination of economic decisions to produce coherent economic behaviour.

Although the Classical economists were aware of the paradox, the origins of the modern treatment of the problem had to await the marginal revolution in economics associated with Leon Walras's (1874) *Elements*, which, along with Jevons's (1871)' *Theory of Political Economy* and Menger's (1870) *Principles of Economics*, attempted to provide the analysis of individual market demand absent in Classical theory. Only when demand was treated on an equal footing with supply could equilibrium be conceived as the combination of prices and quantities at which the 'forces' of supply just offset those of demand.

A general equilibrium system provides a sufficiently complete description of individuals' decisions concerning supply and demand to determine the quantities and prices of all goods and services produced and exchanged. Given the complexity of analysing an economy with a multiplicity of individuals and goods and services, a high level of abstraction is required and most authors appeal to the aid of mathematics. To a large extent, advances in the theory have been linked to advances in mathematical techniques. Leon Walras, generally considered the father of equilibrium theory, envisaged a system composed of households, endowed with specific quantities of factors and preferences over the available consumption goods, facing a budget constraint limiting expenditures to the market value of the factor endowment, and firms who earned zero profit from the entrepreneurial activity of combining factors in fixed proportions (later made to depend on prices) to produce consumption goods. Firms' receipts were thus exhausted by payments for factor services. The desired combination of consumption goods by households was thus determined by preferences and the prices at which endowments could be sold and consumption goods purchased. An equilibrium was constituted by the balance of supply and demand in each market for goods and factor services.

Since the prices considered were relative prices, ratios of quantities exchanged, there could be no more than n-1 such ratios for any number, n, of goods considered; one of them might serve as numeraire to give a common expression to all prices, its ratio equal to unity. The supply and demand relations were thus independent of the measure or level of prices expressed in numeraire, for its absolute quantity had no effect on the ratios of the other goods or its own price equal to unity (that is, the relations are homogeneous of degree zero in prices). Together with the budget constraint on household expenditure, and firms' zero profits, this produces what has come to be known as '*Walras' Law*': since the market value of all goods and services sold is by definition equal to the market value of all goods and services purchased irrespective of prices, the (n) supply-demand relations comprising the system cannot be linearly independent. If supply equals demand in the markets for all but one (n-1) good, then supply must also equal demand in the market for the remaining (nth) good; equilibrium in the markets for any n-1 goods determines prices and quantities exchanged over all n goods' markets.

The use of the idea of an equilibrium or a balance of forces reflected the influence of classical mechanics and the belief that market forces, like those acting on a pendulum, would naturally lead the system to an equilibrium state. Walras describes this process of 'tâtonnement' (groping) by starting from a random set of prices for each good or service, called out in succession by an 'auctioneer', to which households and firms respond with non-binding offers of the quantities they wish to buy or sell at those prices. The auctioneer follows a simple rule of raising prices when buy offers exceed offers to sell, and vice versa. Although the offers for any good are influenced by the price of every other, if its own offers are more influenced by its own price than others (that is, if goods are gross substitutes so that the rise in the price of a good produces excess demand for all others), then the system will converge by successive rounds of price adjustments, or by 'groping', to an equilibrium of prices and quantities at which everyone independently deciding how much to buy or sell at those prices succeeds in completing desired transactions without external directions or control. These adjustments were thought in practice to occur simultaneously in all markets as the result of the forces of household utility maximization and firms' profit maximization.

An alternative formulation of this process was put forward at about the same time by Edgeworth (1881) who emphasized individual bargaining. Letting the length of the two legs of the lower left and upper right corners of an 'Edgeworth box' represent the quantities available of two goods to two traders, and using the corners as the origin of each trader's indifference map for the two goods, a 'contract curve' may be drawn up connecting the tangency points of the two indifference systems. Combinations of the two goods represented by the curve will be preferred by both individuals to any other. A bargaining process over combinations which provides either trader with the possibility of 'recontracting' if a preferable combination of goods (representing a new relative price) which makes the other trader no worse off is discovered, will lead the traders to a combination on the curve. Once the curve has been reached, improved combinations can only be achieved at the expense of the other trader (the combinations on the curve are Pareto optimal) so that further bargaining is blocked. The contract curve thus represents a 'core' of comparative equilibrium combinations, for once one is reached any attempt to change it is blocked. Edgeworth argued that as the number of goods and the number of traders increases, the number of combinations in the core decreases to a limit of a single combination which replicates the price and quantity equilibrium of Walrasian theory. This method of approach was virtually ignored until Shubik (1959) reintroduced it to modern debate.

Neither was Walras's work much studied in his lifetime, except by his successor in Lausanne, Pareto (1896–7): a similar equilibrium formulation in Cassel's *Theory of Social Economy* (published in German in 1918, in English in 1923) gained wider audience, however. Contemporary theory can be traced to elaborations of Cassel's book in the 1930s when Wald, and then von Neumann, both writing in German, proposed the first mathematically satisfactory solutions for the equilibrium of a Walrasian system (see Weintraub, 1983).

Interest in Walras in the English-speaking world had to wait for Hicks's *Value and Capital* (1939), which used general equilibrium theory to recast economic statics in order to build a new theory of dynamics. At about the same time work by Samuelson which was published later in his *Foundations of Economic Analysis* (1947) also sought a theory of dynamic adjustment in support of comparative static stability properties of equilibrum in his 'correspondence principle'. These insights were eventually used as the basis for modern Hicksian IS-LM representations of Keynes's relation to traditional theory and the subsequent 'Neoclassical synthesis' propounded by Samuelson's influential textbook *Economics*. Ironically, it is the descendants of these early general equilibrium formulations of Keynes that have been criticized for their lack of microfoundations.

By the early 1950s, knowledge of the earlier work of Wald and von Neumann amongst others had become known, and a number of economists in the United States took up the formal problems of the existence of equilibrium. Against the background of developments in game theory and linear systems analysis, a series of articles by Debreu, Arrow, and, in an international context, by McKenzie were published nearly simultaneously, providing definitive proofs using modern mathematical methods (see Weintraub, 1983). The theory reached the maturity of textbook treatment in Arrow and Hahn's *General Competitive Analysis* (1971).

Current investigations have returned to the earlier concerns with the stability and the dynamic adjustment process underlying the comparative static analysis. If equilibria are multiple, comparative statics must analyse not only the stability of the new equilibrium, but which one will be established. This extension of stability analysis has grown out of non-tâtonnement analysis initiated by Hahn and is known as the 'disequilibrium' foundations of equilibrium economics (Fisher, 1983); it seeks to investigate 'hysterisis' effects, the possibility that the past history of adjustment affects the set of potential competitive equilibria. Such concerns encompass the analysis of sequential monetary exchange and price setting without an auctioneer.

J. A. Kregel
University of Groningen

References

Arrow, K. J. and Hahn, F. H. (1971), *General Competitive Analysis*, Edinburgh.

Cassel, G. (1923), *The Theory of Social Economy*, trans. J. McCabe, London.

Edgeworth, F. Y. (1881), *Mathematical Psychics*, London.

Fisher, F. M. (1983), *Disequilibrium Foundations of Equilibrium Economics*, London.

Hicks, J. R. (1939), *Value and Capital*, Oxford.

Pareto, V. (1896–7), *Cours d'Economique politique*, Lausanne.

Samuelson, P. A. (1947), *Foundations of Economic Analysis*, Cambridge, Mass.

Shubik, M. (1959), *Game Theory*, Cambridge, Mass.

Smith, A. (1976) [1776]), *Wealth of Nations*, Oxford.

Walras, M. (1954 [1874]), *Elements of Pure Economics*, trans. W. Jaffe, London.

Weintraub, E. R. (1983), 'On the existence of competitive equilibrium: 1930–1954', *Journal of Economic Literature*, 21.

Further Reading

Weintraub, E. R. (1973), *General Equilibrium Theory*, London.

Weintraub, E. R. (1975), *Conflict and Co-operation in Economics*, London.

Weintraub, E. R. (1979), *Microfoundations*, Cambridge.

See also: *economic dynamics; Walras*.

Exchange Rate

The exchange rate is a price: the price of one currency in terms of another. A distinction is made between the *nominal, effective* and *real* exchange rate. The *nominal* rate is a bilateral price expressed and quoted either as the number of units of the domestic currency per unit of another, or vice versa.

The *effective* exchange rate is an index of a currency's value in terms of a weighted basket of other currencies. Movements in this index show how a currency has moved, not against a single currency, but against the group of currencies in the basket. Movement in the effective rate is a weighted average of divergent changes in nominal rates.

The exchange rate (nominal or effective) determines the competitive positions of domestic output in international markets. At constant domestic prices it gives the foreign currency price of a country's exports and hence influences foreign demand for domestically produced goods. Similarly, at constant foreign currency prices, the exchange rate determines the domestic currency price of imports and hence influences the demand for imports. Movements in the exchange rate can, therefore, have a powerful influence on the competitive position of goods and services produced in different countries and thereby influence the pattern of international trade flows.

The *real* exchange rate calculation adjusts movements in either a nominal or effective exchange rate for relative changes in the domestic price of goods in the country of production. Thus, if a currency depreciates by 10 per cent while its rate of inflation is 4 per cent more than its competitors, the real exchange rate has declined by 6 per cent.

The theory and empirical evidence about the determination of the exchange rate are far from settled. Flow theories tend to concentrate on the current account of the balance of payments and therefore on the factors (such as relative price and income movements between countries) influencing trade flows. The exchange rate is viewed as an equilibrating mechanism for the current account. Portfolio theories, or the asset-market approach (of which the monetary theory of the exchange rate is one of many variants), concentrate on the required conditions for equilibrium in wealthholders' portfolios. In these models, movements in the exchange rate reflect an excess supply or demand for financial assets as between countries. A depreciation is viewed as a symptom of an excess supply of domestic financial assets. Stability in exchange rates requires, in these models, consistent monetary policies as between countries.

Governments have an interest in the level and stability of exchange rates. As movements influence the domestic price of imports, they have an effect on the domestic price level and, dependent upon how wage bargainers respond, the rate of inflation also. Through the same mechanism the exchange rate affects the level of real income and wages at each level of output. To the extent that the international competitive position of domestic goods is affected, movements in the exchange rate have implications for the level of output and employment. Thus governments might resist an appreciation because of its adverse employment effects, but also a depreciation because of the prices effect.

David T. Llewellyn
Loughborough University

Further Reading
Isard, P. (1978), *Exchange Rate Determination,* Princeton.
Llewellyn, D. T. (1981), *International Financial Integration*, London.
See also: *balance of payments; devaluation; international monetary system; international trade.*

Externalities, Economic

Economic externalities are (positive or negative) goods or services generated by an economic activity whose costs or benefits do not fall upon the decision-taking agent. Pollution is a leading and important example. They may, alternatively, be thought of as residuals, the difference between 'social' and 'private' costs and benefits. The divergence was first popularized and elaborated by Pigou in *The Economics of Welfare* (1920) and is believed to be a major reason for market failure: for example, the market will over-produce goods with high external costs. For that reason a main principle of cost-benefit analysis is that *all* costs and benefits, no matter to whom they accrue, should be included. Popular discussion rightly emphasizes external costs associated with production, but one should not entirely ignore positive production effects (apples and honey) or effects on the consumption side, either positive (attractive dress) or negative (radio noise).

Various policies are, in principle, available for dealing with externalities. For example, the extent of an activity may be *regulated*, as in the case of the discharge of industrial effluent into estuaries. Using partial equilibrium analysis the regulation should set the amount of discharge at an 'optimum', that is, where marginal social cost and benefit are equal to one another. This is, of course, very difficult to calculate, so rough rules of thumb are used instead. Economists often argue for the direct use of *pricing*: the agent is charged a tax (or paid a subsidy) equal to the value of the externality at the margin. The congestion tax is an example of this. Such taxes and subsidies are referred to as Pigouvian: they are intended to internalize the externality. Internalization may also come about spontaneously by the *merger* of two units inflicting large externalities upon one another (as in industrial integration).

The tax-subsidy solution is often objected to on the ground that it is open to injured parties to bring an action in tort against the offending agent. If agents know this to be the case, they will take expected compensation for damages into account and externalities will automatically be internalized. On this view not only would Pigouvian taxes not be needed but they would, if imposed, lead to an over-restriction of activity (Coase, 1960). Property rights are seen to be crucial, as they define rights to compensation: defenders of the market system therefore argue that externalities do not constitute market failure provided that property rights are adequately delineated. The direction of compensation naturally depends on the initial distribution of legal rights.

The alternative solutions are closely related to one another. Take the case of a major oil spillage which fouls beaches and destroys fishing and wildlife. If spillages are to be 'banned' the fine must be at least equal to the Pigouvian tax. If there is to be a legal contest, it will have to be fought between states and oil companies rather than through improvised groups of holiday-makers, fishermen and wildlife enthusiasts. And fines/compensations must not give an outcome which is totally unreasonable in relation to the optimum (possibly, though not certainly, zero) amount of spillage.

David Collard
University of Bath

Reference
Coase, R. H. (1960), 'The problem of social cost', *Journal of Law and Economics*, 3.

Further Reading
Pearce, D. W. (ed.) (1978), *The Valuation of Social Cost*, London.

Financial Crises

Financial crises are a form of economic difficulty more general than commercial crises, which is what they were called in the nineteenth century, but less so than the more pervasive economic crisis envisaged by Marxist economic thought. The typical financial crises comes after a period of speculation, called 'over-trading' in classical economics, using borrowed money, and occurs when speculators, investors, lenders or depositors try to liquidate all at once. Prices of the asset which had been bid up are driven down, risking bankruptcy of firms and failure of banks.

A typical financial crisis can be divided into several stages. First is an exogenous shock to the economic system, some unexpected change that alters profit opportunities and induces changes in investment. It may be outbreak of war, the end of a war, or political revolution. It may be more narrowly economic, such as discovery of a new resource, a major innovation, good crops, or bad crops. It can be narrowly financial – the unexpected sources of a security issue, conversion of debt to lower interest rates, leading holders to try to maintain their returns in new investments. Whatever the extent that perturbs the system, it alters profit opportunities and leads to new patterns of investment and usually to speculation for capital gains.

If the change is sufficiently pervasive, euphoria and over-trading are likely. The objects traded depend on the nature of the shock, and may consist of many things: commodities, stocks, bonds (foreign or domestic), railroads, factories, mines, office buildings, houses, land, or virtually anything substantial in value. Rising prices leading to further price increases – called 'bubbles' – occur in isolated cases, like the Florida land boom of 1925, without causing financial crisis outside the group of participants. The most recent example of significant excessive lending has been loans by international syndicates of banks, notably to Mexico, Brazil and Argentina. This was initiated by easy money in the United States beginning in 1970, and accelerated by increases in oil prices in 1973 and 1979 that increased both the need for loans by non-oil producing countries and the capacity to borrow of oil producers.

In the typical pattern of overtrading followed by financial crisis, success of early investors induces others to participate. As more and more join with borrowed funds, credit becomes distended, interest rates rise, and some marginal buyers may be forced to liquidate. Some, who anticipate that the aspects in question have risen as far as they are likely to, cash in their gains. Prices stop rising, may level off or may start to slip. There follows a period called 'financial distress', as the confident expectation that prices will continue to climb gives way to doubt. If expectations of a price rise are replaced by expectations of a fall, a financial crisis is likely. A rush from real or financial assets into money drives down the prices of those assets and in acute cases leads to bankruptcy of individuals or concerns still holding them with borrowed funds, and even to bank failures.

Whether financial crises are serious or ephemeral depends to a considerable extent on how they are handled by monetary authorities. The eighteenth century developed a doctrine of supporting a market in crisis by a 'lender of last resort' which stood ready to halt the panicky liquidation and render it orderly by making money available to concerns with debts to pay, and to banks facing deposit withdrawals. The concept was understood by Henry Thornton as early as 1802, but found fuller rationalization in Walter Bagehot's *Lombard Street* in 1873. Other devices to provide the same assurance have been guarantees of a bank's liabilities by other banks, as in the Hamburg crisis of 1857, or the Baring crisis in England of 1890, or mere suspension of a central bank's legal limit on the right of note issue. The crises of 1847, 1857 and 1866 in London were quickly quieted by a letter of indemnity from the Chancellor of the Exchequer to the Bank of England, undertaking to make good to the Bank any hurt it might suffer by reason of violating the limits imposed by the Bank Act of 1844. In 1847 and 1866, so effective was the lifting of the limit that it did not in fact have to be exceeded. When the market in panic found it could get all the money it might want, it wanted less.

If there is no lender of last resort, deflation of asset prices may spread from one type of asset to another, leading to bankruptcies, bank failures and prolonged depression. The leading examples are 1873 and 1929.

There is a disability in using a lender of last resort: the more a financial market knows it will be helped in emergency, the more likely it is to take the chances that will land it in one. This is the 'moral hazard' principle in insurance, that the more insurance one has, the less motivated one is to be careful. It is on this ground that monetary authorities usually leave some doubt as to whether they will rescue markets and banks in difficulty.

A widespread English view holds that financial crises in that country ended with 1866 as the Bank of England learned how to use its policy instruments, particularly the rate of rediscount, so as to prevent overtrading. In 1873, when the Continent and the United States shared a crisis, the Bank of England undertook 24 changes of bank rate and England remained outside the difficulty. This belief tends to overlook the Baring crisis of 1890, the share collapse of 1921 following the overtrading of 1919–20, a potential crisis in foreign lending in 1914 diverted by the outbreak of war, and a 1974 crisis in London real estate which ruined the so-called 'fringe banks'.

A financial crisis may be confined to a single country, such as the series of troubles in France from the crash of the Union générale in 1882, the collapse of the copper corner engineered by the Comptoir d'escompte in 1889, and the bankruptcy and subsequent scandal of the Panama company from 1889 to 1893; or they may be widely shared in several countries. Propagation of the boom takes place through the rise of internationally traded commodities or securities, through capital flows which increase the recipient's monetary base and induce credit expansion, or through the mere communication of euphoria. The boom of 1885 to 1889 occurred simultaneously in South Africa, Latin America and Australia, stimulated by diamond and gold discoveries in South Africa, and rising commodity prices leading to land clearing in Latin America and Australia, and fed by an outflow of capital from London to all three areas. This outflow of capital, in turn, was partly a consequence of the Goschen conversion of national debts from 3 to 2.5 per cent, inducing investors to seek higher returns in brewery shares and foreign mortgage bonds. The financial crisis was precipitated by the halt in British lending which made it impossible for the countries to continue expanding investment.

Writers of various nationalities typically regard financial crises that affect their country strongly as of local origin. In particular, many American economists and economic historians believe that the 1929 depression started primarily in the United States. A more complete view suggests that it is difficult to disentangle the complicated skein of international causality in such a crisis as the Anglo-American one of 1836, the New York-Liverpool-Stockholm-Hamburg crisis of 1857, and without enumerating, several others, especially the world crisis of 1929. Crisis started in Germany and the temperate developing countries when the United States, in its fascination in 1928 with the rising New York stock market, cut off long-term lending to those areas. The stock market crash in 1929 itself was precipitated by short-term capital withdrawals from London in response to the Hatry crisis of September 1929.

International financial crisis requires an international lender of last resort. In the nineteenth century the City of London was the major financial centre from which other centres in trouble borrowed. When London itself faced crisis, it was helped on a number of occasions by the Bank of France (1825, 1836, 1839, 1890 and 1907), by Hamburg (1839) and by the State Bank of Russia (1890). Even so, Britain did not respond to the 1873 crisis in Central Europe and the United States. The classic case, however, seems to have been the 1929 depression when Britain, financially weakened by World War I, had ceased to act as the international lender of last resort, and the United States (and France) were unwilling to take on the role on an adequate scale.

The United States undertook to stabilize the world economy from World War II to about 1971. When the boom in syndicated bank loans to developing countries encountered difficulties in 1981 and 1982 and reached the stage of distress, the world turned not to the United States but to the International Monetary Fund created at Bretton Woods in 1944. The IMF successfully organized rescue operations from Mexico, Argentina and Brazil on a temporary basis by using its own resources, those of the Bank for International Settlements, and advances from the United States Federal Reserve System, and by persuading commercial banks not to halt lending, but in fact to lend more. The resources of the IMF are limited, however, and it is generally recognized that they need to be increased against any further relapse that would lead to financial crisis.

Charles P. Kindleberger
Massachusetts Institute of Technology

Further Reading

Evans, D. M. (1849), *The Commercial Crisis, 1847–48*, London.
Kindleberger, C. P. (1973), *The World in Depression, 1929–1939*, London.
Kindleberger, C. P. (1978), *Manias, Panics and Crashes*, London.
Kindleberger, C. P. and Laffargue, J. P. (eds) (1982), *Financial Crises: Theory, History and Policy*, Cambridge.
Lauck, W. J. (1907), *The Causes of the Panic of 1893*, Boston.
Wirth, M. (1890), *Geschichte der Handelskrisen*, 4th edn, Vienna.

See also: *banking; financial system; international monetary system; securities markets.*

Financial System

Financial systems provide society with a mechanism for facilitating trade, a machinery for transferring resources from savers to investors, and a means of holding wealth in a convenient form. Their origin lies in the need for a satisfactory payments system; further development has had more to do with the requirements of savers and investors, of wealth-owners and those who control the use of physical capital assets.

It is these physical assets – lands, buildings, equipment and other assets comprising the 'physical' capital stock – which form the foundation on which the superstructure of the financial system is created. Financial 'instruments' are claims whose value depends ultimately on physical resources (including human capital) or the income derived from them. The institutions within the financial system attempt to divide up or combine these ultimate claims in ways which match their clients' needs. The result in a sophisticated system is a great variety of instruments, handled by a broad and diverse range of institutions and financial markets.

The provisions of notes and coins as generally acceptable means of payments has usually been regarded as a duty (or profitable right) of the state – the sovereign, government or central bank. These suffice only for small payments and are nowadays supplemented in even the most rudimentary financial system by banks, which take deposits and make payments by effecting transfers between accounts. Allied to this function is the provision of finance for trade – short-term loans to bridge the gap between the despatch of goods and the receipt of payment for them. Though important, activities associated with trade and payments now tend to comprise only a small part of the activities of financial systems.

Much more significant are activities associated with saving, investment, and the ownership of wealth. The financial system enables society to separate the ownership of wealth from the control of physical capital and to ensure that savers and wealthholders have access to financial assets whose characteristics are attractive to them and differ from those of the physical assets which underpin their value. For example, savers frequently seek safety and liquidity in the assets they hold, whereas physical assets are durable, liable to lose their value, and difficult to turn into cash quickly; and the scale of investment is often of an order which dwarfs the amount available from individual savers.

Financial systems thus facilitate effective capital accumulation. By *intermediating* between savers and investors, financial institutions enable surplus resources to be transferred to those who are able to use them. By *mobilizing* saving from many savers, they provide finance for large-scale investment projects. And by *transforming* securities, the system allows the risk inherent in productive activity to be concentrated on wealth-holders who are prepared to take it, while others obtain the safe and liquid assets that they want. In a properly functioning system these activities can be expected both to increase the saving which is available for investment, and to raise the productivity of the investment that takes place.

Most financial systems consist largely of *intermediaries* – institutions which issue their own liabilities, and hold as assets the liabilities of ultimate borrowers or of other intermediaries. They fall into three broad groups: banks and other deposit-taking institutions, such as building societies, savings and loan associations, or credit unions; long-term investing institutions, such as life assurance companies, pension funds and investment companies or trusts; and special credit institutions, usually set up by governments to provide long-term finance for particular purposes. These institutions often compare with each other in the 'market' for savings, loans, or both. In addition, most sophisticated financial systems, and some that are not yet highly developed, contain organized markets. These are security markets, such as the Stock Exchange, where long-term securities are issued and traded, and money markets, where short-term deposits and loans are made.

Economic and political conditions are the principal factors governing the evolution of financial systems. Goldsmith (1969) has suggested that three broad categories of system can be identified, distinguished according to the scale and composition of the economy's financial superstructure: (1) The systems found in Europe and North America up to the middle of the nineteenth century: the total value of financial instruments was low, financial institutions accounted for a low share of the outstanding assets, and commercial banks were pre-eminent. Risk-capital was predominantly in the hands of the owners of (comparatively small-scale) enterprises, and did not play a larger part in the financial system. (2) The structure is similar to the first one, and was found in nonindustrialized countries in the first half of the century. But in this case governments and government-supported institutions played a larger part thanks to the mixed nature of the economies. A similar situation can be found in many developing countries today, with government-supported institutions supplying capital for particular purposes. (3) This category, common amongst industrial countries in this century, shows a considerably greater degree of financial development, a higher proportion of risk-assets, and increased diversity amongst financial institutions. Some (for example, Netherlands, UK, US) have strong long-term institutions supplying risk capital. Others (among them, France and Italy) rely more heavily on special credit institutions. Socialist countries might be thought to form a fourth category: their financial systems are generally less highly developed than in market economies, with banks dominant amongst financial institutions.

While the tendency for financial and economic development to proceed in tandem is well-documented, the direction of causation is still the subject of controversy. Some argue that financial development is a response to economic growth, others (such as Drake, 1980), that improved financial facilities act as an independent stimulus. There is probably some truth in both views: financial innovation, in the form of new instruments or institutions, often results from changes in the economy; but, once created, new facilities are made available to others and help to stimulate further growth. Thus, even if financial development seldom sparks off economic growth, there is a positive feedback from the financial to the economic system.

A. D. Bain
University of Strathclyde

References
Drake, P. J. (1980), *Money, Finance and Development*, Oxford.
Goldsmith, R. W. (1969), *Financial Structure and Development*, New Haven.
See also: *banking; financial crises; securities markets.*

Firm, Theory of

The role of specialization in economic progress was emphasized by Adam Smith. Now specialized activities need to be co-ordinated, either by conscious integration within an organization or through market relationships; and the effects of both organizational forms and market structures on economic performance are topics which date back at least to Smith. But economists rarely try to treat the firm simultaneously as an organization and as a component of an industry or market, and so one can distinguish two major kinds of theory of the firm.

The problems of business enterprise were last treated comprehensively by Marshall (1919, 1920), whose carefully explained decision to give preference to detailed empirically based analyses over further refinement of theoretical structures was rejected by his successors. For Marshall, the problems of the firm were problems of acquiring (or generating) and using knowledge: knowledge of production methods, knowledge of existing and potential markets, knowledge of the ways to construct an organization and to motivate its members to create opportunities for profit. The firm's environment – its customers and its competitors, including potential competitors – at once constrained its actions and provided opportunities to those who had the wit to perceive and the ability to exploit them. (That such ability might be destructive rather than constructive, or perhaps both together, did not escape Marshall's consideration.) For the analysis of this complex evolutionary process the methods of static equilibrium offered some useful guidance, but could be misleading if rigorously pressed; there was no substitute for the detailed investigation of particular organizational and market arrangements, in relation to the technical conditions and demand characteristics of each case.

After Marshall, the study of the firm disintegrated. Economists chose to develop static models of resource allocation in which the major activities of firms were defined away by the assumption of fully specified demand and cost functions, and the firm itself became a unitary decision maker whose actions were completely determined by its situation. Firms as organizations had no reason for existence. The 'theory of the firm' was the label given to a set of exercises in constrained optimization, by which equilibrium price and output were derived for a series of market structures – perfect and imperfect competition, oligopoly and monopoly – and the effects of change read off from shifts in demand or cost curves. Though this style of theorizing began with perfect competition, it was Joan Robinson's *Economics of Imperfect Competition* (1933) which epitomized the triumph of the formal model. (Her diagrams are to be found in many textbooks.) It epitomized too the dominance of problems generated within the theoretical structure: for the origins of imperfect competition theory lay in the logical impossibility of reconciling increasing returns (statically defined) with perfectly competitive equilibrium. Both were concepts which Marshall had avoided.

Though often regarded as an alternative presentation of this model, Chamberlin's (1933) conception of monopolistic competition was very different. Whereas Marshall had insisted that elements of competition and monopoly were usually blended in practice, Chamberlin set out to blend them in theory. In so doing, he tried to incorporate both product variation and selling costs within a formal analysis which used the method (though often not the language) of static equilibrium. Despite his limited success, he provided the primary inspiration for the strong American tradition in industrial economics (even though some of its practitioners borrowed their welfare criteria from Robinson). Chamberlin's approach was also distinguished by the attention he gave to oligopoly, attention which steadily increased over the years. His insistence that oligopolistic behaviour (like all behaviour) depends on expectations, and that there could be no general theory of oligopoly because there could be no general theory of expectations, has haunted theorists ever since.

There are many specific models of oligopoly, though it is noteworthy that most restrict themselves either to relationships within the group (as, for example, the dominant firm and kinked demand models) or to the barriers, natural or artificial, against new entrants, and do not attempt to deal with both issues together – another example of economists' aversion to multilevel analysis. (Andrews (1949) exceptionally tried to argue, significantly in a non-formal way, that the threat of cross-entry and the desire of managers to show themselves worthy of promotion might combine to ensure good value for the customer's money – especially if the customer was another firm.) But the kind of situational determination which is apparently so effective in producing general solutions for other market structures will not work for oligopoly.

This failure was exploited by Baumol, who founded an alternative, though closely related, line of analysis. Instead of varying the environment around a standard firm, why not vary the firms within a standard environment? Baumol's (1959) variation was to assume that a firm's decision makers sought to maximize not profit, but sales revenue; his lead was followed by Williamson (1963), who proposed a managerial utility function, and Marris (1964), who favoured growth. In all three models, the decision makers were constrained not only by the market opportunities but also by their share-holders: in the first two directly by the need to provide an acceptable profit, and in the third by the risk of takeover when share prices were depressed by the low earnings associated with unprofitable growth. Each model generated some plausible contrasts to the results of profit maximization; yet all three were open to a double attack. Although claiming to apply to oligopolistic firms, none attempted to deal seriously with interdependence; and, though they invoked the firm as an organization to justify their choice of managerially oriented objectives, none offered any analysis of organizational influences on behaviour. They considered neither the firm as a system nor the firm within a system.

Williamson has since turned (1975) to firms as organizations, pursuing a research programme adumbrated by Coase (1937), who argued that firms came into existence where they offered a cheaper alternative to the use of costly market transactions, and that the organization of industry could be explained by the comparative advantages, for varying classes of activity, of management and the market. Williamson has extended the costs of transactions to include those arising from differentiated knowledge, which may be exploited by opportunism and guile, but has provided no explanation of the kind of co-operative interdependence between complementary organizations which has been persuasively analysed by Richardson (1972). Complementary to the allocation of activities between markets and firms is the allocation of activities within the organization; here the transactions cost approach converges with the historical studies of organizational structure by Chandler (1962, 1977).

It is perhaps significant that the unit of analysis is called a transaction, for the economics of organization has rather little to say about price and output decisions. Nor is it much concerned with the actual problems and processes of decision making, which are the focus of what is usually called (in economics) behavioural theory. This kind of theory is characterized by its emphasis on the inadequacy of knowledge, and on the limited ability of people to make use even of what knowledge they think they have. Simon's (1976) proposal to substitute procedural for substantive rationality makes obvious sense at a time of much concern over control systems, information systems, techniques of planning, and the machinery of government. So far, such studies of organizational processes and their implications (for example, by Cyert and March, 1963) have centred on short-term decision making, whereas transactions cost theorists write about an organization's structure and scope. Each might borrow from the other, perhaps building on Penrose's (1959) explanation of the growth of firms through the activities of managers who have developed effective decision procedures through their experience of management.

The firm as an agent of discovery and progress has received little attention during the last sixty years. It was a key element in Schumpeter's (1943) theory of economic development through 'creative destruction', but Schumpeter is not usually thought of as a theorist of the firm. There has been some recent interest in the concept of the entrepreneur as the agent of change; and though neo-Austrians have so far studied the entrepreneur only as an individual in the market, Casson (1982) depicts him as the creator of an organization, facing some of the problems discussed by Marshall. Meanwhile, studies of innovation and technical change have increasingly recognized the need to investigate how organizational form as well as market structure influences the generation, transmission and exploitation of knowledge, and also the effects of these processes on markets and organizations. The problems of substance and of method thereby raised are well displayed by Nelson and Winter (1982). There seems no early prospect of any formal apparatus that will handle simultaneously the issues identified by Smith; there may be increasing awareness of the limitations of present models.

Brian J. Loasby
University of Stirling

References

Andrews, P. W. S. (1949), *Manufacturing Business*, London.

Baumol, W. J. (1959), *Business Behavior, Value and Growth*, New York.

Casson, M. (1982), *The Entrepreneur: An Economic Theory*, Oxford.

Chamberlin, E. H. (1933), *The Theory of Monopolistic Competition*, Cambridge, Mass.

Chandler, A. D. (1962), *Strategy and Structure*, Cambridge, Mass.

Chandler, A. D. (1977), *The Visible Hand*, Cambridge, Mass.

Coase, R. H. (1937), 'The nature of the firm', *Economica* (N.S.), 4.

Cyert, R. M. and March, J. G. (1963), *A Behavioral Theory of the Firm*, Englewood Cliffs, N.J.

Marris, R. L., (1964), *The Economics of 'Managerial' Capitalism*, London.

Marshall, A. (1919), *Industry and Trade*, London.

Marshall, A. (1920), *Principles of Economics*, 8th edn, London.

Nelson, R. R. and Winter S. G. (1982), *An Evolutionary Theory of Economic Change*, Cambridge, Mass.

Richardson, G. B. (1972), 'The organisation of industry', *Economic Journal*, 82.

Robinson, J. V. (1933), *The Economics of Imperfect Competition*, London.

Schumpeter, J. A. (1943), *Capitalism, Socialism and Democracy*, London.

Simon, H. A. (1976), 'From substantive to procedural rationality', in S. J. Latsis (ed.), *Method and Appraisal in Economics*, Cambridge.

Williamson, O. E. (1963), *Economics of Discretionary Behavior: Managerial Objectives in a Theory of the Firm*, Englewood Cliffs, N.J.

Williamson, O. E. (1975), *Markets and Hierarchies: Analysis and Anti-Trust Implications*, New York.

See also: *competition; Marshall.*

Fiscal Policy

Book V of J. S. Mill's *Principles of Political Economy* (1848) was labelled 'The Influence of Government', a very apt description of what we mean by fiscal policy. Clearly most important, and the areas which have attracted most attention, are government tax and expenditure policy, and the consequent overall financial impact on the economy. Until the publication of J. M. Keynes's *General Theory* in 1936 it was the impact of individual taxes and expenditures which had been most studied. Keynes's belief that it was not merely the level of tax and expenditure that was important, but that they could be used to bring the economy more quickly to an acceptable equilibrium which it would other-wise only slowly or never achieve, and that active manipulation of the government's budget was vital to the maintenance of a stable economy, revolutionized the analysis of public policy. In the post-war years, discussions of the impact of government policy on the overall level of economic activity became a recognized part of the debate on economic policy in most of the Western world. With hindsight, it seems clear that much of the fine tuning indulged in by many governments had effects which were at best very small and, in some cases, counter-cyclical. The use of fiscal policy for short-term stabilization of the economy was substantially undermined by the economic problems of the early 1970s, which combined spiralling rates of inflation with levels of unemployment unprecedented in the post-war years, and marked the flowering of the so-called monetarist versus Keynesian debate.

Question marks over the use of fiscal policy for macroeconomic stabilization have perhaps helped to heighten the interest in the microeconomic impact of government tax and expenditure policy. Much work has recently been done in the areas of individual responses to taxes; their effect on work effort, investment decisions, risk taking, pricing behaviour, and consumption patterns. The analysis of public expenditure raises questions about the nature of public goods, and the optimum size of the public sector. The latter has recently caused a good deal of controversy, with something of a backlash against the very rapid recent growth in the size of the public sector in many Western countries.

Andrew Dilnot
Institute for Fiscal Studies, London

Reference

Keynes, J. M. (1936), *The General Theory of Employment, Interest and Money*, London.

Further Reading

Bluider, A. S. and Solow, R. M. (1974), 'Analytical foundations of fiscal policy', in A. S. Bluider and R. M. Solow (eds), *The Economics of Public Finance*, London.

Kay, J. A. and King, M. A. (1983), *The British Tax System*, 3rd edn, Oxford.
See also: *public goods; taxation.*

Free Trade

Free international trade became the dominant theory, ideology and trade policy of mid-nineteenth-century Britain. It commanded the support of classical political economists from Adam Smith to David Ricardo and Karl Marx. The theoretical justification was Ricardo's theory of comparative advantage, which assumed internal mobility and international immobility of labour and capital. At the peak of its support free trade implied international mobility of capital and labour. Free trade was also associated with *laissez-faire*, that is, the freedom of enterprise from regulation by the state, although with a commanding British navy this hardly meant the end of state intervention in the struggle for dominance in international trade.

Challenges to the idea of free trade came from Britain's nineteenth-century rivals, the United States and Germany. Hamilton (1957) and List (1904) argued that new industrialized nations required protection before free trade became desirable. By the 1930s, free trade had been abandoned, even in Britain, and international trade theorists acknowledged the case for protection to assist infant industries (sometimes infant nations) or to exploit national monopoly power. But beggar-my-neighbour protectionism in the 1930s crisis gave way in the post-World War II period to a new wave of political and theoretical support for free trade and free international capital mobility, embodied in the institutions of the post-war settlement. Free trade and international capital mobility was embraced by the dominant *pax Americana*, and there was a substantial dismantling of protection between industrial countries.

The theory of international trade was extended to allow for the international mobility of factors and the link between free trade and *laissez-faire* was broken. Protectionist arguments have been rejected by those who use the theory of domestic market distortions as a framework for the analysis of government intervention in the market mechanism. Within this context, protection through intervention in trade is likely to be worse than subsidies or other policies aimed more directly towards policy objectives. Increasingly, it is argued that development of dynamic comparative advantage is better served by imperfect markets than imperfect government policies.

As in the nineteenth century, such ideas have not gone unchallenged. The modern-day counterparts of List and Hamilton successfully argued for protected import-substituting industrialization in many less-developed parts of the world economy in the early post-war period. In Eastern Europe, in spite of considerable integration of their national economies, drives towards import substitution and self-sufficiency, both nationally and as a trading bloc, remained powerful tendencies in their economic mechanisms.

Since the 1960s import substitution policies have been widely questioned. Many developing countries switched to export orientation and benefited from access to world markets and freer trade policies. However, in all twentieth-century late developers, the state has had a strategic and pervasive role in the development process. The export orientated Newly Industrializing Countries (NICs) are no exception, relying on pervasive regulation and control of labour, capital and also trade. With at least 20 per cent of OECD trade directly controlled by multinational corporations (MNCs) as intra-firm trade, freer trade in the twentieth century is a far cry from nineteenth-century free trade of *laissez-faire*.

With a new crisis in the world economy, protectionism is again on the march. New tensions and contradictions are evident in the Western industrial countries, the existing socialist countries and the debt-ridden developing countries. Freedom of exchange, if not free trade, will be a central dimension of political and economic debate for the foreseeable future.

H. David Evans
Institute of Development Studies
University of Sussex

References
Hamilton, A. (1957), 'Encouragement of trade', and 'Encouragement of manufactures', in R. B. Morris (ed.), *Alexander Hamilton and the Founding of the Nation*, New York.
List, F. (1904), *The National System of Political Economy*, London.

Further Reading
Corden, W. M. (1974), *Trade Policy and Economic Welfare*, Oxford.
Evans, H. D. and Alizadeh, P. (1984), 'Trade, industrialisation and the visible hand', *Journal of Development Studies*, October.
Kenen, P. B. and Jones, R. W. (eds) (1984), *Handbook of International Economics*, Vol. 1, Amsterdam.
Roemer, J. E. (1982), *A General Theory of Exploitation and Class*, Cambridge, Mass.
See also: *international trade; laissez-faire.*

Game Theory, Economic Applications

The popularity of game theory has varied considerably since its introduction into economics by J. von Neumann and O. Morgenstern in their 1944 classic *The Theory of Games and Economic Behavior*. Game theory is an attempt to analyse rational strategic behaviour in situations of uncertainty. The initial applications of the theory were to oligopoly theory, and in the 1950s this strand of development seemed to come to an end. After a lull, game theory was applied to general equilibrium theory and has given some fruitful insights into the structure of competitive equilibria through concepts such as 'the core'. Game theorists were able to show that competitive equilibrium was only possible if rational agents could not form blocking coalitions to improve their own position at the expense of the non-coalition actors in the situation. Recently there has been a new wave of interest in game theory. This has had three dimensions, all associated with attempts to analyse economic and social institutions. The three areas are: (1) the analysis of markets and monetary institutions; (2) the analysis of planning processes; and (3) in the area of social choice and welfare economics. Game theory has been used for both analytical and normative problems in all these areas.

One major advance has been the introduction of the concept of incentive compatibility as a constraint on action. The idea is simple: any agent, when designing his strategy, should take account of the fact that the other players will only act in their own best interests. If a player wants others to act, then he should only undertake actions that give others incentives to comply. This analytical concept has been extremely useful in aiding our understanding of bargaining and contracting in labour markets in franchising contracts, and in the analysis of the impact of taxes. It is not so much a new behavioural concept as a recognition of the obvious constraints a rational actor will face. A related set of ideas has been used in the public-choice literature where researchers have been trying to design games where individuals will reveal their true preferences. These ideas have been particularly useful in looking at feasible public utility pricing schemes and in looking at the properties of voting schemes.

Some recent developments in the theory of games have aided our understanding of the market process. The concept of a game can be applied to a process that repeats itself over time. For instance, the problem of oligopolistic pricing can be seen as a repeated game problem. Standard tools can be applied, and it has been discovered that if the length of the game is finite, then in the last period the analysis to apply is that of the one-period game. But if this is known in the period before last, then the same applies to the period before last (this is sometimes known as the chainstore paradox). If one period analysis applies, then the development of 'reputation' and 'reliability' are not possible. It is possible to analyse these concepts in the concept of an infinite (or never-ending) game, where reputation effects change solutions. These concepts have usefully been adopted in the analysis of monetary institutions, in the study of oligopoly, and, most recently, in the analysis of general economic equilibrium.

Often in game theory the results are much less impressive than the techniques used, and new concepts, such as discounted games, are often more useful for telling us where the blind alleys are rather than where they are not. Despite this, clear advances have recently been made in the application of game theory based on agents whose expectations are in some sense 'rational' (in perfect equilibrium games) and whose actions are incentive compatible. After several false starts game theory now appears to be an indispensable part of the economist's tool-kit. An excellent recent survey may be found in *The Journal of Economic Literature*, June 1981, by A. Schotter and G. Schwodjauer.

Ray Barrell
University of Southampton

Health Economics

Health economics is concerned with the analysis of health care inputs such as expenditure and employment, and an appraisal of their impact on that desired outcome, the health of society.

Clearly, many inputs may affect an individual's health. In a world of scarce resources it is necessary to ensure that these resources are used efficiently – that the cost of producing care and health is minimized and the benefits are maximized. At the individual level, this can be modelled in a human capital framework (Grossman, 1972). Grossman's model permits an exploration of the links between inputs (such as education, income, wealth, health care and nutrition) and their impact on health status; this work indicates that the relative importance of income and nutrition on health is greater than that of health care.

The evaluation of health care is seriously deficient. Cochrane (1971) has argued that most health care therapies in use today have not been evaluated scientifically. By 'scientifically', he means the application of randomized controlled trials which administer the therapy under investigation to a randomly selected (experimental) group of patients, and a placebo or alternative therapy (a control) to another randomly selected group of patients. The difference, if any, between the therapeutic results for the experimental and control groups gives an indication of the relative impact of the therapies. Such results require replication to ensure validity, and such methods are noticeable by their relative absence (as documented in Bunker, Barnes and Mosteller, 1977).

Such clinical evaluation informs decision makers about the benefits of health care, but an economic component is needed to assess costs. The economist's role is to elicit the social opportunity costs of the alternative therapies, that is, the costs to all decision makers, both public (the government) and private (for example, the individual and his family). A guide to the application of such techniques and an appraisal of over a hundred case studies is provided by Drummond (1980; 1981).

The dominant (monopolist) role of the medical profession in the health care market-place has resulted in an investigation of physicians' capacity to create demand for their own and other people's services (Department of Health and Human Services, 1981). This, together with the fact that third parties (governments and insurance companies, rather than patients or producers) usually pay for health care, has led to cost containment problems (McLachlan and Maynard, 1982). To control such inflation, user charges (prices) can be introduced, a policy that has both costs and benefits (Maynard, 1979; Newhouse *et al.*, 1981); or more effective incentives must be devised to encourage producers (doctors) to economize, for example, through health maintenance organizations (Luft, 1981).

The inefficient use of health care resources is clearly unethical; it deprives patients of care from which they could benefit. The aim of health economists is to generate information about the costs and benefits of alternative ways of achieving health and health goals. It is hoped that such information will improve the efficiency and equity of health care systems across the world.

Alan Maynard
University of York, England

References

Bunker, J. P., Barnes, B. A. and Mosteller, F. (eds) (1977), *The Costs, Benefits and Risks of Surgery*, New York.

Cochrane, A. L. (1971), *Effectiveness and Efficiency*, London.

Department of Health and Human Services (1981), *Physician Induced Demand for Surgical Operations*, Washington D.C.

Drummond, M. F. (1980), *Principles of Economic Appraisal in Health Care*, Oxford.

Drummond, M. F. (1981), *Case Studies in Economic Appraisal in Health Care*, Oxford.

Grossman, M. (1972), *The Demand for Health*, New York and London.

Luft, H. (1981), *Health Maintenance Organisation*, New York.

McLachlan, G. and Maynard, A. (eds) (1982), *The Public Private Mix for Health*, London.

Maynard, A. (1979), 'Pricing, insurance and the National Health Service', *Journal of Social Policy*, 8.

Newhouse, N. P. *et al.* (1981), 'Interim results from a controlled trial of cost-sharing in health-insurance', *New England Journal of Medicine*, 305.

Human Capital

Human capital is the stock of acquired talents, skills and knowledge which may enhance a worker's earning power in the labour market. A distinction is commonly made between *general* human capital – which is considered as affecting potential earnings in a broad range of jobs and occupations – and *specific* human capital, which augments a person's earning power within the particular firm in which he is employed but is of negligible value elsewhere. An example of the former would be formal education in general skills such as mathematics; an example of the latter would be the acquired knowledge about the workings of, and personal contacts within, a particular firm. In many cases human capital is of an intermediate form, whether it be acquired 'off the job', in the form of schooling or vocational training, or 'on the job' in terms of work experience.

In several respects the economic analysis of human capital raises problems similar to that of capital as conventionally understood in terms of firms' plant and equipment. It is likely to be heterogeneous in form; it is accumulated over a substantial period of time using labour and capital already in existence; futher investment usually requires immedate sacrifices (in terms of forgone earnings and tuition fees); its quality will be affected by technical progress; the prospective returns to an individual are likely to be fairly uncertain, and the capital stock will be subject to physical deterioration and obsolescence. Nevertheless there are considerable differences. Whereas one can realize the returns on physical or financial capital either by receiving the flow of profits accruing to the owner of the asset or by sale of the asset itself, the returns on human capital usually can only be received by the person in whom the investments have been made (although there are exceptions, such as indentured workers), and usually require further effort in the form of labour in order to be realized in cash terms. The stock of human capital cannot be transferred as can the titles to other forms of wealth, although the investments that parents make in their children's schooling and in informal education at home are sometimes taken as analogous to bequests of financial capital.

While the idea of investment in oneself commands wide acceptance in terms of its general principles, many economists are unwilling to accept stronger versions of the theory of earnings determination and the theory of income distribution that have been based on the pioneering work of Becker (1964) and Mincer (1958). This analysis generally assumes that everywhere labour markets are sufficiently competitive, the services of different types of human capital sufficiently substitutable and educational opportunities sufficiently open, such that earnings differentials can be unambiguously related to differential acquisition of human capital. On the basis of such assumptions, estimates have been made of the returns (in terms of increased potential earnings) to human investment (measured in terms of forgone earnings and other costs) by using the observed earnings of workers in cross-sectional samples and in 'panel studies' over time. The rate of return to such investment has usually been found to be in the range of 10 to 15 per cent. However, it should be emphasized that such estimates often neglect the impact of other economic and social factors which may affect the dispersion of earnings.

Frank A. Cowell
London School of Economics and Political Science

Reference
Becker, G. S. (1964), *Human Capital*, New York.
Mincer, J. (1958), 'Investment in human capital and personal income distribution', *Journal of Political Economy*, 66.

Further Reading
Mincer, J. (1974), *Schooling, Experience and Earnings*, New York.
Schultz, T. W. (1972), *Investment in Education*, Chicago.
See also: *capital theory*.

Income Distribution, Theory of

Whilst economists have not always given such primacy to an explicit discussion of distributional questions, income distribution theory has almost always been central to the analysis of economic systems. The theory deals not only with the 'functional distribution of income' but also with the 'size distribution of income'.

Orthodox economic theory treats questions of income distribution as an integral part of the neoclassical analysis of prices, output mix and resource allocation. Briefly, each competitive firm takes the price it can get for its output and the prices it must pay for inputs as given in the market: it selects its level of output and adjusts its demand for inputs so as to maximize profits at those prices. Each household likewise takes as given the prices it must pay for goods and services, and the prices paid to it for goods and services (for example the labour services supplied by members of the household): it adjusts the quantities of the goods and services demanded or supplied in the market so as to maximize satisfaction within the limitations imposed by its budget. All these prices adjust so as to clear the markets: aggregate supply is at least as great as aggregate demand for every good and service. The reward to any factor of production

– whether it be a particular type of labour, a natural resource, or the services of capital equipment – is determined by its market clearing price. If the technology changes, or the stock of natural resources alters, or if there is a shift in the preference patterns of households, this will shift the pattern of supply and/or demand in one or more markets, and in general prices of goods and factors alter accordingly to clear the markets anew. The functional distribution of income is thus apparently automatically determined by the market mechanism. Moreover, the details of the distribution of income between persons or between households can be readily worked out within this framework: the time pattern of consumption and saving by households, and the educational investments which people make in themselves or in their offspring – each of which plays a significant role in the size distribution of incomes that is realized – can each be analysed as particular cases of the household's optimization problem.

However, one other piece of information is required for a complete theory of income distribution within this framework: the system of property rights that prevails within the community. The importance of this as regards the size distribution of income is obvious: the question of who owns which natural resources, of who owns the capital equipment and of who is entitled to a share in the profits of the firms is central to the determination of household incomes. Household budgets are determined jointly by these property rights and the market prices and may be dramatically affected by a change in the pattern of ownership, or by a shift in the *system* of ownership (for example from a system of private property to one of state ownership). But this system of ownership will *also* affect the market prices and thus the functional distribution of income. For if households' rights of ownership are changed, the consequent change in household budgets will change the pattern of demand for goods and services, and hence the market prices of consumption goods and of labour and other resources. Thus orthodox theory might be criticized for evading one of the principal issues of income determination, by passing the question of property rights on to the historian or the political philosopher.

However, the neoclassical orthodoxy has been challanged not only because of such shortcomings, but also on account of its restrictive assumptions concerning the economic processes involved. Because these assumptions lie at the heart of the theory rather than being merely convenient simplifications, many economists have questioned the relevance of various aspects of the standard account of income distribution. We may cite three particular examples which have led to the construction of useful alternative theories.

(1) Note that the orthodox theory neglects barriers to competition and the exercising of monopoly power as being of secondary or transitory importance in the competitive market story. It has been argued that restraints on competition – in the form of segmentation of the labour market and outright discrimination – are of major importance in analysing the lower tail of the size distribution of earnings; and monopoly power may be particularly important in the upper tail, for example in the determination of earnings in professions with restricted entry. Monopolistic pricing by firms has also been seen as of prime importance in the *functional* distribution of income – see for example Kalecki (1939). Indeed such power has an important part to play in the Marxian concept of exploitation and of theories of distribution that are based on 'struggle' between the classes representing different factors of production. The assumption of pure competition is also likely to be inadequate in analysing economics that have a substantial public sector.

(2) Another feature of the orthodox approach which many theorists find unsatisfactory is the assumption of perfect information by individuals and firms. Indeed it is argued that uncertainty is itself a potent force generating inequality in both earned and unearned income alike, in that the rich are not only better able to bear risk but may have superior information which can be exploited in the stock market and the labour market. Moreover, some of the barriers to competition may have been erected by firms in response to such uncertainty.

Hence considerable interest has developed in the distributional implications of recent theories of output, employment and the structure of wages that explicitly incorporate imperfect information.

(3) The last point arises from the second: the predominant interest of the neoclassical orthodox theory of income distribution in smooth adjustments to market clearing equilibria is considered by some writers to be inappropriate to a theory of the functional distribution of income. As a response to this, economists who are strongly influenced by J. M. Keynes's approach to macroeconomics have developed a number of alternative theories of the functional distribution of income using components of the Keynesian system: for example the work of Kaldor (1956) and Pasinetti (1961). Key features of such alternative theories are rule-of-thumb savings decisions by capitalists and workers and a rigid technique by which labour and capital are combined to produce output.

Frank A. Cowell
London School of Economics and Political Science

References
Kaldor, N. (1956), 'Alternative theories of distribution', *Review of Economic Studies*, 23.
Kalecki, M. (1939), *Essays in the Theory of Economic Fluctuations*, London.
Pasinetti, L. L. (1961), 'Rate of profit and income distribution in relation to the rate of economic growth', *Review of Economic Studies*, 29.

Further Reading
Atkinson, A. B. (1983), *The Economics of Inequality*, 2nd edn, London.
Phelps Brown, E. H. (1977), *The Inequality of Pay*, London.
See also: *distribution of incomes and wealth; firm, theory of; prices, theory of.*

Indexation

Indexation represents an attempt to adjust contracts specified in monetary terms for changes in the value in money. It obviously becomes topical at times when prices are rising fairly rapidly. Kendall (1969) refers to the fact that some American states indexed paper during the War of Independence. More recently the French Government has issued loan stocks linked to the price of particular commodities such as electricity or gold, and after some experimental indexed borrowing, in 1981 the UK Government issued indexed loan stocks, whose redemption value and interest payments were indexed to the Retail Price Index. In so far as the index is a good indicator of the value of money, the implication is that it is possible to lend on terms which guarantee a real return.

One might think that indexation is more important for long-term contracts than for short-term ones, because the importance of it depends on the magnitude of movements in prices during the life of the contract. Thus indexation of wages might be seen as unimportant because wages can always be renegotiated. But this argument ignores the link between wages and prices. If wage and salary earners can be persuaded to accept low pay increases because they are also to be compensated for changes in the price level, it may be possible to move smoothly from a state of rapid to one of low inflation. Indexation of wages could therefore form an important part of a policy of disinflation. However, because it has the effect of introducing extra rigidity into real wages, and because it institutionalizes inflation, some authors are highly critical of any form of indexation. A general survey of the topic is provided by Dornbusch and Simonsen (1983).

Martin Weale
University of Cambridge

References
Dornbusch, R. and Simonsen, M. H. (1983), *Inflation, Debt and Indexation*, Cambridge, Mass.

Kendall, M. G. (1969), 'The early history of index numbers', *Journal of the International Statistical Institute*, 37.
See also: *index numbers*.

Index Numbers

Index numbers are constructed essentially as a way of representing a vector of variables by means of a single scalar variable. Clearly there is no uniquely correct way of accomplishing this transformation, and thus a considerable discussion on the implications of different approaches has developed. Economic statisticians have been particularly concerned with two types of scalar representation of vectors: (1) attempts have been made to represent changes in prices by a single price index, and (2) to reduce movements in quantities to a single quantity index, although of course on occasions one may want to reduce other variables to a simple scalar form.

Historically the problem of measuring price movements preceded the quantity analog. The former has always been a more sensitive issue. Early discussion on the subject tended to consider the price of just one commodity, often that of gold. A reduction in the gold content of coinage achieved through debasement of the currency was regarded as the same thing as an increase in the price level. In the last decade of the eighteenth century, the United Kingdom suspended the convertibility of paper money into gold. The subsequent debate on the inflation of prices was then focused on the price of gold bullion in terms of paper money.

The measurement of the price level with reference to one particular price may have been a useful way to determine the magnitude of a sudden marked debasement, and it is still used under circumstances where the value of currency is falling rapidly. (The tendency in Israel to fix prices in US dollars can be seen as an example of this.) However, it is scarcely satisfactory for comparisons over a longer period in which relative prices can change a great deal. It is in order to cope with this problem that the theory of price indices has been developed.

A price index attempts to compare the price level at one time with that of another period, or to compare relative prices in two different places. It is thus always measured relative to a base level (usually 100) and is not absolute in any sense. Early price indices relied on the simple sum of prices divided by the sum of prices in the base period $\Sigma p_t/\Sigma p_0$, or the simple arithmetic average of relative prices $^1/_n\Sigma(p_t/p_0)$ (p_t represents current prices and p_0 base prices). Neither of these is very satisfactory because some commodities are clearly more important than others. If one is trying to measure the change in price of national consumption, it is not very sensible to give the same importance to items which occupy only a small part in the consumption basket as to those which feature prominently. Although the idea of weighting so as to reflect relative importance can be traced back to the early nineteenth century, it is the mid-nineteenth century proposals of Laspeyres and Paasche which remain of great practical importance to the present day. Laspeyres suggested that one should observe the quantities bought in the base period, and derive the price index, I_t^L, as the ratio of their cost in the current period to that in the base period. $I_t^L = \Sigma p_t q_0/\Sigma p_0 q_0$, where p_t, p_0 are as defined above and q_0 are base period quantities. Paasche proposed current rather than base period weights yielding the price index I_t^P as $I_t^P = \Sigma p_t q_t/\Sigma p_0 q_t$.

Most countries which publish consumer price indices adopt the Laspeyres index because, although the prices have to be measured on each occasion an index is calculated, the quantities used as weights only need to be calculated once, usually from an expenditure survey. In any case the time needed to process an expenditure survey means it is not possible to produce a timely Paasche price index. However, it is clear that the weights used in a Laspeyres index can become stale. Expenditure will tend to shift towards goods which become relatively cheaper, and thus a Paasche price index will normally be lower than a Laspeyres index and the gap will tend to increase over time as the Laspeyres weights become increasingly outdated. This problem is usually resolved by updating the weights periodically. A link can be made by calculating indices for one period based on both old and new weights. The United Kingdom is perhaps unusual in updating the weights in its Retail Price Index every year, based on the average consumption pattern in the three previous years. But even here the Laspeyres weights can be very unsuitable if, for example, a seasonal food becomes scarce, with a high price in one particular year.

Quantity indices are constructed in a similar fashion to price indices. When measuring quantities of goods which are broadly similar, simple aggregation is often used. (Steel output is measured by tonnes of steel produced and car output by number of cars, despite the fact that a Mini is very different from a Rolls Royce.) But where very different items are aggregated, some form of weighting is needed. The most common systems used are again derived from Laspeyres and Paasche. The Laspeyres quantity index, J^L_t, is constructed by weighting the quantities by base period prices, $J^L_t = \Sigma q_t p_0 / \Sigma q_0 p_0$, while the Paasche index is calculated using current prices as weights, $J^P_t = \Sigma q_t p_t / \Sigma q_0 p_t$. Since the quantities will tend to be largest for those goods whose prices have risen least, if one is constructing an index of national output, for example, the Laspeyres index will again exceed the Paasche index.

But neither index is completely satisfactory. For multiplying a Laspeyres price index by the same quantity index does not yield the ratio of current to base period values. Instead one must multiply the Paasche price index by the Laspeyres quantity index to obtain the ratio of values. In order to remedy this and a number of other defects, various combinations of the two have been proposed, although these are not greatly used in practice.

Nevertheless, the theoretical development of index numbers has continued. Thus Barnett (1981) deals with the problem of constructing a quantity index of monetary aggregates. Allen (1975) provides a detailed reference on index numbers, while the work of Diewert (1976) and Afriat (1977) contributes further theoretical development of the subject.

Martin Weale
University of Cambridge

References

Afriat, S. N. (1977), *The Price Index*, Cambridge.

Allen, R. D. G. (1975), *Index Numbers in Theory and Practice*, Chicago.

Barnett, W. A. (1981), 'Economic monetary aggregates: an application of index number theory', *Journal of Econometrics (Supplement)*.

Diewart, W. E. (1976), 'Exact and superlative index numbers', *Journal of Econometrics*.

Indifference Curves

Indifference curve analysis is now a standard part of the economist's diagrammatic tool kit. Alongside an indifference curve a consumer is equally satisfied with the different bundles of goods available to him. These curves are normally drawn with quantities of goods on each axis and they are derived from the utility function, say

$$u = u\,(x, y)$$

by taking the total differential and setting the change in utility equal to zero:

$$du = \frac{\partial y}{\partial x}\,dx + \frac{\partial u}{\partial y}\,\partial y = O$$

The slope of the indifference curve:

$$\frac{dy}{dx} = \frac{\partial u/\partial x}{\partial u/\partial y}$$

This is the ratio of the marginal utilities of the two goods and is known as the marginal rate of substitution. It is normally also assumed that the marginal rate of substitution declines as the quantity of a good consumed increases, giving the indifference curves their normal convex to the origin shape. Indifference curve analysis was first introduced by Edgeworth (1881) and was popularized by John Hicks (1937). Although indifference curves are deeply rooted in the theory of utility maximization, attempts were made to demonstrate that they could be derived directly from the axiom of revealed preference without mention of the concept utility. It is now agreed that the existence of indifference curves implies the existence of a utility function. This means that indifference curve analysis must be seen as a teaching tool to illustrate the much wider and deeper results of consumer theory based on utility maximization.

Ray Barrell
University of Southampton

References
Edgeworth, F. Y. (1881), *Mathematical Psychics*, London.
Hicks, J. R. (1937), *Value and Capital*, Oxford.

Industrialization and Deindustrialization

The term industrialization is meant to denote a phase in economic development in which capital and labour resources shift both relatively and absolutely from agricultural activities into industry, especially manufacturing. The rise in the factory system, increasing urbanization, and movement from rural areas partly describe the nature of the process. Agricultural employment undergoes an absolute decline as the rapid growth of productivity, coupled with the relatively slow growth in demand for agricultural output, generate 'surplus labour' in the agricultural sector. The expanding industrial sector, in turn, pulls in the surplus agricultural employment as the output of industry takes on increasing importance. W. Arthur Lewis (1954) was one of the first economists to conceptualize the process of growth and development as the rise of industry made possible by an abundance of cheap labour in agriculture prepared to move to industry when jobs opportunities became available.

Industrialization was a noticeable feature of many economies as early as the second half of the nineteenth century and became a post-Second World War feature of almost all the mature capitalist economies until the late 1960s. Employment in industry and manufacturing in these countries rose both as a share of total employment and absolutely. By the early 1970s, industrial manufacturing employment as a share of total employment began to fall almost everywhere, and in some mature capitalist economies there was a decline in levels of employment. In terms of employment patterns, it can be said that a process of 'deindustrialization' had set in in capitalist (and many communist) countries, even before the period of stagnation and recession of the 1970s and 1980s.

Accompanying these movements in industrial employment has been the rise, both absolutely and relatively, of employment in the service sector. Here the pattern has been universally consistent and pronounced. Relative and absolute employment in the service sector has risen steadily over a period when industrial employment first rose and then fell.

A clue to understanding these employment patterns is found in the relative growths of sectoral outputs and productivities during the growth process. Contrary to the predictions of many, the distribution of final output between goods and services has not shifted appreciably towards services. Nor has the distribution of consumer expenditures shifted noticeably towards the consumption of services. The rates of growth of demand and output for all final goods has been only slightly less than that for final services, and consumer expenditures on goods has grown with expenditures on consumer services. The shifting distribution of employment away from industry towards the service sector can be attributed to lower rates of growth of productivity in the service sector than in the goods-producing industrial sector.

Thus, the process of economic growth in mature capitalist economies can be characterized as one of deruralification and industrialization followed by deindustrialization. Both the shift of labour resources out of agriculture and that eventually out of industry have been caused by very similar underlying forces. Rates of growth of demand for what labour produced in each sector, relative to the rates of growth of productivity, reduced labour requirements, first in agriculture and then in industry.

Much discussion in economics surrounds the question of whether deindustrialization should be a cause of concern. Often those concerned cite the slow rate of growth of labour productivity in the service sector, arguing that as a larger share of the labour force takes employment in this sector, the overall rate of growth of productivity must slow down.

A more serious concern has been voiced by those who

distinguish between a slowing down in the rate of employment of labour in industry because of an acceleration in productivity growth, and a similar retardation due to a slowing down in the rate of growth of demand for industrial output. This distinction is considered important by economists who focus on a possible balance of payments constraint that acts to prevent full employment.

Thus, the lower the rate of unemployment in an economy, the higher will be the demand for imports from abroad. If the rate of growth of exports of this economy is less than the growth of imports at full employment, measures must be taken to reduce import demand. The most effective response is to create unemployment through restrictive demand policies.

If the slow rate of growth of employment in industry is due to an abnormally low growth of demand for industrial output, this will likely be due in part to a slow growth in demand for the country's exports of industrial goods. A payments constraint is likely to be in effect in this case, and high unemployment is the result. In contrast, if productivity growth is abnormally high, contributing to a slow growth in employment, then the growth of demand of industrial output both in the home market and abroad may, and indeed is likely to be, high, allowing the economy to pursue full employment goals. Deindustrialization need not be a cause for concern in this case, as full employment can be maintained at the same time as labour is released from industry for employment in the service sector.

Since the early 1970s deindustrialization has speeded up as a result of world-wide stagnation. This has to a large extent been due to the slowing down in the growth of world trade ultimately caused by the restrictive demand policies pursued almost everywhere. Obviously this source of deindustrialization is also a cause for concern as it too is accompanied by the existence of widespread unemployment. Slowing down world-wide deindustrialization is dependent upon ending the current world-wide recession and reducing unemployment in all sectors.

John Cornwall
Dalhousie University

Reference
Lewis, W. A. (1954), 'Economic development with unlimited supplies of labour', *The Manchester School*.

Further Reading
Blackaby, F. (ed.) (1979), *Deindustrialization*, London.
See also: *economic growth*.

Inflation and Deflation

Inflation is generally taken to be the rise of all or most prices, or, put the other way round, the fall of the general purchasing power of the monetary unit. For almost fifty years inflation had been continuous in the United Kingdom, and nearly continuous in the United States, consumers' prices having in that time risen more than twentyfold in the former country and more than eightfold in the latter. Only the official prices in some of the centrally planned economies have escaped the worldwide trend.

The corresponding sense of deflation – the general fall of prices – is less familiar because it has not been experienced for some time, though deflation prevailed in most countries from the early 1920s to the mid-1930s, and in many for long periods in both the earlier and the later nineteenth century. At present, deflation is perhaps more often used to refer to a fall in total money income or in the total stock of money, or, more loosely, to falls in their rate of growth. Inflation is sometimes used in corresponding, looser, senses.

The idea that the value, or purchasing power, of money depends simply on the amount of it in relation to the amount of goods goes back in a fairly clear form at least to the mid-eighteenth century. So long as money consisted wholly, or mainly, of gold and/or silver coins, the application of this doctrine was easy. A reasonably convincing account of the main changes in price-trend even in the nineteenth century can be given in terms of the gold discoveries of the mid-century and those (together with the ore-processing innovations) of its last decade, set against the continuous rise of physical output of goods. From early on, however, paper claims on trusted debtors began to constitute further means of payment, and such claims, in the form of liabilities of banks and quasi-banking institutions, have now replaced 'commodity money' (coined gold or silver, circulating at virtually its bullion value) almost completely. This makes the definition of money harder – inevitably somewhat arbitrary. Moreover, the supply of 'money', though subject also to other influences, has always been to a considerable extent responsive to the demand for it, so that it cannot be taken as independently given.

The simplest kind of modern inflationary process is that where a government, perhaps for war purposes, needs to acquire an increased flow of goods and services, and pays at least partly for it with newly printed money (in practice, borrowed from the banking system). If the economy was fully employed to start with, and if we exclude the possibility of the need being met by imports, the effect is to raise prices in proportion to the increase in total (government and non-government) expenditure. Since the money spent by the government goes into private hands, private expenditure rises, and the government can get an increased share of the national real output only by printing money faster and faster to keep ahead in the race. In the absence of complications from price rigidities and taxation, an indefinite exponential inflation is generated. In practice, such complications exist and slow the process down; governments often try to increase price-rigidity by price control, which has usually to be supplemented by rationing. Inflation can, however, become completely explosive in the extreme cases of 'hyperinflation', like that in Germany in 1923, and the even bigger one in Hungary in 1946, when prices eventually doubled (or more) each day. These hyperinflations were assisted by special circumstances: their very speed made revenue collection ineffective, so that nearly all government expenditure had to be financed by new money; expectations of their continuation made for very rapid adjustment of wages and salaries to the rate of inflation, and the disruption of the economy (by a general strike in one case, foreign occupation in the other) reduced the real flow of goods for which the government and other spenders were competing. True hyperinflation has occurred only where something like this last condition has been present.

More usually, inflation has to be considered in the light of the fact that prices are formed in different ways. The prices of many raw materials and foodstuffs, in the world market, are flexible and strongly and quickly influenced by supply and demand conditions. The great upward surge of these prices in 1972–4 was induced partly by the boom in industrial production and demand (which, however, was no greater in relation to trend than the one of four or five years earlier), partly by particular conditions affecting mainly cereals – the breakdown a few years earlier of the World Wheat Agreement, the widespread running down of stocks thereafter, and the failure of the harvest in the USSR. Petroleum, the price of which quadrupled, is a special case; its price is 'administered' rather than formed in the market, but the administration of it had passed from the international oil companies to the Organization of Petroleum Exporting Countries (OPEC). In addition, the outlook both for future discoveries of oil and for alternative sources of energy (on which a rational pricing of oil largely depends) had worsened. The immediate occasion for the biggest oil price increase, of course, was the Arab-Israeli war of 1973. (Events in Iran caused another increase in 1979.)

In contrast, the prices of manufactures, though also largely administered rather than determined on 'auction' principles in free markets, seem to be governed fairly closely by costs of production, which depend on wages, raw material and fuel costs, and labour productivity.

The determination of wages is more complex. They are hardly anywhere formed on the 'market-clearing' principle that unemployed workers will underbid current rates until they get jobs; labour solidarity and the need for a minimum of security and trust in the relations of employers with existing employees are too great for that. In fact, collective bargaining determines most wages in some countries (three-quarters of them in the UK), and even where the proportion is lower, as in the US, the main collective agreements exercise widespread influence as 'price-leaders'. The result is that wage claims – and settlements – show considerable sensivity to rises in the cost of living, but that they also show a tendency to creep upward in response to the natural ambitions of trade unionists and their leaders, and sometimes as a result of jockeying for relative position between different trades.

The most noteworthy attempt to generalize about wage-inflation was that of A. W. Phillips (1958), who derived empir-ically, from British data, a negative relation between the level of unemployment and the rate of wage increases, which was for a time thought by some to be practically usable evidence of a possible policy 'trade-off'. Unfortunately, within ten years of its formulation current data began to show that the 'Phillips Curve' in the UK (and also in the US, though the same is not true, for instance, of Germany) was shifting rapidly upwards – the unemployment rate needed to keep wage-inflation down to a given level was rising. At the same time, Milton Friedman (1968) argued that such a relation was inherently implausible; experience of wage-inflation would lead people to expect more of the same, and so raise bids and settlements. The curve would become vertical, only one rate of unemployment (the 'natural' rate) being consistent with a rate of wage-inflation that was not either accelerating upwards or accelerating downwards. Examination of evidence from a number of countries suggests that the extent to which experience leads to expectations which have this effect varies greatly, and the time taken to convince people that inflation will continue, rather than subside, is also variable, but has often been a matter of years or even decades rather than months. Attempts to explain the formation of wages econometrically have been only partially successful.

From early in the post-war years, various governmental attempts were made to curb the tendency towards inflationary wage increases in conditions of low unemployment. Exhor-tation, informal agreements with trade unions or employers' organizations, legislative limits, temporary wage freezes, confer-ences in which potential negotiators were confronted with the average increases the economy was estimated to be able to bear without inflation, have all been tried somewhere, singly or in combination, sometimes in succession, in the United States and the countries of Western Europe. The results have been mixed. The more drastic policies have sometimes been successful, but only temporarily, and there has been some rebound afterwards. Nevertheless, some countries, notably Austria and Germany, have achieved relatively high degrees of wage-restraint and low average levels of inflation over a long period with the help of their institutional arrangements. Japan has also been successful (with one or two lapses), largely because in the large firms, guarantees of employment reconcile employees to arrangements which make their earnings sensitive to conditions in the product markets.

It is important to distinguish between inflation which arises from demand for a country's final output ('demand-pull') and that which comes, immediately at least, from rises in its import prices or in its labour costs of production ('cost push'). The former tends to increase output, the latter to depress it.

It is natural to ask how 'cost-push' can raise prices in a country without a concomitant rise in the supply of money. Indeed, some writers do not recognize cost-push as a useful concept in explaining inflation, and the monetarist school associated with Milton Friedman (but with many and various subdivisions) holds, generally, that the price level varies with the supply of money, and could be controlled, without detriment to the level of real output and employment, by increasing the money supply uniformly in line with the estimated physical capacity of the economy.

The relevant facts are complex. Controlling the supply of money is not easy; money is created by commercial bank lending, which will normally respond in some degree to demand, and central banks cannot fail to act as lenders of last resort to the commercial banks without risking collapse of the monetary system. The need for increased money payments, whether created by a rise in import prices or by an increase in physical output, can be and normally is met, to a substantial extent, by more rapid turnover of money (increase in the velocity of circulation) rather than by increase in the stock of money – though this a short-term accommodation, normally reversed eventually. 'Tightness' in the supply of money curtails spending plans, and normally reduces physical output and employment before (and usually more than) it reduces prices, at least in the short run of two to four years. In the longer run, tightness of money tends to induce a proliferation of 'quasi-monies', the liabilities of institutions outside the banking system as for the time being defined.

Since the mid-1970s, control of the growth of the money stock as a means of controlling inflation has been much in vogue. Experience has shown the difficulty of hitting the target rates of increase, for the reasons just stated, and has demonstrated, not for the first time, that monetary stringency, sometimes combined with parallel fiscal policies, reduces inflation only at the cost of severe unemployment and the reduction of growth in real living standards.

In contrast with the damage to output which seems to be inseparable from deflationary policies (though its severity varies greatly with the institutional arrangements in the country concerned), it is hard to demonstrate any comparable material damage from, at all events, moderate demand-pull inflation (or moderate cost-push inflation which is 'accommodated' by sufficient creation of purchasing power). It can cause arbitrary changes in income distribution, but they are not normally of a kind to depress output (rather the contrary) and they are mostly avoidable by suitable indexing arrangements. The worst aspect of any prolonged inflation is its tendency to accelerate, through the conditioning of expectations, and this is a serious problem, even though, as already noted, the extreme phenomenon of hyperinflation has occurred only where the economy has been disrupted by some external cause. Inflation is, however, unpopular even with those to whom it does no material harm; it is certainly inconvenient not to be able to rely upon the real value of the money unit, and it may create an illusion of impoverishment even when money incomes are periodically and fairly closely adjusted to it.

In the present writer's view, some, at least, of the main market economies can avoid inflation without the depressing concomitants of deflationary policies only if they are able to develop permanent incomes policies, or modify their wage- and salary-fixing institutions, so as to enjoy reasonably full employment without upward drift of labour costs such as became established in them at least by the end of the 1960s. But it must be remembered that the severest general peacetime inflation on record, that of the 1970s, was also largely propelled by supply and demand maladjustments in the world economy, plus special circumstances in the oil industry. This experience points to the need for better co-operation between the main industrial countries to stabilize the growth rate of their total activity, and for some co-ordinated forward planning of aggregate supplies of the main raw materials, fuels and foodstuffs. This would require a programme of international co-operation perhaps even more ambitious than that which, from the end of the Second World War, made possible a generation of unparalleled economic progress.

A. J. Brown
University of Leeds

References

Friedman, M. (1968), 'The role of monetary policy', *American Economic Review*, 58.

Phillips, A. W. (1958), 'The relationship between unemployment and the rate of money wage-rates in the United Kingdom, 1861–1957', *Economica*, 25.

Further Reading

Bosworth, B. P. and Lawrence, R. Z. (1982), *Commodity Prices and the New Inflation*, Washington.

Brown, A. J. (1955), *The Great Inflation 1939–51*, Oxford.

Brown, A. J. (1985), *World Inflation Since 1950*, Cambridge.

Fleming, J. S. (1976), *Inflation*, Oxford.

Organization for Economic Co-operation and Development (1977), *Towards Full Employment and Price Stability* (the 'McCracken Report'), London.

Trevithick, J. A. (1977), *Inflation: A Guide to the Crisis in Economics*, Harmondsworth.

See also: *monetarism; Phillips Curve; stagflation.*

Informal Economy
See Black Economy.

Innovation

The rather specialized meaning given to innovation in economics and other social science disciplines does not correspond precisely to the everyday use of the term. Since Schumpeter, economists generally use innovation to describe the first introduction of any new product, process or system into the economy. In Schumpeter's terminology these include *managerial* and *organizational* innovations as well as *technical* innovations, but in practice the emphasis of most innovation studies has been on technical innovations.

Schumpeter distinguished sharply between *invention* and *innovation*. Many inventions, both patented and non-patented, never reach the point of commercial application. Although Schumpeter's usage is widely accepted, an element of ambiguity remains: the expression 'innovation' is used to describe the whole process of development of an invention and launch of a new product or process (as in the 'management of innovation'); it is also used to identify the precise date of introduction of such new products and processes.

Schumpeter's taxonomy extended beyond the stage of first commercial introduction to the whole process of *diffusion* of innovations through a population of potential adopters. As with all such distinctions, the separation of the three stages (invention, innovation and diffusion) can be overemphasized. Attempts to develop and launch a new product, based on one or several inventions, may lead to still further inventions: the diffusion of any innovation generally involves further improvement, inventions and innovations. Nevertheless, the usefulness of Schumpeter's threefold classification is generally recognized and has been adopted in most social science research which attempts to understand the process of technical change.

All schools of economic theory and sociology have recognized the importance of technical and social innovation for the long-term growth and efficiency of firms and of nations, but in practice only Schumpeter and his followers have placed it at the centre of their analysis. Schumpeter insisted that technological competition through new and improved products and processes was an order of magnitude more important than 'normal' price competition between firms, which was the subject of most orthodox theory. This fundamental insight of Schumpeter's has led ultimately to a drastic revision of the traditional theory of the firm in the work of Nelson and Winter (1982).

An equally important consequence of the recognition of the central importance of innovation in the competitive process is the revision of conventional theories of international trade. Since Posner's first revisionist assault on the factor proportions theory in 1959, empirical research has increasingly confirmed the role of technology innovation in explaining the pattern of international trade. Hufbauer (1966) and Soete (1981) have demonstrated that technological gap theories of foreign trade have far greater explanatory power, both for individual product groups and generally for the greater part of OECD trade in manufactured goods.

The greatly increased emphasis on the management of innovation within firms and of innovation and technology policies at government level is another consequence of the recognition of the role of innovation in effective competition, both at firm level and at international level.

Finally neo-Schumpeterian innovation studies have sought to demonstrate a relationship between the introduction of major innovations (new technology systems) and long-term cyclical developments in the world economy.

Innovation studies remain an active and rapidly developing research area pursued by all branches of the social sciences and technologists as well as by inter-disciplinary groups, such as those at MIT, Sussex, Karlsruhe, Lund and Aalborg.

C. Freeman
University of Sussex

References
Hufbauer, G. (1966), *Synthetic Materials and Theory of International Trade*, Cambridge, Mass.

Nelson, R. R. and Winter, S. (1982), *An Evolutionary Theory of Economic Change*, Cambridge, Mass.

Posner, M. (1961), 'International trade and technical change', *Oxford Economic Papers*, 13.

Soete, L. (1981), 'A general test of technological gap trade theory', *Weltwirtschaftliches Archiv*, Band 117.

Further Reading

Freeman, C. (ed.) (1982), *The Economics of Industrial Innovation*, London.

See also: *Schumpeter*.

Input-Output Analysis

An input-output table records transactions between industries, and input-output (I-O) analysis uses these data to examine the interdependence between sectors and the impact which changes in one sector have on others. This can be seen as a quantitative development of neoclassical general equilibrium analysis used by economists such as L. Walras. Its origins can be traced back to Quesnay's 'Tableau Économique' in 1758. Presently, and for almost half a century, the key figure has been Wassily Leontief, who completed the first I-O table in the US in 1936 and has done much pioneering development work.

An I-O table, such as that shown in figure 1, records in its columns the purchases by each industry, A, B, and C (that is, the inputs into the production process), and in the rows the sales

Payments to \ Payments by	Industry A	B	C	Final demand	Total output
Industry A		20	45	35	100
Industry B	30		30	140	200
Industry C		80		70	150
Factors of production	70	100	75		
Total input	100	200	150		

Figure 1

by each industry. Also included are sales to final purchasers and payments for factors of production (labour and capital) thus showing the necessary integration into the rest of the national accounts.

The production of a commodity requires inputs from other industries, known as *direct inputs*, and from the I-O table a matrix of *technical coefficients* can be derived which shows direct inputs per unit of output, for example, in matrix A below .1 = 20/200. In turn the production of each of these commodities used as inputs requires inputs from the other industries, and this second round of production then imposes demands on other industries, and so on. All these subsequent inputs are known as *indirect inputs*. Tracing all these ramifications is a laborious process in a large I-O system, but it can be shown mathematically that the solution lies in the matrix $(I-A)^{-1}$ where I is the unit matrix and A is the matrix of direct input coefficients. Such a matrix, known as the *Leontief Inverse*, shows in its columns the total direct plus indirect inputs required per unit of output of the column industry. This matrix is the key to I-O analysis as it encapsulates the interdependence of industries in the economy. For instance, a demand from, say, consumers for 1000 units of A requires the production of 1077 units of A, 351 of B and 141 of C (using col. A of matrix $(I-A)^{-1}$). The extra 77 units of A are needed by B and C to produce the inputs which A takes from them and which they take from each other.

Using such a model it is possible to calculate the effect of a change in demand in an economy on the output in all industries. The analysis can be extended to cover the inputs of factors of production which are closely related to the output levels, and in this way the precise effect which a change in demand for one product has on employment in that industry and in all others can be calculated with perhaps additional information on types of skill. The I-O table can be extended to include purchases of imports, thus enabling the import requirements of any given level of demand to be calculated; of particular interest to the balance of payments is the import content of exports.

Just as the production of a commodity has ramifications back through the chain of production, so a change in the price of an input has effects forward on to many other products, both directly and indirectly. The price of any product is determined by the prices of its inputs, and these can all in turn be traced back to the 'price' of labour, capital and imports, using the formal Leontief Inverse. It is thus possible to calculate the effects on final prices of, for example, an increase in wages in one industry or of a change in import prices due perhaps to changes in the exchange rate or changes in foreign prices.

All the above aspects of input-output analysis can be combined into a planning model which will give a comprehensive and internally consistent picture of the economy 5–10 years ahead. This enables policy makers to see the implications which, say, a certain growth in the economy has for particular industries, employment, prices, the balance of payments and so on, and to locate key sectors. Most countries compile I-O tables, usually identifying fifty or more industries, although models have recently lost some of their popularity in Western Europe. They are, however, extensively used in the USSR and Eastern Europe and in developing economies. Here they are well suited to measuring the impact of marked changes in demand and supply patterns which are expected. Further refinements of I-O analysis include disaggregation by region and making a dynamic model so that investment needs are incorporated.

A. G. Armstrong
University of Bristol

Further Reading
Leontief, W. (1966), *Input-Output Economics*, New York.
United Nations (1973), *Input-Output Tables and Analysis, Studies in Methods*, New York.
See also: *Walras*.

Institutional Economics

Institutional economics became prominent in the United States in the late nineteenth and early twentieth centuries after the science of anthropology had become an established scientific discipline. For unlike orthodox economists, who patterned their science after the physical sciences, Thorstein Veblen and later institutionalists patterned their science after anthropology. Institutionalists define economics as a study of a particular aspect of culture concerned with the supplying or provisioning of society with the flow of goods and services needed by individuals to make adjustments to the problems met in the non-social and social environments. In short, institutional economics is the science of social provisioning.

Besides adopting an anthropological approach supported by a pragmatic philosophy, institutionalists have made a basic paradigmatic change. This change involves substituting their concept of process for the orthodox economists' concept of equilibrium as a way of grasping the nature of the real economic world. This substitution relates the current economic situation to a future state of the economy. When the institutionalists take the economic system to be an evolving open-ended process, they explain the nature of this process, the factors that cause it to evolve, and the directions in which it may be moving.

The institutionalists consider the economic system to be a cultural entity that changes its structural and functional features over historical time, and that exhibits considerable social coherence. While this processual entity is not itself a static equilibrium, at any one point in historical time a cross-section of it may be partially analysed from an equilibrium viewpoint. Consequently institutionalists do not dispense with the equilibrium analyses of orthodox economists. Instead they place these inherited analyses in the larger framework of an evolving process.

Institutionalists explain the nature of economic evolution by developing a theory of technological interpretation. They are well aware that many other factors than scientific advance and technological change contribute to economic evolution, but they nevertheless assign special importance to these latter two developmental factors. The institutionalists avoid the charge of excessive technological determination by adopting a multiple factor theory of change, in which scientific advance and technological developments are only two factors leading to structural and functional change.

Since the economic system is an open-ended process, there is the question of the direction in which this process may be moving. It is at this point that the institutionalists introduce the value problem. According to their interpretation, the values of the participants in economic activities play a major role in the course of economic evolution. Rather than imposing their own values on the nation's economy, institutionalists analyse objectively the value systems of individuals and groups which influence economic activities.

Institutionalists view economics as an interdisciplinary cultural science that borrows not only from other social sciences, but also from other types of economics. It draws upon their contributions in the larger cultural framework of an evolving open-ended process.

Allan G. Gruchy
University of Maryland

Further Reading
Veblen, T. (1919), *The Place of Science in Modern Civilisation*, New York.
Clark. J. M. (1936), *Preface to Social Economics*, New York.
Ayres, C. E. (1944), *The Theory of Economic Progress*, Chapel Hill, North Carolina.

Interest

The charge made (or price paid) for the use of loanable funds is called interest. The rate of interest is the amount payable, usually expressed as a percentage of the principal sum borrowed, per period of time, usually per month, quarter or year. Financial intermediaries will commonly both borrow and lend funds, their profitability being dependent on the difference between the rate which they are willing to pay depositors and the rate they charge borrowers. Interest rates may be calculated on a simple or a compound basis. Simple interest involves a percentage return on the principal per period, whereas compound interest involves a return based on both the principal and accumulated interest, already paid in previous periods.

Interest rates may be fixed, in which case they stay constant throughout the period of the loan, or they may be variable, in which case they may be changed during the period of the loan.

The supply of loanable funds will depend on: the level of savings in the private sector; the rate of growth of bank lending; and, less commonly, on the size of the public financial surplus, which depends on the excess of government revenue over its expenditure. Demand for loanable funds can come from consumers, businesses and the government, due to the need to finance the Public Sector Borrowing Requirement.

The charging of interest may be rationalized in a number of ways:

(1) The lender is entitled to a share of the profit resulting from the productive use of the loaned funds.

(2) Savers should be rewarded for abstaining from present consumption, which will probably be worth more to them than future consumption.

(3) Lenders should receive a fee for allowing someone else to borrow an asset which provides the service of liquidity.

(4) Lenders should be entitled to a risk premium, because they face the risk of nonrepayment. These factors may also be used to explain the difference between lending and borrowing rates and the fact that different types of financial asset bear different interest rates. In general the shorter the term of the loan and the lower the risk, the lower the rate of interest.

There have been criticisms of the morality of charging interest in the form discussed above. Marx, for example, regarded interest as an element of surplus value, together with rent and profit, which accrued to finance capitalists and as such it stemmed directly from the exploitation of labour by capitalists. Marxist-Leninist regimes have typically had low interest rates; nominally to cover some of the costs of running banks and the payments mechanism. The charging of interest has also been condemned, at times, by followers of various religions, for example Christianity and Islam, the most reviled practices being those linked to private money lenders, usurers, or 'Shylocks'. Marxist objections, however, stem from social rather than religious ethics.

The present revival of Islamic fundamentalism, in Iran, Pakistan and Sudan, for example, has revived criticism of Western-style interest charges. Islam clearly condemns usury, but there is some theological debate concerning whether this means that interest rate charges in general should be prohibited. It would appear that the fundamentalist interpretation has dominated in Pakistan and, more recently, Sudan. The reasons for condemning interest rate charges, given by the fundamentalists, include: their role in reinforcing the accumulation of wealth in the hands of the few, and thereby reducing man's concern for fellow man; the fact that Islam does not permit gain from financial activity unless the beneficiary is also subject to risk of potential loss; and that Islam regards the accumulation of wealth through interest as selfish compared with that accumulated through hard work. These objections, especially the second, would rule out legally guaranteed regular interest payments. It would not, however, rule out equity investment, since this is subject to a return that varies with profit, and equity holders are subject to loss, although they are commonly protected through limited liability. In Pakistan attempts have been made to develop an Islamic banking system in which returns are based on a profit and loss sharing principle, rather than regular guaranteed interest payments, and which are, therefore, akin to the returns on equities.

We have noted that in Western economies with numerous financial assets there is a whole array of interest rates. These do, however, tend to move up and down together, and so it is possible to consider, in the abstract, the determination of the level of the rate of interest. Keynesian economists regard the interest rate as being determined by the equation of the demand for and supply of money. Classical economists claimed that it was determined by the interaction of the demand for funds, by investors, and the supply of funds, by savers. Keynes criticized this view, arguing that changes in national income were primarily instrumental in bringing about an equilibrium between savings and investment through their influence on the supply of, and demand for, loanable funds.

A distinction is often made between the nominal and the real

interest rate. The real rate is the nominal rate less the expected
rate of inflation; although it is sometimes approximated by
subtracting the actual rate of inflation from the nominal rate.
The concept of the natural rate of interest is also often used. It
is the rate of interest that would hold in an economy which was
in a noninflationary equilibrium. The rate of interest, being the
contractual income expressed as a percentage of the nominal
value of the security, is to be differentiated from the yield of a
security, which is a percentage relationship of its income to its
current market price.

Andy Mullineux
University of Birmingham

Further Reading
Bain, A. D. (1981), 'Interest rates', in *The Economics of the
Financial System*, Oxford.
Karsten, I. (1982), 'Islam and financial intermediation' *IMF
Staff Papers*, vol. 29.
Wilczynski, J. (1978), *Comparative Monetary Economics*, London.
See also: *credit; financial system.*

International Monetary System

The international monetary system encompasses the arrangements and mechanisms governing monetary and financial
relationships between countries. Under alternative 'systems'
these may be either precise and reasonably well defined (as
under the Gold Standard and, to a lesser extent, the Bretton
Woods arrangements in the period 1944–73) or flexible, as has
generally been the case since 1973. The monetary relationships
between countries are different from those between regions of
a country, and raise different issues of analysis and policy.
This is because: (1) countries have degrees of policy autonomy
(particularly with respect to monetary policy) not conferred
upon regions of a nation-state; (2) different currencies are
involved and their exchange values may change in such a way
as to alter the economic and financial relationship between
countries; (3) there is no automatic financing of countries'

payments imbalances unlike between regions within a country, and, for this reason, (4) there is pressure on nation states to adjust balance of payments imbalances.

The arrangements within the international monetary system cover six main areas. In various ways, either explicitly or implicitly, it is these six issues that have dominated developments in the international monetary system and the various debates over reform of prevailing systems:

(1) Central to any system or set of arrangements are *exchange rates* and the extent to which, either because of agreed rules of behaviour or because *ad hoc* decisions are made, central banks intervene in the foreign exchange market to influence the level of exchange rates.

(2) Coupled with the exchange rate is the question of *settlement obligations* when a deficit country's currency is purchased by other central banks. This became a major issue in the early 1970s with the breakdown of the Bretton Woods system following the substantial accumulation of United States dollars by European and Japanese central banks.

(3) A further element in the monetary relations between countries relates to the linked issues of the balance of pressures that exist as between balance of payments *financing and adjustment*, and the extent to which the pressure for adjustment is symmetrical between surplus and deficit countries. Balance of payments adjustment imposes costs on a deficit country both through the particular mechanism adopted, but also because it usually implies a smaller net absorption of real resources from the rest of the world.

(4) The way in which balance of payments *financing* is conducted is a significant issue for international monetary arrangements. In particular, whether financing is undertaken by transferring reserve assets or by borrowing has implications for the growth of international debt and confidence in the international monetary system. One of the factors behind the eventual breakdown of the Bretton Woods system was that a dominant country (the United States) had its persistent payments deficit financed by the central banks of surplus countries purchasing dollars in the foreign exchange market which

were not converted by the American authorities into gold or other reserve asset. A *confidence problem* arose as by the early 1970s the volume of such American liabilities came to exceed the value of the American gold stock. A notable feature of the international monetary system of the 1970s was the financing of balance of payments deficits through borrowing from banks.

(5) The arrangements for satisfying the requirements of central banks to hold *international liquidity* is a significant element. Central in this is the form in which international liquidity is held (and in particular whether certain national currencies are held for this purpose) and the extent to which there are arrangements for the conscious control of the volume of international liquidity, as against conditions where it is largely demand-determined.

(6) Pervading all of the issues identified, there is the question of *management* of the international monetary system and the extent to which it is based upon the acceptance by governments and central banks of agreed rules of behaviour. The 'management' role of supranational organizations (such as the International Monetary Fund) is subject to considerable controversy given its potential implications for the perceptions of national sovereignty.

The several key issues arise because countries (monetary unions) have trade and financial links with one another. This in turn means that policy developments in one country can affect economic conditions in partner countries and, similarly, that the attainment of domestic policy targets can be thwarted by external developments. In practice, most of the problem issues in the international monetary system relate to the consistency of policy targets between countries.

International interdependence necessarily implies that in one way or another *ex post* compatability is secured between countries with respect notably to the balance of payments, the exchange rate and the rate of growth of the money supply. However, these may be secured *ex post* at the expense of some *ex ante* plans not being achieved. This is obvious with respect to the balance of payments, as the sum of separate *ex ante* targets might imply an aggregate world surplus or deficit. In various ways *ex post* these inconsistencies are eliminated. But unless all central banks refrain from foreign exchange market intervention (or can successfully sterilize the monetary effects of such intervention), the same is also true of monetary policies. It is relevant, therefore, to consider how potential conflicts of policy and targets between countries might be minimized through various arrangements for ensuring either *ex ante* consistency, or minimizing the resistance to *ex post* equilibrating mechanisms. Logically, five broad mechanisms or options may be identified: (1) automatic market mechanisms such as floating exchange rates or nonsterilization of balance of payments induced by changes in the money supply; (2) the $(n - 1)$ approach, whereby one country in the system agrees not to have an external target; (3) *ex ante* policy co-ordination designed to ensure consistent targets and compatible means of securing them; (4) an agreement to a precise set of policy rules which indicate what is required of policy makers in specified circumstances; or (5) a multilateral approach, whereby some supranational authority indicates (and possibly enforces) policy measures which have been calculated to ensure consistency and stability in the system. In practice, the mechanisms are likely to be a composite of several.

The Bretton Woods system as it developed in practice was based essentially upon the $(n - 1)$ arrangement with the passive role being played by the United States. Such a system presupposes that the central country agrees not to have an external target, and partners are prepared to accept the hegemony of that country, particularly with respect to monetary policy. It was the latter that proved to be a major weakness in the final years of the Bretton Woods system. The major potential weakness of this mechanism is the moral hazard confronted by the key country, which can largely determine its own policy and targets and in the process impose costs (in terms of nonattainment of targets) on partner countries. For instance, in the monetary sector, with a fixed exchange rate, the rate of growth of the money supply in an integrated group can be determined by the dominant country if, like the United States in the 1960s, it chooses to sterilize the monetary effects of its balance-of-payments position.

For close on thirty years, arrangements in the international monetary system were those outlined in the Bretton Woods agreement of 1944, though the system was operated in practice very differently from the intentions at the outset. The main elements were fixed, but adjustable, exchange rates, with most countries maintaining exchange rates fixed against the United States dollar which became the pivotal currency. International liquidity was held predominantly in dollars which were supplied through a persistent American balance-of-payments deficit.

But the international monetary environment became considerably less certain and predictable over the 1970s, and early in the decade the Bretton Woods arrangements finally disintegrated after almost thirty years. At various times, the fixed-exchange-rate system came under strain as the volume of funds that could move between countries and currencies grew markedly after the general moves towards convertibility in the late 1950s. Towards the end of the 1960s it became increasingly apparent that fixed exchange rates, freedom of international capital flows and independent national control over domestic money supplies were incompatible. The adoption of floating exchange rates in the early 1970s was partly associated with a desire on the part of governments in Europe and elsewhere to determine their monetary policy independently of the United States.

In itself, the Bretton Woods system was potentially stable and had much to commend it. It became, in effect, a dollar standard, and this could have proved durable had Europe been prepared to accept the permanent monetary dominance of America.

Since the breakdown of the Bretton Woods arrangements the international monetary system has operated in an *ad hoc* manner. Attempts at reform in the middle of the 1970s failed to produce a Grand Design new structure similar to that achieved in 1944 which was at the time a response to the turbulance of the 1930s. In the early 1980s, a new 'confidence problem' was emerging and related to the external debt position of a few developing countries. This was a reflection of the shift in the balance of pressures between balance-of-payments financing and adjustment towards the former which had been a notable feature of the previous decade.

David T. Llewellyn
Loughborough University

Further Reading
Tew, J. H. B. (1982), *Evolution of the International Monetary System 1945–81*, London.
Williamson, J. (1977), *The Failure of World Monetary Reform 1971–74*, London.
See also: *balance of payments; devaluation; exchange rate; international trade; reserve currency.*

International Trade

International trade is not intrinsically different from trans-actions in which commodities do not cross national boundaries. Nevertheless, the study of international trade has traditionally constituted a separate branch of microeconomics. It may be distinguished from other branches by its focus on situations where some but not all goods and factors are mobile between countries; and from international macroeconomics by its focus on real rather than nominal variables (trade flows and relative prices rather than exchange rates and money supplies), and by a tendency to examine medium-run issues using equilibrium analysis rather than short-run positions of disequilibrium.

One of the first and most durable contributions to the analysis of international trade is the doctrine of *comparative advantage* due to Ricardo. This is the antecedent of both the normative and positive strands of international trade theory. On the one hand, it postulates that an absolutely inefficient country will neverthe-less gain from trade; on the other hand, it predicts the direction of trade: each country will tend to export those goods which it produces relatively cheaply in the absence of trade. As a positive explanation, the principle has met with some success. However, in its classical form it is open to the objections that it unrealisti-cally assumes production costs are independent of the scale of output, and that it fails to explain why they differ between countries in the first place.

In an attempt to overcome these deficiencies, the Swedish economists Heckscher and Ohlin developed a theory which stressed international differences in *factor endowments* as the basis for comparative advantage and trade. Thus a country which is relatively capital-abundant will tend to export goods which are produced by relatively capital-intensive techniques. Largely through the influence of Samuelson, a highly simplified version of this theory, assuming only two goods and two factors in each country, has come to dominate the textbooks. In this form it is a useful teaching device for introducing some basic concepts of general equilibrium theory but, not surprisingly, it is over-whelmingly rejected by the data. The most notable example of this is the so-called *Leontief Paradox*, an early application by Leontief of his technique of input-output analysis, which found that the presumably capital-abundant United States exported labour-intensive commodities, thus contradicting the theory.

Nevertheless, probably the preferred explanation of trade patterns for most economists is an eclectic theory of comparative advantage along Heckscher-Ohlin lines, allowing for many factors of production, some of them (such as natural resources) specific to individual sectors, as well as for the international differences in technology. Even this theory fails to account adequately for certain features of contemporary international trade, and a variety of special models has been developed to explain different aspects of real-world transactions. Thus, the growth of trade in intermediate goods (as opposed to goods for final consumption) has inspired the theory of *effective protection*, which builds on the insight that an industry benefits from tariffs on its outputs but is harmed by tariffs on its inputs. Attention has also focused on the increased international mobility of factors (in part through the medium of multinational corpor-ations) which in different circumstances may act as a substitute for or a complement to trade. Finally, considerable attention has been devoted to the study of *intra-industry trade*, meaning trade in differentiated products within a single industry cate-gory, typically produced by noncompetitive firms under conditions of increasing returns, and traded between countries with similar technology and factor endowments.

As well as attempting to explain the pattern of trade, positive trade theory also makes predictions about many aspects of open economies. Most notorious of these is the implication of the Heckscher–Ohlin model known as the *factor price equalization theorem*, which predicts that free trade will bring about the equalization of the prices of internationally immobile factors. The empirical irrelevance of this theorem is matched only by the implausibility of the many assumptions required for it to hold. Of greater interest are the predictions of international trade theory concerning such issues as the effects of tariffs and international transfers on foreign and domestic prices, the effects of trade policy on domestic income distribution and the consequences of structural change.

Turning to normative trade theory, its traditional focus has been the merits of free trade relative to autarky, stemming from increased specialization in production and increased efficiency and diversity of choice in consumption. Similar arguments favour partially restricted trade relative to autarky, although the benefits of selective trade liberalization (such as the formation of a customs union) are not as clear-cut. The persistence of protectionist sentiment, despite these theoretical arguments, may be explained by the fact that gains from trade accruing to the economy as a whole are not inconsistent with losses to individual groups, especially owners of factors specific to import-competing sectors.

Two other exceptions to the case for free trade are normally admitted. The *optimal tariff argument* states that a country with sufficient market power can gain by behaving like a monopolist and restricting the supply of its exports. The *infant industry argument* defends transitional protection to enable a new industry to benefit from learning and scale economies. As with many arguments for trade restriction, the latter on closer examination is less an argument against free trade than against *laissez-faire*. Finally, it should be noted that tariffs have declined in importance since the Second World War, due largely to international agreements such as the General Agreement on Tariffs and

Trade (GATT) and the formation of free-trade areas and customs unions such as the European Economic Community (EEC). As a result, many countries now make much greater use of *non-tariff barriers* (such as quotas, health and safety regulations and government procurement policies) as methods of restricting trade.

J. Peter Neary
University College, Dublin

Further Reading
Jones, R. W. and Kenen, P. B. (eds) (1984), *Handbook of International Economics: Volume I*, Amsterdam (see especially Chapter 1: 'The positive theory of international trade', by R. W. Jones and J. P. Neary, and Chapter 2: 'The normative theory of international trade', by W. M. Corden). See also: *free trade; laissez-faire.*

Investment
Investment can be defined as the change in the capital stock over a period of time – normally a year for accounting purposes. It is not to be confused with financial investments; which involves the purchase of financial assets, such as stocks and shares, and is, therefore, more closely connected with the analysis of saving. It is also commonly distinguished from inventory investment, which involves changes in stocks of finished goods, work in progress and raw materials.

Capital investment goods differ from consumption goods in that they yield a flow of services, over a period of time, and these services do not directly satisfy consumer wants but facilitate the production of goods and services, or consumer goods. Although some consumer goods are perishable, a large number provide services over a period of time and are, therefore, akin to investment goods. Such goods are called consumer durables. The existence of various goods that provide flows of services over time presents problems for national income accounting. This is because it is not always clear whether such goods should be classified as investment or consumer goods. Expenditure on land and dwellings, by households, is an example. In the UK such expenditures are treated as investment. Expenditure on plant and machinery is, however, clearly part of (capital) investment, since it either replaces worn-out machinery or adds to productive capacity. Gross investment is total expenditure on capital goods per year and net investment is gross investment net of depreciation – which is the decline in the capital stock due to wear and tear.

A distinction is often drawn between public investment, which is undertaken by the public sector, and private investment. Foreign, or overseas, investment involves the purchase of financial or productive assets in other countries.

A number of theories have been developed to explain the determination of investment demand. These commonly relate to private sector investment demand, since public sector investment may involve other considerations. The importance of investment lies in the fact that a rise in the capital stock of an economy may increase its productive capacity and potential for economic growth. It should be noted that the capital stock is one of a number of factors of production, along with labour and raw materials, which contribute to production and, therefore, that investment is not the sole determinant of growth. Additionally, investment is a major route through which technical progress can be made.

Public investment may be guided by principles other than narrow profit maximization, since the government should take account of social costs and benefits as well as pecuniary ones. Public investment might consequently be undertaken to alleviate unemployment in depressed areas or to encourage technical change. Keynesian economists have argued that public investment can be an important catalyst to economic development and may have a significant role to play in leading an economy out of recession.

Economic literature postulates that there are two major determinants of private investment demand: the rate of interest, and the increase in national income. Other factors clearly influence investment as well: these include wage and tax rates, which affect the relative cost of capital and labour. Assuming that these other influences are constant, however, it is postulated that changes in the rate of interest or national income will cause a change in the desired capital stock and that this will lead to investment.

A change in the rate of interest will influence the desired capital stock by altering the expected profitability of various potential investment expenditures. This can be seen in various ways. Firms may be viewed as forecasting the revenues and costs over the life of the project in which the capital good is to be employed. To do this they must forecast the expected life of the project, the sales volumes and prices and various costs, in each year of the project. The expected project life will depend on both the physical life and the technological life of the capital good. A firm will not wish to operate with obsolete capital goods, since it will be at a cost disadvantage relative to its competitors. Having estimated the expected future flow of profits, and any scrap value that capital good might have at the end of the project's life, the firm will then *discount* this expected income stream. If it discounts it using the market rate of interest, then it will discover the gross present value of the project, and after subtracting the cost of the capital good it will have calculated the net present value. If this is positive, then the profit is acceptable given the risk involved and the attractiveness of alternative projects. A fall in the rate of interest will lead to a rise in the net present value of various projects and will, other things being equal, lead a number of firms to want to buy additional capital goods. In aggregate, the desired capital stock will rise. Keynes explained the influence of the interest rate on investment in a slightly different manner, based on the internal rate of return, or what he called the marginal efficiency of capital. This alternative suggests that firms will find the rate of discount which equates the (discounted) expected flow of returns to the cost of the capital good. If this rate is less than the market rate of interest, then the project is potentially profitable. A fall in the interest rate should, therefore, increase the number of potentially profitable projects and hence the aggregate desired capital stock. If a firm is borrowing funds to finance investment, the interest rate represents the cost of borrowing. If it is financing investment from internal funds, the interest rate represents the *opportunity cost*, since it represents the revenue the firm could, alternatively, receive from financial investment. Such explanations of the determination of investment demand are based on an assumption of fixed interest rates, throughout the life of the project. Financial institutions are, however, increasingly lending at variable rates, and this will further complicate the investment decision by requiring firms to form expectations of interest rates throughout the project's life. It is to be noted that expectations play a major role in determining investment demand, according to this analysis, and that, consequently, a government policy of trying to stimulate investment by reducing the interest rate might not have the desired effect in times of worsening expectations of future profits.

A second major influence on investment demand is believed to be the change in national income. A rise in national income might increase expected sales and lead to a desire to increase productive capacity. The accelerator theory is a more formal explanation of the influence of a rise in national income on investment. It postulates a fixed ratio of capital to output, based on technological considerations, so that output growth should lead to an increase in the desired capital stock. It seems unlikely that an economy's capital to output ratio is fixed over time, since many factors will influence this ratio, such as the relative cost of capital and labour, technical progress, and changes in the relative importance of various sectors of the economy, which may have different capital/output ratios. In its crude form the accelerator theory does not perform well empirically, but in more flexible forms it is more successful at explaining investment.

It is, therefore, clear that a change in the rate of interest or in national income might influence the demand for capital goods and change the aggregate desired capital stock for the economy as a whole. The actual net investment that occurs each year in any economy depends on the rate of depreciation of capital stock, and on the extent to which the increased demand for capital stock is satisfied. This will in turn depend on the ability of the capital goods-producing industry to meet the increased demand; the extent to which the price of capital goods rises in response to the increased demand, thus raising the cost of capital goods and reducing the net present value of investment projects; and the extent to which suitable capital goods can be purchased from abroad.

Andy Mullineux
University of Birmingham

Further Reading

Hawkins, C. J. and Pearce, D. W. (1971), *Capital Investment Appraisal*, London.

Junanker, P. N. (1972), *Investment: Theories and Evidence*, London.

Maurice, R. (ed.) (1968), *National Accounts Statistics: Sources and Methods*, London.

See also: *accelerator principle; capital theory; national income analysis.*

Keynes, John Maynard (1883–1946)

The son of John Neville Keynes, a Cambridge economist, philosopher and administrator, and Florence Ada (Brown), Cambridge's first woman town councillor and later its mayor, Maynard Keynes made contributions that extended well beyond academic economics. After an education at Eton and King's College, Cambridge (BA in mathematics 1905), his first career was that of a civil servant in the India Office (1906–8). Although he soon returned to Cambridge to lecture in economics (1908–20) and be a fellow of King's (1909–46), he never lost his connection with the world of affairs. He served as a member of the Royal Commission on Indian Finance and Currency (1913–14), was a wartime Treasury official eventually in charge of Britain's external financial relations (1915–19), a member of the Macmillan Committee on Finance and Industry (1929–31), a member of the Economic Advisory Council (1930–9), an adviser to the Chancellor of the Exchequer (1940–6) and a director of the Bank of England (1941–6). After 1919, he also had an active career in the world of finance as a company director, insurance company chairman and bursar of King's College, Cambridge. Moreover, under the influence of his Bloomsbury friends, Vanessa Bell and Duncan Grant, as well as Lydia Lopokova of the Diaghilev Ballet whom he married in 1925, he played an active and important role in the cultural life of his time as a patron of the arts, founder of the Arts Theatre, Cambridge (which he gave to the City and University in 1938), trustee of the National Gallery, chairman of the Council for the Encouragement of Music and the Arts, and initiator and first chairman of the Arts Council of Great Britain.

Keynes's reputation as an academic economist arises from work that he started after his fortieth year and published after he was 47. Prior to that, he was much better known as a publicist and commentator on economic affairs, a career he began in 1919 after his resignation as the senior Treasury official at the Paris Peace Conference with his bestselling and influential indictment of the negotiation and terms of the Peace Treaty in *The Economic Consequences of the Peace* (1919). He continued in this popular vein with *A Revision of the Treaty* (1922), *A Tract on Monetary Reform* (1923), *The Economic Consequences of Mr Churchill* (1925), *The End of Laissez-Faire* (1926) and prolific journalism, notably for the liberal *Nation and Athenaeum* (1923–31) and the more socialist *New Statesman and Nation*, for both of which he was chairman of the board. This does not mean that he was unknown as an academic: he was editor of the Royal Economic Society's *The Economic Journal* (1911–45) and the author of *A Treatise on Probability* (1921), a philosophical examination of the principles of reasoning and rational action in conditions of incomplete and uncertain knowledge, the earliest ideas of which date from 1904 when Keynes was strongly influenced by G. E. Moore. Nevertheless, it would be fair to echo Sir Austin Robinson's comment (1947): 'If Maynard Keynes had died in 1925 it would have been difficult for those who knew intimately the power and originality of his mind to have convinced those who had not known him of the full measure of Keynes' ability.'

The bases for Keynes's academic reputation as an economist were his *Treatise on Money* (1930) and *The General Theory of*

Employment, Interest and Money (1936). Both were stages in the development in theoretical terms of the principles which should underlie attempts by governments to achieve economic stability. In the *Treatise*, as in the more popular *Tract*, the main concern was with monetary and price stability and the role that monetary policy alone could play in achieving them. As was common in contemporary monetary economics, Keynes dichotomized the economy into its monetary and real sectors and, on the assumption that money was neutral in the long run, looked for the principles of monetary practice which would ensure price stability, in the *Treatise* case a monetary policy which made the long-term market rate of interest equivalent to the 'natural rate' at which savings equalled investment. This initial approach to the problem was found to be inadequate by Keynes's critics, who included R. G. Hawtrey, F. A. Hayek and D. H. Robertson, as well as a group of younger economists in Cambridge (R. F. Kahn, James Meade, Joan and Austin Robinson, and Piero Sraffa). When convinced of the inadequacies of the *Treatise*, Keynes began reformulating his ideas. The major breakthrough came in 1933 when, contrary to traditional theory, Keynes hit on the crucial role of changes in output and employment in equilibration savings and investment, thus providing the basis for a more general theory than his own or his predecessors' previous work. The new theory seemed to offer the possibility of equilibrium at less than full employment, something missing in previous work. From his 1933 breakthrough, which hinged on the consumption-income relationship implicit in the multiplier, after considerable further work, everything fell into place.

During the last ten years of his life, although his activities were inhibited by a severe heart condition after 1937, Keynes devoted less time to defending and somewhat refining his theoretical views than to seeing them implemented. Even before the outbreak of war in 1939, he had started to influence Treasury thinking in Britain, while his students and his writings were becoming influential in such places as Washington and Ottawa. However, the problems of war finance and post-war planning appear to have been crucial in the spread of his ideas into day-to-day policy making, for as he demonstrated in *How to Pay for the War* (1940) the new ideas when married to another contemporary development – national income and expenditure accounting – provided a powerful new way of thinking about the economy and its management. The resulting 'new economics' put less emphasis than Keynes would have done on the roles of monetary policy and the control of public investment in the achievement of full employment, yet, along with a political determination to avoid the wastes of the inter-war years, it led to widespread official commitments to post-war policies of high or full employment. By then, however, Keynes was less involved in such matters: the last years of his life saw him devoting much more of his efforts to shaping other aspects of the post-war world, most notably the international monetary order of the International Monetary Fund and the World Bank, and to securing Britain's post-war international economic position. Gaining these, or at least a semblance of them, finally exhausted him.

Donald Moggridge
University of Toronto

Reference
Robinson, E. A. G. (1947), 'John Maynard Keynes, 1883–1946', *Economic Journal*, 57.

Further Reading
Harrod, R. F. (1951), *The Life of John Maynard Keynes*, London.
Keynes, J. M. (1971–), *The Collected Writings of John Maynard Keynes*, ed. E. Johnson and D. Moggridge, 30 vols, London and New York. (Those approaching Keynes's ideas for the first time are advised to look at volume 9, *Essays in Persuasion*.)
Moggridge, D. E. (1980), *Keynes*, 2nd edn, London.
Skidelsky, R. (1983), *John Maynard Keynes*, Vol. I, London.
See also: *Cambridge School of economics; Keynesian economics.*

Keynesian Economics

Keynesian economics comprises a body of theory and ways of thinking about the functioning of the aggregate (macro) economy that derives its inspiration from J. M. Keynes's *General Theory of Employment, Interest and Money* (1936), and from the work of Keynes's younger contemporaries such as Sir Roy Harrod, Lord Kaldor, Lord Kahn, Joan Robinson and Michał Kalecki, who extended Keynes's analysis to the growing economy and to the question of the functional distribution of income between wages and profits which Keynes himself had neglected.

There was no formal macroeconomics before Keynes. The prevailing orthodoxy was that economic systems tend to a full employment equilibrium through the operation of the price mechanism, with the distribution of income determined by the payment to factors of production according to their marginal productivity. Growth was assumed to be a smooth continuous process. The twin pillars of classical employment theory were that savings and investment were brought into equilibrium at full employment by the rate of interest, and that labour supply and demand were brought into equilibrium by variations in the real wage. Anyone wanting to work at the prevailing real wage could do so. Keynes's *General Theory* was written as a reaction to the classical orthodoxy. The debate is still very much alive. Keynesians take issue with pre-Keynesian modes of thought relating to such issues as: the tendency of economies to long-run full employment equilibrium; the functioning of aggregate labour markets; the distribution of income, and to other matters such as the relation between money and prices.

There are at least four major differences between Keynesian and pre-Keynesian economics.

(1) In pre-Keynesian economics, investment is governed by decisions to save. Variations in the rate of interest always ensure that whatever saving takes place can be profitably invested. There is no independent investment function. By contrast, Keynesian economics emphasizes the primacy of the investment decision for understanding the level of employment and growth performance. Investment determines output which determines

saving, through a multiple expansion of income (called the multiplier process) at less than full employment, and through changes in the distribution of income between wages and profits at full employment. It is capitalists, not savers, that take the investment decision, and they live in historical time with their present actions determined by past decisions and an uncertain future. By the changing 'animal spirits' of decision makers, capitalist economies are inherently unstable. Keynes brought to the fore the role of expectations in economic analysis, and emphasized their key role in understanding capitalist development.

(2) In pre-Keynesian theory there is a divorce between money and value theory. Money is a 'veil' affecting only the absolute price level, not the relative prices of goods and services in the economic system. There is no asset demand for money. Money is demanded for transactions only, and increases in the money supply affect only the price level. In Keynesian economics, money is demanded as an asset, and in the *General Theory* itself, the rate of interest is determined solely by the supply of and demand for money for speculative purposes, with the effect of money on prices depending on how interest rates affect spending relative to output. Keynesian economics attempts to integrate money and value theory. Keynesian inflation theory stresses the strong institutional forces raising the price level to which the supply of money adapts in a credit economy.

(3) In pre-Keynesian economics, the aggregate labour market is assumed to function like any micro market, with labour supply and demand brought into equality by variations in the price of labour, the real wage. Unemployment is voluntary due to a refusal of workers to accept a lower real wage. Keynes turned classical voluntary unemployment into involuntary unemployment by questioning whether it was ever possible for workers to determine their own real wage since they have no control over the price level. Unemployment is not necessarily voluntary, due to a refusal to accept real wage cuts, if by an expansion of demand both labour supply and demand at the current *money* wage would be higher than the existing level of employment. There are still many economists of a pre-Keyne-

sian persuasion who believe that the major cause of unemployment is that the aggregate real wage is too high and that workers could price themselves into jobs by accepting cuts in money wages to reduce real wages without any increase in the demand for output as a whole.

(4) Keynesian economics rejects the idea that the functional distribution of income is determined by factors of production being rewarded according to the value of their marginal product derived from an aggregate production function. This assumes a constant return to scale production function, otherwise factor income would not equal total output. More serious, since capital goods are heterogeneous they can only be aggregated once the price, the rate of interest or profit, is known. Therefore the marginal product cannot be derived independently. Keynesian distribution theory (as pioneered by Kalecki and Kaldor) shows the dependence of profits on the investment decision of firms and the savings propensities attached to wages and profits. This insight can be found in Keynes's earlier work, *The Treatise on Money* (1930), the story of the widow's cruse.

One unfortunate aspect of Keynes's economics was that, for the most part, it assumed a closed economy. A Keynesian approach to the functioning of capitalist economies cannot ignore the balance of payments, or more precisely the export decision relative to the propensity to import. This is the notion of the Harrod trade multiplier recently revived by Kaldor and Thirlwall. Keynesian economics now embraces analysis of the functioning of the world economy, recognizing the mutual interaction between countries. What unites Keynesian economists, however, is the rejection of the facile belief that we live in a world in which the functioning of markets guarantees the long-run full employment of resources, and even if we did, that it would have any relevance. As Keynes said in his *Tract on Monetary Reform* (1923), 'Economists set themselves too easy a task if in tempestuous seasons they can only tell us that when the storm is long past the ocean is flat again.'

A. P. Thirlwall
University of Kent

Further Reading

Coddington, A. (1983), *Keynesian Economics; The Search for First Principles*, London.

Eichner, A. (ed.) (1979), *A Guide to Post-Keynesian Economics*, London.

Leijonhufvud, A. (1968), *On Keynesian Economics and the Economics of Keynes*, Oxford.

Patinkin, D. and Clarke Leith, J. (1977), *Keynes, Cambridge and the General Theory*, London.

See also: *Cambridge School of Economics; capital theory; employment and underemployment; Keynes; macroeconomics; monetary policy; money.*

Labour Market Analysis

The traditional approach to the demand for labour has been marginal productivity theory, that the firm will demand labour up to the point at which the value of the additonal output attributable to its employment just equals the wage paid. With production subject to diminishing returns, the demand for labour will vary inversely with the wage. The conditions determining its elasticity with respect to the wage were formalized by Alfred Marshall: for any increase in the wage, the demand for labour will fall by less (1) the less easily it can be substituted by other inputs in production; (2) the less price-sensitive the demand for the final product; (3) the lower the proportion of labour costs in the total costs – 'the importance of being unimportant'; and (4) the less elastic the supply of other factors of production.

But in contemporary conditions the cost of labour to the employer is not simply the wages paid, even when redefined to include social insurance levies. In recruiting a new employee the firm incurs once-for-all costs in the form of agency fees, or advertising and interview expenses, plus the diversion of managerial time for his selection and introduction to the new job. The expected value of the new employee's contribution to the firm's output must cover these as well as wage-related costs. The termination of employment, moreover, is increasingly likely to involve the payment of financial compensation, making changes in the firm's work-force not only costly to effect but costly to reverse; labour is increasingly becoming a 'quasi-fixed' factor of production.

However, employees are not passive agents in the production process. In carrying out their duties they acquire familiarity with these and more widely with procedures within the firm; their productivity rises with job-experience, a process which the firm may reinforce by formal or informal training. As a consequence a current employee, particularly one with greater experience, is more valuable to the firm than a new recruit from outside.

The implications of turnover costs and on-the-job training for the employer's demand for labour give rise to a number of special features in the operation of labour markets. Faced with a change in demand of uncertain duration, the efficient strategy for the firm may be to adjust the hours of work of existing employees to avoid the expensive process of recruitment or discharge, even when the extension of hours beyond the standard work-week involves payment at premium rates. In certain contexts, therefore, the demand for hours of work and the demand for workers are separate components of the demand for labour, reflected in the tendency for fluctuations in overtime and short-time working to precede, and be proportionally greater than, changes in the numbers employed.

Additionally, the firm may engage in 'labour-hoarding', retaining experienced or skilled employees, though the fall in market demand means little current need for their services. This reinforces the widely observed tendency for employment to vary much more sluggishly than output, and consequently for labour productivity (output per worker) to rise as output increases, through fuller utilization of the work-week of existing employees, and fall with output as hoarding is renewed.

The importance of turnover costs and experience with the firm varies across groups of employees, tending to rise with level of skill and scope of responsibilities. The greatest care, and expense, in recruitment typically occurs at managerial level, where poor appointments are most damaging. These differences in costs are reflected in the greater stability of employment among managerial and skilled personnel, and the greater frequency of discharges among the less skilled.

Employers have developed a variety of arrangements to minimize turnover by making the employee's experience and seniority directly valuable to him, for example, job ladders with promotions only from among existing workers and with seniority a major criterion; holiday and pension entitlements based on years of service; a redundancy policy of last-in-first-out. These practices have been widely discussed as the 'internal labour market'.

Since the development of demography as a separate discipline, economists' analysis of labour supply tends to start not with population but with participation, the numbers out of any population who are members of the labour force. Unlike labour demand, where economic factors dominate, labour supply is also importantly influenced by wider aspects of the structure of society.

Economic analysis of participation sets the decision in the context of household choice in the use of members' time, where the main alternatives are paid employment outside the home ('market time') and household duties or leisure ('non-market time'). A rise in the wage has two effects on the household supply of labour: it raises the level of income obtained from any given number of hours of work, encouraging an increased demand for leisure as an expression of the higher standard of living (the income effect on labour supply); on the other hand, a rise in the return to market time raises the opportunity cost, in terms of foregone earnings, of non-market time, making this less attractive (the substitution effect). The net effect of a rise in wages on household labour supply is thus ambiguous. Moreover, the changing profile of labour supply over recent decades has been dominated by variations in participation among women which are largely influenced by the greatly reduced burden of work in the home, the smaller size of families, the extension of education among women and evolving social attitudes.

The incidence of formal education contributes an important qualitative dimension to labour supply. Education constitutes 'investment in human capital' undertaken partly by the state and partly by the individual. Unlike on-the-job training, which tends to be firm-specific, formal education provides a general training which is highly transferable between employers, requiring public provision for collective social benefit. Where an individual chooses to continue formal education beyond compulsory schooling, he incurs tuition-related costs and, more importantly, the loss of potential earnings over the period; these costs constitute an investment in himself, to be recouped from his enhanced earnings potential over the remainder of his working life. The impact of education is most marked on the relative supply of labour to different occupations, and hence on pay differentials; the reduction in the overall inequality of earnings is a striking labour-market consequence of the expansion of education in the course of this century.

The level and structure of wages play a central role in balancing demand and supply in labour markets, but the limited flexibility of wages and the complexity of the relationships bring further adjustment processes into play. Typically unemployment and unfilled vacancies coexist. Even at a given wage rate, jobs offered by employers differ in many dimensions – security of employment, promotion prospects, the work environment – the 'net advantages' originally discussed by Adam Smith. Similarly, individuals seeking jobs differ in personal attributes sought by employers, as well as in their own preferences. Hence the process of search, seeking an acceptable match of worker with job, is conducted on both sides. Some of the unemployment among younger-age workers in particular takes the form of repeated spells of short duration, reflecting a process of job-sampling. Longer duration unemployment, however, represents a more profound labour market disequilibrium.

The operation of labour markets has also created the trade union. In most countries, labour has sought to redress the *inequality of power between the employer and the individual* employee by forming trade unions for the purpose of collective *bargaining over wages and working conditions.*

Mary B. Gregory
St Hilda's College, Oxford

Further Reading
Rees, A. (1973), *The Economics of Work and Pay*, New York.
King, J. E. (ed.) (1980), *Readings in Labour Economics*, Oxford.
See also: *employment and underemployment; productivity; trade unions.*

Labour Theory of Value

The labour theory of value is one of the two main intellectual traditions concerned with the issues of the social nature of, as well as the magnitude of prices, in a market, capitalist economy. The other tradition is the utility (or subjective) theory, in which prices are seen as reflecting peoples' subjective feelings of utility, or strengths of subjective preferences. In contrast to the subjective or utility approach, theorists in the labour theory of value tradition see prices as reflecting the social production process generally, and more specifically as reflecting the role of labour in the production process.

Some version or another of the labour theory was espoused by most of the classical economists, who dominated economic thinking from the last quarter of the eighteenth century through the first half of the nineteenth century. Among the classical economists, Adam Smith and David Ricardo were particularly important in developing the theory. From the 1840s until his death, Karl Marx espoused and significantly developed the labour theory of value, and since his death, it has been primarily, although not exclusively, associated with Marxian economics.

Adam Smith argued that in a market society where workers owned their own means of production, prices of commodities would tend to be proportional to the quantities of labour required to produce the commodities. If the price of a particular commodity rose to a level higher than proportional to this labour input, then producers of other commodities could gain by switching to the production of the commodity in question. This self-interested switching of producers would soon create an excess supply of the commodity in question and a shortage of all other commodities. Market competition would lead to a reduction of the price of the commodity in excess supply and to increases in the prices of the other commodities for which shortages existed. This process would continue until the prices were proportional to the quantities of labour. At that point, there would be no incentive for producers to switch to the production of other commodities and therefore no market pressures for prices to change.

Smith noted, however, that all of this would change when a class of people who do not produce acquired ownership of the means of production, and workers without such means, were hired to do the producing. Competition among capitalists would tend to establish a general, average, society-wide rate of profit. By abandoning low profit industries and gravitating toward high profit industries, capitalists' competitive, self-interested behaviour would push the rates of profit in each industry towards this general average profit rate. Therefore, prices would tend to that level at which the capitalist could pay his workers' wages and have enough remaining profit to yield the social average return on his fund of capital. For such prices to be proportional to quantities of labour involved in production, it would be necessary that for any given industry the ratio of the value of capital on which profit is received to the quantity of labour expended in production be identical to that same ratio in every other industry. Otherwise, a profit mark-up that yielded equal rates of return on all capital among all industries would render prices disproportional to labour expended. Smith observed that the ratios of capital to labour are very different from industry to industry. He concluded that private ownership of the means of production by an unproductive capitalist class rendered the labour theory of value a relatively poor approximation of reality.

David Ricardo accepted the fact that unequal ratios of capital to labour would yield prices that were not strictly proportional to quantities of labour. He argued, however, that (1) the deviations from proportionality would be slight and of little importance, and (2) the direction as well as the magnitude of the deviations could be scientifically explained. Therefore, he defended the labour theory of value as a scientific explanation of prices in a capitalist, market society.

Karl Marx argued, however, that the deviation of prices from proportionality could be quite substantial. He believed that this accounted for the inability of most businessmen as well as most economic theorists to see the connections between labour and prices. There were, he asserted, two separate connections: qualitative and quantitative.

The 'qualitative connection' referred to Marx's conception of labour in capitalism. Wage labour was seen as private and not social, thus reflecting the fact that in capitalism there was no conscious, rational control of human productive interdependence. This interdependence was controlled by the blind forces of market supply and demand. Private labour therefore became social labour, Marx argued, only when it appeared in the form of the exchange value of the commodity produced by the labour. Prices were the external visible form of social labour in capitalism in Marx's view.

With this conception of prices, Marx was able to prove that surplus value was created by surplus labour. Surplus labour was defined as that labour performed in excess of the amount of labour embodied in the goods and services the worker purchases with his wages, and surplus value equalled the value of the product created by labourers minus the value of the commodities labourers could purchase with their wages. When labourers produced surplus value they were said to be exploited. Profit, interest and rent were all the outcome of the exploitation of labour.

The 'quantitative connection' between labour and prices in Marxian economics has come to be known as the 'transformation problem' or the problem of transforming quantities of labour into prices.

The labour theory of value remains today the principal alternative to the dominant orthodoxy of the subjective or utility theory of value.

E. K. Hunt
University of Utah

Further Reading
Meek, R. (1973), *Studies in the Labour Theory of Value*, London.
Hunt, E. K. (1979), *History of Economic Thought, A Critical Perspective*, Belmont, California.
See also: *Marxian economics*.

Labour Unions
See Trade Unions.

Laissez-Faire

According to one careful commentator, 'one man's *laissez-faire* is another man's intervention. . . . *Laissez-faire* is in the eye of the beholder: it depends on who he is and where he looks' (Taylor, 1972). Unfortunately this variety of standpoints and interpretations can be found among scholars as well as propagandists. The origin of the concept is usually traced to a seventeenth-century French businessmen's protest against state interference, and it flourished most vigorously among nineteenth-century French, British and American liberals. As a general notion, *laissez-faire* connotes distrust and hostility to government intervention, but it is frequently employed indiscriminately as a description of economic, social and administrative ideas and policy, even of a specific historical era.

The French physiocrats and British classical economists, from Adam Smith onwards, are usually viewed as the leading intellectual spokesmen for *laissez-faire*, whose ideas directly shaped and even dominated nineteenth-century British and American economic and social policy. However, modern historians of economics (for example, Viner, 1927, 1960; Gordon, 1968; Robbins, 1952; Coats, 1971; Samuels, 1966) have conclusively demonstrated that this view is erroneous. Smith and his successors were by no means doctrinaire opponents of state intervention, although Martineau, Wilson, Spencer, and Sumner, and, more recently, von Mises and Friedman, do fall into this category. The classical economists' anti-interventionism was carefully qualified, and increasingly so as time passed. With respect to practice, for example in 1830s England, 'the generation reared in *laissez-faire* doctrines' was systematically engaged in laying 'the foundations of modern collectivism' (Taylor, citing Deane, 1965).

In this century the *laissez-faire* concept is anachronistic, despite a recent revival of anti-interventionist sentiment, for the most important issues concerning the economic and social role of government are questions of degree, not of kind.

A. W. Coats
University of Nottingham
Duke University

References

Coats, A. W. (ed.) (1971), *The Classical Economists and Economic Policy*, London.

Deane, P. (1965), *The First Industrial Revolution*, Cambridge.

Gordon, H. S. (1968), 'Laissez-faire' in *International Encyclopedia of the Social Sciences*, vol. 8, London and New York.

Robbins, L. C. (1952), *The Theory of Economic Policy in Classical Political Economy*, London.

Samuels, W. (1966), *The Classical Theory of Economic Policy*, Cleveland.

Taylor, A. J. (1972), *Laissez-Faire and State Intervention in Nineteenth-Century Britain*, London.

Viner, J. (1927), 'Adam Smith and laissez-faire', reprinted in J. Viner (ed.), *The Long View and the Short, Studies in Economic Theory and Policy*, Glencoe, Ill., 1958.

Viner, J. (1960), 'The intellectual history of laissez-faire', *Journal of Law and Economics*, vol. 3.

Further Reading

Fine, S. (1956), *Laissez-Faire and the General-Welfare State: A Study of Conflict in American Thought, 1865–1901*, Ann Arbor.

See also: *free trade; Smith.*

Land

Economists traditionally classify factors of production into land, labour and capital. The classical economists – notably, Adam

Smith, David Ricardo and John Stuart Mill – attached particular significance to land, as, indeed, the pre-eminence of agriculture at the time warranted. They devoted considerable attention to the implications for the growth and distribution of income of a limited supply of land, combined with diminishing returns in agricultural production. The legitimacy of rents accruing to landowners was also challenged. In particular, Mill, accusing landowners of growing rich as a result of the general progress of society rather than as a result of their own efforts, proposed a scheme for taxing such 'unearned increments'.

The tripartite classification of productive factors, whilst possessing the attraction of expositional convenience, is an uneasy one. Ricardo defined land as 'the original and indestructible powers of the soil'. However, few of the productive powers of land are unambiguously free gifts of Nature; most land has physical and human capital improvements inseparably embodied in it. Moreover, the productive properties of the soil can be, and in places have been, eroded by inappropriate forms of cultivation.

Under neoclassical economics, land has lost the special significance it previously enjoyed. A major reason for this is that land has declined in relative importance as a factor of production in developed economies. Nevertheless, there are still many countries where the ownership of land confers extensive economic, social and political powers. Moreover there has in recent years been renewed pessimism over the possible limits to growth in all countries implied by finite natural resources.

J. M. Currie
University of Manchester

Further Reading

Barlowe, R. (1978), *Land Resource Economics*, 3rd edn, Englewood Cliffs, N.J.

Mill, J. S. (1886 [1848]), *The Principles of Political Economy*, London.

Ricardo, D. (1951), *The Principles of Political Economy and*

Taxation, in P. Sraffa and M. H. Dobb (eds), *The Works and Correspondence of David Ricardo*, vol. 1, Cambridge.

See also: *land tenure; Ricardo*.

Land Tenure

The broad term, land tenure, refers to the relationships betwen individuals and groups in respect of land. The basic rights over land enjoyed by individuals or groups involve rights to use, to exclude others from use, to lease, and to alienate by gift, bequest or sale. However, systems of land tenure differ significantly from society to society; certain types of property rights familiar in one society may be meaningless in another. Moreover, whether based on customary practice, on contract or on legislation, systems of proprietary rights and obligations are usually extremely complex, with several individuals or groups frequently having rights over the same tract of land.

The system of land tenure in a society invariably depends both on the scarcity of land and on the predominant forms of land use. Rights and obligations are much more explicit when land is scarce and where more time is required to reap the fruits of labour expended on the land. In 'primitive' societies practising shifting cultivation, there is seldom any concept of individual 'ownership' of land. An individual household has an inalienable right of access to a share of the community's land and an exclusive right to use whatever land is allocated to it, a use-right which, however, is conditional on actual use.

Even in societies where individuals can own land, rights are typically conditional, not absolute. Indeed, during the present century, there has been in most Western economies a proliferation of statutory controls over changes in land use. Furthermore, freedom of contract has increasingly been restricted by legislation defining in considerable detail the respective rights and obligations of landlords and tenants.

J. M. Currie
University of Manchester

Further Reading

Becker, L. C. (1977), *Property Rights: Philosophic Foundations*, London.

Currie, J. M. (1981), *The Economic Theory of Agricultural Land Tenure*, Cambridge.

Limited Liability

The most common form of capitalist business enterprise, the limited liability company, has a legal status of a *persona* separate from owners or shareholders. Three features arise: (1) debts incurred are the firm's, not the shareholders', whose maximum liability is restricted to their original financial outlay; (2) the identity of the firm is unchanged should one shareholder transfer his ownership title to a third party; (3) the firm's contractual relationships are entered into by its officers (for example, directors or managers).

These characteristics were not originally coexistent. By the fifteenth century, English law had awarded limited liability to monastic communities and trade guilds for commonly held property. In the seventeenth century, joint stock charters were awarded by the Crown as circumscribed monopoly privileges to groups such as the East India and Hudson's Bay Companies.

By the early nineteenth century, a joint stock company could be formed simply by registration, and no monopoly privileges were awarded. The merging of the features was completed by mid-century when incorporation with full limited liability became permissible and common in the UK and the US, and in Europe a decade or so later.

It is widely agreed that the move to large-scale industrial enterprise was facilitated, and indeed made possible, by limited liability. The threat of potential confiscation of an individual's total wealth should he invest part of it in an unsuccessful company was removed. Moreover, his risk could be further reduced if he invested in several and not just one firm. Large sums of untapped personal financial capital became available. Transferability of shares permitted continuity of business operation not present in other forms of enterprise. The existence of the firm as a separate contracting *persona* permitted a productive division of labour between risk-bearing capitalists and business administrators.

Schumpeter (1950) criticized this latter development as having pushed 'into the background all . . . the institutions of property and free contracting . . . that expressed the needs . . . of economic activity'. Hessen (1979) has taken the contrary view: limited liability is a creature of private agreement, not the state. Freely negotiated contractual specialization is a device for greater efficiency in meeting private wants, not a shirking of responsibility, not a Schumpeterian 'absentee ownership' which because nobody is 'left . . . to stand for it' must evolve into a state controlled bureaucracy.

W. Duncan Reekie
University of the Witwatersrand, Johannesburg

References
Hessen, R. (1979), *In Defense of the Corporation*, Stanford, California.
Schumpeter, J. (1950), *Capitalism, Socialism and Democracy*, New York.

Liquidity

Keynes's discussion of the incentives to and consequences of *liquidity* is arguably one of the major innovations of *The General Theory*. Assets are said to be more or less liquid according to the ease and certainty with which they can be converted into money, the ultimate liquid asset. There is no absolute standard of liquidity, as Keynes said, but merely a scale of liquidity, and even the latter is 'a partly vague concept' changing 'from time to time depending on social practices and institutions'. Thus today, for example, building society deposits which are fixed in money terms and convertible on demand or at short notice might be regarded as highly liquid, in contrast to fixed property which might be difficult to sell and the market price of which may vary. In the past, however, land and fixed property have been considered very liquid assets due to their well-developed markets. Thus, while objective standards of liquidity may be difficult to gauge given the essentially *subjective* nature of judgements about liquidity, the latter can be inferred from the liquidity premiums which wealth holders require to tempt them into various assets. In general terms interest is the reward for parting with liquidity, and the less liquid an asset the greater the reward must be, that is, the higher the liquidity premium. Given a positive interest rate the problem is to explain why people hold any money at all, that is, what motivates 'liquidity preference'.

Keynes identified three motives: (1) The so-called *transactions motive* has strong roots in classical monetary theory deriving as it does from the need to finance current net expenditures, and is usually modelled along classical lines as a function of (often assumed proportional to) the level of income. (2) Not all transactions can be anticipated with certainty, hence the need for incremental liquidity to insure against the possibility that unforeseen transactions might be necessary and might therefore impose substantive costs as illiquid assets have to be converted into cash at short notice. This Keynes called the *precautionary motive* and it too is usually related to income levels. (3) The *speculative motive* develops the Keynesian theme of uncertainty and breaks away from the classical identification of money holdings as fixed in relation to income by the prerequisites of the structure of transactions.

The speculative motive for holding money derives from uncertainty as to the future rate of interest and therefore differential expectations about the future prices of fixed interest-bearing assets. This raises the possibility of making capital gains/losses by out-/underguessing the market. Thus, if an investor anticipates a fall (rise) in the interest rate, then capital gains (losses) could be made (avoided) by moving out of cash (bonds) and into bonds (cash) ahead of the market. Assuming that expectations relate to the current interest rate relative to some 'long-run normal level', and that the latter is subjectively determined so that we have a distribution of expectations, then the quantity of money that the general public prefer to hold will vary smoothly and inversely with the rate of interest. This identification of the speculative motive breaks the link between income and money holding which underpins the classical belief in the neutrality of money with far-reaching implications.

In addition, the Keynesian insistence on liquidity as a generalized concept, typified but not exhausted at one extreme by money, has two additional important consequences. First, and less well developed in the literature, is Keynes's deprecation of the speculative motive to hold cash as an obstacle to accumulation and therefore wealth. Second, is the post-Keynesian position that the line between money and debts can be drawn only arbitrarily, and that in an advanced industrial economy they are increasingly close substitutes, with the result that monetary constraint must be widened to encompass the disintermediation into non-monetary but still effectively liquid assets that would follow traditional control. While theoretically convincing, the practical problems involved in this approach are enormous and have contributed to the post-Keynesian mistrust of monetary policy as an important component of demand management.

Jane Humphries
University of Cambridge

Further Reading

Goodhart, C. A. E. (1984), 'The importance of money', in
  Monetary Theory and Practice, London.

Keynes, J. M. (1964 [1936]), *The General Theory of Employment, Interest and Money*, London.

The Committee on the Working of the Monetary System
  (Radcliffe Report) (1969), Cmnd 827, HMSO, London.

See also: *investment; money*.

Macroeconomics

Macroeconomics is concerned with explaining and assessing the performance of the economy in the *aggregate*. Accordingly, it focuses attention upon such magnitudes as the national income, the extent of unemployment, the general level of prices and its rate of change, the rate of economic growth and the overall balance of payments. It is therefore to be contrasted with microeconomics, which is concerned more with *individual* decision making as, for example, the output decision of a particular firm, and with *relative* prices of competing goods and factors of production.

There is almost universal agreement that modern macroeconomics dates from the publication of Keynes's *General Theory of Employment, Interest and Money* in 1936 and which, of course, reflects the experience of the great depression. Prior to this time, economists believed that the economy would naturally tend to approximate the full employment level of income if left to its own devices and if competition was allowed free play. Moreover, it was argued that the governing authorities could do little or nothing to speed up the process towards full employment, since any attempt to promote public works programmes would necessarily draw resources away from the private sector so that the *net* employment impact of such policies would be minimal. This view, the so-called 'treasury view', Keynes sought to deny. The Keynesian revolution produced the theoretical rationale to justify government intervention in the economy and argued that expansionary monetary and fiscal policies could generate increased output and employment. In these Keynesian-oriented *demand management* strategies, changes in government expenditure and taxation became the dominant instrument of control, and accordingly interventionist fiscal policy became strongly identified with Keynesianism.

Despite the apparent success of Keynesian policies in the post-war period, this philosophy was increasingly subject to attack. Monetarist critiques, emphasizing the budgetary consequences of such policies, pointed to the inflationary consequences of budget deficits and suggested that any beneficial stimulus to the economy would be of short duration only. Much of this critique emphasized the inadequate treatment of expectations formation, especially in labour markets, which characterized earlier Keynesian-oriented models. In recent years, a more radical brand of monetarism has emerged which, stressing *rational expectations* formation, has suggested that demand management policies are completely ineffective *even in the short run* in influencing real variables such as output and employment. Accordingly, the *new classical macroeconomics* suggests that macroeconomic policy should be supply-oriented. Supply-side economics argues that the economy will tend to its own 'natural' full employment level of output and that attention should be directed to increasing this natural level by promoting incentives to work effort, risk taking, innovation and so forth. Supply-side strategies are aided by the absence of inflation which generates uncertainty and raises interest rates. Accordingly, attention is focused upon the control of the money supply, and fiscal policy becomes subordinate to the required money supply targets. The new classical macroeconomics is thus, in large measure, a return to pre-Keynesian orthodoxy, albeit in a far more sophisticated guise.

G. K. Shaw
University of Buckingham

Further Reading
Dornbusch, R. and Fischer, S. (1984), *Macroeconomics*, 3rd edn, New York.
Greenaway, D. and Shaw, G. K. (1983), *Macroeconomics: Theory and Policy in the UK*, Oxford.
See also: *Keynesian economics; monetarism.*

Malthus, Thomas Robert (1766–1834)

Thomas Robert Malthus, one of the leading figures of the English classical school of political economy, was born near Guildford, Surrey. He entered Jesus College, Cambridge in 1784, graduated in mathematics in 1788 and was a fellow of his college from 1793 until his marriage in 1804. From 1805 until his death he served as professor of history and political economy at Haileybury College, then recently founded by the East India Company for the education of its cadets. The tranquillity of his life and the gentleness of his personality contrasted sharply with the harshness of his doctrines and the fierce controversies which they evoked.

Malthus's most famous contribution to classical political economy was the theory stated in 1798 in his *Essay on the*

Principle of Population – 'Population, when unchecked, increases in a geometrical ratio. Subsistence increases only in an arithmetical ratio. . . . By that law of our nature which makes food necessary to the life of man, the effects of these two unequal powers must be kept equal. This implies a strong and constantly operating check on population from the difficulty of subsistence.'

In the first edition of his *Essay*, Malthus identified the checks to population as either preventive (keeping new population from growing up) or positive (cutting down existing population); hence followed the bleak conclusion 'that the superior power of population cannot be checked without producing misery or vice'. In the second, much enlarged, edition (1803) he extended the category of preventive checks to include 'moral restraint', thus admitting the possibility of population being contained without either misery or vice as necessary consequences. Even when thus modified, Malthus's doctrine still seemed to impose narrow limits on the possibilities of economic growth and social improvement. Idealists and reformers consequently railed against the implications of the theory, but his fellow economists accepted both its premises and its logic, and for most of the nineteenth century it remained one of the accepted 'principles of political economy'.

Malthus was also one of the first economists to state (in 1815) the theory of rent as a surplus, generally associated with the name of his friend and contemporary, David Ricardo. Both were followers of Adam Smith but Malthus's development of Smith's system differed significantly from Ricardo's, notably in his use of demand and supply analysis in the theory of value as against Ricardo's emphasis on labour-quantities, and in his explanation of the 'historical fall' of profits in terms of competition of capitals rather than by the 'necessity of resort to inferior soils' which Ricardo stressed.

Since the time of Keynes the difference between Malthus and Ricardo which has attracted most attention relates to 'the possibility of a general glut'. In a lengthy debate Ricardo argued the validity of Say's Law, that 'supply creates its own demand', while Malthus asserted the possibility of over-saving (and investment) creating an excess supply of commodities. Ricardo's superior logic won acceptance for Say's Law for over a century, but modern economists now see Malthus's *Principles of Political Economy* as containing many insights which anticipate twentieth-century theories of investment and employment.

R. D. Collison Black
Queen's University of Belfast

References

Malthus, T. R. (1798), *An Essay on the Principle of Population*, London. (Second edn, 1803.)

Malthus, T. R. (1820), *The Principles of Political Economy, Considered with a View to their Practical Application*, London. (Second edn, 1836.)

Further Reading

James, P. (1979), *Population Malthus, His Life and Times*, London.

Petersen, W. (1979), *Malthus*, London.

Marginal Analysis

Marginal analysis in economics attempts to explain the determination of prices and quantities on the basis of the comparisons of rewards and costs 'on the margin', that is, the rewards and costs of extending economic activity by small incremental amounts. It is an approach that follows naturally from the view that economic agents try to maximize some economic goal, such as utility or profits. They are assumed to possess the information that relates their activities to their goals, for example, the extent to which an increase in consumption increases their utility, or the effects of an increase in output on their profits. This is the cornerstone of neoclassical analysis, which dates from the marginal revolution of the 1870s set in motion by the writings of Jevons, Menger and Leon Walras. As opposed to classical analysis, which concentrated on questions of capital accumulation and growth, neoclassical analysis was concerned with the optimal allocation of given resources, and marginal techniques, with their accompanying mathematics of differential calculus, proved to be a fruitful way of dealing with these questions and appeared to provide economics with 'scientific' precision.

Marginal analysis, although it assumed a central role in economic theory from the 1870s, appeared in economics writings in earlier periods. It was prominent in the work of Thünen, whose theory of distribution was based on the marginal productivity of the factors of production. Cournot discussed the behaviour of firms under the assumption of profit maximization, and he made use of marginal revenue and marginal cost to deduce the positions of equilibrium. Dupuit distinguished between the total and marginal utility of goods when he examined the social benefits derived from public goods such as bridges, and on this basis he arrived at measures of consumers' surplus from the existence of such goods. Gossen enunciated the principle of diminishing marginal utility, which he termed his 'First Law'. He went on to state what has been called Gossen's 'Second Law', that the maximization of an individual's satisfaction from any good that can be used in different ways, requires that it be allocated among these uses in such a way that its marginal utility be the same in all its uses.

The marginal approach was also not unknown in classical economics. In Ricardo's theory the rent of land is price-determined, not price-determining, since it is the price of corn, given the wage and interest rates, that determines the extent of cultivation and the rent that can be extracted from the cultivators. His treatment of this question is an example of marginal analysis, since this decision is based on considerations of the effects on the output of corn of incremental changes in inputs. The combined doses of labour and capital on land that is being cultivated are increased until the output from the final, or marginal, dose is just sufficient to cover the wage and interest costs of that dose. Rent can only be extracted from the products of the intramarginal inputs of labour-capital. Similarly, the extent to which less fertile, or more distant, land will be cultivated depends on the marginal product of labour-capital on this land. No-rent land is that land where output is just sufficient to compensate the labour and capital employed. Wicksteed, Wicksell, and J. B. Clark generalized Ricardo's approach to cover the case where all factors of production would be treated as being potentially variable, to arrive at a marginal productivity theory of distribution, and thus Blaug (1978) believes that Ricardo should be credited with 'having invented marginal analysis'.

The independent discovery by different theorists of the marginal productivity theory of distribution can be taken as a high point of marginal analysis, since it appeared to complete the marginal revolution by showing that not only are the prices of goods determined by marginal utility, but the prices of the inputs used to produce these goods are determined in a similar manner by their marginal products. This theory of distribution can, however, also be used to show the limitations of marginal analysis. In order to apply marginal techniques exclusively, it is necessary that there exists a known function linking the variable whose value is to be determined (output of a good in this case) to *all* the variables (inputs of the elements of production in this case) on which its value depends. This function should be continuous and differentiable so that the marginal products of the inputs can be derived. These inputs must be measured in physical units, rather than in terms of money values, if their marginal products are to be taken as independent determinants of their prices. In general, however, these conditions are not all satisfied. If the inputs in any specific production process, whose number will be very large, are measured in physical units, then they are often connected by a relationship of complementarity, and separate marginal products cannot be calculated for them. If these inputs are combined to form the aggregate factors of production, labour and capital, as was done by Clark, then capital can only be measured in money-value terms. This means that the marginal analysis begins with the prices of capital goods, and cannot provide an explanation of their determination. In addition, some essential inputs into the productive activity of firms, such as business organization and ability whose importance was emphasized by Marshall, cannot be measured in physical units and placed in a production function. Even though Marshall made extensive use of marginal analysis, and is often erroneously credited with having a marginal productivity theory of distribution, he was aware of the limitations of marginal productivity as the sole explanation of distribution (Marshall, 1920).

Marginal analysis cannot deal fully with situations where future conditions are not known with certainty, or where they cannot be represented by some well-defined probability distribution, since the effects on the variables of interest of marginal changes cannot be determined. Questions having to do with capital accumulation cannot be handled adequately by these techniques, since investment depends on expectations of future conditions that in a fundamental sense cannot be known in a context of historical time. Those wedded to marginal analysis thus tend to assume conditions that permit marginal techniques to be employed, even though they represent serious departures from the reality the analysis is supposed to illuminate. This may be one reason for the predominance given in neoclassical theory to perfect competition despite the fact that modern manufacturing industry is imperfectly competitive. Only in the case of perfect competition is profit maximization, which is concerned with maximizing the present value of the stream of profits over time, synonymous with short-period profit maximization, the maximization of the current period's profits.

A. Asimakopulos
McGill University

References
Blaug, M. (1978), *Economic Theory in Retrospect*, 3rd edn, Cambridge.
Marshall, A. (1920), *Principles of Economics*, 8th edn, London.

Further Reading
Black, R. D., Coats, A. W. and Goodwin, C. D. W. (eds) (1973), *The Marginal Revolution in Economics*, Durham, North Carolina.

Howey, R. S. (1960), *The Rise of the Marginal Utility School 1870–1889*, Lawrence, Kansas.

Schumpeter, J. A. (1954), *History of Economic Analysis*, New York.

See also: *maximization; Walras.*

Marketing Research

The purpose of marketing research is to provide information which will aid in management decision making. A marketing manager in a large consumer goods company, for example, may want to collect information to assess whether or not to launch a new product or to determine why sales of a product are declining. In collecting this information, five major steps may be identified: (1) establishment of research objectives; (2) development of a research plan; (3) implementation of the research plan; (4) data analysis; and (5) presentation of research findings (Churchill, 1983; Green and Tull, 1978; Lehmann, 1983).

(1) Establishment of Research Objectives

This is the first step, and it requires clear and precise definition by management of the decision problem. This should be expressed not only in terms of problem symptoms such as a decline in market share, but also in terms of possible contributing factors such as changes in competitors' strategies or in consumer interests, as well as the actions management might take based on research findings. Otherwise, much irrelevant information may be collected.

(2) Development of a Research Plan

This stage requires determining what data are to be collected, what research techniques and instruments are to be used, how the sample is to be selected, and how information is to be collected from this sample.

(i)   *Data sources*: The required information may already be available in *secondary* sources such as government or trade reports, company records, or sales-force reports. This will not, however, have been collected with this particular problem in mind. Consequently, *primary* data collection may be required, in other words, collection of information specifically for this purpose.

(ii) *Research techniques*: Where primary data are collected, observational or other qualitative techniques, experimentation or survey research may be conducted. *Observational* and other qualitative techniques, such as projective techniques, (word association or sentence completion tasks, and focus or group interviewing) are most appropriate in the initial stages of research, where little is known about the problem (Webb, Campbell, Schwartz and Sechrest, 1966). The onus of interpretation is, however, placed on the researcher, and, consequently, such techniques are open to criticisms of subjectivity. *Experimental* techniques are also potentially applicable, but they are rarely used except in in-store experiments, studying, for example, the impact of in-store promotions on sales. Test marketing can also be viewed as field experiments. *Survey* research is the technique most commonly used in marketing research. A standard questionnaire can be administered to large samples, and systematically analysed using computerized techniques.

(iii) *Research instruments*: In observational or qualitative research, instruments such as coding schema, recording sheets and other tests may need to be designed. Mechanical devices such as instruments to measure a subject's eye movements or pupil dilation, or optical scanner equipment are also increasingly used. But more common is the questionnaire. For unstructured interviews and focus groups, only an interview guide indicating the topics to be covered may be required. A crucial aspect of survey research is, however, the design of a questionnaire carefully worded to elicit desired information from respondents (Oppenheim, 1966; Payne, 1951). Attention to question form and sequencing is also often essential in order to avoid biased responses.

(iv) *Sampling plan*: This should specify the sample population, its size and sampling procedures to be adopted. The relevant sample population and sample size will depend on the purpose of the research, and the research budget. In qualitative research, small samples are common, but more extensive surveys often require a large sample size. A choice has also to be made between probabilistic sampling techniques, such as random or stratified sampling, and non-probabilistic sampling techniques such as judgemental, quota or convenience sampling (Cochran, 1977). Probability sampling is the only way to obtain a representative sample but requires the availability of a sampling list and entails high costs. Convenience, judgemental or quota sampling techniques are thus often used, particularly where qualitative techniques are applied, or where a specific target segment is to be studied.

(v) *Data collection procedures*: Three principal methods of data collection may be considered: telephone, mail or personal interviewing. *Telephone* interviewing, which is commonly used in the US, is quick and can be conducted from a central location where interviewers are controlled by a supervisor. However, only those with telephones can be interviewed, and a limited number of questions asked. *Mail* questionnaires are the cheapest method of survey administration, but suffer from low response rates, and also assume that the respondent clearly understands and can respond to questions. *Personal* interviewing is the most flexible method since the interviewer can select the sample by judgement or convenience sampling, and is able to explain questions to the respondent. It is, however, an expensive method of data collection, and susceptible to interviewer bias.

(3) Implementation of the Research Plan

This is where major sources of data inaccuracy and unreliability often arise. In the case of surveys, for example, respondents may bias findings by refusal to co-operate, by providing inaccurate answers, for example, on income, or by giving socially desirable responses. Interviewers may also bias results by encouraging a specific response, by inaccurate recording of responses or, in extreme cases, by falsifying responses.

Current developments in telecommunications and computer technology are rapidly changing data collection procedures and improving their efficiency. For example, in both centralized telephone interviewing and in mobile field units, computer terminals can be used by interviewers or interviewees to record responses, thereby eliminating editing and coding errors. The results can also be analysed and updated with each successive response, thus considerably reducing research time and costs.

(4) Data Analysis
The next step is to tabulate, classify, and interpret the information collected. Here, the complexity of the analysis will depend to a large extent on management needs. In many cases, tabulation or cross-tabulation of results with averages and other summary statistics may suffice. In other cases, more sophisticated multivariate techniques such as factor or cluster analysis or multidimensional scaling may be required, if more complex interactions in the data are to be examined (Green, 1978).

(5) Presentation of Research Findings
Presentation of research findings may be verbal and/or written. In either case, the main focus should be on clear presentation of key research findings and their implications for the decisions to be made by management.

Susan P. Douglas
New York University

References
Churchill, G. (1983), *Marketing Research*, 3rd edn, Hinsdale, Ill.
Cochran, W. G. (1977), *Sampling Techniques*, 3rd edn, New York.
Green, P. E. (1978), *Analyzing Multivariate Data*, Hinsdale, Ill.
Green, P. E. and Tull, D. S. (1978), *Research for Marketing Decisions*, 4th edn, Englewood Cliffs, N.J.
Lehmann, D. (1983), *Market Research and Analysis*, 2nd edn, Homewood, Ill.

Oppenheim, A. N. (1966), *Questionnaire Design and Attitude Measurement*, New York.

Payne, S. (1951), *The Art of Asking Questions*, Princeton.

Webb, E., Campbell, D. T., Schwartz, R. D. and Sechrest, L. (1966), *Unobtrusive Measures*, Chicago.

Further Reading

Baker, M. J. (ed.) (1983), *Marketing: Theory and Practice*, 3rd edn, London.

Marshall, Alfred (1842–1924)

The English economist Alfred Marshall was one of the dominant figures in his subject during the late nineteenth and early twentieth centuries. His 1890 masterwork, the *Principles of Economics*, introduced many of the tools and concepts economists use in price theory even today. The book also presented an influential synthesis of received theories of value and distribution.

Marshall was born on 26 July 1842 at Bermondsey, a London suburb, his father William being at the time a clerk at the Bank of England. Alfred was educated at Merchant Taylors' School, revealing there his aptitude for mathematics. Somewhat against his father's wishes, he entered St John's College, Cambridge, to embark on the mathematics tripos, graduating in 1865 as Second Wrangler. He was then elected to a fellowship at St John's. Soon abandoning mathematics for ethics and psychology, his growing interest in social questions led him to economics, which by 1870 he had chosen as his life's work. He took a prominent part in the teaching for the moral sciences tripos until leaving Cambridge in 1877 on marriage to his onetime student, Mary Paley.

Although Marshall published little, these early years were the formative ones for his economic views. He mastered the classical tradition of A. Smith, D. Ricardo and J. S. Mill and was encouraged towards a mathematical approach by early acquaintance with the works of A. A. Cournot and J. H. von Thünen. Priority for the marginal 'revolution' of the early 1870s clearly goes to W. S. Jevons, L. Walras and C. Menger, but

Marshall had been working on similar lines before 1870. However, his attitude towards these new developments remained somewhat grudging, and he was always reluctant to publish merely theoretical exercises. More general influences significant in this early period were those of H. Sidgwick (perhaps more personal than intellectual), H. Spencer and G. W. F. Hegel. The last two, in tune with the spirit of the age, led Marshall towards an organic or biological view of society. He found the early socialist writers emotionally appealing, but unrealistic in their views as to evolutionary possibilities for human nature. Somewhat later, he saw merit in the programme of the German Historical School of Economics, but deplored its anti-theoretical stance. It was from these and other varied sources, including energetic factual enquiry, that he distilled and long pondered his subtle, complex and eclectic approach to economic questions.

Marshall returned to Cambridge in 1885, from exile in Bristol and Oxford, as professor of political economy and the acknowledged leader of British economists. He had already commenced work on his *Principles*. His first two significant publications had appeared in 1879. One was a selection of theoretical chapters from a never-completed book on foreign trade, printed by Sidgwick for private circulation under the title *The Pure Theory of Foreign Trade: The Pure Theory of Domestic Values*. These superb chapters did much to establish Marshall's reputation among British economists. The other was an ostensible primer, the *Economics of Industry*, co-authored by his wife, which foreshadowed many of the ideas of the *Principles*. It was this work that first brought Marshall's views to the attention of foreign economists.

Marshall resided in Cambridge for the rest of his life, resigning his chair in 1908 to devote all his energies to writing. The years were externally uneventful and dominated by the internal struggle to give vent and adequate expression to his vast store of knowledge. The first volume of what was intended as a two-volume work on *Principles of Economics* appeared in 1890 and cemented his international reputation. Although this first volume went through eight editions, little progress was made with the second volume, which had been intended to cover money, business fluctuations, international trade, labour and industrial organization. Among the famous concepts introduced in the *Principles*, as it soon came to be known, were consumer surplus, long and short-period analysis, the representative firm, and external economies. The elucidation and criticism of these and related concepts were to occupy English-speaking economists for many years.

In 1903, under the influence of the tariff agitation, Marshall embarked on a tract for the times on national industries and international trade. This too grew vastly in his hands and, when it eventually appeared in 1919, *Industry and Trade* realized his earlier intentions only incompletely. The book's tone, historical and descriptive rather than theoretical, has made it better known among economic historians than among economists. The years that remained were devoted to a last-ditch effort to salvage some of his unpublished earlier work. Some important early contributions to the theories of money and international trade at last saw the light in *Money, Credit and Commerce* in 1923, but the book remains an unsatisfactory pastiche. Marshall died on 13 July 1924 at the age of eighty-one having failed to do much that he had wished, yet still having achieved greatness.

During his years as professor, Marshall was instrumental in establishing the specialized study of his subject at Cambridge, which eventually became a leading centre for economic study and research. As teacher and adviser he inspired his students with his own high and unselfish ambitions for his subject. Among the several students who were to attain professional prominence and influence, A. C. Pigou and J. M. Keynes should especially be mentioned. Nationally, Marshall was a public figure and played an important role in government inquiries and in the professionalization of economics in Britain. Internationally, he was cosmopolitan in outlook and kept close contact with economists and economic events abroad.

Marshall was anxious to influence events and deeply concerned for the future of Britain, and especially of its poorer and less privileged citizens. Yet he preferred to remain above the fray of current controversy, whether scientific or concerned with policy, trusting that 'constructive' work and patient study would provide the surer if slower route towards the desired goals. His desire for historical continuity and the avoidance of controversy led him frequently to underplay the novelty of his ideas and to exaggerate their closeness to those of his classical forebears.

John K. Whitaker
University of Virginia

Further Reading

Guillebaud, C. W. (ed.) (1965), *Marshall's Principles of Economics, Variorum Edition*, London.
Pigou, A. C. (ed.) (1925), *Memorials of Alfred Marshall*, London.
Whitaker, J. K. (ed.) (1975), *The Early Economic Writings of Alfred Marshall, 1867–1890*, London.
See also: *neoclassical economics*.

Marshall-Lerner Criterion

This criterion is named after the English economist Alfred Marshall and the American economist Abba Lerner. It is a simple condition which shows whether a devaluation of a country's currency will improve the country's balance of trade. Such an improvement need not necessarily follow, since a devaluation will normally cheapen the value of each unit of the country's exports in world currency and may not cheapen the value of each unit of its imports. If the balance of trade is to improve following the devaluation, export sales must increase enough, and/or import purchases diminish enough, to offset any such relative cheapening of exports. The relative cheapening of exports is called a 'worsening of the country's terms of trade'.

The Marshall-Lerner criterion states that 'a country's trade balance will improve following a depreciation of its currency if the [positive value of] the elasticity of foreign demand for its exports and the [positive value of] its elasticity of demand for imports together sum to more than unity'. (An elasticity of demand for a commodity shows the percentage increase in the quantity demanded following a 1 per cent fall in the commodity's price.) The Marshall-Lerner criterion is appropriate if the following simplifying assumptions are applicable: the country's exports are in infinitely elastic supply (export prices are constant in home currency); the world supply of imports to the country is infinitely elastic (import prices are constant in foreign currency); and the balance of trade is initially neither in surplus nor in deficit. In such circumstances an x per cent worsening devaluation will cause an x per cent reduction in the foreign currency revenue from each unit of exports, and no change in the foreign currency revenue for each unit of imports; in other words, it will cause an x per cent worsening of the terms of trade. But it will also cause an increase in export volume and reduction in import volume which together sum to more than x per cent and so outweigh this worsening of the terms of trade.

Qualifications to the Marshall-Lerner criterion are required if the assumptions mentioned in the previous paragraph do not hold. If, for example, the prices of exports in foreign currency are in part tied to foreign competitors' prices in foreign currency, then the terms of trade loss following a devaluation will be smaller, and an improvement in the balance of trade will be easier to obtain. By contrast, a devaluation starting from an initial position of deficit will in general require larger volume responses if it is to improve the trade balance. The export and import elasticities then need to add up to more than unity for a devaluation to be successful.

Modern balance of payments theory, developed since World War II, has suggested some more fundamental modifications to the Marshall-Lerner criterion. Firstly, a devaluation will normally lead to increases in domestic costs and prices. This domestic inflation may partly or fully upset the stimulus to export promotion and import reduction. The second modification is suggested by the techniques of Keynesian 'multiplier' analysis: any improvement in the trade balance will increase domestic incomes and expenditures, sucking in more imports, so partly or fully undoing the initial improvement. The third amendment has been suggested by the 'monetary theory of the balance of payments'. Any improvement in the trade balance may lead to monetary inflow, a stimulus to expenditures at home, and further increases in imports which may undo the initial improvement. These three developments have made it clear that the success of a devaluation depends not only on the size of export and import elasticities, as suggested by the Marshall-Lerner criterion, but also upon the domestic inflationary process, upon domestic income expansion, and upon what happens to domestic monetary conditions.

David Vines
University of Glasgow

Further Reading
Stern, R. M. (1973), *The Balance of Payments: Theory and Policy*, London.
See also: *balance of payments; international trade.*

Marx, Karl Heinrich (1818–83)

Marx was a German social scientist and revolutionary, whose analysis of capitalist society laid the theoretical basis for the political movement bearing his name. Marx's main contribution lies in his emphasis on the role of the economic factor – the changing way in which people have reproduced their means of subsistence – in shaping the course of history. This perspective has had a considerable influence on the whole range of social sciences.

Karl Heinrich Marx was born in the town of Trier in the Moselle district of the Prussian Rhineland on 5 May 1818. He came from a long line of rabbis on both his father's and his mother's sides. His father, a respected lawyer in Trier, had accepted baptism as a Protestant in order to be able to pursue his career. The atmosphere of Marx's home was permeated by the Enlightenment, and he assimilated a certain amount of romantic and early socialist ideas from Baron von Westphalen – to whose daughter, Jenny, he became engaged in 1835 and later married. In the same year he left the local gymnasium, or high school, and enrolled at the University of Bonn. He transferred the following year to the University of Berlin, where he soon embraced the dominant philosophy of Hegelianism. Intending to become a university teacher, Marx obtained his doctorate in 1841 with a thesis on post-Aristotelian Greek philosophy.

From 1837 Marx had been deeply involved in the Young Hegelian movement. This group espoused a radical critique of Christianity and, by implication, a liberal opposition to the Prussian autocracy. Finding a university career closed to him by the Prussian government, Marx moved into journalism. In October 1842 he became editor, in Cologne, of the influential *Rheinische Zeitung*, a liberal newspaper backed by Rhenish industrialists. Marx's incisive articles, particularly on economic questions, induced the government to close the paper, and he decided to emigrate to France.

Paris was then the centre of socialist thought and on his arrival at the end of 1843, Marx rapidly made contact with organized groups of emigré German workers and with various sects of French socialists. He also edited the shortlived *Deutsch-französische Jahrbücher*, which was intended to form a bridge between nascent French socialism and the ideas of the German radical Hegelians. It was also in Paris that Marx first formed his lifelong partnership with Friedrich Engels. During the first few months of his stay in Paris, Marx rapidly became a convinced communist and set down his views in a series of manuscripts known as the *Ökonomisch-philosophische Manuskripte* (*Economic and Philosophic Manuscripts of 1844*). Here he outlined a humanist conception of communism, influenced by the philosophy of Ludwig Feuerbach and based on a contrast between the alienated nature of labour under capitalism and a communist society in which human beings freely developed their nature in co-operative production. For the first time there appeared together, if not yet united, what Engels described as the three constituent elements in Marx's thought – German idealist philosophy, French socialism, and English economics. It is above all these Manuscripts which (in the West at least) reorientated many people's interpretation of Marx – to the extent of their even being considered as his major work. They were not published until the early 1930s and did not attract public attention until after the Second World War; certain facets of the *Manuscripts* were soon assimilated to the existentialism and humanism then so much in vogue, and presented an altogether more attractive basis for non-Stalinist socialism than textbooks on dialectical materialism.

Seen in their proper perspective, these *Manuscripts* were in fact no more than a starting-point for Marx – an initial, exuberant outpouring of ideas to be taken up and developed in subsequent economic writings, particularly in the *Grundrisse* (1857–8) and in *Das Kapital* (1867). In these later works the themes of the '1844 Manuscripts' would certainly be pursued more systematically, in greater detail, and against a much more solid economic and historical background; but the central inspiration or vision was to remain unaltered: man's alienation in capitalist society, and the possibility of his emancipation – of his controlling his own destiny through communism.

Because of his political journalism, Marx was expelled from Paris at the end of 1844. He moved (with Engels) to Brussels, where he stayed for the next three years. He visited England, then the most advanced industrial country in the world, where Engels's family had cotton-spinning interests in Manchester. While in Brussels, Marx devoted himself to an intensive study of history. This he set out in a manuscript known as *The German Ideology* (also published posthumously); its basic thesis was that 'the nature of individuals depends on the material conditions determining their production'. Marx traced the history of the various modes of production and predicted the collapse of the present one – capitalism – and its replacement by communism.

At the same time that he was engaged in this theoretical work, Marx became involved in political activity and in writing polemics (as in *Misère de la Philosophie* (1847) (*The Poverty of Philosophy*) against what he considered to be the unduly idealistic socialism of Pierre Joseph Proudhon. He joined the Communist League, an organization of German emigré workers with its centre in London, for which he and Engels became the major theoreticians. At a conference of the league in London at the end of 1847, Marx and Engels were commissioned to write a *Manifest der kommunistischen Partei* (1848) (*Manifesto of the*

Communist Party), a declaration that was to become the most succinct expression of their views. Scarcely was the *Manifesto* published when the 1848 wave of revolutions broke in Europe.

Early in 1848, Marx moved back to Paris, where the revolution had first erupted. He then went on to Germany where he founded, again in Cologne, the *Neue Rheinische Zeitung*. This widely influential newspaper supported a radical democratic line against the Prussian autocracy. Marx devoted his main energies to its editorship, since the Communist League had been virtually disbanded. With the ebbing of the revolutionary tide, however, Marx's paper was suppressed. He sought refuge in London in May 1849, beginning the 'long, sleepless night of exile' that was to last for the rest of his life.

On settling in London, Marx grew optimistic about the imminence of a fresh revolutionary outbreak in Europe, and he rejoined the rejuvenated Communist League. He wrote two lengthy pamphlets on the 1848 revolution in France and its aftermath, entitled *Die Klassenkämpfe in Frankreich 1848 bis 1850* (1850) (*The Class Struggles in France*) and *Der achzehnte Brumaire des Louis Bonaparte* (1852) (*The Eighteenth Brumaire of Louis Bonaparte*). But he soon became convinced that 'a new revolution is possible only in consequence of a new crisis', and devoted himself to the study of political economy to determine the causes and conditions of this crisis.

During the first half of the 1850s the Marx family lived in three-room lodgings in the Soho quarter of London and experienced considerable poverty. The Marxes already had four children on their arrival in London, and two more were soon born. Of these, only three survived the Soho period. Marx's major source of income at this time (and later) was Engels, who was drawing a steadily increasing income from his father's cotton business in Manchester. This was supplemented by weekly articles he wrote as foreign correspondent for the *New York Daily Tribune*. Legacies in the late 1850s and early 1860s eased Marx's financial position somewhat, but it was not until 1869 that he had a sufficient and assured income settled on him by Engels.

Not surprisingly, Marx's major work on political economy

made slow progress. By 1857–8 he had produced a mammoth 800-page manuscript – a rough draft of a work that he intended should deal with capital, landed property, wage-labour, the state, foreign trade, and the world market. This manuscript, known as *Grundrisse* (or 'Outlines'), was not published until 1941. In the early 1860s he broke off his work to compose three large volumes, entitled *Theorien über den Mehrwert* (1861–3) (*Theories of Surplus Value*), that discussed his predecessors in political economy, particularly Adam Smith and David Ricardo.

It was not until 1867 that Marx was able to publish the first results of his work in Volume One of *Das Kapital*, devoted to a study of the capitalist process of production. Here he elaborated his version of the labour theory of value, and his conception of surplus value and exploitation that would ultimately lead to a falling rate of profit and the collapse of capitalism. Volumes Two and Three were largely finished in the 1860s, but Marx worked on the manuscripts for the rest of his life. They were published posthumously by Engels. In his major work, Marx's declared aim was to analyse 'the birth, life and death of a given social organism and its replacement by another, superior order'. In order to achieve this aim, Marx took over the concepts of the 'classical' economists that were still the generally accepted tool of economic analysis, and used them to draw very different conclusions. Ricardo had made a distinction between use-value and exchange-value. The exchange-value of an object was something separate from its price and consisted of the amount of labour embodied in the objects of production, though Ricardo thought that the price in fact tended to approximate to the exchange-value. Thus – in contradistinction to later analyses – the value of an object was determined by the circumstances of production rather than those of demand. Marx took over these concepts, but in his attempt to show that capitalism was not static but an historically relative system of class exploitation, he supplemented Ricardo's views by introducing the idea of surplus-value. Surplus-value was defined as the difference between the value of the products of labour and the cost of producing that labour-power, that is, the labourer's subsistence;

for the exchange-value of labour-power was equal to the amount of labour necessary to reproduce that labour-power and this was normally much lower than the exchange-value of the products of that labour-power.

The theoretical part of Volume One divides very easily into three sections. The first section is a rewriting of the *Zur Kritik der politischen Ökonomie* (1859) (*Critique of Political Economy*) and analyses commodities, in the sense of external objects that satisfy human needs, and their value. Marx established two sorts of value – use-value, or the utility of something, and exchange value which was determined by the amount of labour incorporated in the object. Labour was also of a twofold nature according to whether it created use-values or exchange-values. Because 'the exchange-values of commodities must be capable of being expressed in terms of something common to them all', and the only thing they shared was labour, then labour must be the source of value. But since evidently some people worked faster or more skilfully than others, this labour must be a sort of average 'socially necessary' labour time. There followed a difficult section on the form of value, and the first chapter ended with an account of commodities as exchange values, which he described as the 'fetishism of commodities' in a passage that recalls the account of alienation in the *Pariser Manuskripte* (1844) (Paris Manuscripts) and (even more) the *Note on James Mill*. 'In order,' said Marx here, 'to find an analogy, we must have recourse to the mist-enveloped regions of the religious world. In that world the productions of the human brain appear as independent beings endowed with life, and entering into relation both with one another and the human race. So it is in the world of commodities with the products of men's hands.' The section ended with a chapter on exchange and an account of money as the means for the circulation of commodities, the material expression for their values and the universal measure of value.

The second section was a small one on the transformation of money into capital. Before the capitalist era, people had sold commodities for money in order to buy more commodities. In the capitalist era, instead of selling to buy, people had bought to sell dearer: they had bought commodities with their money in order, by means of those commodities, to increase their money.

In the third section Marx introduced his key notion of surplus value, the idea that Engels characterized as Marx's principal 'discovery' in economics. Marx made a distinction between *constant* capital which was 'that part of capital which is represented by the means of production, by the raw material, auxiliary material and instruments of labour, and does not, in the process of production, undergo any quantitative alteration of value' and *variable* capital. Of this Marx said: 'That part of capital, represented by labour power, does, in the process of production, undergo an alteration of value. It both reproduces the equivalent of its own value, and also produces an excess, a surplus value, which may itself vary, may be more or less according to the circumstances.' This variation was the rate of surplus value around which the struggle between workers and capitalists centred. The essential point was that the capitalist got the worker to work longer than was merely sufficient to embody in his product the value of his labour power: if the labour power of the worker (roughly what it cost to keep him alive and fit) was £4 a day and the worker could embody £4 of value in the product on which he was working in eight hours, then if he worked ten hours, the last two hours would yield surplus value – in this case £1.

Thus surplus value could only arise from variable capital, not from constant capital, as labour alone created value. Put very simply, Marx's reason for thinking that the rate of profit would decrease was that, with the introduction of machinery, labour time would become less and thus yield less surplus value. Of course, machinery would increase production and colonial markets would absorb some of the surplus, but these were only palliatives and an eventual crisis was inevitable. These first nine chapters were complemented by a masterly historical account of the genesis of capitalism which illustrates better than any other writing Marx's approach and method. Marx particularly made pioneering use of official statistical information that came to be available from the middle of the nineteenth century onwards.

Meanwhile, Marx devoted much time and energy to the First International – to whose General Council he was elected on its foundation in 1864. This was one of the reasons he was so delayed in his work on *Das Kapital*. He was particularly active in preparing for the annual congresses of the International and in leading the struggle against the anarchist wing of the International led by Mikhail Bakunin. Although Marx won this contest, the transfer of the seat of the General Council from London to New York in 1872 – a move that Marx supported – led to the swift decline of the International. The most important political event during the existence of the International was the Paris Commune of 1871, when the citizens of Paris, in the aftermath of the Franco-Prussian war, rebelled against their government and held the city for two months. On the bloody suppression of this rebellion, Marx wrote one of his most famous pamphlets – entitled *Address on The Civil War in France* (1871) – which was an enthusiastic defence of the activities and aims of the Commune.

During the last decade of his life Marx's health declined considerably, and he was incapable of the sustained efforts of creative synthesis that had so obviously characterized his previous work. Nevertheless, he managed to comment substantially on contemporary politics in Germany and Russia. In Germany he opposed, in his *Randglossen zum Programm der deutschen Arbeiterpartei* (1875) (*Critique of the Gotha Programme*), the tendency of his followers Wilhelm Leibknecht and August Bebel to compromise with the state socialism of Ferdinand Lassalle in the interest of a united socialist party. In Russia, in correspondence with Vera Sassoulitch, he contemplated the possibility of Russia's bypassing the capitalist stage of development and building communism on the basis of the common ownership of land characteristic of the village council, or *mir*. Marx, however, was increasingly dogged by ill health, and he regularly travelled to European spas and even to Algeria in search of recuperation. The deaths of his eldest daughter and of his wife clouded the last years of his life, and he died in London on 13 March, 1883.

The influence of Marx, so narrow during his lifetime,

expanded enormously after his death. This influence was at first evident in the growth of the Social Democratic Party in Germany, but reached world-wide dimensions following the success of the Bolsheviks in Russia in 1917. Paradoxically, although the main thrust of Marx's thought was to anticipate that a proletarian revolution would inaugurate the transition to socialism in advanced industrial countries, Marxism was most successful in developing or Third World countries, such as Russia or China. Since the problems of these countries are primarily agrarian and the initial development of an industrial base, they are necessarily far removed from what were Marx's immediate concerns. On a more general level, over the whole range of the social sciences, Marx's materialist conception of history and his analysis of capitalist society have made him probably the most influential figure of the twentieth century.

David McLellan
University of Kent

Further Reading
Avineri, S. (1968), *The Social and Political Thought of Karl Marx*, Cambridge.
Cohen, G. (1978), *Karl Marx's Theory of History: A Defence*, Oxford.
Marx, K. (1977), *Selected Writings*, ed. D. McLellan, Oxford.
McLellan, D. (1974), *Karl Marx: His Life and Thought*, New York.
Ollman, B. (1971), *Alienation, Marx's Conception of Man in Capitalist Society*, Cambridge.
Plamenatz, J. (1975), *Karl Marx's Philosophy of Man*, Oxford.
Suchting, W. (1983), *Marx: An Introduction*, Brighton.
See also: *Marxian economics*.

Marxian Economics

Marxian economics traditionally begins from a general statement of the labour theory of value (GLTV): that value in commodity exchange is grounded on exploitation in production. This leads to an account of the labour process, showing how exploitation takes place and how it can be measured by a rate of exploitation – the hours worked for the employers – divided by the hours worked to support the labourer. From this, a special labour theory (SLTV) is developed: prices, or ratios of exchange between commodities, are proportioned to the hours of direct and indirect labour that went to produce them. These prices are easily calculable from input-output data, and have the important property that they are independent of the distribution of the surplus between the social classes. But, except in special cases, they are not consistent with a uniform rate of profit in capital, such as free competition would tend to establish (Steedman, 1977). (The question of the relation between prices based on labour values and prices based on a uniform rate of profit is known as 'the Transformation Problem'.)

Important as they are, the theories of exploitation and labour value are foundations. The edifice itself centres upon the General Law of Capitalist Accumulation (GLCA), that the accumulation of capital is accompanied, *pari passu*, by an increase in the proletariat, maintaining, therefore, an 'industrial reserve army' of the unemployed, proportioned in size to the total capital. The arguments for this proportion require a way of expressing prices which is independent of distribution (since, for example, when capital accumulates faster than the proletariat grows, wages rise and profits fall, slowing down accumulation), but do not otherwise depend on the SLTV. Having established the GLCA, Marx turned to the theory of circulation, the tendency of the rate of profit to fall, the behaviour of rents, the theory of crises, and the role of money, credit, and interest.

In the last twenty years there has been a great revival of Marxian economics, due chiefly to the work of Piero Sraffa (1960). Sraffa's construction of the 'Standard Commodity' which solves Ricardo's problem of 'the invariable measure of value', provides a way of expressing prices both consistent with a uniform rate of profit and invariant to changes in distribution. Hence, the SLTV can be discarded; the GLTV, on the other hand, remains unaffected, since the rate of exploitation, and the connection between exploitation and profits can be shown more clearly than ever in equation systems based on Sraffa

(Morishima, 1973). Thus, the GLCA can be established on a firm foundation, permitting an analytical treatment of the effects of class conflict on wages and exploitation, although modern work normally gives much greater scope to demand factors than Marx did.

However, the very system of equations which establishes the validity of the basic Marxian scheme – the GLTV and the GLCA – undermines the Marxian argument for the tendency of the rate of profit to fall simply as a result of a rise in the organic composition of capital. For firms will not adapt a new technique unless it is cheaper than the old, at current prices. But it can be shown that if it is cheaper, then when adapted and the new prices are established, the new rate of profit will never be less than the old (Roemer, 1981). Thus, the Marxian theory of crisis needs another foundation. This has led to interesting work on the theory of circulation, money and credit, bringing the Marxian tradition into contact with the work being done by the post-Keynesian school. In particular, Marxists and neo-Ricardians have been concerned with whether the rate of profit determines the rate of interest, or vice versa, or whether they are both determined together.

Questions of circulation and money lead to a re-examination of competition, and the tendency to greater centralization and concentration. Competition has been conceptualized as a form of strategic conflict, but there is as yet no generally accepted theory of the development and behaviour of the corporation. However, this is a rapidly developing field.

Marxian economics has greatly benefited from the Classical Revival instigated by Sraffa. But Marx founded his economic thinking on a critique of the Classics, basically contending that they took relations of social power for the natural order of things, and attributed to mere tokens – money, capital, commodities – power which really resided in class relationships. Modern Marxian economics likewise both learns from the post-Keynesian and modern Classical tradition, and establishes its separate identity through a critique of these schools. Its critique is essentially that of Marx: the economic system works according to laws, but these laws in turn depend on the nature

of the political and social system, and cannot be fully understood apart from the whole. This critique has particular force
when it comes to the theory of economic policy, for the post-
Keynesians, in particular, tend to attribute to the State power
and a degree of neutrality which Marxists do not believe possible under capitalism.

Edward J. Nell
The New School for Social Research, New York

References

Morishima, M. (1973), *Marx's Economics: A Dual Theory of Value and Growth*, Cambridge.

Roemer, J. (1981), *Analytical Foundations of Marxian Economic Theory*, Cambridge.

Sraffa, P. (1960), *Production of Commodities by Means of Commodities*, Cambridge.

Steedman, I. (1977), *Marx after Sraffa*, London.

See also: *labour theory of value*.

Mathematical Economics

Mathematical economics has developed from being a relatively
small branch of economic theory in 1950 to become almost
coextensive with mainstream economic theory. Its success has
been such that economists out of sympathy with the basic
assumptions and models of so-called neoclassical economic
theory have found themselves obliged to provide increasingly
mathematical formulations of radical economic theory derived
from the Marxian and Ricardian traditions. The reasons for
the rapid expansion of mathematical economics after 1950 lie
partly in the influx of ex-mathematicians to academic economics
– Kenneth Arrow, Gérard Debreu, Frank Hahn, Werner
Hildenbrandt – and partly in the increasing concern in all
branches of economics with formal rigour and with the establishment of economics as a 'scientific' discipline. Prior to the
mathematical formalization of economic theory and the introduction of advanced techniques of mathematical analysis, economic theorists had relied primarily on graphical techniques of

analysis and presentation. Up to a point these can be very effective, but they are inherently limited by the two-dimensional character of a piece of paper. More subtly, graphical techniques can introduce implicit assumptions whose significance may be neglected or very difficult to understand.

Historically, among the first applications of mathematical analysis in economics were Leon Walras's use of the theory of simultaneous equations to discuss the problem of equilibrium in several interrelated markets and Edgeworth's use of calculus to analyse consumer behaviour. These subjects remain at the heart of modern mathematical economics, though the mathematical techniques applied have changed totally. They also illustrate the increasingly close relationship between advances in certain areas of mathematical economics and pure mathematics. Walras's problem has stimulated the development of general equilibrium analysis which focuses on the conditions for the existence of a set of prices, or other instruments, which ensure that supply and demand are equal in all markets simultaneously when the resources, technological possibilities and consumer preferences that determine supply and demand are specified in quite general terms. If a unique general equilibrium can be shown to exist, one may then use comparative statistics to examine how the character of the equilibrium is altered if some of the initial conditions are changed. From such comparisons it may – or may not – be possible to infer the response of prices and quantities to a variety of changes in the world. General equilibrium analysis has come to depend heavily on modern developments in topology and functional analysis, so that the dividing line between the more abstract type of mathematical economics and pure mathematics has almost vanished.

The theory of individual consumer – or producer – behaviour has both benefited from and stimulated advances in the theory of mathematical programming and of convex analysis. As a consequence, familiar results derived by the application of calculus have been subsumed within a much more general theory which is based upon the concept of a maximum/minimum value function – that is, a profit or cost function for a producer, an indirect utility or expenditure function for a consumer. This theory exploits a number of powerful duality results which characterize interrelated maximization and minimization problems and can be given straightforward economic interpretations, such as the association of 'shadow prices' with the constraints which limit the set of feasible choices. This approach to consumer and producer theory has important empirical implications which can in principle be tested. For example, the theory of optimal consumer choice implies that compensated price responses must be symmetric – in other words, the change in the consumption of good i with respect to the price of good j must equal the change in the consumption of good j with respect to the price of good i – and that the compensated substitution effect must be negative – an increase in the price of good i should reduce the consumption of i. In both cases the compensated effect refers to the change after income has been adjusted so as to hold utililty constant. This compensation is obviously difficult to measure so that it is not possible to test these predictions directly in experiments, but indirect tests of the hypothesis of maximizing behaviour have been devised. The results have been mixed, but the mathematical developments have stimulated much fruitful empirical work and have provided the basis for modern welfare economics.

The assumptions of equilibrium and maximization which underpin most of economic theory are controversial, especially as descriptions of short-run behaviour. As a result, mathematical economists have sought to construct theoretical models which weaken or dispense with these assumptions. Unfortunately, though these can provide useful insights into particular problems or phenomena, the models are always open to the criticism that they are '*ad hoc*' in the sense that they rely upon specific types of behavioural response, and that their results are not robust to even quite small changes in the characterization of these responses. At present there seem to be no powerful simplifying principles which enable economists to analyse models of disequilibrium or non-maximizing behaviour – or even to agree on what these models should look like. Hence most of the current effort of mathematical economists is devoted to modifying standard equilibrium and maximizing models by incorporating considerations of uncertainty and differential information in the hope that this approach will provide the basis for reconciling the more obvious disparities between observed economic behaviour and theoretical predictions. Nonetheless, the basic philosophical problem of how far useful economic models can be developed without the fundamental assumptions of maximization and equilibrium remains unanswered. What, for instance, does it mean to describe someone as 'choosing' a course of action which *he* judges inferior to some other feasible alternative? Until a convincing solution to this problem is found, mathematical economists are likely to continue to rely upon equilibrium models of maximizing behaviour.

Gordon Hughes
University of Cambridge

Further Reading
Arrow, K. J. and Intriligator, M. D. (eds) (1981, 1983, 1984), *Handbook of Mathematical Economics, Vols I–III*, Amsterdam.
Cassels, J. W. S. (1981), *Economics for Mathematicians*, Cambridge.
Varian, H. R. (1978), *Microeconomic Analysis*, New York.
See also: *equilibrium; maximization.*

Maximization
According to an oft-quoted view, economics is about 'doing the best one can in a situation of scarcity'. Many, if not most, problems in economics fall under this heading. For example, the consumer is assumed to choose the best bundle of commodities out of the range possible given his income constraint. The government is assumed to choose its policies to do the best it can for society as a whole, again given the constraints it faces. Such optimization may be said to be at the heart of economic analysis. The mathematical counterpart of this essentially economic problem is the maximization of an objective function subject to constraints on the choice variables.

The general maximization problem may be written as

Max $W(\underline{x})$ subject to $\underline{x} \epsilon X$
$$\underset{\underline{x}}{}$$

where $W(\cdot)$ is the objective function, $\underline{x}$ is the vector of control (or choice) variables. These are shown to be restricted to the set X, which therefore specifies the constraints of the problem. The *economics* of the problem lies in the specification of the objective function $W(\cdot)$ and the constraint set $\underline{X}$. However, once these are specified, we still have to solve the problem in order to derive further economic results of interest. This is where the mathematical theory of maximization comes in.

If $\underline{x}^*$ satisfies

$W(\underline{x}^*) \geq W(\underline{x})$ for all $\underline{x} \epsilon X$

then $\underline{x}^*$ is said to be a *global* solution to the problem. On the other hand, if the inequality holds only for $\underline{x}$ in a neighbourhood of $\underline{x}^*$, then $\underline{x}^*$ is said to be a *local* solution to the problem. *The Weierstrass Theorem* in mathematics says that, if the set X is compact and non empty, and if the objective function $W(\underline{x})$ is continuous on X, then a global solution exists for the above problem. Most economic problems satisfy these conditions. However, can we say more about the nature of the solution $\underline{x}^*$? The answer is that we can, if we define the set $\underline{X}$ in greater detail.

For many economic problems the constraint set $\underline{X}$ can be specified implicitly as a series of inequalities which the control variable has to satisfy. Consider, therefore, the problem

Max $W(\underline{x})$ subject to $g(\underline{x}) \leq \underline{b}; \underline{x} \geq \underline{0}$

where $\underline{x}$ is a n $\times$ 1 vector. The $\underline{b}$ and the m $\times$ 1 vector of functions g define the constraints on $\underline{x}$. Consider now the following function

$\mathcal{L}(\underline{x}, \underline{\lambda}) = W(\underline{x}) + \underline{\lambda}_*(\underline{b} - g(\underline{x}))$

where $\underline{\lambda}$ is a m $\times$ 1 vector of non-negative auxilliary variables. The m elements of $\underline{\lambda}$ are known as Lagrange multipliers and $\mathcal{L}(\underline{x}, \underline{\lambda})$ is known as the Lagrangian of the problem. The *Kuhn-Tucker theorem* in nonlinear programming then provides the conditions which characterizes the solution to the problem. These conditions are

$$\frac{\partial \mathcal{L}}{\partial \underline{x}}(\underline{x}^*, \underline{\lambda}^*) \leq \underline{0}; \frac{\partial \mathcal{L}(\underline{x}^*, \underline{\lambda}^*)}{\partial \underline{x}} \cdot \underline{x}^* = \underline{0}; \underline{x}^* \leq \underline{0}$$

$$\frac{\partial \mathcal{L}}{\partial \lambda} (x^*, \lambda^*) \geq 0; \; \lambda^*_i \; \frac{\partial \mathcal{L}}{\partial \lambda} \; (x^*, \lambda^*) = 0; \; \lambda^* \geq 0.$$

The first part of the Kuhn-Tucker theorem says that if there exist x^*, λ^* satisfying the above conditions, then x^* is a solution to the problem. The second part say that if $W(\cdot)$ is concave, $g(\cdot)$ are convex and there is some point $\hat{x}$ for which the constraint is satisfied with strict inequality, then, for x^* to be a solution to the problem, there must exist λ^* such that x^*, λ^* satisfy the Kuhn-Tucker conditions.

The Kuhn-Tucker conditions provide the basis for characterizing the optimum in nost economic models. For example, if $x^* \geq 0$, then we must have that

$$\frac{\partial \mathcal{L}}{\partial x} \; (x^*, \lambda^*) = 0$$

or

$$\frac{\partial W(x^*)}{\partial x_i} = \lambda^* \cdot \frac{\partial g(x^*)}{\partial x_i} \text{ for i} = 1, 2, \ldots, n.$$

In the case where the problem is the consumer's problem of choosing quantities x_i to maximize his utility function $U(x)$ subject to a single budget constraint

$$\sum_{i=1}^{n} p_i x_i \leq y$$

these conditions become

$$\frac{\partial U(x^*)}{\partial x_i} = \lambda p_i \qquad i = 1, 2, \ldots, n$$

or

$$\frac{\partial U(x^*)}{\partial x_i} \bigg/ \frac{\partial U(x^*)}{\partial x_j} = \frac{p_i}{p_j}$$

that is, the marginal rate of substitution between any pair of goods must equal the price ratio of those two goods. Similar conditions can be derived and interpreted for other problems. In fact the λ^* have interpretation in terms of 'shadow prices' which tell us the values to the agent of releasing each constraint at the margin.

S. M. Ravi Kanbur
University of Essex

Further Reading
Baumol, W. (1965), *Economic Theory and Operations Analysis*, 2nd edn, Englewood Cliffs, N.J.
Dixit, A. K. (1975), *Optimization in Economic Theory*, London.
Intriligator, M. D. (1971), *Mathematical Optimization and Economic Theory*, Englewood Cliffs, N.J.

Microeconomics

Microeconomics is that portion of economic theory concerned with the economic behaviour of individual units in the economy, and the factors determining the prices and quantities exchanged of particular goods and services. It can be contrasted with *macroeconomics* which is concerned with the determination of values for aggregates for the economy. For example, microeconomics examines the determination of the price of wheat, or the relative prices of wheat and steel, or employment in the steel industry, while macroeconomics deals with the determination of the level of employment in a particular economy, or with the level of prices of all commodities. Although this distinction between two areas of economic analysis is useful for many purposes, and economic theory textbooks are usually devoted either to microeconomics (also known as 'price theory') or to macroeconomics, it should not be taken to imply that these two levels of analysis‑are independent. Micro questions, such as those concerning the relative prices produced in competitive and monopolistic industries, cannot be answered without reference to the level of aggregate demand in the economy, while macroeconomics is built on microfoundations that specify the nature of competition in different industries, for example, competitive or oligopolistic.

The development of microeconomics as a distinct area was part of the marginal or neoclassical approach that came to dominate economic theory after the 1970s. In contrast to classical economics that was concerned with the economic growth of nations due to the growth of their productive resources, and which explained the relative prices of goods on the basis of the 'objective' conditions of their costs of production, neoclassical theory turned its attention to the efficient allocation of given resources (under the implicit assumption of full employment) and to the 'subjective' determination of individual prices based on marginal utility.

The topics dealt with by microeconomic analysis are often presented under the following headings: (1) theory of consumer behaviour; (2) theory of exchange; (3) theory of production and cost; (4) theory of the firm; (5) theory of distribution; and (6) welfare economics. The common theme underlying these topics is the attempt of individual actors to achieve an optimal position, given the values of the parameters constraining their choices. Consumers try to maximize satisfaction (or utility) given their tastes, incomes and prices of all goods; firms try to maximize profits, and this means, among other things, that any rate of output is produced at least cost. The conditions for maximization are expressed in terms of marginal equalities. For example, for profit maximization a firm's rate of output should be such that marginal revenue is equal to marginal cost. In traditional approaches to microeconomics it is assumed that the self-seeking actions of individual units result in equilibrium positions where, given the values of the parameters, all participants are making the best of the situations facing them. They can be concerned either with partial equilibrium analysis (developed by Marshall) that concentrates on the determination of equilibrium values in a particular industry, assuming that the values in other industries are determined independently of these particular values, or with general equilibrium analysis (developed by Leon Walras) that provides full scope for the interdependence of all sectors of the economy, and deals with the simultaneous determination of all prices and quantities in the system. This generality is obtained at some cost, with the treatment being formal and mathematical, and important aspects of economic processes that occupy time are ignored.

A. Asimakopulos
McGill University

Further Reading
Asimakopulos, A. (1978), *An Introduction to Economic Theory: Microeconomics*, Toronto.
Mansfield, E. (1982), *Microeconomics*, 4th edn, New York.
See also: *consumer behaviour; cost-benefit analysis; firm, theory of; welfare economics.*

Mixed Economy

A purely private right to a resource may be said to exist when an individual can select any use for that resource including the option of sale. This may be contrasted with other specifications of property rights like communal access to roads, state owner-ship of railways or, indeed, when any privately-owned resource is subject to restrictions in the range of its use. The degree to which purely private rights prevail in an economy would reflect the degree to which an economy is mixed, but a precise measure has yet to be devised.

There are two broad ways of thinking about the mixed economy. One is to ask how and why the public sector has increased its share of property rights. The other way is to ask why the economy should be mixed, and this has been the main focus of debate in the post-war period up to about the late 1960s. It has been a debate partly about aims, but perhaps more about whether certain economic and social aims are better achieved by non-private rights to resources. In this sense, the mixed economy is the outcome of policies consciously espoused by parties, supported by a majority of voters and executed by governments. To understand the post-1945 growth of the public sector, one needs, in this light, firstly to emphasize the effect of the inter-war years of large-scale unemployment. For many people, the low income levels and social tragedies seemed damning evidence of the inefficiencies and injustices of capi-talism, to be remedied in part by public ownership of the means of production. Doubts that resources would be efficiently allocated in such a system disappeared for some by the demon-stration that public ownership was consistent with the use of a price system (see, for example, Lange, 1936). The efficient allocation of resources which was theoretically obtainable in a perfectly competitive world was obtainable also by public firms adjusting output levels to the point where prices equalled marginal costs, but with the key difference that, with capital publicly owned, profits accrued to the nation rather than to a select few. Similarly, the Keynesian demonstration that unemployment could be an equilibrium feature of capitalism pointed to an enhanced role for the state. While an expansion of private investment would have beneficial effects on income and employment levels comparable to increased public spending, Keynes had stressed the role of pessimistic expectations in preventing a sufficiently low level of interest rates or in inhibiting a business investment expansion independently of interest-rate levels.

In the two decades from 1945, these arguments gradually lost some of their force. Rising living standards in economies where over 60 per cent of GDP still emanated from the private sector, financial losses in public enterprises, waiting-lists for certain public services together with some embryonic doubts, especially by American economists, about whether government deficit manipulation was actually the source of full employment, undermined some of the support for government economic activity. That support was, however, largely sustained, at least intellectually, by several strands of earlier thought receiving increased emphasis. It is clear, for example, that the analysis of public goods has a wider applicability than law, order and defence. In so far as the issue is one of spill-over effects in consumption and production, then, in a world of continuing urbanization, government corrective action for transport congestion, air pollution and safety regulation seemed vital. In a similar technical vein, while public ownership was no longer seen as the best vehicle for improving income distribution, a strand in the early support for such government intervention was to prevent private monopolistic exploitation of economies of scale common in fuel, transport and general infrastructure development. The arguments for public provision of education, health and even housing had never relied solely on the issue of income distribution; rather there were questions about the access to information, to capital markets and to the speed with which the price system could deal fairly with shortages. Finally, though perhaps least convincingly, the differential growth experience of the post-1945 economies entered the economist's agenda in the 1960s with government again seen as an important catalyst.

There has, however, always been the view that the above is a misconception both of how the private competitive system works and how public ownership works. Private monopoly 'in the field' is quite consistent with competiton for the field so that auction bidding for franchises for refuse collection, electricity supply and such services could eliminate monopoly profits. How, secondly, will private decision takers react to the existence of spill-over effects? If there are net gains to be exploited by public action on the height of chimneys or on river pollution by up-stream firms, how can we be sure that private decision takers have not already entered economic dealings to their joint satisfaction? And if the argument is that, especially with large groups, there are transaction costs in private exchange relations, so also are there costs to the government in acquiring information, casting doubt on whether its solution will be any better. More generally, why should the analysis of utility-maximizing behaviour stop at the door of the public sector? Civil servants, public industry managers and politicians are the relevant decision takers. In the Austrian tradition the cost of an activity is the value of the alternative foregone by the decision taker, not by some vague entity like the state. In summary, there is no guarantee on this line of thought that government action will yield a superior solution to the private sector solution with all its warts (see, for example, Demsetz, 1982). Such doubts mounted in the 1970s and 1980s fuelled in part by the increasing growth of government and the part this might have played as the source of monetary expansion in the late 1960s and early 1970s. By the mid 1970s, moreover, Keynesianism as a theoretical framework for analysing unemployment and inflation was under strong attack, precisely because of its deficient analysis of the micro behaviour of agents in the economy.

While such debates on policy have been continually supported by positive studies of how economic systems work, they have not fully confronted the basic question of why the public sector has grown. Indeed, much of the debate has treated the state as an autonomous force, as something separate from the features of the rest of the economy. Doubts about such a characterization should arise when it is recognized that the pre-nineteenth century, early modern European absolutist states had interventionist bureaucracies and armies where the attenuation of private rights, if we could only measure it, might bear comparison to modern state sectors. Many Marxists would certainly want to locate the characterization of the modern state in the capitalist mode of production, in the sense of the state being another form of monopoly capital or a collective form to secure for capitalism what private capital on its own cannot secure -- legal system, control of trade unions, and so on. A longer-term view is also developing in other quarters (North, 1982; Olson, 1982). The industrialization which started in the late-eighteenth century meant a rapidly increasing division of labour, thereby enhancing the role of transaction costs and the supply of organized interest groups. The same forces which have advanced the middleman, the white-collar worker and those engaged in banking, accounting, law, insurance, property and trade are also important in prompting the provision of transaction cost reducing services by government, that is, basic transportation, justice, police, fire, defence, postal services, licensing, quality inspection and measurement standards. The attenuation of purely private rights usually requires group or collective action; there are in-built disincentives to such action which, in democracies, take a long time to overcome. It was in the latter part of the nineteenth century that the significant changes became observable. In 1869–1970 the percentage of the US labour force in government grew from 3.5 per cent to 18.1 per cent matching rises from 7.8 per cent to 19.1 per cent in retail trade, 0.4 per cent to 4.0 per cent in finance, insurance and real estate, and 11.1 per cent to 17.4 per cent in other services. It is probably only by a further analysis of such long-run trends that we shall fully understand the mixed economy.

Robert Millward
University of Salford

References
Demsetz, H. (1982), *Economic, Legal and Political Dimensions of Competition*, Amsterdam.
Lange, O. (1936/7), 'On the economic theory of socialism', *Review of Economic Studies*, 4.
North, D. C. and Wallis, J. J. (1982), 'American government expenditures: a historical perspective', *American Economic Association: Papers and Proceedings*.
Olson, M. (1982), *The Rise and Decline of Nations*, New Haven.

Further Reading
Lord Roll of Ipsden (ed.) (1982), *The Mixed Economy*, London.
See also: *crowding out; nationalization; planning, economic; public goods.*

Monetarism

Although there are probably as many varieties of economic doctrine called 'monetarism' as there are economists who call themselves 'monetarist', there is an agreed central postulate: that the money supply is the most important determinant of the level of aggregate money-income.

The development of monetarism, which began in the 1950s with some articles by Milton Friedman and his associates (Friedman, 1956, 1959), can be seen as a reassertion of the importance of money against a simplified form of Keynesian economics which denied money any significant role.

Monetarism's main postulate has its roots in the quantity theory of money. It shares with older quantity theory the belief that the supply of money is determined 'exogenously', that is, independently of the demand for money, even though the bulk of what we now think of as money consists of bank deposits. In an economy with a relatively small international sector like the United States (where monetarism arose), the supply of money is assumed to be determined by the monetary authorities; implicitly their ability to control bank-created money is not questioned.

Changes in this exogenously-determined money supply affect the economy through the behaviour of those who receive the money, codified in a 'demand-for-money function'. Monetarists see the holding of money as an alternative to holding other assets, but since 'other assets' include all consumption and investment goods, a rise in the quantity of money causes prices to rise and stimulates output, thus preserving the link between money and income which is the hallmark of quantity theory. Direct effects of monetary changes on interest rates are treated as unimportant or transitory, though rises in nominal interest rates to cover for inflation (the 'Fisher effect') figure prominently.

Except at full employment, when there is no scope for raising output, it is always an open question how a change in aggregate income is distributed between price changes and altered levels of production and employment. Monetarists explain this distribution in terms of labour's demand for a wage which embodies their expectations of its purchasing power (the 'real wage'): it is only when labour begins to 'catch on' to the fact that economic activity has risen and to expect rising prices that they make higher wage claims; by thus raising costs the balance between price and output changes shifts towards prices. (This is precisely the argument of Hume in 1752.)

Unless the monetary authorities accommodate the increased prices with more money, the wage rise will also tend to offset previous gains in employment. If the authorities *do* accommodate, labour will once again adjust its expectations and an inflationary situation is set up, no more favourable to employment in the end.

The possibility of permanent gains in employment and output by purely monetary means is thus denied. The level of employment to which the economy tends to return through wage and price rises of the kind described is called the 'natural rate of unemployment', although the air of inevitability that the phrase conveys is misleading. The level of unemployment to which it corresponds is determined jointly by producers, workers and the monetary authorities – human agents, not natural forces. The natural rate of unemployment corresponds to an absence of Keynesian involuntary unemployment, bearing in mind that unemployment at the going money wage due to agreement, open or tacit, amongst workers not to work for less is accounted voluntary.

Monetarists are sceptical of government demand-management policies even as a temporary stimulus to employment and output. They argue that the economy is 'financially constrained' (that is, money is exogenous) and that attempts by government to finance expansionary spending programmes by increasing the public debt will push up interest rates and 'crowd out' intended private expenditure similarly based on borrowing. Financing by means of a monetary expansion is admitted to be efficacious as long as prices are not expected to rise, provoking the wage response explained above, and as long as the existing level of unemployment is above the 'natural rate'.

The more quickly expectations adjust, the less likely is any real benefit, in terms of output and employment, from money-financed expansion. Substantial and prolonged monetary expansion results almost entirely in inflation.

Some monetarists believe that expectations adjust very rapidly even without prolonged experience of a particular rate of monetary change, provided the monetary authorities announce their intentions. These monetarists (often called 'New Classical economists') discount both the potential for short-term expansion and the output and employment costs of monetary contraction. They assume that adjustment will fall chiefly on prices and wages.

Under fixed exchange rates the money supply is not under the control of the monetary authorities of open economies. The money supply can be made to adjust to home demand for money through expenditure on imports or may be determined by events abroad. Most monetarists welcomed flexible exchange rates on the grounds that they afforded some insulation of the home economy.

Victoria Chick
University College London

References

Friedman, M. (1956), 'The quantity theory of money – a restatement', in M. Friedman (ed.), *Studies in the Quantity Theory of Money*, Chicago. (Also in Friedman, M. (1969), *The Optimum Quantity of Money and Other Essays*, London.)

Friedman, M. (1959), 'The demand for money: some theoretical and empirical results', *Journal of Political Economy*, 67. (Reprinted in Friedman 1969, cited above.)

Hume, D. (1752), *Of Money*, in E. Rotwein (ed.) (1955), [*David Hume's*] *Writings on Economics*, London.

Further Reading

Laidler, D., Tobin, J., Matthews, R. C. O. and Meade, J. E. (1981), 'Conference: "Monetarism – An Appraisal" ', *Economic Journal*, 91.

Stein, J. L. (ed.) (1976), *Monetarism*, Amsterdam.

See also: *monetary policy; money; money, quantity theory of.*

Monetary Policy

Monetary policy can be broadly construed to include virtually all aspects of a country's monetary and financial system, or much more narrowly, taking the institutional background as given. Taking the broader perspective first establishes a rationale for monetary policy.

The central question of monetary policy used to be that of the monetary standard – the choice of the monetary metal and the metallic content of the coinage. The purpose of policy was to establish stability and uniformity of the coinage and thus inspire confidence in it and gain general acceptability for it, to the benefit of sovereign and state.

Although obscured by the enormous institutional changes that have taken place, the maintenance of confidence in money and monetary institutions is still the main purpose of monetary policy. Hence the concern, at various points in history, with the maintenance of convertibility (into gold domestically and gold or a 'key currency' internationally), the prevention of 'over-issue' of credit, the avoidance of financial crises and banking panics, and the stability of the price level.

Though monetary policy in the broadest sense is a government matter, many issues of policy and virtually all responsibility for implementation rest with central banks (for example, the Bank of England, the Federal Reserve System). Since 1946, most Western governments have accepted some responsibility for their country's economic performance, and monetary policy became a tool of 'stabilization policy': the promotion of economic growth without severe recession or inflation. Price stability and a 'healthy' balance of payments remained important as contributions to this end. Until the 1970s it was accepted that the burden of stabilization policy should fall on fiscal policy, monetary policy playing a subordinate role. The interrelation between monetary and fiscal policy is now better appreciated.

The distinctive contribution of monetary policy lies in the influence the central bank can exert on the availability of credit, interest rates and the liquidity of the economy, as measured by the money supply or some broader aggregate. The links between these variables and the broader goals of stabilization policy is complex. There are conflicting theories as to which links are important. Keynesians stress interest rates and the availability of credit, because of their influence on expenditures made with borrowed funds. Monetarists favour a money supply target because they see a strong connection between the money supply and aggregate expenditure (income). Monetarists also favour a 'rule' of stable monetary growth rather than discretionary policy, on the grounds that policy-induced variations in the money supply are a source of instability rather than a contribution to stabilization policy.

The instruments used to influence whatever target is chosen vary from country to country according to the structure of their banking systems and financial markets. In countries with developed markets, central bank purchases and sales of securities ('open market operations') are perhaps the most important instruments. These operations may influence both interest rates and the liquidity, and hence the lending capacity, of banks.

Monetary policy is fraught with conflict. There are potential conflicts between the goals of stabilization policy (for example, domestic expansion and balance-of-payments or exchange rate stability) which monetary policy cannot resolve with the limited instruments at its command. In addition the central bank's responsibility for managing the government debt, given the desire of governments to borrow cheaply, may be inconsistent with its stabilization role. Fundamentally, however, both of these roles at times conflict with responsibility, once the sole focus of monetary policy, for the stability of the financial structure. Concern for financial stability limits the amount of pressure which may be exerted on the banks or financial markets at any time, and the central bank must stand ready to provide liquidity when the pressure threatens default on commitments. This role, called 'lender of last resort', was urged on central banks by Bagehot (1873) to avert banking panics.

It has come to be realized that Bagehot's principle has much wider application. Pressure on the financial system will raise interest rates as the affected institutions compete for liquid funds. High interest rates have many undesirable features, and they can even rise high enough to contribute further to instability. Thus central banks have to exercise the lender-of-last-resort function more frequently. An expansionary bias is thereby imparted to the system and also derives from the fact that the financial system is not static but is perpetually growing in complexity and sophistication. Attempts to curb the activities of the financial system are a considerable incentive for those involved in it to find ways round the constraints (Minsky, 1957). Monetary policy's stabilization role must be seen as secondary and limited by the need to maintain confidence in the monetary system.

Victoria Chick
University College London

References
Bagehot, W. (1873), *Lombard Street*, London.
Minsky, H. P. (1957), 'Central banking and money market changes', *Quarterly Journal of Economics*, 71. (Reprinted in

H. P. Minsky (1952), *Inflation, Recession and Economic Policy*, Brighton.)

Further Reading
Chick, V. (1977), *The Theory of Monetary Policy*, Oxford.
Goodhart, C. A. E. (1975), *Money, Information and Uncertainty*, London.
See also: *banking; monetarism; money; money, quantity theory of.*

Money

The ordinary person knows what money is: it is the stuff one uses to buy things with. While money has taken many different concrete forms, both across societies and over time, its defining feature is general acceptability: people are always glad to take it, whether they intend to keep it for a time as a form of saving or to spend it.

The economist, looking at money from a macroeconomic perspective, sees in those two possibilities of disposal what D. H. (later Sir Dennis) Robertson called 'money on the wing' and 'money at rest': money as the medium of exchange which facilitates the circulation of goods and services, and money as the store of value which allows its holder to postpone specific expenditure decisions, thus leaving producers uncertain about future demands for their goods.

In a financially sophisticated society, other assets are close substitutes for money in both these functions. Assets may be ranked by the ease and speed with which they can be converted into money without significant loss of value. The better substitutes are called liquid assets. Money retains distinction, however, in being the asset acceptable as the final means of payment: one may use, say, a credit card ('plastic money'), as the medium of exchange, but one discharges the debt thus incurred with one of the assets which counts as money.

Money itself is not homogeneous. At any point in time in any society there are several different concrete expressions of the functions of money, if only because transactions differ greatly in size. Copper coins coexisted with gold or silver coins to cover small transactions, just as coins and notes coexist with bank deposits in modern economies. Over time, as public confidence in new forms of money develops, a practical definition of money will come to include those new assets. Central banks now collect data on several more or less inclusive monetary aggregates.

Government has done much to establish the general acceptability of particular assets. The sovereign's head on coins was designed to testify to their metallic content. Private coiners were prepared to pay a fee ('seignorage') for this stamp of uniform quality, which enhanced the coins' acceptability. As late as the 1930s, both J. M. Keynes and Irving Fisher hesitated to regard bank deposits as 'proper money', reserving unqualified acceptance only of notes and coin issued by government. As privately-issued forms of money such as bank deposits have usurped coin as the dominant form of money, the precondition for acceptability has been confidence in the convertibility of deposits into state-issued money – notes and coin. This convertibility came to be supported by central banks, providing state money as lenders of last resort. This function of central banks greatly adds to the unification and stability of the monetary and financial system.

Since no single monetary asset is acceptable in all transactions, the criterion of *general* acceptability requires further clarification. There are major acceptors who influence the course of monetary evolution. The state may declare some assets legal tender and may declare what it will accept in payment of taxes. The necessity to raise that particular form of money is an important influence on economic behaviour as long as the exchange of one kind of money for another at par is not assured. Similarly, the use of particular forms of money in the payment of wages both reflects and enhances, in a self-reinforcing manner, acceptability based on social consensus.

These examples represent the polarities of an important debate on the foundations of money: whether money is a creation of the state or of private consensus (see Frankel, 1977). In a modern Western economy, both influences are important. Bank deposits would not be acceptable by workers in payment of wages if deposits were in turn not useful in carrying out transactions, or if deposit money were not convertible in terms of notes and coin at par. Maintaining the par value of state and bank money is a prime objective of prudent banking, but it is underpinned by the actions of the state.

Nor would it be possible to pay wages by cheque had the Truck Acts not been repealed, though that action was taken only when bank deposits had reached a high level of social acceptability. Similarly, it is doubtful if a cheque on a bank deposit would be acceptable in payment of taxes if its value in terms of state-issued notes and coin were uncertain. There is a mutuality of state and social support of money in the modern Western economy: the dichotomy erected by philosophers of money, between state-money and socially-accepted money, needs to be replaced by an appreciation of the interactive support of the two forces in a modern economy.

Victoria Chick
University College London

Reference
Frankel, S. H. (1977), *Money: Two Philosophies*, Oxford.

Money, Quantity Theory of

The quantity theory of money is a rather curious way of referring to the connection between the quantity of money and the general level of prices. The connection was well established by the middle of the seventeenth century: 'It is a common saying that plenty or scarcity of money makes all things dear or good cheap' (Thomas Mun, 1664). A modern version is 'Inflation is too much money chasing too few goods.' In its strongest version, money is not only the cause of price changes but prices are supposed to change in proportion to the monetary change, in the long run.

In the sixteenth and seventeenth centuries discussion of the relation between money and prices could scarcely pass for a *theory*, because there was no articulation of the causal connection. Its status was more that of shrewd observation, the causal role of money made clear by the influx of precious metals from the New World.

The proportionality doctrine was stated by John Locke (1691). His purpose was to refute the mercantilist equation of money with national wealth by showing that money's value varied inversely with its quantity. His reasoning was based on an abstract comparison of the same economy with two different stocks of money (allowing for the velocity of money's circulation). Hume (1752), however, asserted that proportionality applied to ordinary monetary increases and decreases in the long run. It is a plausible enough doctrine in a static, preindustrial society but it is quite unsupported by any reasoning by Hume or anyone since, though it is still widely asserted (as the 'neutrality of money').

Hume's treatment of the short-run effects of monetary changes was, in contrast, good theory – indeed the first *explanation* of the relation between money and prices. (In today's language he explained the 'transmission mechanism'.) An increase of money (from abroad, in exchange for exports) encourages greater output and employment, without, at first, any increase in wages. If workers become scarce, wages will increase (though Hume remarks that the manufacturer will also expect greater productivity). At first, prices of wage-goods are stable and production rises to meet demand. But gradually all prices rise and the situation prior to the monetary increase is restored. This line of reasoning is both congruent with Keynesian export-led growth and similar to the theory put forward by Milton Friedman (1969).

J. S. Mill provides the bridge to modern theory in two ways: he makes clear that the medium-of-exchange function of money is crucial to quantity theory and he deals with nonmetallic, credit money (bank notes, cheques). The older theorists allowed for hoarding, but the advent of credit money, which could not be hoarded in ways which served an alternative purpose, such as plate, simultaneously made hoarding more difficult to justify and gave rise to the possibility that purchases could be made without possessing money (coin).

These problems were new. Irving Fisher (1911) formalized them, but did not solve them, by separating currency from bank-deposit money and postulating a different velocity of circulation for each. It is not obvious which should be the larger, or by how much.

An approach to the hoarding problem is provided by the development, in 'Cambridge quantity theory' (Marshall, 1923), of the concept of a demand for money based chiefly on trans-actions needs. Expected expenditure levels were indicated by one's income and wealth. It was considered plausible that some money might be held idle (hoarded) if one had so little wealth that lending at interest was not open to one. This would affect the velocity of circulation but probably not substantially.

Friedman (1956), though beginning from the antithetical proposition that money is an asset to be held, contrives in the end to arrive at a similar formulation. It is implied that an exogenous change in money will affect aggregate money-income, but the division between price and quantity in the long run is no more resolved than it was in Hume's time and in the short run somewhat less resolved.

Keynes, although originally an adherent of the quantity theory (1923), broke with it in 1936 by providing a rationale for substantial hoarding of money when interest rates were expected to rise.

The problem of credit raised by Mill is not amenable to analysis in the demand-for-money framework and remains an unresolved part of monetary theory generally.

Victoria Chick
University College London

References

Fisher, I. (1911), *The Purchasing Power of Money*, New York.

Friedman, M. (1956), 'The quantity theory of money – a restatement', in M. Friedman (ed.), *Studies in the Quantity Theory of Money*, Chicago.

Friedman, M. (1969), 'The role of monetary policy', *American Economic Review*, 58.

Hume, D. (1955 [1752]), *Of Money*, in E. Rotwein (ed.), [*David Hume's*] *Writings on Economics*, London.

Keynes, J. M. (1923), *A Tract on Monetary Reform*, London.

Keynes, J. M. (1936), *The General Theory of Employment, Interest and Money*, London.

Locke, J. (1823 [1691]), *Some Considerations of the Lowering of Interest and Raising the Value of Money, Works of John Locke*, Vol. V, London.

Marshall, A. (1923), *Money, Credit and Commerce*, London.

Mill, J. S. (1857), *Principles of Political Economy*, 2 Vols, London.

Mun, T. (1928 [1664]), *England's Treasure by Foreign Trade*, Oxford.

Further Reading

Blaug, M. (1978), *Economic Theory in Retrospect*, 3rd edn, London.

See also: *monetarism; money.*

Monopoly

Monopoly in the strictest sense refers to a market where there is only one seller facing a multitude of buyers. Monopoly always attracted the attention of economists, being the exact opposite of the market form which they regarded as normal in capitalist societies: full competition. In competition, with many sellers in the market, each firm has to accept the going price and will try to produce at low costs as far as possible. Output will tend to be high and prices low. The monopolist can influence the price by keeping supplies short. Monopoly, therefore, leads to lower output, higher prices, and higher profits. The exact analysis of this strategy was provided by the French nineteenth-century economist Antoine Augustin Cournot.

Monopoly and full competition are two extreme cases. They are rarely found in pure form in the real world. Pure monopoly is hardly possible, because substitute commodities will exert competitive pressures on monopolists. Alfred Marshall recognized in the nineteenth century that in reality we normally find various mixtures of monopoly and competition. This was incorporated into economic theory in the 1930s through the work on 'monopolistic competition' by E. H. Chamberlin and Joan Robinson.

'Normative' economics has usually condemned monopoly

because it leads to an inefficient allocation of resources. Some economists have pointed to possible dynamic advantages of monopoly. In J. A. Schumpeter's theory, adventurous entrepreneurs can establish temporary monopolies by creating new products, and this is seen as the source of economic progress. Also, large-sized firms with safe monopolistic profits may be more research-oriented. Against this has to be set the room for inaction and inefficiency (through lack of competitive pressure). Empirical work on these questions has not led to definite results.

Kurt W. Rothschild
Johannes Kepler University, Linz

Further Reading
Hunter, A. (1969), *Monopoly and Competition. Selected Readings*, Harmondsworth.
Machlup, F. (1952/67), *The Political Economy of Monopoly*, Baltimore.
See also: *cartels and trade associations; competition; oligopoly.*

Multinational Enterprises
A multinational enterprise owns and controls productive activities located in more than one country. It owns the outputs of these activities even though it may not own the assets used – these may be hired locally in each country. The multinational does not necessarily transfer capital abroad: finance can often be obtained locally as well. The multinational is thus first and foremost an *international producer*, and only secondarily a *foreign investor*.

The activities of the multinational enterprise form an integrated system; they are not usually a mere portfolio of unrelated operations. The rationale for integration is that managerial control within the enterprise co-ordinates the activities more profitably than would arm's length contractual relations (Buckley and Casson, 1976).

The antecedents of the modern multinational enterprise are found in the late nineteenth century, in British direct investments in the colonies, and in the merger movement in the US from which the modern corporation evolved. In the interwar period, multinational operations focused upon backward integration into minerals (especially oil). Horizontal integration was effected through international cartels rather than multinational firms. After World War II, many US enterprises began to produce in Western Europe, particularly in high-technology industries producing differentiated products. They transferred to Europe new US technology, together with improved management and accounting practices, and the experience of selling to a multicultural market of the kind that was developing within the European Community. In the 1970s European firms began to produce in the US on a larger scale than before, often in the same industries in which US firms were producing in Europe. At the same time, Japanese firms began to produce abroad on a large scale in low-wage South-East Asian countries, particularly in low-technology industries such as textiles.

The value added by some of the world's largest multinationals now exceeds the gross national products of some of the smaller countries in which they produce. On the other hand, there are increasing numbers of very small multinational firms: not all multinationals conform to the popular image of the giant corporation.

Multinational operations provide firms with a number of benefits in addition to the operating economies afforded by integration. Intermediate products transferred between the parent company and its overseas subsidiaries – or between one subsidiary and another – can be valued at 'transfer prices' which differ from those prevailing in arm's length trade. The transfer prices can be set so as to minimize *ad valorem* tariff payments, to reallocate profits to subsidiaries in low-tax countries, and to allow the enterprise to bypass exchange controls by disguising capital transfers as income. Transfer prices are particularly difficult for fiscal authorities to detect when the resources transferred are inherently difficult to value: this is particularly true of payments for technology and management services which are very common in firms in high-technology industries. Reliable evidence on transfer pricing is difficult to obtain, though there are some proven instances of it.

Multinational operations also give the enterprise access to privileged information through membership of producers' associations in different countries, and enable it to co-ordinate internationally the lobbying of government for favourable changes in the regulatory environment. Multinationals are often accused of enlisting the support of powerful governments in the pursuit of their interests in foreign countries, though once again reliable evidence is difficult to obtain. The United Nations actively monitors the behaviour of multinationals through its Centre on Transnational Corporations.

Mark Casson
University of Reading

Reference
Buckley, P. J. and Casson, M. C. (1976), *The Future of the Multinational Enterprise*, London.

Further Reading
Caves, R. E. (1982), *Multinational Enterprise and Economic Analysis*, Cambridge.
Dunning, J. H. and Pearce, R. D. (1981), *The World's Largest Industrial Enterprises*, Farnborough, Hants.
Stopford, J. M., Dunning, J. H. and Haberich, K. O. (1980), *The World Directory of Multinational Enterprises*, London.
See also: *business concentration; cartels and trade associations; international trade.*

Multiplier

A multiplier is a coefficient which relates the change brought about in one variable, considered endogenous, to the change in another variable considered determinant. A large number of multipliers have been defined in modern economics: the bank credit multiplier, which relates the change in total bank deposits to a change in the high-powered money base; the export multiplier, which relates a change in equilibrium real income to a change in exports; and so on. The term was originally used by Richard Kahn and John Maynard Keynes to refer to the coefficients relating ultimate employment and equilibrium real income to an exogenous change in primary employment in the investment goods industries or investment demand respectively.

The concept of the investment multiplier can easily be illustrated:

Given a consumption function:

$$C = a + by \quad \ldots \ldots 1$$

Where
C = aggregate consumption
a = autonomous consumption i.e. consumption that is independent of income
b = the marginal propensity to consume (mpc)
y = income

and an investment function:

$$I_p = \bar{I} \quad \ldots \ldots \ldots 2$$

Where
I_p = planned investment
$\bar{I}$ = exogenously determined investment

and characterizing equilibrium by the realization of all plans, then in equilibrium planned savings must equal planned investment

i.e. $S_p = I_p \ldots \ldots \ldots 3$
or $Y = C_p + I_p \ldots \ldots 4$

substituting 1 and 2 into 4 and solving for Y

$$Y = a + b_y + \bar{I}$$
$$Y(1 - b) = a + \bar{I}$$
$$Y = [a + I] \times \frac{1}{1-b}$$

The expression in square brackets is all spending which is independent of income, and equilibrium income is the product of this expression and a second term: $\frac{1}{1-b}$ i.e. $\frac{1}{1-mpc}$. As the marginal propensity to consume is assumed a positive fraction the value of the whole expression exceeds unity, and as the mpc and the marginal propensity to save, mps, must, by definition, sum to one the expression can be rewritten as $\frac{1}{mps}$.

Now consider an increase in exogenously given investment, $\Delta\bar{I}_p$. Denote the derived change in equilibrium income by Δy. We define

$\frac{\Delta Y}{\Delta I_p}$ as the multiplier.

Using equation 5. for the initial equilibrium income now called y_0:

$$y_0 = [a + I] \frac{1}{1-b} \quad\text{...} \quad 5a$$

If $\bar{I}$ increases by $\Delta\bar{I}$ the new equilibrium, y_1, is given by

$$y_1 = [a + I + \Delta I] \frac{1}{1-b} \quad\text{..} \quad 6$$

so that $\Delta y = y_1 - y_0 = \Delta I \frac{1}{1-b}$ 7

and $\qquad\qquad \frac{\Delta y}{\Delta I} = \frac{1}{1-b}$ 8

Thus $\frac{1}{1-mpc}$ is the multiplier. As it exceeds unity and change in investment, spending (or indeed in autonomous spending of any kind in the current simple model), it has an amplified or '*multiplier*' effect. To give this algebra an intuitive interpretation, consider the effects of the rise in investment: incomes will be created for the producers of the investment goods who in turn will allocate this incremental income according to their propensities to consume and save, hence generating new income for yet other groups who produce the goods and services purchased. This interpretation of the multiplier emphasizes the underlying practical proposition that one person's expenditure constitutes another person's income and that a change in exogenous spending will precipitate a cycle of income creation and expenditure. Given the marginal propensity to consume b, we know consumer demand at each round of income creation and therefore the income which is passed on:

Summing up we obtain an estimate of ΔY thus:

$$\Delta Y = \Delta I_p + b\ \Delta I_p + b^2\ \Delta I_p + b^3\ \Delta I_p \ldots \ldots + b^n \Delta I_p.$$

The sum of such an expansion, that is, ΔY, is given by $\Delta I_p \times 1 - b^{n+1}/1 - b$ which in the limit becomes $\Delta I_p \times 1/1 - b$ which confirms our earlier result.

It now becomes clear that the restoration of equilibrium requires that the new income level be large enough that, given the savings propensity, just enough new savings will be forthcoming so that the equilibrium condition $\Delta S_p = \Delta I_p$ is satisfied.

The underlying rationale of a multiplier relationship, although worked out here in a specific context, is readily generalized to the other cases identified above.

Jane Humphries
University of Cambridge

References

Kahn, R. F. (1931), 'The relation of home investment to unemployment', *Economic Journal*, June.

Keynes, J. M. (1964 [1936]), *The General Theory of Employment*, London.

National Income Analysis

In any economy millions of transactions take place each year which combine to give the overall level of economic activity. It is the classification, presentation and study of statistics relating to such transactions which is the concern of national income analysis. Such information is vital to policy-makers in assessing what changes are needed in short-term economic policy and in assessing long-term performance of the economy, the latter being of particular interest to developing economies. International organizations may use national income as a basis for allocating aid or demanding contributions to their budget.

The first works in national income were by Sir William Petty and Gregory King in England in the seventeenth century. Modern pioneers include Kuznets in the US and Bowley, Stamp and Clark in the UK. The development and use of Keynesian economics gave a great impetus to national income analysis during and after the Second World War with Richard Stone, Nobel Laureate 1984, as the leading figure (Stone and Stone, 1965).

The central point of national income analysis is the measurement of the amount of economic activity or national product: that is, the value of all goods and services crossing the production boundary. There are three methods of arriving at this aggregate figure: (1) The *income method* totals all incomes earned in economic activity in the form of wages, rent and profits (including undistributed amounts). Old-age pensions and similar transfer payments are excluded as not representing economic activity. (2) The *expenditure method* totals all items of final expenditure – private and government expenditure on current consumption and industrial and government purchases of capital equipment. Payments by one firm to another for raw materials or components or other inputs must be excluded. Such items of *intermediate expenditure* are 'used up' in the production process and do not cross the production boundary. (3) The *production method* looks at each firm and industry and measures its *value added* – the value of its output less the value of intermediate purchases from other firms. This represents an individual firm's contribution to the national product.

When due allowance is made for imports and exports, these three methods will, in principle, yield identical estimates of national income. In practice this is not always the case due to a less than perfect supply of information to government statisticians who are required often to reconcile three slightly differing estimates.

It is generally agreed that national income is a measure of economic activity. Unfortunately there is no general agreement about what constitutes economic activity, that is, where to draw the production boundary. Transfer payments and intermediate expenditures have been noted as transactions which are excluded because they do not cross the production boundary. Many countries follow the UN System of National Accounts (S.N.A.) and include all goods and services (including the services of government employees) for which there is a payment, either in money or in kind. The principal difference occurs in the Soviet Material Product System (M.P.S.) which emphasizes material output and excludes government services and many personal services such as entertainment and hairdressing.

Whatever definition is adopted, there are three different pairs of concepts of national income which can be used: (1) A measure of *gross national product* makes no allowance for depreciation – wear and tear of capital equipment. *Net national product* subtracts an estimate of depreciation from the gross measure, and is a more accurate reflection of the achievement of the economy. (2) If expenditures are valued at the prices paid by purchasers, they will include indirect taxes and will yield a measure of national income at *market prices*. For many purposes of comparison, both internally and externally, it is desirable to deduct indirect taxes (and add on any subsidies) and obtain a measure at *factor cost*, which is the essential costs of production. Such a measure is obtained automatically using the income or production methods. (3) The third pair are measures of gross *domestic* product (GDP) and gross *national* product (GNP). The former relates to all economic activity taking place within the geographical limits of the economy. The latter measures economic activity carried out by the resources – labour and capital owned by national members of the economy. In many developing countries dependent on foreign capital, the outflow of profits means that GDP can exceed GNP by up to 20%. These pairs of concepts can be combined in various ways, the most common being gross domestic product at factor cost.

The three methods of measuring national income serve as a focus for different analyses of the aggregate. The income accounts can be used to analyse the shares of wages and profits in total national income and the equality, or otherwise, of the distribution of this income to individuals. The details of the production accounts enable one to examine the relative importance of different industries (for example, manufacturing and services), of different regions in the country, or of privately and publicly-owned production. On the expenditure side, much attention has focused in Western Europe on the split between private and public spending. In general economists are interested in the division between consumption and investment (the

Table 1 Social accounting matrix UK 1982 (£ billion)

Payments by:- \ Payments to:-	PRODUCTION Goods & Services	PRODUCTION Taxes on goods & services	CONSUMPTION Private Sector	CONSUMPTION Public Sector	CAPITAL ACCUMULATION	REST OF THE WORLD	TOTALS
PRODUCTION — Goods & services	—	—	136.5 CH	55.6 CG	37.8 V	67.8 X	299.7
PRODUCTION — Taxes on goods & services	—	—	30.6	4.5	3.2	3.3	41.6
CONSUMPTION (INCOME AND OUTLAY) — Private Sector	192.3 YH	—	—	50.4 HG	—	1.6 E	244.3
CONSUMPTION (INCOME AND OUTLAY) — Public Sector	7.2 YG	41.6	58.4 GH	—	—		107.2
CAPITAL ACCUMULATION	33.0 D	—	18.5 SH	−5.1 SG	—	—	46.4
REST OF THE WORLD	67.2 M	—	0.3 TH	1.8 TG	5.4 B	—	74.7
TOTALS	299.7	41.6	244.3	107.2	46.4	74.7	

CH – Household consumption; CG – Government current expenditure; V – capital formation; X – exports of goods and services YH – Private sector incomes (wages, profit, rent); HG – Transfers from government to private sector (including Social Security benefits) E – Net income from abroad; YG – Public sector trading surplus; GH – Payments by private sector to government (taxes on income; social security contributions); D – depreciation or capital consumption; SH – private sector saving; SG – public sector saving; M – imports of goods and services; TH – private transfers abroad (net); TG – government transfers abroad; B – net investment abroad (= balance of payments on current account)

Gross domestic product at factor cost = YH + YG + D = 232.5

purchase of new capital equipment). Here national income analysis is very closely related to macroeconomics and the study of what determines the size of these items and how changes in them affect the overall level of national income.

All transactions are measured in money terms and give national income in *current prices*, but it is necessary to allow for price changes when making comparisons between years. Values at current prices are adjusted by an appropriate index of prices in order to obtain estimates in *constant prices*. Any observed changes will then reflect only changes in quantity and not in price.

National income analysis originated in the measurement of production, income and expenditure aggregate flows, but gradually more and detailed transactions have been included. The analysis of transactions between firms and industries known as *input-output analysis* is a separate topic. Borrowing and lending, that is, transactions in financial assets, are analysed in a *flow-of-funds table*, and the accounting system can be extended to include stocks as well as flows. *National balance sheets* record the value of assets, financial and physical, held by members of the economy at the end of each accounting period. The presentation and analysis of this more complicated system of accounts is greatly facilitated by showing the data in a large square table (see Table 1) recording transactions between sectors of the economy in the columns and those in the rows. Known as a social accounting matrix, this is the most recent methodological development in this field.

A. G. Armstrong
University of Bristol

Reference
Stone, R. and Stone, G. (1965), *National Income and Expenditure*, 7th edn, London.

Further Reading
Abraham, W. I. (1969), *National Income and Economic Accounting*, Englewood Cliffs, N.J.

Beckerman, W. (1976), *An Introduction to National Income Analysis*, London.
See also: *deflation as a statistical device; national wealth.*

Nationalization

At the heart of the term nationalization is the act of converting a privately-owned resource into one owned by the central government (or local government in the case of 'municipalization'). One might then ask how the use and development of the resource and the economic organization of production may be predicted to change. Instead of exploring this issue, many economists in both Europe and North America have taken an essentially prescriptive stance. What advice can one give about the use of the resources? they have asked, invariably on the presumption that the managers, civil servants and ministers are disinterested recipients of that advice. Since no one would want to deny that resources should be used efficiently, economists have translated their own concept of efficiency into guidelines of behaviour. Publicly-owned industries should, as a first approximation, set user prices and extend the use of resources up to the point where the marginal cost of output equals price. The rationale for this is that no gains could then be made by switching resource usage in or out of the industry, since consumer valuation of the marginal dose of resources is just equal to its valuation in other activities. The implications of such a rule are quite striking, suggesting, for example, different electricity tariffs for different times of day, high fares and tariffs for transport, gas and electricity to high-cost rural areas, low fares and freight rates for bulky, long-distance rail journeys. Much work has been undertaken on the detailed implementation of these policy proposals, in terms of identifying short and long-run marginal costs, demand elasticities and time-stream aspects of investment projects. While many economists have not felt that the price at marginal cost rule should be modified to take into account questions of income distribution – on the grounds that the tax system is the way to handle that – they have not advocated the simple rule when spill-over effects exist or when information flows have been regarded as deficient.

Health and education are therefore viewed as areas raising other considerations.

The forgotten question about how the use of resources would actually change under public ownership re-emerged in the 1970s, partly as a product of the growing influence of a persistent element in American economic thinking – the study of institutional behaviour – and partly because the economists' policy prescriptions were either ignored or found too difficult to implement. The restriction of a private interest to the end of promoting a public interest can be achieved in a variety of ways. Such 'regulation' has a long history in Britain embracing areas like the factory inspectorate and the control of private railway and fuel companies in the inter-war period. The shift in the immediate post-1945 period to public ownership of strategic industries may itself be a reflection of the siege mentality of the 1930s and 1940s. Study of such issues is still awaited. Instead the main thrust of 'positive' theories has come from American thinking on the property rights characteristics of public firms. For example, one approach stresses that citizen-owners can dispose of their rights in publicly-owned activities only by engaging in high-cost activities like migration or concerted political action. This is contrasted with private ownership, where each owner has the unilateral ability to buy and sell shares, an act viewed as a capitalization of the expected results of current management action. A significant wedge between owner and management therefore arises in public firms, the nearest approximation to which for private firms is the cost to owners of monitoring management behaviour. In the former case the wedge permits scope for discretionary behaviour by civil servants, management and politicians. The precise outcome in each public firm would depend on the way in which property rights are specified and the constraints on the various parties in the pursuit of their own utility maximizing position. But the broad expectation is that productivity will be lower and unit costs higher in public than in private firms. Testing such theories is difficult, for when public firms have product monopolies there is no contemporaneous private firm to act as benchmark, and in the absence of monopoly one has to separate the effects of competition from the effects of ownership. Because of the wide variety of institutional types within many of its industries, America is proving a fruitful data source with comparisons between publicly-owned firms (municipal rather than national) and private firms, some of which are regulated. The evidence on productivity and unit costs shows a very varied pattern, with public firms coming out better in electricity supply, private firms in refuse collection and water supply, and with no clear-cut differences in transport. Pricing structures in public firms seem unambiguously to be less closely geared to the supply costs of particular activities, though whether this is due to electoral influences, empire building or a disinterested pursuit of fairness is not yet clear. Little work has yet been done on explaining why some activities are taken into public ownership whilst others are not.

Robert Millward
University of Salford

Further Reading
Chester, N. (1975), *The Nationalisation of British Industry 1945–51*, London.
Millward, R. and Parker, D. (1983), 'Public and private enterprise: relative behaviour and efficiency', in R. Millward and M. T. Sumner (eds), *Public Sector Economics*, London.
See also: *mixed economy; public goods*.

National Wealth

The wealth of a nation comprises a wide range of assets including both physical capital and net claims on other countries. The physical capital itself is not easily quantified. The United Nations System of National Accounts (1968), however, provides conventional guidelines for building up an inventory of physical assets. Broadly, vehicles, plant and machinery, and buildings are entered at their market value, after allowing for depreciation. Land is valued at its improved value, but no allowance is made for unextracted minerals or growing crops and forests. Equally, and perhaps most importantly, no allowance is made for the human capital possessed by the nation, despite the fact that the productive skills of its people may be its most important resource. Wealth estimates for the United Kingdom are to be found in Revell (1967), while for the United States they are provided by Goldsmith (1982). In both cases annual statistical estimates are provided of some of the components of national wealth.

In an attempt to measure national wealth, net claims on other nations represent real resources available to the home country, and thus net fixed and portfolio investment must be counted together with foreign currency reserves and other lending to the rest of the world, net of borrowing from the rest of the world. But the network of financial claims within a country has no direct bearing on its national wealth. A country is not richer because the government has borrowed a large national debt from the private sector (although it may be if the government has invested the money it has borrowed more productively than the private sector would have). Individual holders of the national debt are, however, richer because they hold the debt, and in a full analysis of national wealth the economy is broken up into institutional sectors. The wealth of each sector includes not only its physical assets and its net claims on the rest of the world but also its net claims on the other sectors in the economy. Because only net claims are included, the sum of the net wealth of each institutional sector will equal the national wealth, in the same way as transfer payments have to be netted out when adding up institutional income to arrive at national income.

Just as some physical assets are conventionally omitted in the estimation of national wealth, so some financial claims are omitted in the compilation of estimates of sectoral wealth. Buiter (1983) presents a more general accounting framework which includes the capitalized value of social security and national insurance benefits as a liability of central government, and the capitalized value of future tax receipts as an asset, although such an approach can be criticized because future tax rates can change, and there is no obvious reason to capitalize these flows on the basis of any particular future path of tax and payment rates.

Martin Weale
University of Cambridge

References
Buiter, W. M. (1983), 'Measurement of the public sector deficit and its implications for policy evaluation and design', *International Monetary Fund Staff Papers*.
Goldsmith, R. W. (1982), 'The National Balance Sheet of the United States, 1953–1980', NBER.
Revell, J. L. (1967), *The Wealth of the Nation*, Cambridge.
United Nations (1968), *System of National Accounts*, New York.
See also: *national income analysis*.

Neoclassical Economics

The term neoclassical economics refers to the enhanced version of classical economics that was promoted and developed in the late nineteenth century, primarily by Alfred Marshall and Leon Walras. The most familiar versions were developed in the twentieth century by John Hicks and Paul Samuelson. Despite what 'neoclassical' might usually imply, neoclassical economics differs from the classical only in matters of emphasis and focus. Unlike classical methods of explaining the state of any economy in terms of seemingly mysterious forces like the 'invisible hand', neo-classical economics tries to provide a complete explanation by focusing on the actual mechanisms which lead to the explained state.

The pure world that neoclassical economists attempt to explain consists of independently-minded individuals making decisions which can be completely rationalized in terms of aims and means, interacting with one another only by means of market competition, and limited only by the constraints provided by Nature. It is important to note what is omitted from this world view. There is no necessary role for social institutions such as churches or governments, except those that can be explicitly explained as the consequences of individual market choices. Likewise, there is no role for authorities. The individual or the decision-making unit such as a firm always knows what is best for him, her or it.

In the neoclassical world, whenever any individual is not satisfied with some aspect of his current situation (say, not consuming enough bread), he allegedly enters the market and competes with other buyers by bidding up the price (of bread), thereby creating an incentive for at least one producer to sell to him rather than anyone else. This process of increasing the going market price raises the average selling price and thereby indicates to producers that more is wanted, and to other buyers that they should consider cheaper substitutes (for bread). If sufficient time is allowed for all such market activity to be worked out, eventually all individuals will be satisfied relative to what they can afford (to afford any more may mean they would have had to work more than they considered optimal). The market process is worked out to a point where one individual can gain only by causing others to lose and thereby leaving them unsatisfied. In other words, in the long run everyone is happy relative to their own personal aims and to their natural givens (for example, to their inherited resources or skills).

Over the last fifty years, formal analyses of this very stylized neoclassical world have frequently demonstrated that any attempt to interfere with its preconceived free market mechanism – either by manipulating prices or by restricting market trading – can only lead to a situation where some people are not being allowed to choose what they want and thus lead to a non-optimal state of affairs. It has often been pointed out by critics, such as John Maynard Keynes, that the amount of time necessary for the market activity to be worked out is unrealistic. Other critics, such as Thorstein Veblen, claimed that the neoclassical world was fundamentally unrealistic as some individuals do not act independently, and thus there is no guarantee, even if there were enough time, that everyone will be satisfied. While there are exceptions, most neoclassical economists have been concerned with either the formal analytics of the special neoclassical world or the applicability of its many formal theorems to everyday world problems.

Few of the economists who focus on the analytical aspects of economic theory are actually attempting to answer such critics. Rather, most neoclassical economic theorists have been concerned with other equally important questions. Can we confidently rely on a world view that allows only independent decision making and only free competition? How can one specify the details of the formal neoclassical world so as to justify such confidence? Critics still question the sufficiency of any purely competitive, individualist world and ask whether other specifications are necessary. Does this world require that there be numerous individuals participating as buyers and as sellers? Does it require an infinity of time for the 'long run' and thus by doing it so render an impossible world? While the necessity of such additional conditions remains somewhat in doubt, a few logically sufficient views of a world of individual decision makers have been worked out in great, yet tedious, detail.

Since, by methodological commitment, all events are ultimately to be explained in neoclassical economics as being the logical consequences of individual decision making guided by market events, the elements of individual decision making have required extensive formal analysis. Unfortunately, despite many impressive displays of mathematical agility and prowess, not much has been accomplished beyond what can be learned from any elementary calculus textbook. Every individual is thought to be maximizing with respect to some particular quantitative aim (for example, utility, profit, net income) while facing specified natural constraints (such as technical knowledge or capabilities, personal skills). It follows, then, whenever utility (the quantity representing the level of satisfaction achieved by consuming the purchased goods) is maximized, the formal relationship between the quantity of any good and the utility (the 'utility function') must be one where, over the relevant range of choice, each additional unit of the good must add slightly less to the total utility than did any previous unit. This is termed 'diminishing marginal utility' and it (or some multidimensional version such as 'diminishing marginal rates of substitution') is a necessary condition for each individual's utility function. Why any individual's marginal utility is diminishing has never been adequately explained using economics principles alone. It can only be asserted that it is a necessary condition for the viability of any neoclassical world. Similar analysis has been provided for the other aims that individuals might have (such as profit, wealth, welfare), although virtually all aims can be reduced to the analytics of utility maximization (see Samuelson, 1947).

Other neoclassical economists have been trying indirectly to answer the critics by showing that, even without assurance that the neoclassical world is realistic or possible, it can be used to provide detailed explanations of current economic events. Countless academic articles have been written which demonstrate the 'robustness' of neoclassical theories. All are of a form that implies that any desirable economic event must be the logical consequence of the aims and choices of individuals and any undesirable event must be the result of unforeseen natural events or the consequence of interference in the market by 'well-meaning' governments or corporations.

Lawrence A. Boland
Simon Fraser University

References
Hicks, J. (1939/1946), *Value and Capital*, 2nd edn, Oxford.
Samuelson, P. (1965 [1947]), *Foundations of Economic Analysis*, New York.

Further Reading
Boland, L. (1982), *Foundations of Economic Method*, London.
See also: *equilibrium; Marshall; prices, theory of; Walras.*

Oligopoly

Oligopoly is defined as an industry or market in which there are only a few sellers. Evidence on levels of market concentration suggests it to be the prevailing market structure in most Western industrial economies. The central feature of oligopoly is the *interdependence* of firms' activities. Thus any action by one oligopolist will significantly affect the sales, profitability and so on, of its rivals, who might therefore be expected to react or retaliate. Correspondingly, most oligopoly theory posits behaviour in which the oligopolist sets his decision variables (including advertising, research and innovation, as well as the traditional price or quantity decision) on the basis of specific conjectures about rivals' reactions. At one extreme lies the Cournot model, in which zero reactions are assumed, and at the other is the view, most persuasively articulated by Chamberlin, that a recognition of mutual independence will lead oligopolists to maximize their joint profits (thus making oligopoly virtually indistinguishable from monopoly). A major post-war development was the Structure-Conduct-Performance paradigm which extended traditional oligopoly theory to incorporate the effects of entry barriers and product differentiation. A multitude of empirical studies ensued, usually with results pointing to a need for strong antitrust policies. The theoretical basis of much of this work was, however, *ad-hoc*, and only recently have significant developments been added (for example, on strategic entry deterrence and contestable markets) to our theoretical understanding of oligopoly. Dissenting voices to the mainstream include Schumpeter and the Austrians, viewing competition as a dynamic process, and, latterly, Chicago economists, doubting the general existence of significant entry barriers.

S. W. Davies
University of East Anglia

See also: *antitrust legislation; business concentration; cartels and trade associations; competition; monopoly.*

Phillips Curve

The Phillips curve, named after its originator A. W. Phillips in 1958, depicts an inverse relationship between wage inflation and unemployment – usually extended to link price inflation and unemployment. This relationship has attracted more attention and generated more economic discussion than any other simple macroeconomic hypothesis. There has been research into its theoretical foundations, its empirical validity, its policy implications and its estimation problems. As originally set forth by Phillips, it was no more than a statistical relationship based on weak historical data. But so pervasive was its attraction that a theoretical foundation was soon sought, although without much success. The main attraction of the Phillips curve was in indicating that policy makers can choose lower unemployment only at the cost of higher inflation, and in suggesting that it could be possible to calculate the terms of the trade-off between the policy objective of full employment and stable prices. A series of articles trying to estimate such a relationship for various countries demonstrated not only the indeterminate foundations of the relationship, but also the many methodological problems involved in estimating it. As a policy tool, however, it is useful only to the extent that it is a stable relationship, and the relationship was evidently highly unstable for most countries from the late 1960s through the 1970s. This instability was then attributed to the revision of price expectations upwards as governments persisted in running economies at high levels of aggregate demand.

Ronald Shone
University of Stirling

Further Reading

Phillips, A. W. (1958), 'The relationship between unemployment and the rate of change of money wage rates in the United Kingdom, 1861–1957', *Economica*, 22.

Frisch, H. (1983), *Theories of Inflation*; Cambridge Surveys of Economic Literature, Cambridge.

See also: *employment and underemployment; inflation and deflation.*

Planning, Economic

Economic planning is the use of a systematic alternative method of allocating economic resources either to replace or supplement the market mechanism. Its main justification is when the market mechanism fails to supply the right signals to decision-makers; this may be because economies of scale render the atomistic market mechanism ineffective, or because the market is incapable of taking into account the long-run needs of the economy. The state may possess knowledge which the market does not, whether about general economic uncertainties, the preferences of the community as a whole, or the longer run future. Alternatively, the state may simply reject the validity of the individual preferences which underlie the market system. Critics of planning have focused on the insuperable quantities of information that must be processed if the entire economy is to be organized by one body, and on the undemocratic implications of the state's overruling individuals' choices.

In common usage 'planning' can mean either 'control' or 'forecasting', and 'economic planning' can be anything from consultation to coercion. It is possible in principle to distinguish three types of economic planning: (1) 'Directive planning' involves administrative regulation from a central body entirely replacing autonomous profit-seeking behaviour in the market. (2) 'Incentive planning' – the state attempts to achieve a desired outcome by using monetary rewards without coercion. (3) 'Indicative planning' – the state confines itself to forecasting or consultation, hoping that persuasion and the provision of superior economic information will lead to better economic performance.

In reality no single system falls into one only of the above categories. The Soviet system is in principle 'directive' with respect to enterprises, but the market mechanism is in fact allowed considerable sway in the USSR. Consumer goods are not administratively distributed and enterprise managers actually have considerable freedom of manœuvre which the state tries to manipulate by incentives schemes. In practice the state gives instructions to firms in annual operating plans rather than the Five Year Plan which is very general. The Soviet state cannot in practice direct the whole of the production side of the economy because of the vast amount of information that it would need to handle even if there were no uncertainty.

Many proposals have been made and continue to be made

for reforming planning in the USSR and Eastern Europe (most of which copied the Soviet model after 1945) in order to replace the directive element by incentive-based systems. But despite continuing discussions the only major result has been Hungary's 'market socialism'. A major problem with such reforms is that if the price incentives are set wrongly the decentralization may lead to undesirable actions by enterprises. Other schemes involving the use of computers and mathematical techniques have foundered on the computational complexity and the difficulty of coping with uncertainty.

After World War II the idea of incentive or indicative planning was favoured by many in the West as a way of obtaining the benefits of the co-ordinating powers of both the market and the plan. But actual attempts at planning often lacked the coherence of policy instruments both among one another and between them and desired objectives which would have to exist for real planning. State intervention in many countries and periods has been entirely *ad hoc*. Indicative planning was attempted in France. In principle the planners simply calculated what amounted to an optimal balanced growth path for the economy, the mere revelation of which was supposedly sufficient to induce people to follow it. French planning appears to have had some real success before 1965, but it has atrophied since then. In practice it always involved far less coherence and considerably more compulsion than the pure model of indicative planning. A misunderstanding of French experience led to total failure of the UK National Plan (1965–70); too much weight was placed on the idea that a plan could be virtually self-fulfilling merely by being highly optimistic. Planning as forecasting continues in a number of countries, notably the Netherlands and Scandinavia, and was hotly debated in the US during the mid–1970s. Planning in Western industrial economies (outside wartime) typically does not try to forecast or control every micro-economic variable but rather to regulate the major aggregates such as inflation, overall investment, etc. Incomes policies are a form of macro-economic planning where the free play of market forces in the labour market is held to be socially undesirable.

Economic planning may be carried out at a lower level than the national economy. There is regional and sectoral planning, which may or may not be made consistent with national planning. Large corporations also engage in planning, and there have been suggestions that the planning activities of large corporations can be building blocks for the creation of national plans. Critics of this view point out that usually corporate 'plans' are speculative scenarios rather than fully worked out operational programmes.

Less developed countries have often engaged in development planning. This has rarely attempted to follow the directive model, because agriculture does not lend itself well to central planning and because the political and bureaucratic preconditions are such as to make it very hard to manage. India in the 1950s announced an intention to combine Western parliamentary democracy with Soviet-type planning. In the end planning became little more than a system of forecasting designed to clarify national economic priorities alongside a widely criticized system of bureaucratic regulations. Some countries have been more successful (e.g. South Korea or Tunisia) though attempting less than India did initially.

Probably the most fruitful use that can be made of economic planning lies in attempts to simulate the likely consequences of alternative future scenarios for the economy, and discussing and negotiating on the likely responses of major economic actors. Rigid plans are much more easily overturned by events than ones which constitute strategic reflection and consultation.

Peter Holmes
University of Sussex

Further Reading
Bornstein, M. (ed.) (1979), *Comparative Economic Systems*, 4th edn, Homewood, Ill.
Cave, M. E. and Hare, P. G. (1981), *Alternative Approaches to Economic Planning*, London.
See also: *mixed economy; prediction and forecasting*.

Political Economy

Economic science was first called political economy by an unimportant mercantilist writer, Montchrétien de Watteville, in 1615 (*Traicté de l'oeconomie politique*). The word 'economy' dates back to ancient Greeks for whom it meant principles of household management (οἰκος = house, νόμος = law). Montchrétien argued that 'the science of wealth acquisition is common to the state as well as the family' and therefore added the adjective 'political'.

The term had not been accepted immediately, but in 1767 it reappeared in the *Inquiry into the Principles of Political Economy* by James Steuart, the last precursor of classical economists. With the advent of classical economics, the term came into general use and remained so throughout the entire nineteenth century. It meant economics as it had just emerged as one of the social sciences. English and French authors used the term almost exclusively, while German authors vacillated between *Staatswirtschaft* (Schlözer, 1805–7; Hermann, 1832), *Nationalökonomie* (von Soden, 1804: Hildebrand, 1848) or *Volkswirtschaft* (Eiselen, 1843; Roscher, 1854–94; Menger, 1871; Schmoller, 1900–4), *Politische Ökonomie* (Rau, 1826; List, 1840; Knies, 1855) and *Sozialökonomie* (Dietzel, 1895; M. Weber).

Like any new discipline, political economy included both theoretical principles and practical policies, scientific proofs and political advocacies; it was a combination of science, philosophy and art. In his *Wealth of Nations* (1776, Book IV) Adam Smith wrote: 'Political economy, considered as a branch of the science of a statesman or legislator, proposes two distinct objects: first, to provide a plentiful revenue or subsistence for the people . . . and secondly, to supply the state . . . with a revenue sufficient for the public services.' The titles of some of the later treatises reflect similar ideas (Hufeland, *Neue Grundlagen der Staatswirtschaftskunst*, 1807–13; J. S. Mill, *Principles of Political Economy with Some of Their Applications to Social Philosophy*, 1848). Also, like many other sciences in the nineteenth century, political economy passed through a process of catharsis: it gradually liberated itself from the political and ideological baggage, the concepts used became more rigorously defined, the analysis and proofs imitated procedures in exact sciences, and art (which advises, prescribes and directs) was distinguished from science (which observes, describes and explains). Commenting a century later (1874) on Smith's definition, Leon Walras observed that 'to say that the object of political economy is to provide a plentiful revenue . . . is like saying that the object of geometry is to build strong houses . . .'.

This development proceeded in two different directions: towards pure economic theory unrelated to social relations, and towards social economics stressing production relations as the main task of analysis. The former is sometimes (very conditionally) denoted as bourgeois economics, the latter (equally conditionally) as Marxist economics. Both were equally critical of inherited doctrines, but from different perspectives. Bourgeois economists took capitalism as an established social order (as data exogenously given) and tried to develop economic science by reducing the immense complexity of social phenomena to some manageable proportions. Marx and the socialists, on the other hand, questioned the established social order itself (and treated production relations as endogenous variables).

Nassau Senior (*An Outline of Political Economy*, 1836) was probably the first to stress explicitly the abstract and hypothetical character of economic theory and to distinguish theoretical economics from policy advice useful for the statesmen. J. B. Say provided the definition of political economy in the title of his book *Traité d'économie politique, ou simple exposition de la manière dont se forment, se distribuent et se consomment les richesses* (1803). While Smith's definition referred to an art, 'from Say's definition it would seem that the *production*, *distribution* and *consumption* of wealth take place, if not spontaneously, at least in the *manner* somehow independent of the will of man' which means treating political economy as a 'natural science' (Walras). Marx also talks of natural laws in economics, though, unlike Say, he also subsumes production relations under the governance of these laws. Although the econometricians – as Schumpeter calls them – of the seventeenth and eighteenth century, Petty, Boisguillebert, Cantillon and Quesnay, tried to measure economic phenomena, it was only Cournot (*Recherches sur les principes mathématiques de la théorie des richesses*, 1838) who successfully introduced mathematics into economics. And 'a science becomes really developed only when it can use mathematics' (Marx). The marginalist revolution of the 1870s gave the purification tendencies full swing. In the last great work under the title of political economy – *Manuale di economia politica* by Pareto, 1906 – the author scorns 'literary economists and metaphysicians' and defines his discipline by enumerating its three component parts: the study of tastes, the study of obstacles and the study of the way in which these two elements combine to reach equilibrium. This type of reasoning led to the most popular definition of economics in the first of the two intellectual traditions: economics as the study of the allocation of scarce resources among competing uses. Starting from this definition, it is logical to conclude, as L. Robbins did, that 'the generalizations of the theory of value are applicable to the behaviour of isolated men or the executive authority of a communist society as they are to the behaviour of men in an exchange economy' (*An Essay on the Nature and Significance of Economic Science*, 1932). Economics has thus become applied praxiology (study of rational behaviour). Most of what goes for the contemporary economic theory is in fact not theory but analysis. The difference between the two consists in economic analysis being *identically* true: if the rules of logic are observed, the conclusions follow with certainty and cannot be refuted. Economic theory, like any other theory, cannot be proved but can be refuted. As a result of these developments, political economy disappeared from the titles of economic treatises and also from Western encyclopaedias.

The Marxist tradition uses the following definition: political economy is the science of the laws governing the production, exchange and distribution of material means for living in the human society (Engels, *Anti-Dühring*, 1878). Since the conditions under which people produce and exchange are different in different epochs, there must be different political economies. Political economy is basically an historical science. Marx's chief work, *Das Kapital. Kritik der Politischen Ökonomie* (1867), was a critique of bourgeois society and was intended to 'discover the law of economic development' of this society. In an earlier work he links political economy with the dominant class in a particular society and draws attention to the 'blind laws of demand and supply, of which consists the political economy of bourgeoisie, and social production governed by social forecast, of which consists the political economy of the working class' (1864). Political economists of Marxist persuasion start from the observation that means of production together with appropriately skilled labour power make up the forces of production. The latter, together with the corresponding relations of production, determine modes of production which represent the proper subject of study for political economy. Marxist economists have preserved the term and the approach, but have not contributed much to the development of political economy after the master's death.

After the Second World War, the emergence of many new nations, substantial political and social changes, and widening gaps in economic development made the usefulness of pure economic theory rather questionable. Models that implied Western *Homo economicus* proved inapplicable in many parts of the world and, increasingly so, in the West itself. The interest in political economy was revived. The subject was reintroduced into curricula, and studies bearing the title began to reappear (A. Lindbeck, *The Political Economy of the Left*, 1971; H. Sherman, *Radical Political Economy*, 1972). The current tendency is to bridge the gap between the two strands of thought: the most sophisticated analytical techniques are applied to analyse social relations. The term 'political economy' came to denote that part of economic theory which deals with the functioning of entire socioeconomic systems. In a somewhat looser sense it is also used to denote political-economic doctrines or comprehensive sets of economic policies such as liberal, conservative and radical. The increasing exactness of economics and the development of other social sciences make it possible to extend the task of political economy from merely explaining the functioning of economic systems to the design of basically new economic systems. In order to achieve this, an attempt has been made to

integrate economic and political theory into one single theory
of political economy (Horvat, 1982).

Branko Horvat
University of Zagreb

Reference
Horvat, B. (1982), *Political Economy of Socialism*, New York.

Further Reading
Lange, O. (1963), *Political Economy*, New York.

Prediction and Forecasting

The periods and time horizons considered in relation to specific
forecasting procedures may be short term (1 to 18 months),
medium term (½ to 5 years) or long term (over 5 years). Very
long-term projections (15–25 years) tend to be more in the
nature of perspective plans about the social and physical infrastructure of the country and, apart from the demographic
projections, more politically conjectural.

There are two basic analytical approaches to forecasting:

(1) One method tries to outline a pattern of responses by
relating the variable to be predicted, such as prices or sales, to
all the other significant variables, such as output, wage costs,
exchange rate variation, imports, that policy makers believe
exert a strong influence on its behaviour. This approach rests on
a view of what factors are important and the interrelationships
between them. A major problem, however, is that most
endogenous and exogenous variables are not, in practice, independent. Directly and indirectly the various explanatory and
dependent variables react on each other. For example, interest
rates in the US affect interest rates and prices in Europe which
lead to exchange-rate adjustments. These influence capital
flows, which in turn have repercussions on interest rates. The
interaction between prices and wages is also well-known and
has led to bitter disputes as to 'cause' and 'effect'. To a certain
extent, however, such difficulties can be handled (or their
importance recognized) in the mechanical techniques chosen.
Other features of a more psychological nature, involving expec-

tations motivated by feelings of political uncertainty and individual caution, are less easy to accommodate in any mathematical schema.

(2) An alternative approach produces forecasts on the basis of historical trends and patterns. The procedure tries to quantify and 'formalize' experience in order to replicate, reproduce and extrapolate future trends in the socioeconomic variables of interest (income, production, crime, and so on). The length of past time series, the interval of the observations and their regularity should be closely related to the time horizon considered important. The relationships are rarely of a simple linear or quadratic form and will inevitably reflect a combination of trend, cyclical, seasonal and random shock disturbances.

A particular example of a large and complex economic model of the first kind concerned with short and medium-term projections is the OECD's INTERLINK model. This adopts relatively simple techniques to try and assess the overall international impact of various policy stimuli in different countries. The system links together a large number of individual country models through their international trade relations. Although the specifications of these large-scale national models differ widely, their approach is fundamentally Keynesian and mainly expenditure oriented. They are concerned essentially with the impact of government policies on consumption, investment and the balance of payments. This means that although the INTER-LINK system focuses primarily on the broad macroeconomic aggregates necessary to produce the OECD's current individual country and overall economic projections, it still retains the same basic multiplier properties of the official national models. The significance of INTERLINK is that it draws the attention of policy makers to the fact that, increasingly, other countries' policies have an important impact on their own nation's demands and the levels of activity in the domestic economies. In the highly interrelated areas of budgetary finance, interest rates and currency exchange rates, such issues assume particular importance. The model also takes into account international feedback effects such as those that occur when the imports of certain countries (for example, Britain and the US) are affected by the production and exports of another country (for example, Japan), to the extent that these adversely affect the output and exports of the importing countries (Britain and the US). This leads to lower incomes in the importing countries as well as discriminatory trade policies, so that the demand for the goods produced by the exporting country is reduced and production (in Japan) has to be cut back (unless other new markets are found). National models, however sophisticated, rarely take into account these 'echo' effects, where economic disturbances elsewhere in the international system are subsequently transmitted back to their origin through related variables.

Fluctuations in economic activity associated with expansion, contraction and recovery in production and employment regularly occur in industrial countries, and many internal and external factors have been advanced for the existence of such cycles. Whatever the reasons, it is apparent that the fluctuations touch on a wide range of statistical series: income, investment, prices, construction, share values, and so on. Some of these series appear to turn consistently a certain number of months before aggregate economic activity in general. This is not purely by chance; businessmen themselves look for various 'signs' to guide their current production, pricing and marketing strategies, and they react accordingly – often bringing about the particular outcomes they foresee.

In the area of short-term forecasting especially – the field which tends to dominate official policy concerns at the national level – systems of leading indicators are increasingly complementing the use of specified forecasting models. This is not so much because such indicators more accurately predict the values of economic variables but because they better identify when and where cyclical changes are likely to take place. Leading indicators are also a convenient and economical way of obtaining an overall perspective of an economy from a large amount of detailed and potentially interconnected data. 'Good' leading indicators should refer to variables which, historically, have had a strong and stable timing relationship with the turning points of certain economic aggregates during the phases of a business cycle. Such indicators are therefore designed to provide very specific (interval) estimates of the dates for particular cyclical turning points.

A leading indicator system is usually built around a basic economic aggregate or reference series, such as the Gross Domestic Product (GDP) or total industrial production. Other economic series are then classified as to whether they are 'leading', 'coincident' or 'lagging' with respect to this predetermined benchmark variable. Among leading indicators are stock market prices (business confidence proxy), interest rates (investment and credit), inventories and orders (sales), overtime and short-time working (employment adjustment) and the money supply. Conceptually, all such variables must satisfy the requirement of some theoretical justification for the observed relationship. As more evidence is gathered over time and the links appear more sound, confidence in certain indicators increases and some series can be further refined to become better 'predictors'.

Michael Ward
Institute of Development Studies, University of Sussex

References
OECD Economic Outlook (1979), *The OECD International Linkage Model*, Occasional Studies, Paris.
OECD (1982), *OECD Interlink System* vol. 1, *Structure and Operation*, Paris.

Further Reading
Forrester, J. W. (1971), *World Dynamics*, Cambridge, Mass.
Meadows, D. *et al.* (1972), *The Limits to Growth*, New York.
Theil, H. (1961), *Economic Forecasts and Policy*, Amsterdam.

Prices, Theory of
The theory of prices lies at the heart of neoclassical economics. Its twin components of optimization and equilibrium form the basis of much of modern economic analysis. Not surprisingly, then, the theory of prices is also a showcase for economic

analysis – reflecting its strength but also exposing its weaknesses.

The neoclassical theory of prices considers a stylized economy consisting of consumers and producers and the set of commodities which are consumed and produced. The object of the theory is to analyse the determination of the prices of these commodities. Given a set of prices, one for each commodity, consumers are assumed to decide on their consumption pattern in order to maximize a utility function representing their tastes between the different commodities. They are assumed to take prices as parametric and to choose commodity demands and factor supplies in order to maximize utility, subject to a budget constraint which says that expenditure (on commodities consumed) cannot exceed income (from selling factors, which are included in the list of commodities). Producers also take prices as parametric, but they maximize profits (revenue from selling commodities minus costs of purchasing factors of production), subject to technological constraints, these profits being distributed back to consumers. Consumers' commodity demands and factor supplies can be seen as functions of the parametric prices and producers' commodity supplies, and factor demands can also be seen as functions of these prices. Given these functions, derived from utility maximization and from profit maximization, we can ask the following question: does there exist a set of *equilibrium* commodity and factor prices, such that all markets clear, that is, the aggregate demand for each commodity and each factor equals aggregate supply?

If such a set of prices existed and if the economy tended towards these prices, then the above theory of prices (that they are determined in a manner so as to balance supply and demand) would have relevance. The existence question was settled in the early post-war period, culminating in the work of Debreu (1959) – for which he has been awarded the Nobel Prize in Economics. Mathematically, the problem is one of finding a solution to a set of non-linear equations in the price vector. The major mathematical theorem that is invoked is the Fixed Point Theorem – which says that any continuous map from a compact convex set into itself has a fixed point, that is, there is an element such that that element is mapped back into itself. The requirement that prices lie in a compact convex set is met if we notice that the entire system described above is homogeneous of degree zero in prices – scaling all prices by a given number leaves all decisions unaltered. For example, doubling all commodity and factor prices would not alter the optimal combinations of commodity supplies and factor demands – the profit at the old combinations would merely be doubled. Consumers' profit income would, therefore, double, as would their factor incomes and expenditures on commodities – the pattern of consumption and factor supply would be the same as it was before. Given such homogeneity of the system, we can in effect restrict prices to be such that they add up to unity. This, together with the fact that they are not allowed to be negative, restricts the price vector to lie in the unit simplex, which is a compact, convex set.

The next key requirement is that of continuity; we need individual demand and supply functions to be continuous in the prices which form their arguments. As shown in the diagrams below for a *single* market, a discontinuity in supply or demand functions could lead to there being no price at which supply equals demand. Continuity, along with the other assumptions of the fixed point theorem, guarantees existence of an equilibrium set of prices. But what guarantees continuity? Since the demand and supply curves are derived from the maximization decisions of producers and consumers, the answer must lie in the objective functions and in the constraints of these problems. In fact, it is convexity of individual indifference curves that guarantees continuity of commodity demands and factor supplies as functions of the price vector. The diagrams above show convex and concave indifference curves, together with the corresponding continuous and discontinuous demand functions. A similar analysis would apply to production technology, profit maximization and the continuity of the resulting supply functions.

If the equilibrium price vector exists, then we have a theory of prices – a theory which relies on the role of prices as co-ordinating the independent demand and supply decisions of

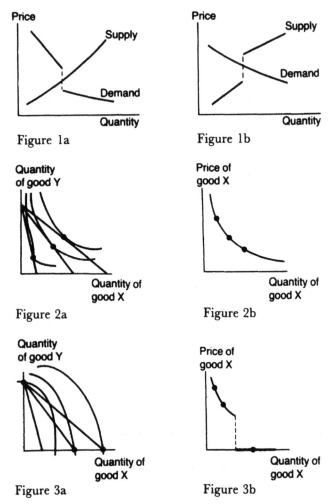

Figure 1a

Figure 1b

Figure 2a

Figure 2b

Figure 3a

Figure 3b

individuals, which are based in turn on quite independent optimization. But will the equilibrium price vector be attained? For
this we need to consider *dynamics*, how the economy moves when
it is out of equilibrium. The simple way of thinking about this
is to consider what happens in a given market when the price
is such that supply exceeds demand. Then, it is argued, there
will be a downward pressure on prices as the excess supply

makes itself felt. Similarly, when price is such that demand exceeds supply, the price will rise and reduce this gap. The limit of this process, occurring in all markets simultaneously, will be to move the price vector to its equilibrium pattern. The 'Invisible Hand' of Adam Smith leads the market to a state of rest.

If the above account were acceptable, then we would have a theory of the determination of prices – the forces of supply and demand would move the economy towards a price such that all markets clear. There are, however, at least two flies in the ointment: (1) Recall the assumption of price taking behaviour, which formed the logical basis for deriving supply and demand curves. As Arrow once remarked, if everybody is a price taker, then who changes the price? (2) If a market does not clear at the going price, some agents will be rationed – they will either not be able to purchase what they wish to purchase or to sell what they wish to sell. It then seems plausible that they will recalculate their demands on the basis of these new constraints – which, again, destroys the earlier basis for calculation of supply and demand curves.

Orthodox theory has invented the fiction of an 'auctioneer' who performs the twin tasks of adjusting prices in response to disequilibrium, along with the fiction that no trade can take place out of equilibrium, in order to overcome the above problems. But this is no more than a device to maintain the formal structure of the theory. Once the artificial construct of the auctioneer is removed, the theory breaks down. Since the theory cannot guarantee convergence to equilibrium prices within its own logical framework, it is a theory of prices only in so far as the economy is in equilibrium. This is fine for the theory, but supply and demand equilibrium has certain features which are directly at variance with observed reality – involuntary unemployment, for example. Since supply of labour equals demand for labour in equilibrium, and the theory of prices only permits considerations of supply and demand equilibrium, the theory which claims to account for the determination of prices cannot account for the phenomenon of unemployment. These features have been stressed recently by Malinvaud (1977).

The orthodox theory of prices outlined here can and has been extended to cover time, by use of the device of 'dated goods'. A commodity is now defined in terms of its consumption characteristics as well as in terms of its location in time. The number of goods is thus increased by a factor equal to the number of time periods considered in the analysis. Markets are supposed to exist *now* for all future goods, and an equilibrium set of prices is determined in exactly the same way as before. A similar device is used to introduce uncertainty. Uncertainty is captured in terms of a probability distribution over which 'state of nature' will rule at a given point in time. Goods are then distinguished according to the time and the state of nature in which they are consumed – an umbrella today if the sun shines is a different good from an umbrella today if it rains, and each of these is, in turn, different from an umbrella tomorrow if it rains, and so on. Once again, markets are assumed to exist *now* for these future 'contingent' commodities, and prices for these goods are determined by equilibrium of demand and supply. It is, of course, a major requirement of the theory that these markets for state contingent goods exist now. If they do not, then equilibrium may not exist, as shown, for example, by Hart (1975).

To summarize, the modern neoclassical theory of prices attempts to provide a rigorous basis for Adam Smith's claim that an 'Invisible Hand' leads markets to a situation in which the optimizing decisions of agents are rendered consistent with each other. The modern theory demonstrates precisely the conditions under which this must be true. In doing so in a formal and rigorous way, it shows how implausible it is that equilibrium, even if it exists, will be obtained. Of course, in conducting this analysis, the modern theory neglects institutional features of actual economics – the analysis is in an abstract setting. But it seems unlikely that if the validation of the co-ordinating role of markets is questionable in the abstract setting, it will be any more plausible once the institutional constraints have been introduced.

Ravi Kanbur
University of Essex

References
Debreu, G. (1959), *Theory of Value*, New Haven.
Hart, O. (1975), 'On the optimality of equilibrium when the market structure is incomplete', *Journal of Economic Theory*.
Malinvaud, E. (1977), *The Theory of Unemployment Reconsidered*, Oxford.

See also: *neoclassical economics*.

Production Function

A production function is a representation of the technical relationship between the rate of output of a good (measured in physical units), and the rates of inputs of the elements of production (measured in physical units) required to produce the specified rate of output. The production functions utilized in economic theory are assumed to be 'efficient', that is, for any set of values for inputs, they show the maximum possible rate of output, given technical knowledge. When presented in the form of an equation, for example $x = f(v_1, v_2, \ldots v_n)$, then only the output (x) and the variable inputs (the v_i's) are shown explicitly, while the fixed inputs (for example, the factory building and machinery) are implied in the form of the function along with the given technical knowledge. These fixed inputs determine the productive capacity of a factory, and the extent to which given increases in the variable inputs can increase output.

Many different types of production processes can be represented formally in terms of a production function. There can be joint products; some inputs may be complements while there is a degree of substitutability between others. With substitutability there is more than one efficient combination of inputs that can be used to produce a particular rate of output, and the choice of input combination to use is based on the economic criterion of least cost. The least cost of producing any given rate of output is determined by utilizing the technical information contained in a production function and the prices of the inputs. If there are no fixed inputs, then the shape of the average cost curve as the rate of output increases will indicate 'returns to scale'. Constant average costs reflect constant returns to scale, decreasing average costs reflect increasing returns, and increasing average costs reflect decreasing returns.

In neoclassical analyses, production functions are assumed to allow for some substitutability between inputs, and these functions are also often taken to be homogeneous of degree one. That is, if all inputs are varied in the same proportion, then output is also varied in the same proportion. Output would increase in a proportion greater (smaller) than the proportionate increase in the inputs if the degree of homogeneity were greater (smaller) than one. If only one input is varied, the values for all the other inputs being kept constant, then it is assumed that the marginal product of the variable input (the increase in output due to a small unit increase in the input) will eventually diminish as the rate of employment of the input is increased. These functions have an important role in the neoclassical theory of distribution. It is deduced that, in a perfectly competitive system, competition will ensure that each input will be paid its marginal product, and, further, if the production function is homogeneous of degree one, payment of all inputs according to their marginal products will exhaust the total product. The assumption of substitutability, which is required to enable marginal products to be calculated, is made to appear reasonable by use of aggregate inputs, or factors of production, such as labour and capital, each of which combine many specific elements of production. However, the attempt to explain factor payments using aggregate production functions has been shown in *Some Cambridge Controversies in the Theory of Capital* (Harcourt, 1972) to lack a consistent theoretical foundation, because capital must be measured in value terms that presume a particular distribution of income. As Sraffa (1960) noted, '[There] is not an independent measure of the quantity of capital which could be used, without arguing in a circle, for the determination of prices and of shares in distribution.'

A. Asimakopulos
McGill University

References

Harcourt, G. C. (1972), *Some Cambridge Controversies in the Theory of Capital*, Cambridge.

Sraffa, P. (1960), *Production of Commodities by Means of Commodities*, Cambridge.

Further Reading

Asimakopulos, A. (1978), *An Introduction to Economic Theory: Microeconomics*, Toronto.

Frisch, F. (1965), *Theory of Production*, Chicago.

Robinson, J. (1953–4), 'The production function and the theory of capital', *Review of Economic Studies*.

Walters, A. A. (1963), 'Production and cost functions', *Econometrica*.

See also: *capital theory; microeconomics.*

Productivity

Productivity represents a relationship between the inputs used in a productive process and the output they generate. It is increases in productivity which make possible growth in income per head. A considerable amount of work has gone into an analysis of the historic growth process in the Western world, in an attempt to unravel the extent to which the growth in output has been achieved through growth in productivity rather than through increases in inputs. Thus Kendrick (1961) looks at the United States, Denison (1967) tries to analyse the reasons for different growth rates in different countries, and Matthews, Feinstein and Odling-Smee (1982) analyse the growth process in the United Kingdom. More recently, particularly since the oil crises of 1973–4, growth rates in many Western countries have slowed down. Attempts to find explanations for what, to a casual observer, seems to be a reduction in productivity growth are found in Denison (1979) and Matthews, ed. (1982).

The essence of productivity analysis is a production function of the type $Y = f(K, L)$ where K, L are inputs of capital and labour respectively and Y is output. A simple notion of productivity growth would be one in which productivity grows in the same way as manna appears from heaven. Thus one may find the production function is in fact $Y = e^{at}f(K, L)$. Here output grows at the rate a, even though there need be no increase in the measured inputs. In his analyses Denison attempts to decompose this growth in productivity into changes arising from sources such as education, economies of scale, advances in knowledge, and so on. Courbis (1969) presents a clear framework showing how the index number problems of productivity measurement fit into a general scheme of index numbers.

The above production function led to attempts to analyse neutral progress as that which is capital and labour saving in equal proportions. If there are constant returns to scale it can be written as $Y = f(e^{at}K, e^{at}L)$, and this represents Hicks's neutral technical progress (Hicks, 1965). But the above approach does not take account of the fact that capital is a produced good. Rymes (1972, 1983) argues that Harrod (1961) produced a more suitable framework in order to allow for this. In such a framework one comes close to arguing that all increases in productivity are attributable to increases in labour productivity. Finally, Bruno and Sachs (1982) make the obvious point that capital and labour are not only inputs to production. Any analysis which fails to take account of changes in raw material inputs may give misleading results.

Martin Weale
University of Cambridge

References

Bruno, M. and Sachs, J. (1982), 'Input price shocks and the slowdown in economic growth: the case of UK manufacturing', *Review of Economic Studies*.

Courbis, R. (1969), 'Comptabilité nationale à prix constants et à productivité constante', *Review of Income and Wealth*.

Denison, E. F. (1967), *Why Growth Rates Differ*, Washington, D.C.

Denison, E. F. (1979), 'Accounting for slower growth: the United States in the 1970s', Washington.

Harrod, R. F. (1961), 'The neutrality of improvements',
  Economic Journal.

Hicks, J. R. (1965), *Capital and Growth*, Oxford.

Kendrick, J. W. (1961), 'Productivity trends in the United
  States', *National Bureau for Economic Research*, New York.

Matthews, R. C. O., Feinstein, C. H. and Odling-Smee, J. C.
  (1982), *British Economic Growth, 1856–1973*, Oxford.

Matthews, R. C. O. (ed.) (1982), *Slower Growth in the Western
  World*, London.

Rymes, T. K. (1972), 'The measurement of capital and total
  factor productivity in the context of the Cambridge theory
  of capital', *Review of Income and Wealth.*

Rymes, T. K. (1983), 'More on the measurement of total
  factor productivity', *Review of Income and Wealth.*

Profit

In terms of business accounting, gross profit is the difference
between total sales revenue and expenditure on wages and
salaries, rents and raw materials, and any other outlays
incurred in the day-to-day operation of the firm. Net profit is
gross profit net of money costs, such as interest payable on
loans and depreciation allowance. After deduction of tax, profit
may be distributed amongst the firm's owners or retained to
contribute to reserve and investment funds.

In economics, profit is also regarded as revenue net of cost,
where the costs concerned include imputed costs, as well as
expenditures on inputs to the production process. A distinction
is drawn between normal and supernormal (or excess) profit.
Normal profit is regarded as the income accruing to the entrepreneur. It is the return that the entrepreneur must receive to
cover the opportunity costs of the inputs employed. If actual
profits are less than normal profits, then the entrepreneur will
be able to switch his resources to a more profitable activity. The
imputed costs, referred to above, are, therefore, the opportunity
costs, namely the returns that could be earned by employing or
hiring out the entrepreneur's assets to gain maximum pecuniary
gain. Supernormal profits are profits earned in excess of normal
profits. In competitive markets these should be zero, in the long

run, but in markets with elements of monopoly (or oligopoly) they may be non-zero, hence they are often called monopolistic profits. In pure, perfectly, or imperfectly, competitive markets, excess profits can be made in the short run but, given the assumption of freedom of entry into the market, these will not persist in the long run. Similarly, less than normal profits may be earned in competitive markets, in the short run, provided that variable costs are being covered, but the assumption of freedom of exit will ensure that normal profits are made in the long run. A major factor leading to the persistence of excess profits in the long run, in monopolistic markets, is therefore the existence of barriers to entry to the market.

Profit has been variously regarded as the wages paid to the entrepreneur; as the rent paid for specialist knowledge possessed by the entrepreneur; as the interest on the entrepreneur's capital; as recompense for risk taking; as payment for management skills; and as surplus value expropriated by capitalists from workers.

With reference to modern firms, the view that profit is the return to entrepreneurial risk taking is complicated by the fact that the ownership of the firm is often divorced from its control. In the simple case of an entrepreneur who is both owner and manager of the firm, this return to risk view is attractive. For a limited company, however, the problem arises that it is not easy to see how the risk is divided between the shareholders, who receive the distributed profits, and the management, which may be regarded as essentially salaried employees. The matter is further confused when some of the management holds shares, in the form of directorships, and when the management is responsive to the wishes of shareholders, expressed at shareholders' meetings. It is also to be noted that not all risks need be borne by the firm, since many of them can be converted into a known cost through insurance.

F. H. Knight (1971) distinguished between risk and uncertainty. Risk entails events that occur with known probability and which can be insured against, in principle. Uncertainty occurs due to a change in the environment and entails unforeseeable events. The existence of uncertainty creates an environment in which, even in competitive markets, excess profits may be made in the short run. In the long run, when the change is understood, profits will return to normal. If the world is such that change is continually creating unforeseen events, or shocks, then there will always be newly created profitable opportunities. Change will be signalled by movements in the market price or in quantities, such as sales or inventories, and the firm must decide how to respond to such changes in order to take advantage of profitable opportunities. In order to do this the firm must form expectations of future changes and respond rapidly once prices or quantities deviate from expectations. In a competitive market, if a firm waits until the change is fully understood it will have missed the profitable opportunity, since others will have taken it up already. Lucas (1977) has developed a theory of the business cycle based on responses, in pursuit of profit, to price changes in the presence of rationally formed expectations.

Marx (1898) took a very different view of profit and its source. He argued that labour was paid wages only sufficient to maintain its labouring power. Normal profit then resulted from selling the product at its real value, which included surplus value resulting from unpaid labour. The whole of the expropriated surplus value or 'profit' is not necessarily pocketed by the employing capitalist, however. The landlord may take one part, namely rent, and the money-lending or finance capitalist may claim a portion of surplus value, in the form of interest. The surplus value remaining in the hands of the employing capitalist may then be called industrial or commercial profit. Profit is not derived from land or capital as such, but is due to the fact that ownership of these factors enables capitalists to extract surplus value from workers. Clearly this view has had to be modified by Marxian theorists in the light of increasing ownership of capital, through direct or indirect shareholding, by workers.

Andy Mullineux
University of Birmingham

References
Knight, F. H. (1971), *Risk, Uncertainty and Profits*, Chicago.
Lucas, R. E. (1977), 'Understanding business cycles', in R.
  E. Lucas (1981), *Studies in Business Cycle Theory*, Oxford.
Marx, K. (1898), *Wages, Prices and Profit*, London.
See also: *entrepreneurship*.

Project Analysis

Project analysis is the evaluation of investment proposals in terms of the balance between benefits accruing to and costs incurred by the investor. The discounting of cash flows (x) generated (the net differences between cash flows, 'with' and 'without' the project) in each year (i) over the planning horizon (n), at a rate determined by the opportunity cost of the funds involved (r), produces the net present value (NPV). Broadly, a positive net present value implies that the project should be accepted; the internal rate of return (the rate of discount which brings the NPV to zero) and the cost-benefit ratio (the ratio of discounted benefits to discounted costs) can also be used as decision criteria.

$$NPV = \sum_{i=0}^{n} \frac{x_i}{(1+r)^i} > 0$$

Further developments include: the application of an overall capital budget constraint, within which alternative projects are chosen so as to maximize the sum of their NPVs; the optimization of capacity expansion over time, maximizing NPV for a particular product line; and the application of probability distributions to uncertain cash flows to produce an 'expected' NPV.

The application of such a criterion to public investment implies a different objective function, which involves the assessment of costs and benefits to the whole economy, as well as to the state budget itself. The modern approach is derived from neoclassical welfare theory, but the first exponent was the French engineer Dupuit in 1844 (benefits of bridges to hauliers). This was further developed by the US Corps of Engineers in the New Deal years to calculate the 'indirect' benefits of hydroelectric projects in the form of increased farm yields from irrigation. In the post-war years, the methodology was again advanced in developed market economies, towards a full estimation of secondary costs and benefits. This is a complex process, involving not only partial equilibrium analysis of changes in other economic sectors (for example, the value of time savings to commuters on improved highways) in the context of 'second-best' situations (e.g. government pricing policies), but also attempts to quantify the value of non-economic factors such as loss of amenity (e.g. noise from airports), and the inclusion of 'social' criteria such as regional balance. This 'cost-benefit analysis' remains highly controversial, because it relates to political debate.

In developing market economies, the imbalances of the industrialization process (principally foreign-exchange shortages and surplus labour) require that 'shadow prices' be used in order to reflect the true opportunity cost of inputs and net value of outputs; multilateral aid agencies such as the IBRD have been particularly influential in this respect. The dominant method at present is to value commodities at their international ('border') price if so traded, and according to costs of production if nontraded, while labour costs are revalued to reflect underemployment (the 'shadow wage rate'). The application of suitable weights to reflect income-distribution criteria, and the adjustment of the discount rate to reflect fiscal constraints on accumulation, extend the scope of such investment criteria. In socialist planned economies, the discounting criterion is closely paralleled by the 'investment efficiency index', which reflects the reduction in input costs over time for a planned output, as a result of the investment project, with the return on other investments providing the equivalent of the opportunity cost of capital. Indirect costs and benefits are simply computed in a planned economy, where production is in any case programmed; a more recent development is the evaluation of foreign trade effects at international prices. Project appraisal criteria are brought to their logical conclusion in the

'economic calculus' as the basis for decentralized state enterprise operation with centrally managed prices.

E. V. K. Fitzgerald
Institute of Social Studies, The Hague

Further Reading

Dasgupta, A. K. and Pearce, D. W. (1972), *Cost-Benefit
Analysis: Theory and Practice*, London.

Little, I. M. D. and Mirrlees, J. A. (1974), *Project Appraisal
and Planning for Developing Countries*, London.

Merret, A. J. and Sykes, A. (1963), *The Finance and Analysis of
Capital Projects*, London.

Radowski, M. (1966), *Efficiency of Investment in a Socialist
Economy*, Oxford.

See also: *cost-benefit analysis*.

Public Choice

Public choice, or the economic theory of politics, is the application of the economist's way of thinking to politics. It studies
those areas in which economic and political forces interact,
and is one of the few successful interdisciplinary topics. The
behaviour of the individual is taken to be rational, an assumption which political scientists and sociologists have also found
to be fruitful.

While the term public choice was coined in the late 1960s,
the type of politico-economic analysis has a long history.
Condorcet was the first to recognize the existence of a voting
paradox: in a system of majority voting, the individual preferences cannot generally be aggregated into a social decision
without logical inconsistencies. Italian and Scandinavian public
finance scholars have also explicitly dealt with political
processes, in particular in the presence of public goods. Another
forerunner is Schumpeter, who regarded the competition
between parties as the essence of democracy.

The following four areas are central to public choice:

(1) *Preference aggregation.* Condorcet's finding of a voting

paradox has been generalized to all possible methods of aggregating individual preferences. The impossibility result remains in force, in particular when many issue-dimensions are allowed for.

(2) *Party competition.* Under quite general conditions, the competition of two vote maximizing parties leads to an equilibrium: both parties offer the same policies in the median of the distribution of voters' preferences. The programmes proposed differ substantially when there are more than two parties competing, and when they can form coalitions.

(3) *Interest groups.* The product of the activity of a pressure group is a public good, because even those not participating in its finance may benefit from it. Consequently, economic interests are in general not organized. An exception is when the group is small, when members only receive a private good from the organization, or when it is enforced by government decree.

(4) *Public bureaucracy.* Due to its monopoly power in the supply of public services, the public administrations tend to extend government activity beyond the level desired by the population.

In recent years, the theories developed have been empirically tested on a wide scale. The demand for publicly provided goods and services has been econometrically estimated for a great variety of goods, periods and countries. An important empirical application is *politico-economic models* which explicitly study the interaction of the economic and political sectors. A vote maximizing government, which has to take into account the trade-off between inflation and unemployment, willingly produces a political business cycle. More inclusive politico-economic models have been constructed and empirically tested for various representative democracies: economic conditions such as unemployment, inflation and growth influence the government's re-election requirement, which induces in turn the government to manipulate the economy to secure re-election.

Viewing government as an endogenous part of a politico-economic system has far-reaching consequences for the theory of economic policy. The traditional idea of government maximizing the welfare of society has to be replaced by an emphasis on the consensual choice of the appropriate rules and institutions.

Bruno S. Frey
University of Zurich

Further Reading
Frey, B. S (1978), *Modern Political Economy*, Oxford.
Mueller, D. (1979), *Public Choice*, Cambridge.
See also: *public goods*.

Public Goods

Public goods are characterized by non-excludability (individuals not paying for the good cannot be excluded) and by non-rivalry in consumption (that is, it does not cost anything when, in addition, other persons consume the good). The supply of a public good is Pareto-optimal (efficient) if the sum of the marginal utilities (or the sum of the marginal willingness to pay) of the persons benefiting equals the marginal cost of supply. This efficiency condition differs from the one of the polar opposite, private goods, where marginal utility has to equal marginal cost of supply.

The basic problem of public goods is that the prospective consumers have no incentive to reveal their preferences for such a good and are thus not ready to contribute towards financing the provision of the good. In the extreme case this incentive to act as 'free rider' leads to no supply of the public good at all, although everyone would potentially benefit from its provision.

Public goods is one of the few theoretical concepts in modern economics often used by other social sciences. One of the most important applications is to the problem of organizing economic interests. Pressure groups largely provide a public good because all persons and firms sharing these interests benefit from the activity. For that reason, there is little or no incentive to join. The (pure) public goods conditions apply, however, only when the interests are shared by a large number of persons or firms, for example by consumers and taxpayers, and when there are no exclusive benefits offered to members only.

The incentive to act as a free rider in a market setting may (partly) be overcome by resorting to the political process. The direct use of simple majority voting does not guarantee that the resulting public-good supply is Pareto-optimal. This is only the case if the median voter (who throws the decisive vote) has a 'tax price' equal to his marginal willingness to pay. This will rarely be the case. In a representative democracy the competition between two parties leads under ideal conditions to the same outcome for public goods supply as simple majority voting. With more than two parties and/or imperfect political competition, the resulting public goods supply cannot in general be determined. Public goods should not be identified with public provision: some public goods are privately provided, and there are many non-public goods which are politically provided.

Decision-making procedures have been devised which solve the free-rider problem. These 'preference-revealing mechanisms' result in no one gaining by understating his preference for the public good. However, these proposals are difficult to understand by the participants and violate the principle of anonymity of voting.

In laboratory experiments, it appears that individuals are ready to contribute to the cost of providing a public good to some extent, even in the large number setting. Ethical considerations seem to play a significant role in the public goods context; many people appear to have moral qualms about behaving as free-riders.

Bruno S. Frey
University of Zurich

See also: *public choice*.

Rational Expectations

Expectations of the future play an important part in economics. Investment, for example, is affected by expectations of demand and costs. The foreign exchange rate is affected by expectations of inflation and interest rates. The rational expectations hypothesis embodies the assumption that people do not make systematic errors in using the information available to them to predict the future. Some errors in prediction are generally inevitable, due to lack of information and the inherent uncertainties of economic affairs. The rational expectations hypothesis postulates that, given the information used, the prediction errors are random and unavoidable.

Rational expectations are on average self-fulfilling, the term rational expectations equilibrium being used to describe situations in which expectations lead to actions that confirm the original expectations. For example, the expectation of a rise in stock market prices may itself generate the rise. The absence of systematic prediction errors in rational expectations equilibrium suggests that people have no incentive to change the way they make predictions, and hence that the equilibrium is likely to persist unless disturbed by outside events.

The rational expectations hypothesis is seen by some economists, including Muth, who coined the term rational expectations in 1961, as the extension to expectation formation of the assumption that people act 'rationally' in pursuit of their own self-interest, which forms the basis of neoclassical economics. In this context rational behaviour is that which achieves the highest possible level of an objective (generally utility for a household, and profits for a firm), given the constraints imposed by economic and technological conditions. People fare less well in reaching their objectives if they do not have rational expectations. This identification of the rational expectations hypothesis with the more general rationality postulate has been criticized on the grounds that although people may seek to pursue their interests, they may make systematic mistakes in predictions owing to lack of understanding of their economic environment, particularly when that environment is changing rapidly. Nevertheless the rational expectations hypothesis is more appealing to many economists than any of the available alternatives, providing as it does a relatively simple and plausible description of expectation formation which can be readily incorporated into mathematical economic models.

The rational expectations hypothesis has been very widely used in the 1970s and 1980s in both theoretical and empirical research in economics. The earliest applications were to markets for assets, such as stock and futures markets, where demand depends upon expectations of the future value of the asset. More recently, the rational expectations hypothesis has been adopted in some macroeconomic theories, which also employ the hypothesis that, in the absence of unanticipated inflation, there is a unique 'natural rate' of output and employment. The conjunction of the natural rate and rational expectations hypotheses is the basis for the controversial claim of policy neutrality, that monetary policy can have no systematic and predictable effect on output and employment, and hence that there is no long-term trade-off between inflation and unemployment.

Margaret Bray
University of Cambridge

Further Reading
Begg, D. K. H. (1982), *The Rational Expectations Revolution in Macroeconomics Theories and Evidence*, Oxford.

Reserve Currency

Governments hold reserves of foreign currencies to enable them to intervene in the foreign exchange markets, in order to try to influence the exchange rate of the domestic currency against foreign currencies, by buying and selling various currencies. The need for such reserves would not arise if currencies were allowed to float freely. The fixed exchange-rate system existed from 1944, following the Bretton Woods Agreement, until 1973; it was succeeded by the 'dirty' floating system in which governments frequently intervene to influence exchange rates rather than let them float freely. Both systems require governments to hold foreign exchange reserves in order to be able to influence exchange rates. Reserve currencies are currencies widely held by governments as part of their foreign exchange reserves.

Given that the Bretton Woods Agreement resulted in the

major countries fixing the exchange rates of their currencies, against the US dollar, and given the significance of the US in the world economy, the US dollar became the major reserve currency throughout the world. Sterling had been a major reserve currency prior to the Second World War but its role declined significantly in the post-war period. Following the collapse of the fixed exchange-rate system in 1973, there has been a move to diversify foreign currency holdings by governments. The Deutschmark, the Swiss franc and the Japanese yen have all emerged as widely held reserve currencies.

There is some debate concerning whether this diversification of foreign currency holdings is optimal or whether some internationally created reserve asset might provide a better basis for the international monetary system, such as the Special Drawing Right or the European Currency Unit or some other specially created asset.

Andy Mullineux
University of Birmingham

Further Reading

Grubel, H. (1984), *The International Monetary System*, 4th edn, Harmondsworth.
Kenen, P. B. (1983), *The Role of the Dollar as an International Currency*, New York.
Roosa, R. V. *et al.* (1982), *Reserve Currencies in Transition*, New York.
See also: *international monetary system*.

Returns, Laws of

Among the abstract generalizations for which economists have at some time or another claimed explanatory or predictive powers analogous to those inherent in the natural or scientific laws of the physical sciences, the laws of returns have the longest history. They describe the relationship between the rate of growth of output for an expanding industry and the rate of increase in the inputs of the required factors of production (land, labour and capital); and they provide an instructive illustration of the way so-called economic 'laws' are in practice circumscribed by the organizational and technological conditions in which they operate.

In principle there are three ways in which the output of an industry might expand as a result of the injection of additional inputs into the production process. In the case of constant returns, output increases in proportion to the increase in total inputs. In the case of increasing returns, the rate of growth of output is greater than the rate of increase in inputs. In the case of diminishing returns, the rate of growth of output will fall short of the rate of growth in inputs. In practice an expanding industry may be subject to successive phases of increasing, constant and diminishing returns. In the early stages of its growth, when all factor inputs are in elastic supply and there are economies to be gained by increasing the scale of operations, increasing returns would be the norm. Where there is an important factor of production in limited supply (for example, land in the case of agriculture), there will come a point beyond which adding equal doses of the other factors to a fixed quantity of, say, land, will yield a declining rate of return to the variable factors – unless of course there are advances in knowledge (technological progress) compensating for the scarcity of land and possibly generating further economies of scale.

Cases of increasing returns in manufacturing were noticed by seventeenth- and eighteenth-century observers. Adam Smith, for example, explained a tendency for output to grow faster than inputs in manufacturing industry partly in terms of the scope offered for division of labour (improved organization) in factory industry, and partly in terms of what would now be classified as technological progress (advances in knowledge, improved machinery, and so on). Other eighteenth-century writers were more concerned with the evidence for diminishing returns in agriculture and its implications for an economy experiencing a rising population. Turgot, for example, pointed out that if increasing amounts of capital are applied to a given piece of land the quantity of output resulting from each additional dose of capital input will first increase and then, after a certain point, decrease towards zero.

Most English nineteenth-century classical economists readily accepted the assumption that diminishing returns prevailed in agriculture, and increasing returns in manufacturing. Few of them expected much technological progress in agriculture and were consequently pessimistic about the long-term consequences of a sustained increase in population. According to J. S. Mill, for example, 'This general law of agricultural industry is the most important proposition in political economy.' The neoclassical economists, such as Alfred Marshall, writing later in the century when it was evident that economic progress involved a high degree of industrialization, were more optimistic about the outcome of what they saw as the conflict between the two forces of diminishing returns in the primary product industries and increasing returns, reinforced by technical progress, in the manufacturing sector. Their problem, however, was that the only assumption about laws of returns which was consistent with the long-term competitive equilibrium analysis on which the neoclassical theory of value depended was the unrealistic assumption of constant returns. For as Piero Sraffa showed, in an article published in the 1926 *Economic Journal*, if increasing returns to scale prevailed, the profit-maximizing firm would be driven to expand indefinitely, thus destroying the basis for perfect competition; while the existence of diminishing returns would mean that costs and prices would be interdependent for all those industries competing for a factor in scarce supply, thus invalidating the Marshallian technique of partial equilibrium analysis.

Meanwhile, however, leading economic historians had already questioned the empirical validity of the laws of returns. In a famous article on 'empty economic boxes' published in the 1922 *Economic Journal*, Clapham had complained that, 'A great deal of harm has been done through omission to make clear that the Laws of Returns have never been attached to specific industries, that we do not, for instance, at this moment *know* under what conditions of returns coal or boots are being produced.'

Today the concept of diminishing returns is still sometimes invoked in support of Malthusian polemics by those who insist on the limits to growth, or as ready-made explanations for such events as the spectacular rise in commodity prices in the early 1970s; similarly those wishing to promote policies favouring some branch of manufacturing may justify their case by categorizing it as subject to increasing returns. However, modern economic theorists have effectively abandoned the idea that it is either useful or possible to formulate a theoretical justification for broad, generalizable laws of returns. More significant has been recent research focused on whether and when particular industries experience constant or increasing or decreasing returns to scale; these are essentially empirical issues which raise complex technical and analytical problems and yield results valid only for highly differentiated sectors of industries. In this context the laws of returns are demoted to tentative hypotheses which provide the starting point for a programme of theoretical and/or empirical research into the characteristics of a particular production function.

Phyllis Deane
University of Cambridge

Ricardo, David (1772–1823)

David Ricardo, political economist and politician, was born in London on 18 April 1772, the third son of a Dutch Jew who had moved to England around 1760 and worked on the London Stock Exchange. Ricardo's education reflected his father's wish that he join him in business, which he did at the age of 14; he is reported by his brother not to have had a 'classical education', but one 'usually allotted to those who are destined for a mercantile way of life'. At the age of 21, following a period of waning attachment to Judaism, he married a Quaker, became a Unitarian and was estranged from his father. Thrown back on his own resources, he pursued a brilliant career as a Jobber, within a few years amassing considerable wealth. At this time, his leisure hours were spent studying mathematics, chemistry, geology and minerology.

In 1799, Ricardo happened to peruse Adam Smith's *Wealth of Nations*. The subject matter interested him, although it was ten years before he published anything himself on it. His first article appeared anonymously in the *Morning Chronicle*, addressed to the 'Bullion Controversy'. Briefly, he argued that the low value of the pound on the foreign exchanges and the premium quoted on bullion over paper resulted from an over-issue of paper currency. His views were elaborated in published letters and pamphlets.

The 'Bullion Controversy' brought Ricardo into contact with, among others, James Mill, Jeremy Bentham and Thomas Malthus. Mill remained a close friend, encouraging the reticent Ricardo to publish, giving advice on style, and eventually persuading him to enter Parliament, which he did in 1819 as the independent member for the pocket borough of Portarlington in Ireland; with Bentham, Mill was also responsible for tutoring Ricardo in Utilitarianism. As for Malthus, he too became an enduring friend, although his intellectual role was mainly adversarial: something which provided Ricardo with a mental stimulus which, in the sphere of political economy, his more admiring friends were largely incapable of supplying.

In 1814, Ricardo began a gradual retirement from business, taking up residence in Gatcombe Park, Gloucestershire. One year later he published *An Essay on the Influence of a Low Price of Corn on the Profits of Stock*, one of many pamphlets spawned during the 'Corn Law Controversy'. Borrowing Malthus's theory of rent – that rent is an intra-'marginal' surplus and not a component of price, itself determined at the agricultural 'margin' – Ricardo inveighed against protection, claiming it would result in a rise of money wages, a reduced rate of profit, and a consequent slackening in the pace of capital accumulation. This was predicated on a theory of profitability at variance with Adam Smith's 'competition of capitals' thesis; taking the social propensity to save as given, Ricardo argued that 'permanent' movements in general profitability would uniquely result from changes in the (real) prices of wage-goods.

These views were developed in *On the Principles of Political Economy and Taxation* (first edition, 1817). In particular, Ricardo wanted to disseminate a single proposition, that the only serious threat to the unconstrained expansion of free-market capitalism came from the less productive cultivation of domestic land.

To illustrate this proposition Ricardo had developed a 'pure' labour theory of value, with 'permanent' changes in exchange relationships between competitively produced, freely reproducible commodities, the sole consequence of altered direct or indirect labour inputs (always assuming uniform profitability). He had also discovered limitations, eventually reduced to one of differences in the time structures of labour inputs. Pressed by Malthus to justify his use of the theory in the face of problems which he had himself unearthed, Ricardo departed on his celebrated quest for an 'invariable measure of value' which, if 'perfect', would magically obviate all variations in exchange relationships not the result of 'labour-embodied' changes, and this *without* assuming identical time-labour profiles. This futile search found expression in a new chapter 'On Value' in the third edition of the *Principles* (1821). Ironically, the impossibility of finding a 'perfect' measure of value was only recognized in a paper Ricardo was finalizing immediately before his sudden death on 11 September 1823.

Adumbration of a theory of comparative advantage in international trade (*Principles*, all editions) and of the possibility of net labour displacing accumulation (*Principles*, third edition) constitute further distinctive Ricardian contributions. Generally, he was a vigorous and fairly uncompromising advocate of *laissez-faire* capitalism: relief works schemes would be abolished, since they involved taking capital from those who knew best how to allocate it; taxation should be minimal, with the National Debt speedily paid off; the Poor Laws should be scrapped, because they distorted the labour market; and monopolies were *necessarily* mismanaged.

These views were promulgated from the floor of the House of Commons, where Ricardo also campaigned against religious discrimination and in favour of a meritocratic society. His guiding legislative principle was that it be for the public benefit and not in the interest of any particular class, with the 'public benefit' rigidly identified with the outcome of a private property, *laissez-faire* system. To this end, he favoured a gradual extension of the electoral franchise, immediately in order to weaken the legislative power of the landed aristocracy.

In his lifetime, Ricardo's political economy reigned supreme. But after his death, perhaps owing to the inability of followers. such as James Mill and J.R. McCulloch to work to the same high level of abstraction, 'Ricardian' economics was rendered platitudinous and diluted to little more than free-trade sloganizing. At the same time, Ricardo's labour theory of value was used by 'Ricardian Socialists' (such as Piercy Ravenstone and Thomas Hodgskin) to justify labour's claim to the whole product – a view Ricardo would have abhorred. Later, his writings exerted a powerful influence on Karl Marx which, if only by association, had the effect of placing Ricardo outside the mainstream of economic thought: a view which Alfred Marshall (and, more recently, Samuel Hollander) attempted to rebut. Following publication of Piero Sraffa's *Production of Commodities by Means of Commodities* (1960) Ricardo again achieved prominence as primogenitor of a 'Neo-Ricardian' school of thought, this identification resting on Sraffa's interpretation of Ricardo in his Introduction to *The Works and Correspondence of David Ricardo*. Sraffa's interpretation has increasingly been challenged, and a consensus has not yet been reached. It is, however, a tribute to Ricardo's complex genius that he should still evoke controversy.

Terry Peach
University of Manchester

Further Reading

Blaug, M. (1958), *Ricardian Economics: A Historical Study*, New Haven, Conn.

Hollander, J. H. (1910), *David Ricardo: A Centenary Estimate*, Baltimore.

Hollander, S. (1979), *The Economics of David Ricardo*, Toronto.

Ricardo, D. (1951–73), *The Works and Correspondence of David Ricardo*, edited by P. Sraffa with the collaboration of M. H. Dobb, Cambridge.

Say's Law of Markets

Say's Law of Markets is named after the French economist Jean-Baptiste Say. It refers to the belief that a free, competitive market automatically creates full employment of both labour and capital. The Law states that unemployment of either labour or capital is a result of a market disequilibrium and that the unfettered operation of the forces of supply and demand will eliminate all market disequilibria.

Say's Law was accepted by most of the classical economists, particularly Adam Smith and David Ricardo, and by most adherents to the orthodox neoclassical school of economic theory (from 1870 to the present). Economists who have rejected the law include Thomas Robert Malthus, Karl Marx, and John Maynard Keynes.

Say's Law presumes that in a market economy at any point in time there is a clearly defined set of prices for all items capable of being exchanged. Within the context of this set of prices, a desire to engage in exchange by someone who owns an exchangeable commodity is defined as a supply of the commodity the individual wishes to give up and a demand for a quantity of another commodity which represents *the value equivalent* of the amount of the commodity that is being supplied (the value equivalence being defined only with respect to the existing set of prices). Therefore, each desire to exchange is simultaneously a supply and a demand of identical value magnitudes. If such desires to exchange are the only components of the social aggregate supply, it follows that aggregate demand and aggregate supply must be equal.

In this view, there can be a market disequilibrium in which an excess supply for any commodity exists or an excess supply of labour exists, but given the necessary equality of aggregate demand and aggregate supply, it follows that the value of all excess supplies in all such markets must be exactly offset by a corresponding set of markets in which excess demands exist. The problem is then seen as a wrong or disequilibrium set of prices. The prices in markets with excess supply are too high and the prices in markets with excess demand are too low.

It is argued, however, that excess supply tends to lower

prices, while excess demand tends to raise prices. Therefore, the problem is self-correcting and the market tends to an equilibrium in which there is full employment of capital and labour. It follows that Say's Law tends to support the *laissez-faire* economic philosophy which generally provides an intellectual rationale for minimizing the role of government in the market place. Those who reject Say's Law (for example, the followers of Keynes) often support a more active role for government in the market place.

E. K. Hunt
University of Utah

Schumpeter, Joseph Alois (1883–1950)

Schumpeter, who belongs to the top layer of eminent twentieth-century economists, cannot be easily assigned to a definite school or branch of economics. His outstanding characteristics were his broad erudition, his interdisciplinary thinking, combining economic theory with sociology and history, and his immense capacity for mastering plentiful and difficult materials.

Throughout his life he was attracted by the problem which dominated the thinking of the classical economists and of Marx: the long-term dynamics of the capitalist system. He saw one of the main sources of growth (and profits) in the existence of 'risk-loving' entrepreneurs who, by pioneering new products, new production methods and so on, are destroying old structures and inducing change. This idea was already propounded in his early *Theorie der wirtschaftlichen Entwicklung*, 1912, (*Theory of Economic Development*, 1951), and then came up repeatedly, particularly in his monumental two-volume study on all aspects of the business-cycle – theoretical, statistical, historical (*Business Cycles*, 1939). The intertwining of economic, sociological and political factors and their influence on long-term trends was treated in a more popular fashion in *Capitalism, Socialism and Democracy* (1942), which became an outstanding success. After Schumpeter's death, his widow. Elizabeth Boody, edited the unfinished *History of Economic Analysis* (1954), an enormous and unique tableau of economic thought from earliest times till today.

The numerous economic and sociological publications by Schumpeter, which included seventeen books, were produced in his academic career which led him from provincial universities in the Habsburg Empire (Czernowitz, Graz) to the University of Bonn (1925), and finally to Harvard University (1932). In between he had an unlucky spell as Minister of Finance and private banker in inflation-ridden Austria just after World War I.

Kurt W. Rothschild
Johannes Kepler University, Linz

Further Reading
Frisch, H. (ed.) (1981), *Schumpeterian Economics*, Eastbourne.
Harris, S. E. (ed.) (1951), *Schumpeter: Social Scientist*,
    Cambridge, Mass.
See also: *Austrian School; entrepreneurship; innovation.*

Securities Markets

Securities may be distinguished by the type of issuer. *Primary securities* are issued by nonfinancial deficit-spending units to acquire real assets. *Secondary securities* are issued by financial intermediaries which issue their own secondary securities chiefly to households, typically through their retail outlets, in order to acquire primary securities from ultimate borrowers. Due to economies of scale in lending and borrowing, they are able to endow their own secondary securities with low risk, high divisibility, high liquidity, and a variety of assorted services-in-kind that make them more attractive than primary securities in the portfolios of ultimate wealth-owners. Intermediaries make a profit by lending at higher rates than they borrow. Commercial banks, savings institutions (such as building societies and savings and loan associations), insurance companies, pension funds, and mutual funds are the most important types of financial intermediaries.

Securities markets is a broad term embracing a number of

markets in which securities are bought and sold. The broadest classification is based upon whether the securities they handle are new issues, or are already outstanding. New issues are sold in *primary markets*; securities that are already outstanding are bought and sold in *secondary markets*. Another classification is between fixed and variable income securities. Fixed income securities are traded in the *bond* or *bill markets*. Variable income securities are traded in organized *stock markets*, or *over-the-counter markets*. A final classification is by maturity. Securities with maturities of less than one year trade in the *money market*; those with longer maturities are bought or sold in the *capital market*.

Primary securities may be sold to lenders directly, but ordinarily, due to the high transactions costs involved in borrowers seeking out lenders, they are sold by businesses that specialize in selling securities: security underwriters (investment or merchant banks). Underwriters purchase securities directly from borrowers at one price, and sell them to lenders at a higher price. The difference is referred to as the underwriter's spread, which represents compensation for undertaking the distributional activities, and for absorbing the risk that goes along with guaranteeing the borrower a fixed price before the securities are actually placed in the hands of lenders.

New issues of common stock are sold by way of 'public offerings', that is to say, reoffered to the general public, with no one investor buying more than a small proportion of the issue. In contrast, a significant proportion of bond issues of corporations and municipalities are sold by 'direct placement' to one of a few large financial investors, usually insurance companies and pension funds. Common stock and many corporate bonds are sold on a negotiated basis, while most bonds of state and local governments and public utilities are sold on the basis of competitive bidding, in the expectation that this will lead to lower borrowing costs.

The prices and yields established in secondary markets provide the basis for the terms and conditions that will prevail in the primary markets. The yield of a bond is the return to an investor buying the bond at its current market price. If a bond sells in the market for more (or less) than its face value, the yield is less (or more) than the coupon rate which the bond bears. The return of a common stock is the dividend yield (dividend-price ratio) plus the expected capital gain, which if the dividend yield is constant will be equal to the rate of growth of the dividend stream. In addition, the existence of secondary markets permits securities to be liquidated, that is, turned into cash at relatively low cost. It is in this manner possible for the economy to make long-term commitments in real capital that are financed by savings of a short-term nature. By endowing financial assets with the characteristics of high liquidity, low risk and high marketability, secondary security markets, like financial intermediaries, enhance the attractiveness of securities for the portfolios of ultimate wealth-owners, and thus encourage saving by surplus spending units.

Secondary markets for corporate stock play an important role in guiding corporate investment decisions. Corporate managements must decide how much of their after-tax earnings they should pay out to the shareholders in dividends, and how much they should retain to reinvest in the business. In making this judgement, the expected returns from reinvestment in real assets must be compared with the return which shareholders could earn on the stock market. There is considerable evidence that mature corporations continue to reinvest internally-generated funds even when few profitable investment opportunities exist. Managers are likely to act in pursuit of their own self-interest, and their salaries and perks may be more closely related to corporate size. However, if corporate managers consistently reinvest when the expected return falls below the cost of funds, the value of the company's shares will fall on the stock markets, rendering the company increasingly attractive as a takeover candidate. This market for corporate control thus operates to ensure that overall capital allocation is efficient, by compelling inefficient managers to face the likelihood of takeover.

The stock market and the market for government bills and bonds are the most active secondary markets in terms of the volume of transactions. In contrast, the secondary markets for corporate and local government bonds are relatively inactive, even though brokers and dealers stand ready to make markets by quoting buying and selling prices for those who want to engage in exchange. For nonmarketable securities, such as bank loans, no secondary markets exist. In stock markets '*specialists*' stand ready to trade with those who demand immediate servicing of their orders, and thus improve a market's continuity and resilience or depth, by reducing the variability of transaction prices over time.

Secondary markets comprise both *organized exchanges* and *over-the-counter* markets. Brokers operating on the floor of the exchange receive, buy and sell orders from the public, and then trade with Jobbers (specialists) who act both as agents and principals in a continuous auction process. Over-the-counter markets have no centralized location or limited number of members or 'seats'. They are characterized by freedom of access, and trading takes place through a complex system of telephone and teletype linkage, now being automated to keep a consolidated book of unfilled limit orders, and do a myriad of record-keeping and communication chores. Technology is likely to reduce the costs of search to the point where market perfection is closer at hand, so that all trades will be exposed simultaneously to all participants. What remains as yet unclear is whether computers will be used to replace dealers and specialists in the market-maker function.

As stated, market makers stand ready to provide liquidity in secondary markets by holding a buffer or inventory of securities in which they act as principals. However, in order to ensure the continuous liquidity of financial markets, a central bank must stand ready continually to purchase securities on demand in exchange for cash, in its central role of lender of last resort. Ultimately, in a crisis, the only securities which possess liquidity are those which the central bank is willing to purchase.

Basil J. Moore
Wesleyan University, Connecticut

Smith, Adam (1723–90)

Adam Smith was born in Kirkcaldy, on the East Coast of Scotland, in 1723. After attending the Burgh School Smith proceeded to Glasgow University (1737–40) where he studied under Francis Hutcheson. Thereafter he took up a Snell Exhibition in Balliol College, Oxford (1740–6). In 1748 Henry Home (Lord Kames) sponsored a course of public lectures on rhetoric and Smith was appointed to deliver them. The course was successful and led, in 1751, to Smith's election to the chair of logic in Glasgow University where he lectured on language and on the communication of ideas. In 1752 Smith was transferred to the chair of moral philosophy where he continued his teaching in logic, but extended the range to include natural theology, ethics, jurisprudence and economics.

Smith's most important publications in this period, apart from two contributions to the *Edinburgh Review* (1755–6), were the *Theory of Moral Sentiments* (1759, later editions, 1761, 1767, 1774, 1781, 1790) and the *Considerations Concerning the First Formation of Languages* (1761).

The *Theory of Moral Sentiments* served to draw Smith to the attention of Charles Townsend and was to lead to his appointment as tutor to the Duke of Buccleuch in 1764, whereupon he resigned his chair. The years 1764–6 were spent in France, first in Bordeaux and later in Paris where Smith arrived after a tour of Geneva and a meeting with Voltaire. The party settled in Paris late in 1765 where Smith met the leading *philosophes*. Of especial significance were his contacts with the French economists or Physiocrats, notably Quesnay and Turgot, who had already developed a sophisticated macroeconomic model for a capital using system.

Smith returned to London in 1766, and to Kirkcaldy in the following year. The next six years were spent at home working on his major book, which was completed after a further three years in London (1773–6). The basis of Smith's continuing fame, *An Inquiry into the Nature and Causes of the Wealth of Nations*, was published on 9 March 1776. It was an immediate success and later editions (of which the third is the most important) appeared in 1778, 1784, 1786 and 1789.

In 1778 Smith was appointed Commissioner of Customs and of the Salt Duties; posts which brought an additional income of £600 per annum (to be added to the continuing pension of £300 from Buccleuch) and which caused Smith to remove his household to Edinburgh (where his mother died in 1784). Adam Smith himself died, unmarried, on 17 July 1790 after ensuring that his literary executors, Joseph Black and James Hutton, had burned all his manuscripts with the exception of those which were published under the title of *Essays on Philosophical Subjects* (1795). He did not complete his intended account of 'the general principles of law and government', although generous traces of the argument survive in the lecture notes.

The broad structure of the argument on which Smith based his system of social sciences may be established by following the order of Smith's lectures from the chair of moral philosophy. The ethical argument is contained in *Theory of Moral Sentiments* and stands in the broad tradition of Hutcheson and Hume. Smith was concerned, in large measure, to explain the way in which the mind forms judgements as to what is fit and proper to be done or to be avoided. He argued that men form such judgements by visualizing how they would behave in the circumstances confronting another person or how an imagined or 'ideal' spectator might react to their actions or expressions of feeling in a given situation. A capacity to form judgements on *particular* occasions leads in turn to the emergence of *general rules* of conduct which correct the natural partiality for self. In particular Smith argued that those rules of behaviour which related to justice constitute the 'main pillar which upholds the whole edifice' of society.

Smith recognized that rules of behaviour would vary in different communities at the same point in time as well as over time, and addressed himself to this problem in the lectures on jurisprudence. In dealing with 'private law' such as that which relates to life, liberty or property, Smith deployed the analysis of *The Theory of Moral Sentiments* in explaining the origin of particular rules in the context of four socioeconomic stages – those of hunting, pasture, agriculture and commerce. In the lectures on 'public' jurisprudence he paid particular attention to the transition from the feudal-agrarian state to that of commerce; that is, to the emergence of the exchange economy and the substitution of a cash for a service nexus.

The economic analysis which completed the sequence and which culminated in the *Wealth of Nations* is predicated upon a system of justice and takes as given the point that self-regarding actions have a social reference. In fact the most complete statement of the psychology on which the *Wealth of Nations* relies is to be found in Part VI of *The Theory of Moral Sentiments* which was added in 1790.

The formal analysis of the *Wealth of Nations* begins with an account of the division of labour and of the phenomenon of economic interdependence before proceeding to the analysis of price, the allocation of resources and the treatment of distribution. Building on the equilibrium analysis of Book I, the second book develops a version of the Physiocratic *model* of the circular flow of income and output before proceeding to the analysis of the main theme of economic growth. Here, as throughout Smith's work, the emphasis is upon the unintended consequences of individual activity and leads directly to the policy prescriptions with which Smith is most commonly associated: namely, the call for economic liberty and the dismantling of all impediments, especially mercantilist impediments, to individual effort.

Yet Smith's liberalism can be exaggerated. In addition to such necessary functions as the provision of defence, justice and public works, Jacob Viner (1928) has shown that Smith saw a wide and elastic range of governmental activity.

The generally 'optimistic' tone which Smith uses in discussing the performance of the modern economy has also to be qualified by reference to further links with the ethical and historical analyses. Smith gave a great deal of attention to the social consequences of the division of labour, emphasizing the problem of isolation, the breakdown of the family unit, and that mental mutilation (affecting the capacity for moral judgement) which follows from concentrating the mind on a restricted range of activities. If government has to act in this, as in other spheres, Smith noted that it would be constrained by the habits and prejudices of the governed. He observed further that the type of government often found in conjuction with the exchange or commercial economy would be subject to pressure from particular economic interests, thus limiting its efficiency, and, also, that the political sphere, like the economic, was a focus for the competitive pursuit of power and status.

A. S. Skinner
Glasgow University

References
Works by Adam Smith:

I   *Theory of Moral Sentiments*, ed. D. D. Raphael and A. L. Macfie (1976).
II   *Wealth of Nations*, ed. R. H. Campbell, A. S. Skinner and W. B. Todd (1976).
III   *Essays on Philosophical Subjects*, ed. W. P. D. Wightman (1980).
IV   *Lectures on Rhetoric and Belles Lettres*, ed. J. C. Bryce (1983). This volume includes the *Considerations Concerning the First Formation of Languages.*
V   *Lectures on Jurisprudence*, ed. R. L. Meek, D. D. Raphael and P. G. Stein (1978). This volume includes two sets of students notes.
VI   *Correspondence of Adam Smith*, edited by E. C. Mossner and I. S. Ross (1977).

Further Reading
Campbell, T. D. (1971), *Adam Smith's Science of Morals*, London.
Haakonssen, K. (1981), *The Science of the Legislator: The Natural Jurisprudence of David Hume and Adam Smith*, Cambridge.
Hollander, S. (1973), *The Economics of Adam Smith*, Toronto.
Rae, J. (1965 [1895]), *Life of Adam Smith*, London. (Reprinted with an introduction by J. Viner, New York.)
Scott, W. R. (1937), *Adam Smith as Student and Professor*, Glasgow.
Skinner, A. S. and Wilson, T. (1975), *Essays on Adam Smith*, Oxford.

Winch, D. (1978), *Adam Smith's Politics*, Cambridge.
See also: *classical economics*.

Social Welfare

The adjective 'economic' is perhaps more appropriate, since when it is discussed by economists, *'social' welfare* encompasses goods and services but not wider social issues. The modern approach is a fusion of two earlier approaches, a rough-and-ready 'statistical' approach and a finely-honed welfare analytic approach.

The statistical approach measures social welfare in terms of just two parameters: real income and its distribution. One's overall judgement is then to some degree subjective, depending upon how real income gains (or losses) are valued as against egalitarian losses (or gains). To capture the whole income distribution in one parameter is, of course, extremely arbitrary, but for many purposes (for example, cross-country comparisons) it is reasonably safe to take some measure of real income per head and an index of inequality like the Gini coefficient. The measurement of real income itself is not unambiguous because its composition changes over time as does its distribution. The composition aspect is intimately connected with both the theory of index numbers and the theory of consumer behaviour. To use current prices as weights for the different commodities is, however, a reasonable practical approximation to changes in real income. Distributional changes are more serious, and only in the rare case where real income had increased to the same degree for everyone could they be ignored. All this is essentially an elaboration of Pigou's double criterion that real income increase without the poor being worse off *or* that the poor be better off and real income not decrease.

It was thought for some time – by Kaldor and Hicks – that it would be desirable to use real income alone, without distributional judgements, to evaluate economic policies. This is because interpersonal comparisons were said to be 'unscientific'. The 'new welfare economics' advocated the use of a compensation principle: if adoption of a policy enabled the gainers to compensate the losers and still be better off, then the policy would bring an improvement. Later, due to Scitovsky, it had to be added that the losers could not then bribe the gainers to return to the original position. Controversy arose as to whether the principle was merely a test for real income increases or a criterion for improvement. Part of the difficulty lay in whether compensation was to be actual or merely hypothetical. In the 1950s, Little insisted, successfully, that distributional considerations would have to be reintroduced. Though the attempt to jettison distribution failed, there is still a feeling that real income is somehow more important and more fundamental, especially in the longer term (it is, after all, a *sine qua non*). The compensation principle was intended to be a test of economic efficiency from which it is not desirable to depart too far.

The other, welfare analytic, approach starts from the preferences of individuals rather than from aggregate income. Individual utilities are a function of individuals' goods and services, and social welfare is a function of individual utilities (Bergson, 1938). Together with competitive theory, this construction enables one to draw out certain optimality properties of markets – this is especially so if lump-sum redistributions (almost impossible in practice) are permitted. Most of these propositions, except those to do with redistribution, are independent of distributional weights and therefore robust against distributional preferences. Whatever these preferences, efficiency requires equality of marginal rates of substitution in production and consumption. So if lump-sum redistributions are possible, social welfare is maximized under competition with distribution being a separate 'political' matter. Unfortunately the dichotomy cannot be sustained, and there are no truly simple rules for maximizing social welfare.

A second use of the welfare analytic approach which has so far proved to be strongly negative (though usefully so) is relating social choice to individual preferences. There should, it was felt, be some method for moving from the latter to the former. Arrow (1951) showed that no such transition rule was possible. Starting from individual preference orderings, it is impossible to derive a social ordering without violating at least one of a number of perfectly reasonable axioms, for example, that the ordering be not imposed, not dictatorial, not restricted in domain, and so on. To give examples, a competitive mechanism has to be rejected because the domain is restricted to Pareto-improvements on the original allocation and a Bergsonian welfare function because it would have to be imposed (by an economist?). Social choice cannot therefore be grounded in individual preferences except for relatively trivial cases.

The modern reaction to these two weaknesses of the welfare analytic approach (the impossibility of lump-sum redistributions or of acceptable transition rules) is to be very much more explicit about distributional judgements and interpersonal comparisons. Failing that, work on social choice remains barren and formal. Following Atkinson (1970), a great deal of technical work has been done on the relationships between social-welfare functions and indices of inequality. There is scope within the approach for a whole spectrum of value judgements running from a zero preference for equality to Rawlsian emphasis on the income of the poorest. The modern approach moves away from Arrow's assumption that we have only ordinal information about individuals, without reverting to crude utilitarianism. In the same spirit it ventures to make statements about equivalence between individuals and to compare 'needs'. Social welfare can then be indexed (always provisionally) by statistical measures which certainly carry recognized value judgements with them but have good foundations in consumer theory. The measures are a compromise between statistical convenience and (possibly sterile) theoretical purity.

David Collard
University of Bath

References

Arrow, K. J. (1951), *Social Choice and Individual Values*, New York.

Atkinson, A. B. (1970), 'On the measurement of inequality', *Journal of Economic Theory*, 2.

Bergson, A. (1938), 'A reformulation of certain aspects of welfare economics', *Quarterly Journal of Economics*, 52.

Further Reading
Mishan, E. J. (1981), *Introduction to Normative Economics*, Oxford.
Sen, A. K. (1982), *Choice, Measurement and Welfare*, Oxford.
See also: *social welfare policy; welfare economics*.

Social Welfare Policy

In the long boom succeeding World War II, social welfare policy was widely seen as the state's intervention in society to secure the well-being of its citizens. This progressivist interpretation of increasing social expenditure by the state was sustained by the writings of key post-war welfare theorists such as Titmuss (1950) and Marshall (1967). The former welcomed increasing collectivism as a necessary and desirable means of enhancing social integration; the latter saw in the developing British Welfare State the extension of citizenship through the acquisition of social rights. The Beveridge-Keynes Welfare State, which had been called into existence by the exigencies of war and the balance of social forces in the post-war situation, came to assume an ideological significance, both as the exemplar against which other Welfare States were to be assessed, and also as an explanation of the development of the Welfare State itself. This ideological construction had few means of accounting for developments in other countries such as the pioneering achievements in social policy in New Zealand, nor of specifically conservative political strategies such as those of Bismarck's Germany, in which social insurance was conceived of as a mechanism to weaken the working-class movement and inhibit the spread of socialist ideas. For that matter, its emphasis on the peculiarly British nature of the achievement led to difficulties in explaining the rather better performance by most indicators of Britain's new partners when she joined the European Community, a phenomenon which was received with some shock by British political culture.

Relatively early on in the post-war period, social democratic theorists such as Crosland (1964) acknowledged the significance of social welfare policy and the achievement of the full employment economy in modifying a basically capitalist social formation. Nonetheless, redistribution was to be secured through growth, thus avoiding the political opposition of the rich – a strategy which was thrown into question as economic growth faltered and even declined. The significance of these policies for structuring sex-gender relations within the home and within the labour market was grasped very much more slowly (Wilson, 1977). Nonetheless, the achievement of the Welfare State or welfare capitalism, as it has been variously termed, was aided by the discourse and practices of social policy in which 'need' was set as morally and administratively superior to the market as the distributive principle for welfare. Thus integral to the achievement of welfare capitalism and institutional welfare was a concept of need which stood as an antagonistic value to that of capitalism with its, at best, residual welfare.

Need was at the same moment emancipatory and constrained within the dominant social relations. In its emancipatory aspect, need fostered the language of rights, not only in theoretical writing but within the popular demands of the new social movements which rose during the late 1960s and early 1970s within North America and Europe (Piven and Cloward, 1971; Rose, 1973). Aided by the 'rediscovery of poverty' in the 1960s (Harrington, 1962; Abel-Smith and Townsend, 1965), large-scale mobilization around income maintenance and housing exerted substantial pressure on governments to offer more, and more responsive, welfare provision. Thus, the new social movements shared with institutional welfare an opposition to mere residual welfare, but continuously sought to go beyond not only the level of existing provisions but also the organizational forms through which they were realized. Instead – and this tendency was to become magnified as the welfare movements were joined by the 1970s wave of feminism – existing forms of welfare were seen as coercive, inadequate and statist. In contrast, the oppositional forms developed by the movements themselves emphasized democratic accountability, and nonhierarchical ways of working. Freire's (1972) thesis of conscientization as the politically creative strategy for the poor in the Third World was shared by the new social movements as they sought to develop an alternative practice of welfare to what was usual in the old industrialized societies. At their most radical the new movements sought that society itself should be organized around the meeting of human need.

While the boom lasted, this critique of institutional welfare as statist and bureaucratic made relatively little impact on either mainstream social welfare policy thinking or on political culture: ideological support for a more or less institutional welfare overlaid the deeper antagonism between need and the market. The separation of need from market values was further facilitated by the separation between economic and social policy discourses. Social policy felt able to ignore economic policy, since it was confident that Keynesian demand management techniques had delivered and would continue to deliver the precondition of the Welfare State, namely the full employment economy. Economists largely ignored the discussion of social welfare policy as of no interest to other than social ameliorists, until the crisis of the mid-1970s during which the loss of confidence in Keynesian techniques fostered a return to an endorsement of the market and an increasingly open opposition to state welfare expenditure (Friedman, 1962). Where institutional welfare had seen expanded welfare policies as socially integrative, a radical political economy had emphasized their contribution to capital accumulation and social control (O'Connor, 1973; Gough, 1979); now monetarism and the advent of a new right saw such expenditures as harming individualism and competitiveness and thus weakening the central dynamic of capitalism. With considerable populist skill the new right acknowledged the critique of the coercive character of public welfare, and offered an increase in personal liberty through rolling back the (Welfare) State, restoring the market and the family as the paramount providers of welfare.

The very depth of the current crisis, which has provided the conditions for the rise of the new right, nonetheless serves as a major constraint for its remedies. Global restructuring of manufacturing is associated with widespread and foreseeably long-term unemployment in the de-industrializing countries.

Unemployment, averaging around 12 per cent in the OECD countries in 1982 and with few clear indications of a significant improvement, requires, even in the most residual conception of welfare, substantial expenditure for both maintenance and control of an expanding surplus population. This situation is aggravated by the large numbers of young people among the unemployed, among whom ethnic and racial minorities are over-represented.

Despite these political constraints, since 1975 most Western governments have reduced the rate of growth of their social welfare budgets. Thus, up to 1975 the real rate of social expenditure growth in the seven largest OECD countries was no less than 8 per cent per annum (15 per cent growth at current prices); between 1975 and 1981 the real rate was halved. While all countries have experienced difficulties in maintaining their social welfare budget in the face of the reduction of the growth of the overall economy, governments with a specifically anti-welfare ideology such as the US and Britain have made substantial inroads. Thus, in the case of Britain an institutional system of welfare moves increasingly towards a residual model, particularly in the area of social security. The Nordic countries stand apart as the last bastion of the most highly developed expression of the old Welfare State, although the mix of labour market and social policies through which they achieve this varies substantially between them. Given the double significance for women of the existence of the Welfare State, as potential provider of both employment and services, it is perhaps not by chance that those Nordic countries with a continuing commitment to welfare have also an unusually high proportion of women representatives in their parliaments and upper houses. It is noteworthy that writers from these countries, such as Himmelstrand (1981) and his co-workers, are taking an active part in the current international debate concerning the possible future direction open to a post-Welfare State society. These writers seek to develop a theory which looks beyond welfare capitalism, to a new but very much more democratically based corporatism. Such post-Welfare State theorists are typically not unsympathetic to the claims of the new social movements (Gorz,

1982). However, they seem not to have fully appreciated the significance of feminist theorizing concerning the relationship between paid and unpaid labour within the development of the Welfare State, and thus the advantage to the dominant gender of retaining the present arrangements. Thus, even though the precondition of the old Welfare State, the full employment of one gender with welfare flowing through the man to the dependent family, no longer fits the actuality of either domestic or labour market structures, the ideological defence of those arrangements persists. Faced with the growing 'feminization of poverty' (Pearce, 1978), and the profoundly segregated (by both occupation and between full and part-time employment) labour market, there is a serious question concerning the extent to which the needs of women are met by the new post-Welfare State theorizing.

These are cautious, even sceptical, reflections on the debate around the Welfare State and the place of social welfare policy (Glennister, 1983). How far any of the new theories can offer to serve as the new fusion of the social and the economic, the contemporary historical equivalent of the old Welfare State of Keynes and Beveridge is not yet clear. What is clear, however, is that social welfare policy having spent its years of greatest growth relatively detached from economic policy has now been forcibly rejoined by circumstance. Together they occupy the centre of an intensely debated political arena.

Hilary Rose
University of Bradford

References

Abel-Smith, B. and Townsend, P. (1965), *The Poor and the Poorest*, London.

Crosland, C. A. R. (1964), *The Future of Socialism*, London.

Freire, P. (1972), *Cultural Action for Freedom*, Harmondsworth.

Friedman, M. (1962), *Capitalism and Freedom*, Chicago.

Glennister, H. (ed.) (1983), *The Future of the Welfare State*, London.

Gorz, A. (1982), *Farewell to the Working Class*, London.

Gough, I. (1979), *The Political Economy of Welfare*, London.

Harrington, M. (1962), *The Other America*, Harmondsworth.

Himmelstrand, U., Ahrne, G., Lundberg, L. and Lundberg, L. (1981), *Beyond Welfare Capitalism; Issues Actors and Social Forces in Societal Change*, London.

Marshall, T. H. (1967), *Social Policy*, 2nd edn, London.

O'Connor, J. (1973), *The Fiscal Crisis of the State*, New York.

Pearce, D. (1978), 'The feminization of poverty: women, work and welfare', *Urban and Social Change Review*.

Piven, F. F. and Cloward, R. (1971), *Regulating the Poor: The Functions of Public Welfare*, New York.

Rose, H. (1973), 'Up against the Welfare State: the claimant unions', in R. Miliband and J. Saville (eds), *The Socialist Register*, London.

Titmuss, R. M. (1950), *Problems of Social Policy*, London.

Wilson, E. (1977), *Women and the Welfare State*, London.

See also: *social welfare; welfare economics*.

Stagflation

Stagflation is a form of inflation which occurs or persists despite the presence of a substantial or even increasing percentage of measured unemployment of the labour force. The measured inflation rate may, however, be decreasing. Stagflation is therefore not inconsistent with a substantial degree of disinflation, provided only that the residual inflation rate remains significantly positive.

The term stagflation (stagnation plus inflation) came into common usage in the United States in the late 1960s and early 1970s to describe the state of the American economy as American involvement in Indochina was reduced substantially, and the American government sought to reduce or reverse the so-called 'Vietnam' inflation by fiscal and particularly by monetary measures. But aspects of the stagflation phenomenon itself were known earlier under other names, such as 'cost-push inflation', 'sellers' inflation', 'administered-price inflation', and even 'new inflation'. The novelty was that the inflation rate seemed resistant to reductions in aggregate demand from whatever source.

Stagflation is in any case inconsistent with thoroughgoing price flexibility in input and output markets – in other words, with pure competition. But such flexibility had been assumed, as regards outputs though not the wages of labour, by the expository or 'textbook' Keynesianism of the immediate post-war period (1945–55). Its policy recommendation had been for fiscal and monetary expansion (particularly the former, in the form of higher public expenditures and deficits) as a remedy for unemployment, and for fiscal and monetary contraction as a remedy for inflation, which was itself assumed to arise from the excess demand of 'too much money chasing too few goods'. The uselessness and irrelevance of such recommendations in the face of unemployment with inflation (that is, of stagflation) led to widespread public, political and journalistic dissatisfaction with both Keynesian theory and macroeconomics generally, and to demands of its complete scrapping or restructuring.

Macroeconomics offers no unified counsel as to how stagflation should be dealt with. In particular, counsel which assumes low employment as the major problem, which concentrates on short-run solutions, which is not averse to 'living with inflation', differs from counsel which assumes inflation to be the major problem, which concentrates on long-run solutions to 'squeeze inflation out of the economy', and which is not averse to 'living with unemployment'. The problem, in short, is one of social and economic priorities.

In this discussion we shall deal separately with two related sorts of scenarios of stagflation. The first type begins with a failure or refusal of the monetary and fiscal systems – particularly the former – to respond to or 'accommodate' an exogenous and often external inflationary shock. The second type begins with monetary and fiscal measures – again, primarily the former – to decelerate or reverse an inflation already in progress. These two stagflation scenarios are often found together, and much of the technical analysis of the two cases is quite similar.

A standard example of Type I stagflation, the exogenous shock, begins with a rapid and unanticipated rise in the price of an imported raw material like petroleum (the OPEC oil shocks of 1973 and 1979), although a domestic catastrophe like drought or earthquake could serve as well on the supply side. (On the demand side, the US involvement in Vietnam provided a similar shock to the Canadian economy in the middle and later 1960s.) To make the analysis clearer but at considerable cost in realism, we suppose a starting position marked by both high employment and price-level stability. The price of crude oil and petroleum-intensive products (fuels, petrochemicals) rises. The reduced supply of petroleum also lowers the country's real income. Nothing, however, is done to ease either fiscal policy (by tax cutting or increased expenditures) or monetary policy (higher monetary growth rates or lower interest rates). The price increase in the economy's petroleum-intensive sector leads to inflation unless other sectors cut their prices and allow their profit margins to be squeezed, and unless labour accepts some part of the real income cost in lower money and real wages. In these circumstances, any inflation is of the stagflation variety because there is no monetary or fiscal 'validation' of the higher price level at the going high level of employment. Without such validation, the employment and capacity-utilization levels will fall.

In a pressure-group economy, a price rise in one sector does not in the short run trigger price declines in other sectors, in profit margins, or in the wages of organized labour. And as we have said, without increased purchasing power to carry the higher price level at the previous level of employment, the employment level will fall. The stagflation scenario is then largely complete. Not entirely complete, however, for we can inquire further into the reasons and rationalizations for the failure of non-oil sectors and of labour to accept price, profit and wage reductions and maintain employment despite the higher oil price and its repercussions through the economy. There are three explanations: (1) forecasting; (2) distributional considerations; and (3) a 'strike' against the monetary and fiscal policy of the government in power. These three reactions are often simultaneous, and it is difficult to distinguish between them.

(1) The 'forecasting' reaction is nothing more than a rational belief (in the light of recent history in many countries) that

government monetary and fiscal policy will soon 'accommodate' higher oil prices. In which case, prices and wages lowered now would shortly rise again anyway, and patience is preferable to controversial concessions. (We should also remember that much of the initial unemployment consequent upon stagflation is concentrated upon youth not yet hired, youth employed only recently, temporary employees, and employees of concerns in financial difficulty. The bulk of the labour force is protected by 'seniority' institutions.)

(2) As for the 'distribution' reaction, it is very well to argue in the abstract for wage-price-profit concessions in non-oil sectors to maintain employment and avoid inflation, or for the equitable sharing of the real income loss which results from reduced oil supplies. But what does all this mean in the concrete? What constitutes 'equity'? How much of the cost is to be borne by whom? What wages and profit margins are to be cut, and by how much? The purely competitive market has its own rough-and-ready, quick-and-dirty solutions for such problems, but these are solutions which, for reasons of 'fairness', 'equity', and/or 'compassion', pressure-group economics and collective bargaining are designed to avoid. The 'distribution' argument against deflationary adjustment is, in simple terms, that the group bargaining and negotiation procedures necessary to allocate the oil-shock losses are too costly in time, acrimony, nervous strain, and possible output losses through strikes and bankruptcies, to be undertaken before they have become practically necessary as well as theoretically desirable.

(3) The 'strike' reaction can be understood if we suppose a monetarist government in power, which cannot be expected to yield to group pressure or 'adjust' its fiscal and especially its monetary policies to the higher price of oil. But if we also suppose a regime of parliamentary democracy, subject to periodic elections, then there is likely to exist, or to arise if stagflation persists, an opposition party or faction which advocates accommodative policies of monetary and fiscal ease. Does it not then make good *Realpolitik* deliberately to refuse concessions to the current hard-nosed, anti-inflationist regime, and even facilitate its overthrow by making the stagflation worse

and its alternative more attractive? This is what I mean by a political 'strike' against government fiscal and monetary policies, to facilitate the government's replacement by the 'accomodationist' opposition. Until the accommodationist pressure groups have faced and lost at least one general election, it is unlikely that they will themselves accept the adjustments required to end stagflation.

We turn now to stagflation of Type II (which is not fundamentally different), namely, a situation in which a government tightens its monetary and fiscal policy, particularly the former, with the aim of decelerating or reversing an inflationary process in being. We again assume initial high employment and also a situation when some prices (including wages and interest rates) have already been adjusted to next year's anticipated inflation, while others have not yet been adjusted for last year's inflation. Relative prices, wages, and interest rates, in other words, are 'wrong' from the viewpoint of the omniscient economist. In this situation stagnation results from the 'leading' prices and (especially) wage rates being too high and rigid downward. The inflation results from the 'lagging' prices and wages receiving an additional upward fillip in the interests of 'fairness', 'equity', or simply high inflationary expectations. The stagflation results, of course, from the conjunction of the stagnation and inflation factors.

Once again, competitive market forces would provide a rough-and-ready solution if unchecked. This solution would presumably feature the decline of those prices and wages that had risen too high under the influence of over-sanguinary expectations, and the rise of those which had been restrained by caution, money illusion, or long-term contracts. But, once again, power or pressure economics have partially replaced market forces in the short run. The rationalizations of Stagflation Type I, which we have classified as forecasting, distributional disagreement and strikes against controls, take over just as in Stagflation Type I. There is however a minor difference, in that any distributional 'losses' to be allocated are not actual losses as in Type I but the non-achievement of the gains anticipated from outpacing inflation.

Incomes policies are advocated widely as remedies for stagflation, as well as for inflation in the large by writers fearing stagflation. Some of these involve direct controls over prices, wages, interest rates, and/or profit margins. Others are associated with tax penalties for firms raising the wages they pay or the prices they charge beyond levels approved by government agencies. (In the US, such systems are known generically as TIPs or Tax-Induced Incomes Policies.) The only reason why stagflation requires different remedies than inflation generally, is that the greater need to avoid increasing unemployment demands greater delicacy in tightening constraints. Similarly, remedies for the unemployment aspects of stagflation are no different from those for unemployment generally, except for a greater delicacy required to avoid igniting or accelerating inflation.

Martin Bronfenbrenner
Duke University, North Carolina
Aoyama Gakuin University, Tokyo

Further Reading
Cornwall, J. (1983), *Post-Keynesian Analysis of Stagflation*, London.
See also: *employment and underemployment; inflation and deflation.*

Stock-Flow Analysis
Economic variables can be classified into two basic forms: flow variables (such as income), and stock variables (such as wealth). Other variables may be formed as a ratio between flows (such as the proportion of income saved), a ratio between stocks (such as proportion of wealth held as liquid assets), or a ratio between a flow and a stock (such as the ratio between capital and output). Clarity in economic analysis requires that a clear distinction between flows and stocks be maintained at all times. A flow should always have attached to it the relevant time period *during* which the flow occurs (to say that a person's income is $500 is meaningless until one adds 'per week' or 'per month' or whatever the relevant period). For precision, a stock variable should always have attached to it the date at which

the stock existed or was valued. A change between a stock at one date and the stock at a later date will be a flow during the period covered by the dates (see Fisher, 1906).

Stock-flow analysis is concerned with the relationship between stock variables and flow variables: there are two basic branches. The first branch comprises causal stock-adjustment models in which a flow is causally related to changes in a 'desired' or 'equilibrium' stock. The second branch is concerned with valuation models in which a stream of future flows is discounted and summed to a present-value stock equivalent.

An important feature of stock-adjustment models is that adjustment to change may be spread over several time periods, so giving rise to lags, distributed variously over those time periods, in the impact on flows. Hence the analysis of distributed lags tends to be a feature of stock-adjustment models.

Examples of stock-adjustment models are, in macroeconomics, the accelerator principle in which the aggregate flow of fixed-capital formation is related to changes in the 'desired' stock of fixed capital, and, in microeconomics, the relationship of the flow of demand for new cars to the pre-existing stock of cars (partly because of replacement demand). Bringing stocks into the analysis of flows has proved a powerful explanatory device and has served greatly to elucidate the variance in flows. For example, it is likely that a full understanding of personal sector savings flows (particularly in conditions of inflation) will require more information on personal sector stocks of financial assets, and for this we will have to await the regular compilation of national and sectoral balance sheets to complement the national income flow accounts.

Valuation models, based on the operation of discounting, are a form of stock-flow analysis in which a stream of future flows is rendered into a stock-equivalent at the present date. In this way, a series of flows (or entitlement thereto) may be given a single valuation or 'price'. Accordingly, discounting is a common technique of financial analysis.

Dudley Jackson
University of Wollongong, Australia

Reference
Fisher, I. (1906), *The Nature of Capital and Income*, New York.
See also: *capital consumption*.

Stockholm School

The Stockholm School – known also as the Swedish School –
refers to a group of Swedish economists who were active in the
late 1920s and the 1930s. Its members were Dag Hammar-
skjöld, Alf Johansson, Erik Lindahl, Erik Lundberg, Gunnar
Myrdal, Bertil Ohlin and Ingvar Svennilsson. Their interests
centred on macroeconomic theory and its application to economic policy. (Although they did not all work in the same university, they were nevertheless a 'School' in that they all influenced
one another in these two areas of economic science.) They
were themselves influenced by the older generation of Swedish
economists, in particular Knut Wicksell and Gustav Cassel,
who developed the cumulative process.

The School's origins can be traced back to exploration of
the economists into dynamic methods and its application of
macroeconomics. Dynamic method developed in four separate
stages, the first of which was Myrdal's dissertation (1927) which
used the concept of long-run equilibrium where anticipations
had been included as a datum. The next two stages were
marked by Lindahl's notion of intertemporal equilibrium (1929)
and temporary equilibrium (Lindahl, 1939). The final stage
represented a protracted evolution from Lindahl's temporary
equilibrium to Lundberg's disequilibrium-sequence analysis
(Lundberg, 1937).

The ideas of the Stockholm School concerning fiscal policy
were similar to those of Keynes as contained in his *General
Theory*. However, the Swedes did not develop Keynes's principle
of effective demand where savings and investment are made
equal via quantity changes. While the ideas of the School were
still prevalent in the 1940s and 1950s, they were by this time
heavily mixed with other ideas that were current at the time.

Björn Hansson
University of Lund

References
Lindahl, E. (1939), *Studies in the Theory of Money and Capital*, London.
Lundberg, E. (1937), *Studies in the Theory of Economic Expansion*, London.
Myrdal, G. (1927), *Prisbildningsproblemet och föränderligheten* (Price Formation and Economic Change), Stockholm.

Further Reading
Hansson, B. A. (1982), *The Stockholm School and the Development of Dynamic Method*, London.
Myrdal, G. (1939), *Monetary Equilibrium*, London.
Ohlin, B. (1978), 'On the formulation of monetary theory', *History of Political Economy*, 10 (Swedish original, 1933).

Subsidies

Subsidies are negative taxes which may be put on consumption goods or investment goods or factor services. Specific examples include subsidies on welfare goods and housing, accelerated depreciation provisions for investment, general wage subsidies, wage subsidies for specific purposes such as training, deficiency payments to farmers, and payments to public utilities for providing services in sparsely-populated areas.

Whereas taxes generally reduce taxed activities, subsidies normally increase the subsidized activity and are sometimes justified because the activity concerned generates external benefits. For example, a training subsidy might be introduced to encourage a better-trained labour force. When subsidies are introduced to aid the poor, an important issue is whether the subsidy should be paid in cash or in kind – for example, through food vouchers. Payments in kind make it more likely that the subsidy is used as desired, such as on food purchases, but is open to objections on paternalistic grounds and because such payments prevent people from spending their income as they themselves prefer.

Subsidies frequently present problems of public account-ability because it may be difficult to discover or control the extent of the subsidy. For example, support for a subsidy to a branch railway line does not necessarily mean unlimited support for losses on railway lines. Subsidies are of course open to all sorts of political pressures, but the force of this argument is for subsidies to be open and known. It may, for example, be difficult to discover if housing subsidies go mainly to those who live in publicly-owned housing or who have subsidized rents, or to owner-occupiers with subsidized mortgages and who escape income taxation on the implicit income from home ownership. In the absence of knowledge, both renters and owner-occupiers may feel the other group is the more heavily subsidized.

C. V. Brown
University of Stirling

See also: *taxation*.

Taxation

Taxes are the main source of government revenue. Amongst the OECD countries in 1981 taxes accounted for between one-fifth (in the case of Turkey) and one-half of gross domestic product (in the case of Sweden).

There is considerable variation in the relative importance of different kind of taxes. In 1981 France raised only 13 per cent of tax revenue from personal income tax, while New Zealand raised 61 per cent. Neither the United States nor the United Kingdom appear unusual either in the total amount of tax that they collect or in the composition of the tax burden, except that both raise a high share of revenue from property taxes, and the US raises a low share from taxes on goods and services.

It is assumed here that it has been decided how much total revenue the government requires. This makes it possible to concentrate on how best this revenue requirement can be met. This question is considered under three headings: allocative effects, distributional effects and administrative effects.

Allocative Effects

Taxes will in general cause people to change their behaviour. If there are two activities (or goods) A and B, and A is taxed while B is not, then, unless their incomes change, people will normally do (or buy) less of A and more of B. An important exception is where it is not possible to do less of A. For example, a tax on each person (a head or poll tax) cannot be avoided except by dying.

If A is an activity which has harmful side effects – for example, a chimney that smokes – then reducing activity A may be desirable. In general, however, it is preferable to tax activities where the reduction in production or consumption will be small. One aspect of this concerns the effects of taxes on prices of goods. Taxes will normally raise prices (though not usually by the amount of the tax). The increase in price will cause people to reduce consumption, especially where the quantity demanded is very sensitive to price. Because high consumption is generally to be preferred to low consumption, this leads to the proposition that taxes should tend to be concentrated on goods where demand is relatively insensitive to price changes.

It is also interesting to look at an example where people's incomes are *not* held constant, for instance, a tax on income from work. A tax on the income from work will have two effects on the amount of work people will want to do. It will reduce take-home pay and thus encourage them to want to work more to maintain their real income (the 'income effect'). But it will also reduce the amount that people receive for giving up an hour of their leisure and so encourage them to work less (the 'substitution effect'). This means that an income tax distorts the work–leisure choice. If the tax base included leisure as well as income, this distortion could be avoided, as in the case of the head tax mentioned above. The difficulty with head taxes is that it is impractical to vary them in accordance with a person's capacity to earn income.

Distributional Effects
Taxes generally change the distribution of income. This is fairly obvious if we think about the distribution of income after tax, but taxes can also influence the distribution of income before tax. If, for example, income taxes change the amount of work people do, this will change the distribution of pre-tax income.

A common fallacy is that in order to redistribute income towards the poor, it is necessary to have a schedule of rates which increase as income rises. However, provided that tax receipts are used to finance a benefit which is equally available to all, there is no need for a rising schedule of tax rates.

Many people would like to see taxes make the distribution of net income more equal. 'More equal' is of course a very vague phrase, and there are clearly differences as to how far towards equality people would like society to go.

Achieving the balance between allocative and distributional effects of taxes is the subject matter of the field of optimal taxation. In the case of income tax, the problem is to find the structure of rates that provides the best balance between high rates to provide revenue for redistribution and low rates to ensure that the income available for redistribution does not fall too much. More crudely, the problem is to balance the size of the cake against its distribution. It has been argued that the schedule of tax rates against income should start at zero, rise, and then at some high level of income fall again to zero. This optimal schedule thus looks rather like an upside down U, whereas the actual tax schedule in some countries is U-shaped if one includes means-tested state benefits on low incomes as well as income taxes.

Administrative Effects

Collecting taxes imposes costs on both the public and private sector which can vary widely. For example, the US and UK have very nearly the same number of people collecting income tax, but the US population is roughly four times the UK population. (It may be that private sector costs of income tax compliance are lower in the UK than in the US.)

One of the main determinants of administrative costs is the complexity of the tax law. Very often these complexities are introduced to attempt to make the law fairer, but ironically the complexities may reduce public awareness to the point where, for example, the poor do not make full use of provisions that could benefit them.

One of the most important sources of complexities is multiplicity of rates as between different kinds of income such as earnings and real capital gains. Where the rate of tax on capital gains is relatively low, there is a strong incentive for those with high earnings to convert income into capital gains. A single uniform rate on all income would be a considerable simplification. It would also be a move in the direction of the optimal schedule of income tax rates discussed above.

C. V. Brown
University of Stirling

Further Reading

Kay, J. A. and King, M. A. (1983), *The British Tax System*, 3rd edn, London.

Brown, C. V. (1983), *Taxation and the Incentive to Work*, 2nd edn, London.

Blinder, A. S. *et al.* (1974), *The Economics of Public Finance*, Washington DC.

See also: *distribution of incomes and wealth; fiscal policy; subsidies.*

Technical Assistance

Technical know-how, along with tools, has been transmitted from one society to another throughout history. The use of wind power or of a device such as the stirrup provide early examples of what amounts to a spontaneous diffusion of knowledge.

The deliberate adoption of techniques was undertaken when continental Europe strove to emulate England's early Industrial Revolution. The US subsequently relied on European expertise to initiate her industrialization; in turn, American engineers familiarized their Latin-American counterparts with the new skills.

In the late nineteenth century, Dutch officers taught the Japanese how to cast cannon; even the Chinese eventually deigned to solicit foreign technological advice (Nakaoa, 1982). In addition, merchants, pilgrims and missionaries transferred various crafts, occasionally in defiance of bans imposed by governments anxious to preserve their comparative advantage.

All such instances of technical assistance were, of necessity, incidental and *ad hoc*.

But after World War II a conscious, large-scale effort was introduced to impart industrial and agricultural expertise, with the object of inducing growth of the economy of underdeveloped countries; for the work of empiricists such as Denison and Solow had made it clear that technological knowledge was a major factor in development (Mansfield, 1982). Technical assistance, accordingly, came to be looked upon as a considered strategy, whereby industrial countries transfer knowledge, skills and even complementary attitudes to economically backward nations, in order to assist them in their efforts to improve living standards. These activities were henceforth largely undertaken and financed by institutions for the disbursement of foreign aid. The Food and Agricultural Organization of the United Nations (FAO) was among the first of the agencies to implement a programme of technical assistance. Subsequently, the UN Economic and Social Council (UNESCO) was assigned the preparation of an industrial assistance policy. A resolution was carried in 1948, outlining the principles of such a strategy and calling for the training of experts and supply of the requisite equipment. The following year, the Council launched an Expanded Programme of Technical Assistance (Vas-Zoltán, 1972). Meanwhile, President Truman delivered his 'Point Four' address, urging 'a wider and more vigorous application of modern and technical knowledge' in the interest of poor nations. Thus, the scene was set and the institutional framework provided for a new angle on the Third-World problem.

Early experience soon showed the mere transference of objective information as contained in manuals and instruction leaflets to be inadequate. For the effective operation and maintenance of sophisticated equipment, an element of 'bricolage', some sort of tinkering attitude, apparently needs to be imparted. A communication gap became apparent, and this could be bridged only by subjecting would-be recipients to an elaborate learning-by-doing process which, incidentally, conformed with the 'modernization' approach to development then prevalent (Inkeles and Smith, 1974).

Also, a suitability gap was revealed: factor proportions as embodied in modern machinery reflect the high wage levels and low capital costs prevailing in advanced industrial countries. Modes of production in these countries are geared to mass markets where substantial purchasing power is brought to bear. Transplantation to the alien economic environment of a poor country entails maladjustment: there labour is abundant and, therefore, cheap; investments funds are scarce and costly. Consumer aspirations may have been raised, but incomes as yet are low and potential markets, consequently, limited. The realization of the suitability gap has given rise to a new approach to technical assistance, advocating the adaptation of technology to conditions peculiar to the receiving economy. This has become known as the 'appropriate technology' movement.

H. J. Duller
University of Leiden

References
Inkeles, A. and Smith, D. H. (1974), *Becoming Modern – Individual Change in Six Developing Countries*, London.
Mansfield, E. (1982), *Technology Transfer, Productivity and Economic Policy*, New York.
Nakaoa, T. (1982), 'Science and technology in the history of modern Japan: imitation or endogenous creativity?', in A. Abdel-Malek, G. Blue and M. Pecujlic (eds), *Science and Technology in the Transformation of the World*, Tokyo.
Vas-Zoltán, P. (1972), *United Nations Technical Assistance*, Budapest.

Further Reading
Bradbury, F. (1978), *Transfer Processes in Technical Change*, Alphen aan den Rijn.
Duller, H. J. (1982), *Development Technology*, London.
Maddison, A. (1965), *Foreign Skills and Technical Assistance in Economic Development*, Paris.
See also: *aid; economic growth; technological progress.*

Technological Progress

The importance of technological progress for economic and social development is undeniable, but it is a field where understanding and analytical effort have lagged far behind other areas, such as short-term supply-demand analyses. This is due at least partly to the complexity of the process of technical change and the difficulty of obtaining precise definitions and measurements of it. Important advances have been made in recent years, but it remains a relatively neglected field.

Schumpeter, one of the few distinguished economists to put technological progress at the centre of his analysis, stressed the importance of new products, processes, and forms of organization or production – factors which have clearly been associated with enormous changes in the economic structures of developed economies since the Industrial Revolution. The rise of major new industries, such as railways and steel in the nineteenth century, and automobiles, synthetic materials and electronics in the twentieth, depended upon a complex interaction of inventions, innovations and entrepreneurial activity, which Freeman (1982) has aptly described as 'technological systems'. Since the onset of the post-1973 recession, the idea that developed capitalist economies are subject to 'long waves' of alternating periods of prosperity and stagnation, each wave being of around fifty to sixty years' duration, has been revived: some commentators argue that new technological systems are primarily responsible for the onset of an upswing, which begins to slow down as the associated technologies and industries reach maturity. Other economists, while accepting the notion of such cycles, argue that technological progress is a consequence, rather than a cause, of them. Outside the long-wave literature, there is an ongoing debate concerning the direction of causality regarding observed statistical associations between the growth of an industry and the pace of technical innovation.

At the macroeconomic level, the traditional, neoclassical growth models treat technological progress as part of a residual factor in 'explaining' increases in output, after accounting for the effects of changes in the volume of the factors of production (capital, labour and so on). This residual is normally large, and implicitly incorporates factors such as the education of the workforce and management expertise which contribute to improvements in efficiency, in addition to technological progress. In such approaches technological change is purely 'disembodied', that is, unrelated to any other economic variables. The class of so-called vintage capital models, which have become quite widely used over the last decade or so, treat technological progress as at least partly 'embodied' in new fixed investment: plant and machinery are carriers of productivity improvements and the gains from technological progress depend on the level of investment in them. Even the latter approach, however, does not go far in capturing the processes and forces by which new techniques are absorbed into the production system; the 'evolutionary' models pioneered by Nelson and Winter (1982) attempt to explore the conditions under which entrepreneurs will strive to adopt improved techniques. Such approaches are, however, in their infancy.

Discussion of how new techniques are generated and adopted is typically conducted at a more microeconomic case-study level. An *invention* is a new or improved product, or a novel procedure for manufacturing an existing product, which may or may not become translated into an *innovation*, that is, the (first) commercial adoption of the new idea. In many cases, scientific discoveries pave the way for inventions which, if perceived as having potential market demand, are adopted commercially; in the nineteenth century, the inventor/innovator was frequently an independent individual, but in the twentieth century the emphasis has moved to scientific and technological work being carried out 'in-house' by large firms. If an innovation is successful, a period of *diffusion* often follows, where other firms adopt or modify the innovation and market the product or process. It is at this stage that the major economic impact frequently occurs. Freeman has illustrated this process in the case of plastics, where fundamental scientific research work in Germany in the early 1920s on long-chain molecules led directly to the innovation of polystyrene and styrene rubber, and indirectly to numerous other new products in the 1930s. Further innovations and massive world-wide diffusion took place after the Second World War, facilitated by the shift from coal to oil as the feedstock for the industry. In the 1970s the industry appears to have 'matured' with a slow-down in demand and in the rate of technological progress.

The measurement of inventive and innovative activity is beset with difficulties. Input measures include the manpower employed and financial expenditure, although there is necessarily a degree of arbitrariness in defining the boundary of research and development activity. Output measures of invention include patent statistics, but these need to be interpreted with caution, owing to the differences in propensity to patent between firms, industries and countries with different perceptions of whether security is enhanced by patent protection or not, and differences in national patent legislation. The use of numbers of innovations as an output measure normally requires some – necessarily subjective – assessment of the relative 'importance' of the individual innovations. Despite their limitations, however, the use of several indicators in combination can provide a basis for comparisons between industries or between countries.

Over the post-war period, governments have increasingly recognized the importance of attaining or maintaining international competitiveness in technology. The emergence of Japan as a major economic power owes much to a conscious policy of importing modern foreign technology and improving it domestically. Most countries have a wide variety of schemes to encourage firms to develop and adopt the new technologies, and policies for training or retraining the workforce in the skills needed to use new techniques. In the current context attention is, of course, focused particularly on microelectronics-related technologies; and – whatever their validity – fears that these technologies could exacerbate unemployment problems generally take second place to fears of the consequences of falling behind technologically, in the eyes of governments and trade unions alike.

Forecasts of the impact of new technologies are notoriously unreliable. The cost-saving potential of nuclear power was dramatically overstated in the early stages, while the potential impact of computers was first thought to be extremely limited. For good or ill, we can however say that technological progress shows no sign of coming to a halt.

J. A. Clark
University of Sussex

References
Freeman, C. (1982), *The Economics of Industrial Innovation*, 2nd edn, London.
Nelson, R. R. and Winter, S. G. (1982), *An Evolutionary Theory of Economic Change*, Cambridge, Mass.

Further Reading
Heertje, A. (1977), *Economics and Technical Change*, London.
See also: *automation; innovation.*

Trade Unions

A trade union is a combination of employees for the purpose of regulating the relationship between employees and employer so that the pay and conditions of the employees may improve. Such regulation can be brought about in three main ways: (1) unilateral regulation by the trade union; (2) bargaining with the employer by the employees collectively; (3) statutory regulation (Clegg, 1976).

Historically, unilateral regulation was used by unions of skilled craftsmen who would agree among themselves not to accept employment unless certain terms were met by the employer. Subsequently, with the extension of trade unions to cover nearly all sections of the work force, collective bargaining over pay and conditions became the major activity of trade unions in most countries, with trade union officers also acting to resolve any grievances of individual members, or of small groups, within the work-place. The process of collective bargaining now has very wide scope, and trade union officers frequently exert considerable control and management of the 'internal labour markets' of the members' employing organization (in regard to such things as recruitment, promotion, discipline, and task allocation). The state has tended to intervene both in the employee-employer relationship and also in the process of collective bargaining by legislation and through judicial or quasi-judicial procedures. Thus trade unions have developed their legal expertise and their political connections to operate (and occasionally to resist) and to influence legislation in their members' interests.

Most countries have some statutory legislation concerning the formation of a trade union and the conduct of its affairs (paralleling company or partnership legislation). Generally, a trade union is required to be registered, to have rules conforming to certain standards (for example, for the election of a governing body and the appointment of officers), and to keep and submit (audited) accounts. In return, a registered trade union may be granted certain legal immunities or privileges, the most important being the right not to be sued for breach of contract as a result of action taken in the course of collective bargaining. In some countries, deregistration (or the threat thereof) has been used by governments to influence the behaviour of trade unions.

The logic of collective bargaining (and of its corollary, that agreements must be honoured by both sides) requires that, when necessary, the employee members of a trade union will act together in a united front and that no members will break ranks either by refusing to take, say, strike action when instructed by trade union officers or by taking strike action when this has not been instructed. A trade union must, therefore, have some method of ensuring that each member does what is required of him. A trade union can usually rely on voluntary compliance based on fraternal solidarity or ideological commitment, but the use of sanctions against recalcitrant members always raises difficult questions of the rights of individuals against the needs of the collectivity.

In general, trade unions have become an integral and accepted part of the economies in which they work. This has caused controversy among those who have other views of the functions of trade unions. Marx and Engels saw trade unions as developing inevitably and together with capitalism and (optimistically from their viewpoint) as being in the vanguard of the revolutionary process to overthrow the capitalist system. Marx and Engels subsequently observed the tendency of trade unions, especially in Britain, to become 'corrupted': by concentrating on improving the condition of workers through collective bargaining, they were, by implication, accepting the capitalist system.

Although Marx and Engels observed these tendencies towards the 'embourgeoisement' of the working class, it was Lenin who argued that trade unions tended to become integrated into the capitalist system and that there was therefore a need 'to divert the working-class movement from this spontaneous, trade-unionist striving to come under the wing of the bourgeoisie, and to bring it under the wing of revolutionary Social-Democracy' (Lenin, 1902). Subsequently, Trotsky extended Lenin's thesis of trade union integration into the capitalist system to an attack on trade union leaders who used their authority actively to assist capitalism in controlling the workers, so ensuring trade unions' full incorporation into the system. Seen from another point of view, Trotsky's attack is simply a criticism of the role of trade unions in enforcing collective agreements. The view that trade unions render capitalism 'safe' by institutionalizing conflict may meet with approval or disapproval, but it is central in understanding the role of trade unions in many countries.

Given that trade unions, as an integral part of the market economy, bargain effectively, the question arises as to their economic impact. There are two broad issues of interest: their impact on the general level of wages and their impact on the structure of earnings within the labour market. In situations of full employment, the process of collective bargaining (or the 'power' of trade unions) has been blamed for causing inflation by increasing remuneration per employee by more than the increase in real output per employee, so leading to rising unit labour costs, rising prices, and loss of 'competitiveness' (at an unchanged exchange rate) in world markets with consequent loss of jobs. In response, governments have sometimes attempted to agree with (or to impose on) trade unions an incomes policy, usually comprising some limitation on collectively bargained pay increases together with other measures more acceptable to the unions.

On the issue of pay structures, there is evidence to show that (at least during certain periods – especially of high unemployment) average earnings for unionized groups of employees tend to be higher than average earnings for employees who are not unionized. Some argue that trade unions (or rather, the consequences of collective bargaining) have been at least partly responsible, in co-operation with many other influences, for creating and maintaining labour market 'segmentation'. This is the situation where employment is divided between a relatively unionized 'primary' labour market comprising well-paid jobs with good conditions of employment (short hours, holidays with pay, promotion prospects, pensions) in large firms and in the public sector, and a peripheral relatively non-unionized 'secondary' labour market with low pay and inferior conditions. This strand of criticism of trade unions has been developed both in industrial countries and also in Third-World countries where, it has been argued, trade unions serve to enhance the real incomes of an employed urban élite at the expense of the rural peasantry: incomes policies in Third-World countries have as often been aimed at this problem as at controlling inflation.

D. Jackson
University of Wollongong, Australia

References
Clegg, H. (1976), *Trade Unionism under Collective Bargaining: A Theory Based on Comparisons of Six Countries*, Oxford.
Lenin, V. I. (1902), *What Is To Be Done?*

Further Reading
Clegg, H. A. (1979), *The Changing System of Industrial Relations in Great Britain*, Oxford.
Hyman, R. (1977), *Strikes*, Glasgow.
Nichols, T. (ed.) (1980), *Capital and Labour*, Glasgow.
See also: *labour market analysis*.

Transport Economics and Planning

Traditionally economists' interest in transport focused on the transport industries (the railways, shipping, airlines, and so on) and specifically on ways in which the market mechanism could be improved to maximize the benefits derived from public and private transport operations. The emphasis has changed in recent years, with more attention given to the environmental and distributional aspects of transport, while market efficiency is seen as only one dimension in a broader decision-making process.

The demand for transport is a derived demand since transport is seldom wanted for its own sake but rather for the benefits which can be obtained when reaching a final destination. In addition, transport provision can affect where firms locate or where people decide to live. Consequently, it is unrealistic to treat transport in isolation from the broader industrial and spatial environment in which it is provided. This interface with, for example, industrial and residential location and with economic development more generally means a practical involvement in subjects such as regional economic policy and urban land-use planning.

The expansion of urbanization poses particular problems for the transport system. The central location of many employment opportunities, the inflexible nature of much existing transport infrastructure, and the pollution and noise associated with concentrated traffic flows generate problems both of pure economic efficiency and of extensive external costs which free-market mechanisms are thought incapable of resolving. Costs of providing major new road and urban rail systems, combined with the need for co-ordinated decision making in an environment of imperfect knowledge and diverse interest groups, has further pushed policy away from free-market provision. The resultant introduction of urban transport planning has attempted both to meet wider social objectives and retain traditional economic concepts of efficiency.

Urban transport planning in the immediate post-World War II period was primarily concerned with drawing up physical plans for the utopian transport system. Modern structure planning, in contrast, is more concerned with the interaction of transport with the urban economy in general and with the operations of all modes of transport, rather than with narrow, engineering questions of infrastructure design. Such planning is co-ordinated with policies for the development of land use and the improvement of the urban environment.

Economics contributes to the modern urban transport planning process in several important ways, but two are of specific relevance: (1) It provides the theoretical economic underpinnings for travel demand forecasts which offer guidelines to the traffic impacts of alternative planning strategies. Many models in current use (especially of the disaggregate type) originate from the microeconomic work of Kelvin Lancaster on attributal demand analysis. (2) Social investment appraisal procedures, generally involving variants on the cost-benefit analysis (CBA) methodology, now form the basis for the evaluation of alternative urban transport plans. While conventional CBA approaches involve reducing all aspects of decision making to common monetary units, the specific concern with distributional implications and the diverse effects of modifications to the urban transport network have substantially changed the conventional framework. Thus, the Planning Balance Sheet methodology developed by Nathaniel Lichfield (1962) presents details of the costs and benefits associated with alternative plans in an accountancy framework. It emphasizes the specific impacts on various affected parties, while not reducing all items to monetary terms.

Inter-urban transport tends to be the subject of less control, mainly because its indirect consequences are smaller, but also because long-distance mobility is not considered to be a social necessity. Infrastructure (such as the motorway network in the UK or the Interstate Highway System in the US) does tend to be planned, but transport operations are increasingly left to market forces operating within defined legal boundaries designed for safety, fuel economy, and so on. Recently the regulatory framework built up during the inter-war period in the US and the UK has been dismantled and entry to transport markets has become much freer. But this trend is less pronounced in much of continental Europe, where inter-urban road and rail transport is treated as an input into wider, macroeconomic policies – transport efficiency in these countries is, for example, treated as secondary to regional and industrial objectives.

Political considerations necessitate a high level of capacity control in international transport fields. Capacity in international air transport, for instance, is regulated, and national planning of airport and airline policy revolves more around questions of national image than pure economic efficiency. International shipping is less regulated since much of the traffic moves outside of national waters. However, in an attempt to protect the interests of Third-World countries, there have in recent years been moves by UNCTAD to regulate and plan the growth of the shipping cartels or 'conferences' which provide much of the capacity on major routes.

Transport is regarded as very important in economic development. Substantial international aid is directed towards improving the transport infrastructure of Third-World countries, on the premise that good transport is a precondition for take-off into self sustained growth. But some economists argue that there is little evidence that improved transport *per se* necessarily results in economic growth and, in some instances, by allowing market penetration by competitors, it may stifle it. The role of planning in less-developed countries should, therefore, be seen not in terms of improving general mobility but rather in terms of integrating transport investment into a larger development programme designed to achieve the fastest growth in Gross National Product.

K. J. Button
Loughborough University

References
Lancaster, K. (1971), *Consumer Demand: A New Approach*, New York.
Lichfield, N. (1962), *Cost-Benefit Analysis in Urban Development*, Berkeley and Los Angeles.

Further Reading
Button, K. J. (1982), *Transport Economics*, London.
Glaister, S. (1981), *Fundamentals of Transport Economics*, Oxford.
See also: *cost-benefit analysis; planning, economic.*

Underdevelopment

The original meaning of underdevelopment was a neutral one, simply defining the condition of poorer countries which then were called underdeveloped countries. However, this term was felt to be derogatory and has since disappeared from the international vocabulary, being replaced by the more euphemistic 'developing countries'. As a result the term underdeveloped has now assumed a specific and rather different meaning. It is now closely associated with the so-called dependency school, and it indicates a belief that in the world economy there are centrifugal forces at work, strengthening the position of the already rich 'core' while keeping the 'periphery' poor and in a state of permanent underdevelopment. The chief author using and building on this term was André Gunder Frank (Frank, 1967). Frank was also the first to speak of 'development of underdevelopment', meaning the development of a rich country/poor country or core/periphery relationship which results in the impoverishment of the poor or periphery partner.

There are a number of variants within the underdevelopment school. These range from the radical wing which identifies underdevelopment with neocolonial relationships and is an outgrowth of Marxist thinking, to nonpolitical or non-ideological explanations such as the principle of 'cumulative causation' developed by Gunnar Myrdal (Myrdal, 1956). The principle of cumulative causation states that in the case of poor countries or poor groups a vicious circle is at work keeping them poor (for example, low income causing low savings and low investment, in turn causing low income in the next round; or low income leading to poor health leading to low productivity and low income). By contrast, in rich countries, or among rich groups, a reverse beneficial circle enables them to go from strength to strength and to improve their condition progressively. The strict Marxian view is perhaps best represented by

W. Rodney in *How Europe Underdeveloped Africa* (1972): 'An indispensable component of modern underdevelopment is that it expresses a particular relationship of exploitation: namely the exploitation of one country by another.' This view logically also leads to the use of the concept in describing domestic relations within developing countries (as in relations between an urban élite and the rural poor), but in practice the term is now associated with an international context of relations between countries. In between these two extremes are various other schools of thought explaining that the system of international trade relations has a tendency to benefit rich countries more than poor countries. The best known of these schools is the Prebisch-Singer theory according to which the terms of trade of primary products tend to deteriorate in relation to the prices of manufactured goods (Prebisch, 1964; Singer, 1950).

The radical view that any international contact between rich and poor countries will be to the disadvantage of the latter, obviously leads to the policy conclusion that poorer countries should either try to be self-sufficient or inward-looking in their development; while in the case of smaller countries, where this is not feasible, regional groupings of developing countries are advocated. One does not have to be an advocate of the underdevelopment school, however, to support such policies; it is clear that trade, investment and other economic relations among the developing countries are conspicuously and abnormally sparse compared with relations between rich and poor countries. It can be argued that it is also in the interest of the richer industrialized countries to support such closer South-South cooperation.

The milder variation is that international contacts are advantageous for both partners, in accordance with liberal doctrine and the law of comparative advantage, but that the benefits are unequally distributed.

The belief of the more radical underdevelopment school that international relations are positively harmful to the poorer partners can in turn lead to two different policy conclusions. One is to reduce North-South contacts and instead develop South-South relations; the other is to reform the international system so that its benefits are more equally distributed. The latter approach is implied in the pressure of the developing countries for a New International Economic Order which has dominated the international discussions during the last decade, and also in such reform proposals as the two Brandt Reports (Brandt I, 1980; and Brandt II, 1983).

H. W. Singer
Institute of Development Studies
University of Sussex

References

Brandt I (1980), *North-South: A Programme for Survival*, (The Report of the Independent Commission on International Development Issues under the Chairmanship of Willy Brandt), London.

Brandt II (1983), *Common Crisis, North-South: Co-operation for World Recovery*, The Brandt Commission, London.

Frank, A. G. (1967), *Capitalism and Underdevelopment in Latin America*, New York.

Myrdal, G. (1956), *Development and Underdevelopment*, Cairo.

Prebisch, R. (1964), *Towards a New Trade Policy for Development*, New York.

Rodney, W. (1972), *How Europe Underdeveloped Africa*, Dar-es-Salaam.

Singer, H. W. (1950), 'The distribution of gains between investing and borrowing countries', *American Economic Review*.

See also: *economic development*.

Walras, Marie-Esprit Léon (1834–1910)

Léon Walras, one of the founders of the marginal utility theory of value in the 1860s, was inspired to devote his life to the development of economic science by the teaching of his father, Antoine Auguste Walras (a French professor of political economy who was one of the first economists to perceive that value derived from marginal utility rather than total utility). The subsequent work of the younger Walras in General Equilibrium Theory was to establish him as a leading modern economist.

Denied a teaching post in France, he became the first occupant of a newly-founded chair in economics at the University of Lausanne, Switzerland in 1870, where he remained until his retirement in 1892. Through his work, together with that of his successor, Vilfredo Pareto, a new school of thought was established, which became known as the Lausanne School of Political Economy.

Walras's approach to political economy consisted of his trilogy – pure economics, applied economics, and social economics – each part constituting a particular aspect of political economy. The first was essentially developed in his *Eléments d'économie politique pure* (1874–7) (*Elements of Pure Economics*, London, 1953) when he presented the theory of general economic equilibrium, with its emphasis upon the interdependence of economic phenomena. Through a method of successive approximations, he began with the theory of exchange, then production, followed by his theory of capital, and, finally, monetary theory. In the process, he made significant contributions to each of these fields. Taken as a whole, his *Eléments* has often been recognized as one of the greatest theoretical achievements in the history of economic science.

The other two components of his trilogy – applied and social economics – dealt with economic policy and economic justice respectively. These two works did not achieve the same status as his pure economics among his contemporaries, and have all but been forgotten by modern economists, reflecting a current preference for narrow scope of economics.

Vincent J. Tarascio
University of North Carolina, Chapel Hill

Reference
Walras, L. (1874), *Eléments d'économie politique pure*, Paris.

Further Reading

Hicks, J. R. (1934), 'Leon Walras', *Econometrica*.

Jaffé, W. (ed.) (1965), *Correspondence of Léon Walras and Related Papers*, 3 vols.

Walker, D. A. (ed.) (1983), *William Jaffé's Essays on Walras*, London.

Welfare Economics

If economics is the study of how to make the best, or optimal, use of limited resources, welfare economics is concerned with the meaning of the term 'optimal' and with the formulation of statements that permit us to say that a given policy or event has improved or reduced social welfare.

Optimality is defined in terms of maximizing social welfare, so that the focus of concern is on what compromises the latter concept. Typically, it is taken to be the sum of the welfares of all members of a defined society. By adopting the value judgement that it is individuals' own judgements of their welfare that is to count in the formulation of a measure of social welfare, we have the basis for Paretian welfare economics (after Vilfredo Pareto). In this case, to say that individual A's welfare has improved is to say no more than A prefers one situation to another. To say that *social* welfare has improved requires a further definitional statement, namely that the improvement in A's welfare has occurred without any other individual being worse off. Thus social welfare has improved if, and only if, at least one individual's welfare has improved and no one's has decreased. It may be noted that while the first requirement is a value judgement, the second is a matter of definition. It is not an additional value judgement.

Paretian welfare economics is almost self-evidently sterile, since we can envision few situations in which no one is harmed by a policy. Some individuals gain and some lose. The sterility of the pure Paretian principle arises because of the alleged difficulty of comparing one person's gain in welfare and another's loss: the so-called fallacy of interpersonal comparisons of utility. If this is accepted, there are obvious difficulties for the formulation of criteria for a gain in social welfare. The principle emerging from the work of Kaldor and Hicks declares that there is a net gain in social welfare if those who gain can use part of their gains to compensate the losers and still have something left over. In other words, *if* compensation occurred, those who stand to lose would be fully compensated and their welfare would accordingly be the same before and after the policy in question. Gainers would still be better off provided the required compensation is less than their gross gains. This is the Kaldor-Hicks compensation principle.

Scitovsky (1941) pointed out that a further condition is required, since a policy may alter the distribution of income in such a way that those who lose may be able to pay those who gain sufficient to induce them back to the initial situation. The requirement that this should *not* be the case defines the Scitovsky reversal test for a state of affairs to be defined as a (modified) Pareto-improvement. Since *actual* compensation mechanisms are complex, all compensation criteria are typically formulated in terms of the potential for compensation. There is no requirement for the compensation to occur. This provides the complete separation from the Pareto principle: the compensation principle may sanction a policy that leads to a (strict) Pareto deterioration in social welfare. Scitovsky's work opened the way for an explicit treatment of the distribution of income. Little (1957) defined various alternatives whereby social welfare can be said to increase according to the fulfilment of the compensation criterion (the efficiency test) and an improvement in the distribution of income (an equity test). The seminal work of Rawls (1971), however, best defines the turning point in welfare economics, whereby there is explicit and simultaneous attention paid to both efficiency and equity through the adoption of Rawl's 'maximin' principle of benefiting the least well off in society.

The historical oddity of welfare economics remains that it has survived as an elaborate framework in itself, and as the foundation of practical techniques such as cost-benefit analysis, despite severe and arguably fatal criticism in the 1950s – notably in the work of de Graaf (1957). Arrow's famous 'impossibility theorem' (Arrow, 1963) also indicates the problems of defining any social welfare function based on the fundamental Paretian value judgement about consumer sovereignty. Tendentiously, one might suggest that the survival and health of welfare economics arises from its preoccupation with social decision rules which, if not embraced by economics, renders the science inconsistent with its own functional definition of making the 'best' use of scarce resources. 'Best' implies a criterion for judging alternative states of affairs, and this is the concern of welfare economics.

David W. Pearce
University College London

References
Arrow, K. (1963), *Social Choice and Individual Values*, 2nd edn, New York.
Graaf, J. de V. (1957), *Theoretical Welfare Economics*, Cambridge.
Hicks, J. (1939), 'Foundations of welfare economics', *Economic Journal*, 49.
Kaldor, N. (1939), 'Welfare propositions of economics and interpersonal comparisons of utility', *Economic Journal*, 49.
Little, I. M. D. (1957), *A Critique of Welfare Economics*, 2nd edn, Oxford.
Rawls, J. (1971), *A Theory of Justice*, Oxford.
Scitovsky, T. (1941), 'A note on welfare propositions in economics', *Review of Economic Studies*.

Further Reading
Ng, Y.-K. (1979), *Welfare Economics*, London.
Sudgen, R. (1981), *The Political Economy of Public Choice: An Introduction to Welfare Economics*, Oxford.
Just, R. E., Hueth, D. H. and Schmitz, A. (1982), *Applied Welfare Economics and Public Policy*, Englewood Cliffs, N.J.